Clive Oxenden
Christina Latham-Koenig
Paul Seligson
with Lindsay Clandfield
Francesca Target

New
ENGLISH FILE

Elementary
Teacher's Book

Paul Seligson and Clive Oxenden are the original co-authors of
English File 1 (pub. 1996) and *English File 2* (pub. 1997).

OXFORD
UNIVERSITY PRESS

OXFORD
UNIVERSITY PRESS

Great Clarendon Street, Oxford OX2 6DP

Oxford University Press is a department of the University of Oxford.
It furthers the University's objective of excellence in research, scholarship,
and education by publishing worldwide in

Oxford New York

Auckland Cape Town Dar es Salaam Hong Kong Karachi
Kuala Lumpur Madrid Melbourne Mexico City Nairobi
New Delhi Shanghai Taipei Toronto

With offices in

Argentina Austria Brazil Chile Czech Republic France Greece
Guatemala Hungary Italy Japan Poland Portugal Singapore
South Korea Switzerland Thailand Turkey Ukraine Vietnam

OXFORD and OXFORD ENGLISH are registered trade marks of
Oxford University Press in the UK and in certain other countries

© Oxford University Press 2004

The moral rights of the author have been asserted

Database right Oxford University Press (maker)

First published 2004
2009 2008 2007 2006
10 9 8 7 6 5

Photocopying

ISBN-13: 978 0 19 438426 1
ISBN-10: 0 19 438426 8

Printed in China

ACKNOWLEDGEMENTS

Designed by: Holdsworth Associates, Isle of Wight, and Newton Harris Design
Partnership

The Authors would like to thank all the teachers and students around the
world whose feedback has helped us to shape *New English File*. We would also
like to thank Carla Guelfenbein, Cristina Mayo, Russell and Anna, Ben
Silverstone, and Annabel Wright for agreeing to be interviewed, and Joaquin
for the short story *It's written in the cards*. The Authors would also like to thank
all those at Oxford University Press (both in Oxford and around the world),
and the design team who have contributed their skills and ideas to producing
this course.

*The Publisher and Authors would like to thank the following for their invaluable feedback
on the materials*: Beatriz Martin; Michael O'Brien; Lester Vaughan; Tom Stutter;
Wendy Armstrong; Javier Santos Asensi; Tim Banks; Brian Brennan; Xosé
Calvo; Susanna Di Gravio; Jane Hudson; Carlos Leite; Norma Sheila Botelho;
Paulo Pimenta Marques; Katarzyna Pawłowska; Graham Rumbelow; Blanca
Sanz; Yolanda Gomez; Ágnes Szigetvári; Judit Gadanecz né Szarka

Finally, very special thanks from Clive to Ma Angeles and from Christina to
Cristina for all their help and encouragement. Christina would also like to
thank her children Joaquin, Marco, and Krysia for their constant inspiration.

Lindsay Clandfield would like to thank Oxford TEFL for its support.

*The authors and publisher are grateful to those who have given permission to reproduce
the following extracts and adaptations of copyright material*: p.222 *Eternal Flame*
Words & Music by Billy Steinberg, Tom Kelly & Susanna Hoffs © Copyright
1988 & 1989 Billy Steinberg Music/Sony/ATV Tunes LLC/Bangopile Music, USA.
Sony/ATV Music Publishing (UK) Limited (66.66%) Universal Music Publishing
Limited (33.34%). Lyrics used by permission of Music Sales Ltd. All Rights
Reserved. International Copyright Secured.

p.223 *Somethin' Stupid* Words and Music by C. Carson Parks © Copyright 1967
Greenwood Music Company, USA. Montclare Music Company Limited (UK &
Eire). Warner/Chappell Music Ltd (World excluding North America, UK &
Eire). Reproduced by permission of Music Sales Limited & International Music
Publications Ltd. All Rights Reserved. International Copyright Secured.

p.224 *Oh Pretty Woman* Words and Music by Roy Orbison and Bill Dees © 1964
(renewed 1992) Roy Orbison Music Company, Barbara Orbison Music
Company and Acuff-Rose Music Inc, USA (50%) Warner/Chappell Music Ltd,
London W6 8BS, (50%) Sony/ATV Music Publishing Ltd., London W1F 7LP.
Reproduced by permission of International Music Publications Ltd and
Sony/ATV Music Publishing Ltd. All Rights Reserved.

p.225 *Dancing Queen* – Benny Andersson/Bjorn Ulvaeus. By permission Bocu
Music Ltd, 1 Wyndham Yard, London W1H 2QF.

p.226 *Waterloo Sunset* by Ray Davies © 1967 Davray Music Ltd & Carlin Music
Corp, London NW1 8BD – All Rights Reserved – Used by kind permission.

p.227 *La Isla Bonita* Words and Music by Madonna Ciccone, Bruce Gaitsch and
Patrick Leonard © 1986 Webo Girl Publishing, Bleu Disque Music Co Inc,
Johnny Yuma Music and Orangejello Music, USA (60%) Warner/Chappell
North America Ltd, London W6 8BS (20%) EMI Music Publishing Ltd, London
WC2H 0QY. Reproduced by permission of International Music Publications
Ltd. All Rights Reserved.

p.228 *The Best* Words and Music by Holly Knight and Mike Chapman
© Copyright 1989 Knight-Knight Music, Mike Chapman Publishing entre.
Zomba Music Publishers Ltd (62.5%) / IQ Music Ltd (37.5%). Used by
permission of Music Sales Limited. All Rights Reserved. International
Copyright Secured.

Illustrations by: Emma Dodd/Black Hat Ltd pp.164, 171, 191, 208, 211; Mark
Duffin pp.160, 193, 206, 214; Martina Farrow, pp.223, 226, 227; Spike Gerrell.
pp.142, 143, 147, 155, 165, 192, 194, 199, 202; Neil Gower pp.169, 217; Conny
Jude pp.222, 224, 225, 228; Ellis Nadler pp.144, 146, 150, 162, 167, 170, 195,
201; Kath Walker pp.140, 141, 145, 148, 152, 153, 157, 159, 189, 203.

*The publishers would like to thank the following for permission to reproduce
photographs*: Alamy Images pp.158 (drinking coffee), 205; Corbis pp.156 (Marie
Antoinette/Ali Meyer), 158 (beach/Danny Lehmann), 186 (Martin Scorsese);
Rex Features pp.156 (Che Guevarra/SIPA), 186 (Christina Aguilera, Pierce
Brosnan, Celine Dion, Nicole Kidman/Matt Baron, Ricky Martin/Giuseppe
Aresu, Ewan McGregor/Colin Garvie, Shakira).

CONTENTS

- **What do Elementary students need?**
- **Study Link**
- **Course components**
  Student's Book Files 1–9
  Back of the Student's Book
- **For students**
  Workbook
  MultiROM
  Student's website
- **For teachers**
  Teacher's Book
  Video
  Class cassettes / audio CDs
  Teacher's website
  Test booklets

Contents
Grammar activity answers
Grammar activity masters
Communicative activity instructions
Communicative activity masters
Song activity instructions
Song activity masters

Quicktest instructions and answers
End-of-course test instructions and answers
Quicktests
End-of-course test

Syllabus checklist

Pronunciation	Speaking	Listening	Reading
vowel sounds: /ɪ/, /iː/, /æ/, /uː/, /aɪ/, word stress	saying hello, saying goodbye	saying hello, saying goodbye	
vowel sounds: /ɑː/, /ɒ/, /ə/, /e/, /əʊ/, /eə/	*Where are you from? Where is it from? Where are they from?*	*Where are you from? Where is it from? Where are they from?*	
the alphabet, /ɜː/ and /aʊ/	an interview, famous actors	an interview, personal information	
vowel sounds: /ɔː/, /ʊ/, /ʌ/, /ɔɪ/, /ɪə/, /ʊə/	classroom language	classroom language, song: *Eternal Flame*	
consonant sounds: /v/, /d/, /s/, /z/, /l/, /w/; third person -s	a typical family in your country		Typically British?
consonant sounds: /k/, /g/, /ð/, /ʃ/, /ʒ/, /r/	Meeting People interview	Natasha and Darren, song: *Something Stupid*	Natasha and Darren
consonant sounds: /p/, /f/, /tʃ/, /dʒ/, /j/, /ŋ/	guess my job	guess my job	A Double Life
consonant sounds: /b/, /θ/, /ð/, /m/, /n/, /h/	your family	family photos	
vowel sounds: /ɪː/, /uː/, /aɪ/, /əʊ/, /e/	describing famous people	fast speech, song: *Oh Pretty Woman*	
the letter *o*	*Who is more stressed?*	How stressed are these people?	How stressed are these people?
the letter *h*	Do you live the Okinawa way?		The mystery of Okinawa
word stress, /ð/ and /θ/	your favourite times	Times you love	Fascinating festivals, Times you love
sentence stress	Are you creative, physical, or practical?		
/ŋ/, sentence stress	activities you like	Do you like shopping?	Shopping: men and women are different
/ɪ/ and /iː/	What do you think of …?		Five classic love stories
rhyming words	music questionnaire	song: *Unchained Melody*	
sentence stress	the top people from your country	American presidents	famous statues
pronunciation of -ed endings	Find a person who …		A tale of two Sydneys
sentence stress	A night out	Girls' night out, song: *Dancing Queen*	Girls' night out
past simple verbs	police interview	Murder in a country house	Murder in a country house

Pronunciation	Speaking	Listening	Reading
/ð/ and /eə/, sentence stress	Is there a … in your house?	Larry and Louise rent a house	
silent letters	What was there in the room?	Did Stephen see the ghost?	Would you like to spend a night in this room?
verb + -ing	noisy neighbours, They're having a party	What's happening?	
city names	tourism in your town	song: *Waterloo Sunset*	The London Eye

the letters *ea*	a food diary	Can men cook?	
/w/, /v/, and /b/	How much water do you drink?		Water – facts and myths
sentence stress	play *Changing Holidays*	Changing Holidays song: *La Isla Bonita*	holiday diaries
/ʊ/, /uː/, and /ʌ/	fortune telling	It's written in the cards	It's written in the cards

/ə/, sentence stress	the True False Show car colours and personality	the True False Show,	
consonant groups	How well do you know your country?	song: *The Best*	Extreme living
sentence stress	choosing and buying presents	a parachute jump	a really special present
word stress in adjectives and adverbs	They drive dangerously in …		The inside story

sentence stress	Are you jealous?, Find a person who …	Who phones Rob?	Are you jealous?
irregular past participles	cinema experiences, films and books	films and books	

We have met and spoken to many different teachers in many different countries over the years, and we are very aware that no teaching situations are ever the same. For this reason we have tried to make *New English File Elementary* as flexible as possible. Apart from the main Student's Book lessons, there is a wealth of other material which can be used according to your students' needs and the time available, for example:

- the Writing and Revise & Check pages.
- over 80 pages of photocopiable extras in the Teacher's Book.
- extra self-study support for students both on the MultiROM and the *New English File* website.

The Teacher's Book also suggests different ways of exploiting many of the Student's Book activities depending on the level of your class.

We believe that this flexibility makes the course suitable both for elementary students and real and false beginners.

We very much hope you enjoy using *New English File*.

What do Elementary students need?

It is no coincidence that when we talk about language knowledge and ability, we use the verb *speak*: *Do you speak English?*, *How many languages do you speak?* What most students want above all is to be able to speak English and this is why our aim is to get students talking.

Grammar, Vocabulary, and Pronunciation

If we want students to speak English with confidence, we need to give them the tools they need – Grammar, Vocabulary, and Pronunciation (G, V, P). We believe that 'G + V + P = confident speaking', and in *New English File Elementary* all three elements are given equal importance. Each lesson has clearly stated grammar, vocabulary, and pronunciation aims. This keeps lessons focused and gives students concrete learning objectives and a sense of progress.

Grammar

Elementary students need

- clear and memorable presentations of new structures.
- plenty of regular and varied practice.
- student-friendly reference material.

We have tried to provide contexts for new language that will engage students, using real-life stories and situations, humour, and suspense.

The **Grammar Banks** give students a single, easy-to-access grammar reference section, with clear rules, example sentences, and common errors. There are then two practice exercises for each grammar point.
◌ Student's Book *p.122*.
The photocopiable Grammar activities in the Teacher's Book can be used for practice in class or for self-study, especially with slower or weaker classes or real or false beginners.
◌ Teacher's Book *p.140*.

Vocabulary

Elementary students need

- to expand their knowledge of high-frequency words and phrases rapidly.

- to use new vocabulary in personalized contexts.
- accessible reference material.

Every lesson in *New English File Elementary* focuses on high-frequency vocabulary and common lexical areas, but keeps the load realistic. Many lessons are linked to the **Vocabulary Banks** which help present and practise the vocabulary in class and provide a clear reference so students can revise and test themselves in their own time.

Where we think the pronunciation of a word may be problematic, we have provided the phonemic script.
◌ Student's Book *p.142*.
Students can practise the pronunciation of all the words from the **Vocabulary Banks** using the **MultiROM** and the *New English File* student's website.

Pronunciation

Elementary students need

- a solid foundation in the sounds of English.
- systematic pronunciation development.
- to see where there are rules and patterns.

Elementary learners want to speak clearly but are often frustrated by English pronunciation, particularly the sound–spelling relationships, silent letters, and weak forms. In the first two Files we introduce the 44 vowel and consonant sounds of English through *New English File's* unique system of sound pictures, which give clear example words to help students to identify and produce the sounds. *New English File Elementary* has a pronunciation focus in every lesson, which integrates clear pronunciation into grammar and vocabulary practice.
◌ Student's Book *p.9*.
This is often linked to the **Sound Bank**, a reference section which students can use to check the symbols and to see common sound–spelling patterns.
◌ Student's Book *p.156*.
Throughout the book there is also a regular focus on word and sentence stress where students are encouraged to copy the rhythm of English. This will help students to pronounce new language with greater confidence.

Speaking

Elementary students need

- topics that will arouse their interest.
- achievable tasks.
- regular opportunities to use new language.

The ultimate aim of most students is to be able to communicate in English. Every lesson in *New English File Elementary* has a speaking activity which activates grammar, vocabulary, and pronunciation.
◌ Student's Book *p.81*.
The Communication section of the Student's Book provides 'information gap' activities to give students a reason to communicate.
◌ Student's Book *p.108* and *p.111*.
Photocopiable Communicative activities can be found in the Teacher's Book. These include pairwork activities, mingles, and games.
◌ Teacher's Book *p.185*.

Listening

Elementary students need

- confidence.
- to understand the gist of what is being said.
- to make sense of connected speech.

Many students say that they find understanding spoken English one of the hardest skills to master. This can be especially demotivating at lower levels where students often find the speed of the listening material too fast and the tasks too difficult. We feel that students need confidence-building, achievable tasks that help them understand the gist even though they will not understand every word.

Students also need a reason to listen. As with the reading texts, we have chosen listenings that we hope students will want to listen to.
○ Student's Book *p.67*.

Receptive work on pronunciation also helps students get used to speakers of English and gives them practice in decoding rapid speech.

New English File Elementary also contains eight songs which we hope students will find enjoyable and motivating. For copyright reasons, these are cover versions.

Reading

Elementary students need

- engaging topics and stimulating texts.
- manageable tasks that help students to read.

Many students need to read in English for their work or studies, and reading is also important in helping to build vocabulary and to consolidate grammar. The key to encouraging students to read is to give them motivating but accessible material and tasks they can do. In *New English File Elementary* reading texts have been adapted from a variety of real sources (the British press, magazines, news websites) and have been chosen for their intrinsic interest.
○ Student's Book *p.34*.

The Revise & Check sections also includes a more challenging text which helps students to measure their progress.
○ Student's Book *p.99*.

Writing

Elementary students need

- clear models.
- the 'nuts and bolts' of writing on a word- and sentence-level.

The growth of the Internet and e-mail means that people worldwide are writing in English more than ever before both for business and personal communication. *New English File Elementary* has one Writing lesson per File, where students study a model before doing a guided writing task themselves. These writing tasks focus on a specific text type and provide consolidation of grammar and lexis taught in the File.
○ Student's Book *p.13*.

Practical English

Elementary students need

- to understand high-frequency phrases that they will hear.
- to know what to say in typical situations.

Many Elementary students will need English 'to survive' if they travel to an English-speaking country or if they are using English as a *lingua franca*. The eight *Practical English* lessons give students practice in key language for situations

such as checking into a hotel or ordering a meal in a restaurant. To make these everyday situations come alive there is a story line involving two main characters, Mark (American) and Allie (British).

The **You hear / You say** feature makes a clear distinction between what students will *hear* and need to understand, for example *Are you ready to order?*, and what they need to *say*, for example *I'd like the pasta please*. The lessons also highlight other key 'Social English' phrases such as *Let's go, OK, It doesn't matter*.

The Practical English lessons are also on the ***New English File Elementary Video*** which teachers can use with the same Student's Book exercises instead of the class cassette / CD. Using the video will provide a change of focus and give the lessons a clear visual context. The video will make the lessons more enjoyable and will also help students to roleplay the situations.

Extracts from the video (the first dialogue from each lesson) are also on the MultiROM.
○ Student's Book *p.12*.

Revision

Elementary students need

- regular review.
- motivating reference and practice material.
- a sense of progress.

However clearly structures or vocabulary are presented, students will usually only assimilate and *remember* new language if they have the chance to see it and use it several times. Grammar, Vocabulary, and Pronunciation are recycled throughout *New English File Elementary*.

At the end of each File there is a Revise & Check section. **What do you remember?** revises the grammar, vocabulary, and pronunciation of each File. **What can you do?** provides a series of skills-based challenges and helps students to measure their progress in terms of competence. These pages are designed to be used flexibly according to the needs of your students.
○ Student's Book *p.14*.

The photocopiable Grammar and Communicative activities also provide many opportunities for recycling.
○ Teacher's Book *p.140* and *p.185*.

(Study Link)

The Study Link feature in *New English File Elementary* is designed to help you and your students use the course more effectively. It shows **what** resources are available, **where** they can be found, and **when** to use them.

The Student's Book has these Study Link references:

- from the Practical English lessons ○ MultiROM.
- from the Grammar Bank ○ MultiROM and website.
- from the Vocabulary Bank ○ MultiROM and website.
- from the Sound Bank ○ MultiROM and website.

These references lead students to extra activities and exercises that link in with what they have just studied.

The Workbook has these Study Link references:

○ the Student's Book Grammar and Vocabulary Banks.
○ the MultiROM.
○ the student's website.

The Teacher's Book has Study Link references to remind you where there is extra material available to your students.

Student's Book Files 1–9

The Student's Book has nine Files. Each File is organized like this:

A, B, C, and D lessons Four two-page lessons which form the core material of the book. Each lesson presents and practises **Grammar** and **Vocabulary** and has a **Pronunciation** focus. There is a balance of reading and listening activities, and lots of opportunities for spoken practise. These lessons have clear references > to the Grammar Bank, Vocabulary Bank, and Sound Bank at the back of the book.

Practical English One-page lessons which teach functional 'survival' language and vocabulary (situations like checking into a hotel or ordering a meal) and also social English (useful phrases like *Nice to meet you, Let's go.*). The lessons have a story line and link with the *New English File Elementary Video*.

Writing One-page focuses on different text types (for example, informal and formal e-mails) and writing skills like punctuation and paragraphing.

Revise & Check A two-page section – the left- and right-hand pages have different functions. The **What do you remember?** page revises the **Grammar**, **Vocabulary**, and **Pronunciation** of each File. The **What can you do?** page provides **Reading**, **Listening**, and **Speaking** 'Can you…?' challenges to show students what they can achieve.

! File 9 has two main lessons (A and B, which present the Present Perfect), and then four pages of revision of the whole book: a two-page **Grammar** section and a two-page **Vocabulary** and **Pronunciation** section.

The back of the Student's Book

In the back of the Student's Book you'll find these three Banks of material:

Grammar Bank (*pp. 122–139*)
Two pages for each File, divided into A–D to reflect the four main lessons. The left-hand page has the grammar rules and the right-hand page has two practice exercises for each lesson. Students are referred > to the Grammar Bank when they do the grammar in each main A, B, C, and D lesson.

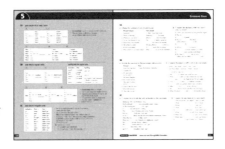

Vocabulary Bank (*pp. 140–153*)
An active picture dictionary to help students learn, practise, and revise key words. Students are referred > to the Vocabulary Bank from the main lessons.

Sound Bank (*pp. 156–159*) A four-page section with the *English File* sounds chart and typical spellings for all sounds. Students are referred > to the Sound Bank from the main lessons.

You'll also find:

- **Communication activities** (*pp. 108–113*) Information gap activities and role plays.
- **Listening scripts** (*pp. 114–121*) Scripts of key listenings.
- **Irregular verb list** (*pp. 154–155*)

For students

New English File Elementary gives your students everything they need for successful learning and motivating home study.

Workbook Each A–D lesson in the Student's Book has a two-page section in the Workbook. This provides all the practice and revision students need. Each section has:

- **More Words to Learn**, which reminds students of new vocabulary from the lesson which is not in the Vocabulary Bank.
- **Question time**, five questions for students to answer, which show them how their communicative competence is developing. (These questions also appear on the MultiROM.)

For each File there is a **Study Skills** tip on how to learn Vocabulary.

Each Practical English lesson has a one-page section in the Workbook, and includes 'Practical English reading'. There is also a Key Booklet.

MultiROM

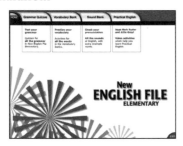

The MultiROM works in two ways:

- It's a CD-ROM, containing revision of **Grammar, Vocabulary, Pronunciation**, and functional language (with Practical English video extracts from the Video).
- It's an audio CD for students to use in a CD player. They can listen to, repeat, and answer the questions from the **Question time** sections of the Workbook.

Student's website

www.oup.com/elt/englishfile/elementary

The *English File* website gives your students extra learning resources, including more grammar activities for every lesson, more vocabulary activities for every Vocabulary Bank, Practical English audio activities, weblinks, and games and puzzles.

For teachers

New English File Elementary gives you everything you need to teach motivating, enjoyable lessons, to save you time, and to make your life easier.

Teacher's Book The Teacher's Book has detailed lesson plans for all the lessons. These include:

- an optional 'books-closed' lead-in for every lesson.
- **Extra idea** suggestions for optional extra activities.
- **Extra challenge** suggestions for ways of exploiting the Student's Book material in a more challenging way if you have a stronger class.
- **Extra support** suggestions for ways of adapting activities or exercises to make them more accessible for complete or false beginners.

All lesson plans include keys and complete tapescripts. Extra activities are colour coded in red so you can see where you are at a glance when you're planning and teaching your classes.

You'll also find over 80 pages of photocopiable materials in the Teacher's Book:

Photocopiable Grammar activities see *pp. 140–174*
There is a photocopiable Grammar activity for each A, B, C, and D lesson. These provide extra grammar practice, and can be used either in class or for self-study.

Photocopiable Communicative activities see *pp.185–219*
There is a photocopiable Communicative activity for each A, B, C, and D lesson. These give students extra speaking practice.

Photocopiable Song activities see *pp.222–228*
New English File Elementary has a song for every File. In File 4 the song is in the Student's Book, and the other seven songs are in the Teacher's Book.

Photocopiable Quicktests and End-of-course test see *pp.231–240*
There are eight photocopiable one-page Quicktests which cover the **Grammar**, **Vocabulary**, and **Pronunciation** of each File. There is a two-page End-of-course test which also includes reading, writing, listening, and speaking.

All the photocopiable material is accompanied by clear instructions and keys.

Video This is a unique 'teaching video' that links with the Practical English lessons in the Student's Book. The video has stylised minimalist sets which help students to concentrate on the language, and there is a story line which features Allie (British) and Mark (American). Each video section can be used with the tasks in the Student's Book Practical English lessons as an alternative to using the  Class cassette / audio CD. There's no extra video print material, and you don't need to find extra time to use it. It shows students language in clear contexts and will help them to role play each scene.

The speed of delivery is slightly faster than on the cassette / audio CD, as video is easier for students to understand. Extracts of the video also appear on the MultiROM.

The *New English File Elementary* package also includes:

- **Three Class cassettes / audio CDs**
  Contain all the listening materials for the Student's Book.
- **Teacher's website www.oup.com/elt/teacher/englishfile**
  This gives you extra teaching resources, including wordlists, listening and reading texts from the Student's Book (including ideas for how to use them in class), syllabus information, and weblinks.
- **Test booklets**
  These contain full-length tests for each File of *New English File Elementary*.

1
A

G verb *be* ☐+, personal pronouns: *I, you*, etc.
V numbers 1–20, days of the week
P vowel sounds: /ɪ/, /iː/, /æ/, /uː/, /aɪ/, word stress

Nice to meet you

Lesson plan

This first lesson covers basic greetings and farewells, and the verb *be* in positive sentences, as well as numbers and days of the week. Depending on whether your SS are real or false beginners you may want to spend more or less time on each section. The lesson also introduces SS to the *New English File* system of teaching the forty-four sounds of English. Here they begin by learning six vowel sounds. Both false and real beginners should be motivated by working systematically to improve their pronunciation.

Optional lead-in (books closed)

- Pre-teach the first conversation in a by introducing yourself. Say *Hi/Hello, I'm* (…), and ask three or four SS *What's your name?* When they answer, pretend sometimes not to have heard them properly and say *'Sorry?'* and put your hand to your ear.

1 SAYING HELLO

a ◖ **1.1** ◗

- Books open. Focus on the four pictures. Then tell SS to listen to and read the four conversations and match each one to a picture.
- Play the tape/CD once or twice. Check answers.

> **A** 2   **B** 1   **C** 4   **D** 3

> ◖ **1.1** ◗   CD1 Track 2
>
> 1   **A** Hi, I'm Tom. What's your name?
>   **B** Anna.
>   **A** Sorry?
>   **B** Anna!
> 2   **A** Hi, Dad. This is Dave.
>   **B** Hello. Nice to meet you.
>   **C** Nice to meet you.
> 3   **A** Good evening. What's your name?
>   **B** My name's Janet Leigh.
>   **A** You're in room 5.
> 4   **A** Hello, John. How are you?
>   **B** I'm fine, thanks. And you?
>   **A** Very well, thank you.

b ● Focus on the chart. Explain that *Hello/Hi* mean the same, but *Hi* is more informal.
- Get SS in pairs to complete the chart with words from the list. Check answers and highlight that in the second row the words/phrases are more informal than in the first.

Hello	My name's	Very well	Thank you
Hi	**I'm**	**Fine**	**thanks**

c ● Explain that in English some words are said more strongly than others, e.g. in <u>Nice</u> to <u>meet</u> you, *nice* and *meet* are pronounced more strongly than *to* and *you*. Encourage SS to try to copy the rhythm on the

tape/CD. Getting the rhythm right is one of the most important aspects of good pronunciation.
- Go through each line of the conversations, getting SS to repeat after the tape/CD. Take this opportunity to elicit/explain the meaning of any words or phrases that SS don't understand.
- When you go through conversation **3**, focus also on the box with *Good afternoon* and *Good evening*. Model and drill the pronunciation. Explain the times when these expressions are used. There is no fixed time for when *afternoon* becomes *evening*, but *Good afternoon* is generally used between lunchtime and about 5.00 p.m. and *Good evening* after that. Tell SS that they are more formal than *Hello*, especially *Good afternoon* and *Good evening*. Use body language to demonstrate formal and informal greetings, e.g. shaking hands for more formal greetings.

d ◖ **1.2** ◗

- Put SS in pairs. Tell them to focus on the pictures. Explain that they are going to act out the conversations with the sound effects.
- Play all the sound effects for conversations **1–4** for SS to understand what they have to do. Then play for conversation **1** and demonstrate the activity with a good student.

> ◖ **1.2** ◗   CD1 Track 3
>
> 1 disco music
> 2 doorbell
> 3 footsteps and bell
> 4 birdsong

- Now play sound effects for conversation **1** again, getting SS to roleplay it in pairs. Repeat with the other three conversations. If time get SS to change roles.

Extra idea

Get SS to practise the conversations first by *reading* their roles with the sound effects. Then they could try to act them out from memory.

e ● Focus on the example sentences in the speech bubbles. Tell SS to imagine that they're at a party or a conference where they don't know anyone. Get them to stand up.
- Now tell SS to introduce themselves to at least five other students. Encourage SS to shake hands, or use a locally appropriate gesture, say *Nice to meet you*, and *Sorry?* if they don't hear the other student's name.

2 GRAMMAR   verb *be* ☐+, pronouns

a ● Focus on the first sentence, *I'm Tom*. Explain that *I'm* is the contraction of two words, and elicit that the missing word is **am**.
- Give SS a minute to complete the other two gaps and check answers.

> I **am** Tom.
> My name **is** Janet Leigh.
> You **are** in room 5.

b ● Tell SS to go to **Grammar Bank 1A** on *p.122*. Explain that all the grammar rules and exercises are in this section of the book.

● Go through the rules with the class. Model and drill the example sentences. Model and drill the pronunciation of the contractions, especially *You're* /juə/, *We're* /wɪə/, and *They're* /ðeə/.

Grammar notes

● Highlight that fluent speakers of English nearly always use contractions in conversation.

● In English there is only one form of *you*, which is used for singular and plural and for formal or informal situations. In your SS' language(s) there may be different pronouns for second person singular and plural and also formal and informal forms.

● Focus on the exercises for **1A** on *p.123*. SS do the exercises individually or in pairs.

● Check answers.

> **a** 1 is 2 are 3 am 4 are 5 is 6 are 7 is
> **b** 1 It's…   5 They're…
> 2 We're…   6 She's…
> 3 You're…   7 I'm…
> 4 He's…

● Tell SS to go back to the main lesson on *p.4*.

c ● Point to a male student whose name you remember and say *He's (Antonio)*. Then point to a female student and elicit *She's (María)*. Continue with several other SS to give more practice with *He's/She's*.

3 PRONUNCIATION vowel sounds, word stress

● Focus on the cartoon. Tell SS that English has twenty vowel sounds, and they are going to learn an example word to help them remember each sound. In File 1 they are going to learn the vowel sounds of English and in File 2 the consonant sounds. Learning the sounds will help them to pronounce words more clearly and confidently.

a **1.3**

● Focus on the six sound pictures (*fish, tree,* etc.). Explain that the phonetic symbol in the picture represents the sound. The phonetic alphabet is used worldwide to help you know how words are pronounced. Learning to recognize these symbols will help SS to check the pronunciation of a word in a dictionary.

● Play the tape/CD once for SS just to listen.

● Then play the tape/CD again pausing after each word and sound for SS to repeat.

1.3		CD1 Track 4
fish	/ɪ/	boot /uː/
tree	/iː/	train /eɪ/
cat	/æ/	bike /aɪ/

Pronunciation notes

● It is important to point out to SS that with the vowels, i.e. *a, e, i, o, u,* there is no one-to-one relation between a letter and a sound, e.g. the letter *a* can be pronounced in several different ways. However, there are common combinations of letters which are usually pronounced the same way and these will be pointed out to SS as the course progresses.

● Tell SS that the two dots in the symbols /iː/ and /uː/ mean that it's a long sound.

● You could also tell SS that /eɪ/ and /aɪ/ are diphthongs, i.e. two sounds together (/e/ and /ɪ/, /æ/ and /ɪ/), if you think this will help them.

● Focus especially on sounds which are difficult for your SS and model them yourself so that SS can see your mouth position. Get SS to repeat these sounds a few more times.

b **1.4**

● Now focus on the example words in the column under each sound picture, e.g. *it* and *this*. Explain that the pink letters are the same sound as the picture word they're under. Demonstrate for SS, e.g. say *fish, it, this; tree, he, she,* etc.

● Now focus on the words in the list. Tell SS in pairs to decide what the sound of the pink letter is, and to write the word under the corresponding sound picture. Encourage them to say the words out loud.

● Play the tape/CD for SS to check their answers.

● Play the tape/CD again pausing after each group of words for SS to repeat them.

1.4			CD1 Track 5
fish	it, this, **is**	boot	you
tree	he, she, **we**	train	they, **name**
cat	am, **thanks**	bike	I, Hi, **my**

Study Link SS can find more practice of these sounds on the MultiROM and on the *New English File Elementary* website.

Extra idea

If SS have dictionaries with them get them to look up a few words with these vowel sounds and see how the phonetics are always given after the words and how this helps them to pronounce better. If SS don't have dictionaries, you could write the words and the phonetics on the board.
Possible words: key /kiː/, sky /skaɪ/, eight /eɪt/, food /fuːd/

c ● Write COFFEE up on the board. Elicit/teach that it has two syllables. Then explain that all words of two or more syllables have one which is stressed (pronounced more strongly than the other(s)). Then say coffee both ways (COffee and coFFEE) and ask SS which way is right (COffee). Underline CO on the board, and tell SS to underline the stressed syllable when they learn new words, especially if it's not where they would expect it.

● Now focus on the words in the pictures. These are words that most SS will probably already know, and some are 'international', e.g. *hotel, Internet*.

● Tell SS in pairs to say the words out loud and underline the stressed syllable.

⚠ Warn SS that even if the same or similar word exists in their language, the stress may be on a different syllable.

d 🔊 **1.5**

- Play the tape/CD and check answers. The two words not stressed on the first syllable are ho<u>te</u>l and com<u>pu</u>ter. Point out to SS that the majority of English words are stressed on the first syllable.

🔊 1.5		CD1 Track 6
<u>co</u>ffee	<u>In</u>ternet	<u>pi</u>zza
<u>sand</u>wich	<u>toi</u>let	<u>air</u>port
<u>e</u>-mail	ho<u>te</u>l	com<u>pu</u>ter

Extra idea

If SS have dictionaries with them get them to look up, e.g. *coffee*, and show them that stress is marked in dictionaries with an apostrophe before the stressed syllable, e.g. /ˈkɒfi/. If not, copy a dictionary entry onto the board or an OHT.

e ● Get SS to write the words from **c** in the chart under the correct heading. Check answers.

food	travel	communication
coffee	toilet	e-mail
sandwich	hotel	Internet
pizza	airport	computer

f ● Write the three categories on the board. Then give SS in pairs one minute to try to add two more English words to each column.

● Feedback their answers, writing the words on the board. Underline the stressed syllable and model and drill the correct pronunciation.

(Suggested answers)		
food	**travel**	**communication**
<u>bur</u>ger	bus	<u>mo</u>dem /ˈməʊdem/
coke	car	<u>mo</u>bile (phone)
<u>ap</u>ple	plane	<u>te</u>levision
chips	<u>sta</u>tion	<u>web</u>site

4 VOCABULARY numbers 1–20

a 🔊 **1.6**

- Most SS will probably know how to count to ten, but may be less confident with 11–20. Get the class to try to count from 1 to 20. You start with the number 1 and get a student to say the next number. Try to elicit all numbers from 1–20. Then do the same counting backwards, starting from 20.

- Play the tape/CD and get SS to repeat each number. Explain/elicit that numbers 13–19 are stressed on the second syllable. Give extra practice with any numbers that are difficult for your SS.

🔊 1.6	CD1 Track 7
1 2 3 4 5 6 7 8 9 10 11 12 13 14 15 16 17 18 19 20	

⚠ When we count in a list, 1, 2, 3, 4, etc. we usually stress numbers 13–19 on the first syllable. However, at all other times, when we say them in isolation, e.g. room 13, they are stressed on the second syllable.

We recommend that you teach this pronunciation as it is important for SS to later distinguish between e.g. 13 and 30.

b ● Tell SS to go to **Vocabulary Bank *Numbers 1–20*** on *p.140*. Explain that these pages (Vocabulary Banks) are their vocabulary section where they will first do the exercises as required by the Student's Book, and will then have the pages for reference to help them remember the words.

● Here they check the spelling of numbers 1–20. Give SS a couple of minutes to do **1** in pairs.

● Check answers. Highlight the spelling changes between *three* and *thirteen* and *five* and *fifteen*. You could also point out to SS that numbers in English don't change (i.e. they never become masculine or feminine).

3 three
5 five
7 seven
11 eleven
12 twelve
15 fifteen
18 eighteen
20 twenty

Study Link SS can find more practice of these words on the MultiROM and on the *New English File Elementary* website.

Extra idea

Give SS more practice by saying simple sums to them, e.g. *What's 4 and 4?* They could also practise this way in pairs.

● Tell SS to go back to the main lesson on *p.5*.

c 🔊 **1.7**

● Focus on the four places (airport, sandwich bar, etc.) Tell SS they're going to listen to four short conversations. The first time they listen they should just try to understand *where* the conversation is taking place and write a number 1–4 in the boxes.

⚠ Make sure SS write 1–4 in the boxes, and not in the spaces, e.g. after *Gate number*.

● Play the tape/CD once and check answers.

1 sandwich bar	**2** airport	**3** taxi	**4** hotel

d ● Now tell SS to listen again but this time to focus on the numbers they hear in each conversation. Play the tape/CD again, pausing between each conversation to give SS time to write the numbers in the gaps.

● Get SS to compare their answers in pairs and then check answers.

Gate number 9	€3.20	Room 12	16 Manchester Road

Extra support

If SS want to know exactly what was said in each conversation, get them to turn to the tapescript on *p.114*. Play the tape/CD again and explain/translate any unknown vocabulary.

fe5195en

1.7   CD1 Track 8

(tapescript in Student's Book on *p.114.*)

1 **A** A cheese and tomato sandwich please.
  B That's **3** euros and **20** cents.
2 British Airways flight to Madrid is now boarding at gate number **9**.
3 **A** Where to, love?
  B Manchester Road, please. Number **16**.
4 **A** Here's your key sir. Room **12**.
  B Thank you.

Extra idea

Another numbers game which SS always enjoy is 'Buzz'. You may want to play it now or at any other moment when you want to revise numbers.

– Get SS to sit or stand in a circle and count out loud. When they come to a number which contains 3 (e.g. 13) or a multiple of 3 (e.g. 3, 6, 9, etc.) they have to say 'Buzz' instead of the number.

– If a student makes a mistake, either saying the number instead of 'Buzz', or simply saying the wrong number, he/she is 'out', and the next player begins again from 1.

– Carry on until there is only one student left, who is the winner, or until the group have got to thirty without making a mistake.

– When SS have done numbers 20–1,000 (in the next lesson) you can also play 'Buzz' with 7 as the 'wild' number and go up to 50.

5 SAYING GOODBYE

a **1.8**

• Focus on the cartoon and ask SS *Who are they?* (Tom and Anna from **1a**).

• Focus on the six different ways of saying goodbye. Model and drill the expressions for SS to repeat, and highlight the stressed syllables (Good<u>bye</u>, Good<u>night</u>) and words (<u>See</u> you, <u>See</u> you on <u>Sat</u>urday, <u>See</u> you to<u>mor</u>row). Elicit/explain the meaning of any words SS don't know.

⚠ We only say *Goodnight* as another way of saying goodbye at the end of an evening, or before going to bed. We never use it as a greeting. For a greeting at night, use *Hello* or *Good evening* (more formal).

• Tell SS they're going to hear the two people in the picture saying goodbye to each other. They must number the expressions in the order they hear them. Play the tape/CD once or twice.

• Check answers.

> **1** Bye.
> **2** Goodbye.
> **3** See you tomorrow.
> **4** See you on Saturday.
> **5** See you.
> **6** Goodnight.

Extra idea

Get SS to roleplay the conversation (Phrases 1, 3, 4, and 6 are said by Tom, 2 and 5 by Anna.)

1.8   CD1 Track 9

(tapescript in Student's Book on *p.114.*)

TOM   OK, bye.
ANNA Yes, goodbye.
TOM   See you tomorrow.
ANNA Not tomorrow, Saturday.
TOM   Oh yeah. See you on Saturday.
ANNA See you.
TOM   Goodnight.

b **1.9**

• Ask SS if they know/remember which day Saturday is, and which syllable is stressed (the first).

• Focus on the capital letters. Tell SS that in English, days of the week always start with a capital letter.

• Give SS in pairs a few minutes to complete the days, and then play the tape/CD and get SS to repeat them. Ask them where the stress is (always on the first syllable). Give more pronunciation practice as necessary. SS may have problems with *Tuesday* /ˈtjuːzdeɪ/, *Wednesday* /ˈwenzdeɪ/, and *Thursday* /ˈθɜːzdeɪ/.

1.9   CD1 Track 10

Monday	Friday
Tuesday	Saturday
Wednesday	Sunday
Thursday	

• Ask SS *What day is it today?* and *When's your next class?* At the end of the class, remember to say *Goodbye. See you on (...)* and encourage SS to do the same.

Extra photocopiable activities

Grammar
pronouns + verb *be* *p.140* (instructions *p.175*).
Communicative
Fancy dress party *p.185*.

Homework

Study Link Workbook *pp.4–5*.

G verb *be* ⊟ and ⁇
V countries and nationalities: *Spain, Russian*, etc. numbers 20–1,000
P vowel sounds: /ɑː/, /ɒ/, /ə/, /e/, /əʊ/, /eə/

I'm not English, I'm Scottish!

Lesson plan

In this lesson a world quiz provides the context for SS to learn/revise countries and nationalities. The lesson also covers all present simple forms of the verb *be*, numbers, and six more vowel sounds.

Optional lead-in (books closed)

- Write the three questions in **VOCABULARY a** on the board. Elicit/teach the answers and write them on the board. (In a monolingual class you could draw a simple map of your SS' country and its neighbours. In a multinational class you may prefer just to ask the first two questions.)
- Model and drill pronunciation.

1 VOCABULARY countries and nationalities

a • Elicit the answers to the three questions onto the board.

b • Tell SS to go to **Vocabulary Bank *Countries and nationalities*** on *p. 141*.
   • Give SS five minutes to do exercise **a** in pairs. Check answers. Model and drill pronunciation. Point out that the stress on country and nationality words sometimes changes and sometimes doesn't, e.g. Germany, German (no change) Italy, Italian (change).

1 the United States	9 Italy
2 Argentina	10 Japan
3 England	11 Poland
4 Spain	12 Russia
5 Brazil	13 Scotland
6 France	14 Thailand
7 Germany	15 China
8 Ireland	

- Focus on instructions for **b**. If SS' own country is not in the list, get them to draw the flag here and write the words. Elicit ideas for other countries to add.
- Focus on instructions for **c**. Get SS to cover the words with a piece of paper leaving the flags visible. SS look at the flags and try to remember both the country and nationality/language.
- Finally, focus on the information box and go through it with the class.

Study Link SS can find more practice of these words on the MultiROM and on the *New English File Elementary* website.

- Tell SS to go back to the main lesson on *p.6*.

c 1.10
   • Focus on the example and elicit that Ja<u>pan</u> has the stress on the second syllable.
   • Play the tape/CD twice. SS repeat the words and underline the stressed syllables. SS compare with their partner. Check answers.

1.10	CD1 Track 11
Japan	Japa<u>nese</u>
Germany	German
China	Chi<u>nese</u>
Italy	I<u>tal</u>ian
the U<u>nit</u>ed <u>States</u>	American
Russia	Russian

- Play the tape/CD again and get SS to repeat the pairs of words.

d • Here SS recycle the country and nationality words that they have just learnt above.
   • Put SS in pairs. Give them a minute to do question **1** but don't check answers yet.
   • 1.11
   Focus on question 2. Play the tape/CD. SS write the languages that they think they hear.
   • 1.12
   Focus on question 3. Play the tape/CD and SS write which country they think the music is from.

1.11	CD1 Track 12
a (In Russian) My name's Anna and I'm from Moscow.	
b (In Italian) My name's Giovanni and I'm from Firenze.	
c (In Spanish) My name's Pilar and I'm from Salamanca.	
d (In Japanese) My name's Takashi and I'm from Osaka.	

1.12	CD1 Track 13
a *Irish folk music*	
b *Brazilian samba*	
c *French accordion music*	
d *Argentinian tango*	

- Check answers.

1 **a** Poland
b Scotland
c the USA
d China
e Thailand
2 **a** Russian **b** Italian **c** Spanish **d** Japanese
3 **a** Ireland **b** Brazil **c** France **d** Argentina

2 LISTENING & SPEAKING

a 1.13
   • Focus on the four pictures and get SS to cover the gapped conversations in **b**.
   • Play the tape/CD and SS number the pictures. Check answers.

3 1 4 2

b • Play the tape/CD again. This time SS fill the gaps with a country or nationality. Check answers.

1.13   CD1 Track 14

1 A Are you **English**?
  B No, I'm **Scottish**. I'm from Edinburgh.
2 A Where are you from?
  B We're from **the United States**.
  A Are you on holiday?
  B No, we aren't. We're on business.
3 A Where's she from? Is she **Spanish**?
  B No, she isn't. She's **Argentinian**. She's from
      Buenos Aires.
4 A Mmm, delicious. Is it **German**?
  B No, it isn't. It's **French**.

c ● Play the tape/CD again and use the pause button. SS
       repeat the conversations line by line trying to copy the
       rhythm. Elicit/explain any words or phrases that SS
       don't understand, e.g. *on business/holiday, delicious.*
d ● Give SS two minutes to memorize the conversations.
       Then in pairs they roleplay each conversation, using
       the pictures in **2 a** as a memory aid.

3 GRAMMAR   verb *be* ⊟ and ?

a ● Give SS two minutes to try and complete the grammar
       chart.
   ● Check answers, writing the missing words on the
       board.

Question	Short answer	Negative
Are you English?	No, **I'm not**.	**I'm not** English.
Are they from Spain?	Yes, they **are**.	
Is she Portuguese?	No, she **isn't**.	She **isn't** Portuguese.
Is he on business?	Yes, he **is**.	

   ● Tell SS to go to **Grammar Bank 1B** on *p.122.*
   ● Go through the rules with the class. Model and drill
       the example sentences.

Grammar notes

● Remind SS that in conversation it is more common to
   use contractions than the full form.
● In the negative the verb *be* can be contracted in two
   ways, e.g. *You aren't Italian* (contracting *not*); *You're
   not Italian* (contracting *are*). Throughout *New English
   File* the first way (contracting *not*) has been used, but
   accept either from your SS, who may have learnt the
   other way.
● With short answers, explain to SS that although native
   speakers often use *Yes, I am* instead of just *Yes,* both
   ways of answering are perfectly correct.

● Focus on the exercises for **1B** on *p.123.* SS do the
   exercises individually or in pairs.

a 1 I'm not British.
  2 They aren't Brazilian.
  3 It isn't Mexican food.
  4 She isn't Italian.
  5 We aren't from England.
  6 You aren't Japanese.
  7 He isn't from the USA.

b 1 Am I in room 13?	Yes, you are.
2 Is it German?	No, it isn't.
3 Are they from Italy?	No, they aren't.
4 Are we in Class 2?	Yes, you/we are.
5 Is she Chinese?	Yes, she is.
6 Are you Irish?	No, I'm not.
7 Is he from Scotland?	No, he isn't.

● Tell SS to go back to the main lesson on *p.7.*

4 PRONUNCIATION   vowel sounds

● Quickly revise the previous six vowel words and
   sounds on *p. 5.*

a **1.14**
   ● Focus on the six sound pictures (*car, clock,* etc.).
       Remind SS that the phonetic symbol in the picture
       represents the sound.
   ● Play the tape/CD once for SS just to listen.
   ● Then play the tape/CD again, pausing after each word
       and sound for SS to repeat.

1.14		CD1 Track 15
car	/ɑː/	
clock	/ɒ/	
computer	ˈ/ə/	
egg	/e/	
phone	/əʊ/	
chair	/eə/	

Pronunciation notes

● The /ə/ sound occurs twice in *computer.* The /ə/ sound
   occurs before or after stressed syllables and is the most
   common sound in English.
● Remind SS that the two dots in /ɑː/ means that this
   sound is long.
● You could also point out that /eə/ is a diphthong, i.e.
   two sounds, /e/ and /ə/ if you think this will help.

● Focus on sounds which are difficult for your SS and
   model them yourself so that SS can see your mouth
   position. Get SS to repeat these sounds a few more
   times.
b ● Focus on the instructions and the example. Explain
       that SS have to match the sentences to the pictures in **a**
       according to the pronunciation of the letters in pink.
c **1.15**
   ● Play the tape/CD and check answers.

2 egg   **3** clock   **4** computer   **5** car   **6** phone

d ● Play the tape/CD again for SS to repeat the words and
       phrases.

1.15		CD1 Track 16
1 Where's he from?	chair	
2 Ben's French.	egg	
3 I'm not Scottish.	clock	
4 I'm American.	computer	
5 Are you from France?	car	
6 No, I'm Polish.	phone	

Study Link SS can find more practice of English sounds on the MultiROM or on the *New English File Elementary* website.

5 SPEAKING

a • Focus on the example exchange in the speech bubbles and model and drill the question. Get SS to ask you the question.

⚠ The answer to *Where are you from?* is usually *I'm from (town)* when you're in your own country and *I'm from (country)* or *I'm (nationality)* followed by the town when you're abroad.

• Get SS to stand up and ask five other students the question. In a monolingual class where SS are all from the same town, encourage SS to say their nationality and then the area of the town or the village that they're from, to make this more communicative.

b • Focus on the pictures and the example exchanges in the speech bubble and model and drill pronunciation. Demonstrate the activity with the first picture and then get SS to work in pairs.

> 1 Mercedes-Benz is from Germany.
> 2 The dolls are from Russia.
> 3 The women are from Japan.
> 4 The cheese is from France.
> 5 Guinness is from Ireland.
> 6 The trainers are from the USA.
> 7 The sunglasses are from Italy.
> 8 The football fans are from Brazil.

6 VOCABULARY numbers 20–1,000

a 〔1.16〕

• Focus on the cartoon and the question. Then play the tape/CD twice and elicit the answers. Highlight that 0 is usually pronounced /əʊ/ in telephone numbers, although *zero* can also be used.

> Double seven 'Oh'

> 〔1.16〕   CD1 Track 17
>
> ANNA What's your phone number?
> TOM   It's 6347750.

b • Model and drill the question. Get SS to ask three students sitting near them for their phone number and to try to write it down correctly.

c • Tell SS to go to **Vocabulary Bank** *Numbers 20–1,000* on *p. 140* and do the exercise.

• Check answers by writing the numbers on the board, and model and drill pronunciation. Highlight *and* in e.g. *two hundred and fifty*.

> 31 40 47 50 59 60 63 70 72 80 86 90 94 100   ·
> 250 1,000

• Write some more high numbers on the board (100–1,000) and give SS practice saying them.

Study Link SS can find more practice of these numbers on the MultiROM and on the *New English File Elementary* website.

• Tell SS to go back to the main lesson on *p. 7*.

---

d 〔1.17〕

• Play the tape/CD and get SS to repeat the numbers. Ask *What's the difference between a and b?*

⚠ The answer is that 13, 14, etc. are stressed on the second syllable and 30, 40, etc. are stressed on the first syllable. This means that the pairs of numbers can be easily confused and this can be a problem, even for native speakers.

> 〔1.17〕   CD1 Track 18
> 13, 30 14, 40 15, 50 16, 60 17, 70 18, 80 19, 90

e 〔1.18〕

• Play the tape/CD twice and SS circle **a** or **b**.

> 1 a   2 b   3 a   4 b   5 a   6 b   7 b

> 〔1.18〕   CD1 Track 19
> (tapescript in Student's Book on *p.114.*)
> 1 The train waiting at platform **13** is the Eurostar to Paris.
> 2 A Excuse me! How far is it to San José?
>   B It's about **40** kilometres.
>   A Thanks a lot.
> 3 **15** love.
> 4 Will all passengers on flight BA234 to New York please go to gate 60 immediately.
> 5 A How much is that?
>   B A pizza and a coke. That's **17** Euros.
> 6 A What's your address?
>   B It's **80** Park Road.
>   A Sorry? What number?
>   B **80**, 8 oh.
> 7 TEACHER OK. Can you be quiet, please? Open your books on page **90**.
>   S1 What page?
>   S2 Page **90**.

f • Draw this bingo card on the board for SS to copy.

• SS in pairs complete their bingo card with six numbers from **d**. They must only choose one from each pair, either 13 or 30 but not both.

• Call out random numbers choosing from the pairs of numbers in **d**.

• If SS have one of the numbers you call out on their card, they should cross it off. Keep calling until one pair have crossed off all the numbers, at which point they should call out 'Bingo!'

• Check the winning pair's card. If it's correct they have won. If it isn't, continue the game. Once there is a winner, you can play 'Bingo' again if there is time.

Extra photocopiable activities

Grammar
verb *be* ☐ and ? *p.141.*
Communicative
Where are they from? *p.186* (instructions *p.175*).

HOMEWORK

Study Link Workbook *pp. 6–7.*

G possessive adjectives: *my, your,* etc.
V personal information: *address, phone number,* etc.
P the alphabet, /ɜː/ and /aʊ/

His name, her name

Lesson plan

The topic of where SS go to study English abroad and an interview in a Dublin language school provide the context for SS to revise countries, learn how to give personal information, and practise the alphabet. The grammar focus here is possessive adjectives and the different elements of the lesson are brought together in the final activity, where SS identify famous actors who have unusual names.

Optional lead-in (books closed)

- Put SS in pairs. Give them two minutes to write down five countries where the first language is English.
- Feedback the countries onto the board. Ask them what the nationality is for each country, and where the stress is on both words.

(Possible answers)	
Britain	British
Scotland	Scottish
Ireland	Irish
the USA	American
Canada	Canadian
Australia	Australian

1 LISTENING

- Write these numbers on the board: 40,000, 80,000, 120,000, 500,000, 600,000 and elicit/teach the pronunciation.

a • Books open. Focus on the five countries, and tell SS that they are all countries where people go to study English. Go through the introductory sentence (*Every year...*) with them, and then get them in pairs to guess the missing numbers.

- Check answers, getting SS to say the whole sentence to practise the high numbers, e.g. *Six hundred thousand people study English in _____ .* You could teach them *We think...* to preface their answers.

600,000	**Britain**
500,000	**Ireland**
120,000	**the USA**
80,000	**Australia**
40,000	**Canada**

- Ask some individual SS where *they* would like to go to study English.

b 🔊 **1.19**

- Focus on the picture of the language student and on the map and elicit the country where he is going (Ireland).
- Now focus on the language school enrolment form. Explain (in SS' L1 if necessary) that Mario is a new student at a language school in Dublin. Tell SS that they are going to listen to him being interviewed by the school secretary, and must complete the form with his information.

- Go through the different headings on the form and make sure SS understand them. (They may not know *age* and *postcode*).
- Play the tape/CD once the whole way through. Then play it again, pausing from time to time to give SS time to write.

Extra support

This is the first quite long listening that SS have had. Reassure them by telling them just to relax and listen the first time, without trying to complete the form, but just trying to follow the conversation. Ask *Where are they? Who's speaking? Two men, a woman and a man, or two women?* (A woman and a man.) Then tell them to try to complete some of the form, and play the tape/CD as many times as you think they need, pausing where necessary, e.g. after the phone numbers. They could also listen again at the end with the tapescript on *p. 114.*

- Give SS time to compare their answers in pairs, and then check answers.

First name	Mario
Surname	Benedetti
Country/city	**Italy/Rome**
Student	**Yes**
Age	**20**
Address	Via Foro **25**
Postcode	**Rome 00132**
E-mail address	mario.benedetti@hotmail.com
Phone number	**06 8405 517**
Mobile phone	**348 226 7341**

1.19   CD1 Track 20

(tapescript in Student's Book on *p.114.*)
R = receptionist, M = Mario
R Hello. Are you a new student?
M Yes, I am.
R Sit down, then. I'm just going to ask you a few questions.
M OK.
R Right. **What's your first name?**
M Mario.
R **What's your surname?**
M Benedetti.
R Benedetti. **How do you spell it?**
M B-E-N-E-D-E-double T-I.
R B-E-N-E-D-E-double T-I. OK. **Where are you from?**
M I'm from Italy. From Rome.
R **Are you a student?**
M Yes, I am.
R And **how old are you?**
M I'm 20.
R **What's your address?**
M In Rome?
R Yes.
M It's Via Foro 25.
R **What's your postcode?**
M Sorry?

19

R Is there a postcode? You know, a number?
M Ah yes. It's Rome 00132.
R 00132. Great. **What's your e-mail address?**
M It's mario.benedetti@hotmail.com.
R And **what's your phone number?**
M My mobile number or my home number in Rome?
R Both – home and mobile.
M My phone number in Rome is 06 840 5517.
R 06 840 5517.
M Yes. And my mobile number is 348 226 7341.
R 348 226 7341. That's great, Mario. Thank you. Now come and meet the Director of Studies, we need to give you a test...

c 1.20
- Now focus on the receptionist's questions. Give SS a couple of minutes to read through them before they listen.

Extra challenge

Get SS to guess the missing words first, and then listen and check.

- Play the tape/CD once all the way through. SS try to complete the missing words. Play it again, pausing if necessary. Check answers, and elicit the meaning of *How do you spell it?* and *How old are you?*

⚠ The question *How old are you?* and the answer *I'm 20* are with the verb *be*. In your SS' L1 a different verb may be used, e.g. *have*.

1.20	CD1 Track 21
1 What's your first name?	
2 **What's** your surname?	
3 **How** do you spell it?	
4 Where are you **from**?	
5 **Are** you a student?	
6 How old **are** you?	
7 **What's** your address?	
8 What's **your** postcode?	
9 **What's** your e-mail address?	
10 What's your **phone number**?	

2 PRONUNCIATION the alphabet

a 1.21
- Ask SS what question the receptionist asks after *What's your surname?* (How do you spell it?) and *Why?* (Because for her it's a difficult name). Explain that it's important to know the English alphabet because you often need to spell names, surnames, town names, etc. (especially when you're talking on the phone).
- Focus on the alphabet and ask SS *Can you say the alphabet?* Unless your SS are complete beginners they should be able to pronounce some of the letters.
- Now get SS to repeat the alphabet letter by letter after the tape/CD. Play it at least twice.

1.21	CD1 Track 22
A B C D E F G H I J K L M N O P Q R S T U V W X Y Z	

b 1.22
- Focus on the chart. Explain that the letters are in columns according to the pronunciation of each letter. Elicit the seven picture words and sounds (SS have

seen them all before). Play the tape/CD for them to listen and repeat them.

1.22			CD1 Track 23
train	/eɪ/	phone	/əʊ/
tree	/iː/	boot	/uː/
egg	/e/	car	/ɑː/
bike	/aɪ/		

- Then show SS how the letters in each column have the same sound, e.g. *train*, A, J, *tree*, B, C, etc.

c 1.23
- Put SS in pairs. Get them to go through the alphabet, stopping at the letters that are missing from the chart, and writing them in the right column. Do the first one with them (D). Write it on the board and ask SS how to say it and which column it goes in (*tree*). Give SS a time limit, e.g. three minutes, to complete the chart.
- Play the tape/CD once for them to listen and check answers (you may want to copy the complete chart onto the board). Then play the tape/CD again pausing after each sound for SS to repeat the group of letters.

1.23			CD1 Track 24
train	AHJK	phone	O
tree	BCDEG**PTV**	boot	QUW
egg	FLMN**SXZ**	car	R
bike	I**Y**		

d - Focus on the abbreviations. Explain that in English we usually say abbreviations by saying the individual letters. Give SS a few moments in pairs to practise saying them. Then feedback answers round the class and ask SS if they know what any of them mean.

PC = personal computer
OK = yes, fine
CD = compact disc
VIP = very important person
DVD = digital versatile disc or digital video disc
MTV = Music Television
USA = the United States of America
UK = the United Kingdom
BMW = Bavarian Motor Works
FBI = Federal Bureau of Investigation

Extra idea

- Play *Hangman*. Think of word SS know, preferably of at least eight letters, e.g. NATIONALITY. Write a dash on the board for each letter of the word:

— — — — — — — — — — —

- SS call out letters one at a time. If the letter's in the word (e.g. A) fill it in each time it occurs, e.g.
__ A__ __ __ __ A__ __ __ __. Only accept correctly pronounced letters. If the letter is **not** in the word, draw the first line of this picture on the board:

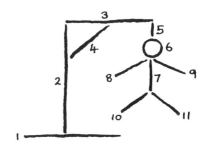

- Write any wrongly-guessed letters under the picture so that SS don't repeat them. The object of the game is to guess the word before the man is 'hanged'. SS can make guesses at any time, but each wrong guess is 'punished' by another line being drawn.
- The student who correctly guesses the word comes to the board and chooses a new word.
- SS can also play in pairs/groups drawing on a piece of paper.

3 SPEAKING

a 1.24
- Focus on the cartoon, and remind SS that getting the rhythm right when they speak will help them to understand and be understood.

Pronunciation notes
- SS have already seen how within a word one syllable is stressed more strongly than the others. They also need to be aware that within a sentence, some words are stressed more strongly than others. Stressed words are usually 'information' words, i.e. nouns, adjectives, verbs. Unstressed words are usually pronouns, articles, prepositions, and auxiliary verbs in *Wh-* questions.
- This mixture of stressed and unstressed words is what gives English its rhythm. It is this rhythm SS need to try to copy.

- Focus on the questions in **1c**. Play the tape/CD and get SS to listen and repeat. Pause after each question if SS need the extra time.

Extra idea
Get SS to underline the stressed words (see tapescript below).

1.24	CD1 Track 25
1 <u>What's</u> your <u>first</u> <u>name</u>?	
2 <u>What's</u> your <u>surname</u>?	
3 <u>How</u> do you <u>spell</u> it?	
4 <u>Where</u> are you <u>from</u>?	
5 <u>Are</u> you a <u>student</u>?	
6 <u>How</u> <u>old</u> are you?	
7 <u>What's</u> your <u>address</u>?	
8 <u>What's</u> your <u>postcode</u>?	
9 <u>What's</u> your <u>e</u>-mail <u>address</u>?	
10 <u>What's</u> your <u>phone</u> number?	

b
- Put SS in pairs, A and B, and get them to sit so that they are facing each other. Explain that they're going to roleplay the interview. A is the receptionist, and B is a new student. A is going to interview B.
- Tell SS to go to **Communication** *Interview* on *p. 111*. Focus on the registration form, and elicit the questions. Then tell A to start the interview: *Hello. What's your first name?...*
- ⚠️ Tell SS they can invent their ages and phone numbers if they prefer.

Extra challenge
Get B to listen and answer the questions with his/her book closed.

c
- SS swap roles.
- Get some quick feedback by asking a few SS about their partners, e.g. *What's his address? What's her e-mail address?*
- Tell SS to go back to the main lesson on *p. 9*.

4 GRAMMAR   possessive adjectives

a
- Focus on the two sentences and the questions.
- Check answers.

> you = a pronoun
> your = an adjective

b 1.25
- Focus on the chart and give SS in pairs two minutes to try to fill the gaps. Then play the tape/CD once or twice for SS to check their answers.

Extra support
If your SS are complete beginners and have never seen these adjectives before, you could do this as a listening presentation. Drill the pronunciation of the words. Then play the tape/CD once or twice for them to fill the gaps.

1.25	CD1 Track 26

I'm Italian. **My** family are from Rome.
You're in level 1. This is **your** classroom.
He's the Director of Studies. **His** name is Michael.
She's your teacher. **Her** name is Lucy.
We're an international school. **Our** students are from different countries.
They're new students. **Their** names are Tina and Daniel.

c
- Tell SS to go to *p.122* and focus on **Grammar Bank 1C**.
- Go through the rules with the class. Model and drill the example sentences.

Grammar notes
- In some languages the possessive adjective agrees with the following noun, i.e. it can be masculine, feminine, or plural depending on the gender and number of the noun that comes after. In English nouns don't have gender, so adjectives don't change, and the use of *his/her* simply depends on whether we are talking about something belonging to a man or to a woman.
- Remind SS that *your* is used for singular and plural.
- If SS don't know the difference between an adjective and a pronoun, explain (in their L1 if you prefer) that we use a pronoun **in place of** a name or noun, e.g. *James = he*, but an adjective goes **with** a noun, e.g. *his name, French food*, etc.

- Focus on the exercises for **1C** on *p. 123*. SS do the exercises individually or in pairs.
- Check answers.

> **a** 1 your 2 Their 3 its 4 her 5 Our 6 His 7 My
> **b** 1 What's his name?
>   2 Is her mother German?
>   3 Where are your parents from?
>   4 Is your surname Zablowski?
>   5 How do you spell your name?

- Tell SS to go back to the main lesson on *p. 9*.

5 PRONUNCIATION /ɜː/ and /aʊ/

- Quickly revise the previous 12 vowel sounds and pictures from *p. 5* and *p. 7*.

a 🔊 **1.26**

- Focus on the two new sound pictures, *bird* and *owl*. Play the tape/CD once for SS just to listen to the words and sounds.
- Then play the tape/CD again pausing after each word and sound for SS to repeat.

🔊 1.26	CD1 Track 27
bird /ɜː/ owl /aʊ/	

Pronunciation notes

- Remind SS that the two dots in /ɜː/ means that this sound is long.
- You could also point out that /aʊ/ is a diphthong i.e. two sounds, /ə/ and /ʊ/, if you think this will help them.

- If either of these sounds are difficult for your SS, model them yourself so that SS can see your mouth position, and get SS to repeat them a few more times.

b 🔊 **1.27**

- Now focus on the words in the box. Explain that the letters in pink are pronounced either /ɜː/ or /aʊ/. Give SS a few minutes, in pairs, to write the words in the chart.
- Check answers. Then play the tape/CD once or twice for SS to listen and repeat.

🔊 1.27		CD1 Track 28
bird	**her**, **first**, **surname**	
owl	**how**, **our**, **now**	

Study Link SS can find more practice of English sounds on the MultiROM or on the *New English File Elementary* website.

6 SPEAKING

- Focus on the photos. Ask SS *Do you know the films?* and elicit some/all of the titles in English, if SS know them.

1 Bridget Jones's Diary
2 Monster's Ball
3 Shakespeare In Love
4 Star Wars
5 Amélie
6 A Beautiful Mind
7 Life Is Beautiful
8 All About My Mother
9 Schindler's List

⚠ They may well be different in SS' L1.

- Now focus on the flow chart. Go through the questions, making sure SS are clear that those on the right are for a woman and on the left for a man. Focus also on the expressions *I don't remember, I don't know. I think...* and *about* (= more or less, approximately). Teach/elicit their meaning and drill the pronunciation.
- Now ask SS the questions for photo 1. Get SS to spell the man's name on the board, and when SS have

guessed his age/nationality, tell them the answers (see key below).

- In pairs (or small groups) SS continue asking and answering about the other people.
- Feedback their ideas and check answers.

1 Hugh Grant - England - Born 1966
  Renée Zellweger - USA - Born 1969
2 Halle Berry - USA - Born 1966
3 Gwyneth Paltrow -USA - Born 1972
4 Ewan McGregor - Scotland - Born 1971
5 Audrey Tautou - France - Born 1978
6 Russell Crowe - New Zealand - Born 1964
7 Roberto Benigni - Italy - Born 1952
8 Penélope Cruz - Spain - Born 1974
9 Liam Neeson - Northern Ireland - Born 1952

Extra photocopiable activities

Grammar
possessive adjectives *p. 142*.
Communicative
Personal information *p. 187* (instructions *p.175*).

HOMEWORK

Study Link Workbook *pp. 8–9*.

G articles: *a / an / the*, regular plurals, *this / that / these / those*
V the classroom, common objects, classroom language
P vowel sounds: /ɔː/, /ʊ/, /ʌ/, /ɔɪ/, /ɪə/, /ʊə/

Turn off your mobiles!

Lesson plan

In this lesson, SS learn or revise the vocabulary of the classroom environment and personal possessions. This lexis is then used to practise articles, plurals, and *this / that / these / those*. The lesson ends with a focus on classroom language, which helps SS to understand and respond to common classroom instructions, and to ask the teacher in English for information and clarification.

Optional lead-in (books closed)

- Play 'Hangman' with the word CLASSROOM (see *p.20*).

1 VOCABULARY the classroom, common objects

a • Focus on the instructions. Demonstrate the activity with the first two items in the list. Check answers saying *Can you see (a table)? Where?* Get SS to point and teach *There* as the answer.

b (1.28)
- Play the tape/CD for SS to repeat the words. Drill any words which SS find difficult, using yourself as a model.

1.28		CD1 Track 29
a table	a light	
a board	a picture	
a TV	a video	
a CD player	walls	
a window	chairs	
a door		

c (1.29)
- Focus on the photos and get SS to match the words and pictures.

1 tissues	5 an address book
2 an identity card	6 a mobile (phone)
3 a lipstick	7 a purse
4 keys	8 coins

- Play the tape/CD for SS to check their answers. Then play it again to drill the pronunciation of the words.

1.29		CD1 Track 30
1 tissues	5 an address book	
2 an identity card	6 a mobile	
3 a lipstick	7 a purse	
4 keys	8 coins	

d • Tell SS to go to **Vocabulary Bank** *Common objects* on p. 142. In pairs they do **a**. Check answers and model and drill pronunciation.

1 a magazine	15 a diary
2 a book	16 a photo
3 cigarettes	17 a file
4 a mobile (phone)	18 a wallet
5 coins	19 stamps
6 a newspaper	20 matches
7 a purse	21 glasses
8 a comb	22 sunglasses
9 a pen	23 a lipstick
10 an identity card	24 a watch
11 tissues	25 keys
12 an address book	26 an umbrella
13 a credit card	27 a lighter
14 a pencil	28 a dictionary

- Focus on **b**. Model and drill the two questions *What's this?* (for singular objects) and *What are these?* (for plural objects). Demonstrate the meaning by holding up classroom objects, e.g. one pencil, two pens.
- Get SS to cover the words and test each other's memory.

Study Link SS can find more practice of these words on the MultiROM and on the *New English File Elementary* website.

- Tell SS to go back to the main lesson on *p. 10*.

e • Put SS in pairs and focus on the instructions. Demonstrate the activity first with a student, taking turns to be **A** and **B**.

2 PRONUNCIATION vowel sounds

- Quickly revise the previous fourteen vowel words and sounds on *p.5*, *p.7*, and *p.9*.

a (1.30)
- Here SS learn the final six vowel sounds. Focus on the six sound pictures (*horse*, *bull*, etc.) and play the tape/CD once for SS just to listen to the words and sounds.
- Now play the tape/CD again pausing after each word and sound for SS to repeat.

1.30			CD1 Track 31
horse	/ɔː/	boy	/ɔɪ/
bull	/ʊ/	ear	/ɪə/
up	/ʌ/	tourist	/ʊə/

Pronunciation notes

- Remind SS that the two dots in /ɔː/ mean that this sound is long.
- You could also point out that /ɔɪ/, /ɪə/ and /ʊə/ are diphthongs, i.e. two sounds, if you think this will help them.
- Focus especially on sounds which are difficult for your SS and model them yourself so that SS can see your mouth position. Get SS to repeat these sounds a few more times.

b 🔊 **1.31**

- Focus on the word *horse*. Get SS to say the three words aloud and elicit which one is different. Now focus on the groups of three words to the right of the sound pictures. Play the tape/CD. SS circle the word in each group which has a different sound from the sound picture. Pause after each group to give SS time to circle the word. Play the tape/CD again if necessary.

- Check answers.

🔊 **1.31**		CD1 Track 32
horse	wall, door, **glasses**	
bull	book, **photo**, look	
up	**purse**, sunglasses, umbrella	
boy	coins, **board**, toilet	
ear	here, we're, **there**	
tourist	/ʊə/	euro, Europe, **e-mail**

c • Play the tape/CD again for SS to repeat the words.

Study Link SS can find more practice of English sounds on the MultiROM or on the *New English File Elementary* website.

3 GRAMMAR *a / an, plurals, this / that / these / those*

- Tell SS to try to do **a** and **b** without looking back at exercise **1 VOCABULARY**.

a • Focus on the exercise. SS complete it in pairs. Check answers.

> 1 a   2 an   3 a   4 an   5 a

b • Focus on the exercise. SS complete it in pairs. Check answers.

> 1 stamps   2 matches   3 keys

c • Demonstrate the difference between *this* and *that* by putting one object near to you and one in the distance. Focus on the cartoons and the four questions. SS complete the captions with *this, that, these,* or *those*. Check answers.

> 1 this   2 that   3 those   4 these

⚠ SS should be able to work out that *those* is the plural of *that* by a process of elimination.

d • Tell SS to go to **Grammar Bank 1D** on *p.122*.
- Go through the rules with the class. Model and drill the example sentences. Highlight particularly the pronunciation of *es* (/ɪz/) in *watches* and *boxes*.

Grammar notes

a/an (indefinite article), *the* (definite article)
- Articles are very easy for some nationalities and more difficult for others, depending on their L1. If articles are a problem for your SS, give more examples to highlight the difference between *a* and *the*, e.g. *It's a door* (explaining what it is), and *Open the door* (talking about a specific door), and give them extra practice with the Extra Photocopiable Activity. They will also see more examples of the use of *the* in exercise **4 CLASSROOM LANGUAGE**.

Plural nouns
- The system in English of making regular nouns plural

is very straightforward, simply adding an *s*. The *s* can sometimes be pronounced /s/, e.g. *books*, and sometimes /z/, e.g. *keys*, depending on the previous sound. The difference is small and you may not want to focus on it too much, but if you do, see **Extra challenge** below. *es* (/ɪz/) is added to some nouns when it would be impossible to pronounce the word by adding just an *s*, e.g. *watches*. Irregular plurals are dealt with in lesson 2A.

this/that/these/those
- The meaning of *this / these* (for things within reach) and *that / those* (for things out of our reach or far away) is easier to demonstrate than it is to explain. They can be adjectives (*this book*) or pronouns (*What's this?*).

Extra challenge

If SS want to know when the final *s* in plurals is pronounced /s/ and when it is pronounced /z/, you could give them further rules by explaining that it is pronounced /s/ after words ending with these unvoiced sounds: /k/, /p/, /f/, /t/, e.g. *books, lips, cats*. After all other endings the *s* is pronounced /z/ or /ɪz/.

- Focus on the exercises for **1D** on *p. 123*. SS do the exercises individually or in pairs.
- Check answers.

a	1	a	bags		5	an	e-mails
	2	a	countries		6	a	sandwiches
	3	an	identity cards		7	a	keys
	4	a	watches		8	an	umbrellas
b	this		these	This	that		those

Study Link SS can find an end-of-File grammar quiz on the MultiROM, and more grammar activities on the *New English File Elementary* website.

- Tell SS to go back to the main lesson on *p.11*.
e • Put SS in pairs, A and B. Tell them to ask each other the questions in **c**. They can point to the objects in **1c** on *p.10* for *this/that* and to objects in the classroom for *that/those*.

4 CLASSROOM LANGUAGE

a • Here SS learn to recognize and respond to common instructions used by the teacher in the classroom.
- Focus on the twelve pictures and phrases. Get SS in pairs to match the phrases and pictures. Check answers and make sure the meaning of each phrase is clear by miming or getting SS to mime.

> 1 Close the door.
> 2 Go to page (84).
> 3 Read the text.
> 4 Don't speak (Spanish).
> 5 Listen and repeat.
> 6 Look at the board.
> 7 Open your books.
> 8 Sit down.
> 9 Stand up.
> 10 Turn off your mobile (phone).
> 11 Don't write.
> 12 Work in pairs.

• Focus on the box **GIVING INSTRUCTIONS** and highlight:
– to give ⊞ instructions we use the infinitive form of the verb, e.g. *Look!*
  For ⊟ instructions we use *Don't* + the infinitive, e.g. *Don't look!*
– *Don't* is the contracted form of *Do not* and is used to make the verb negative.
– These forms are the same for singular and plural.
– To make instructions more polite add '*please*' or use *Can you* + infinitive?

b 🔘 **1.32**

• Play the tape/CD at least twice. SS listen and write the number (1–10) next to the instructions they hear. Check answers.

🔘 **1.32**   CD1 Track 33

(tapescript in Student's Book on *p.114*.)
T = teacher, S = student
1 T Hello. Hello. Can you **close the door** please, Susanna?
   S Sorry?
   T Close the door, please.
2 T Can you **sit down**, please? Can you sit down? SIT DOWN!
3 T OK, **open your books.** It's lesson 1C. Lesson 1C.
4 T OK, now **read the text**. You can use your dictionary for any new words.
5 T Miguel and María, **don't speak Spanish**, this is an English class! Please speak in English.
6 T All right now, **stand up**. STAND UP. OK, now ask What's your name? to five other students.
7 T OK, now **go to page 84.**
   SS What page?
   T 84, page 84.
8 T OK, can you **look at the board**, please? Look at the board.
9 T All right, now **listen and repeat** the letters. A (A), B (B) C…
10 T D (D), E (E), F (F), María, please **turn off your mobile phone!** TURN OFF YOUR MOBILE, MARIA!

---

c 🔘 **1.33**

• Here SS learn phrases they themselves may need to use in class.
• Focus on the seven phrases. In pairs SS try to fill the gaps with one word.
• Play the tape/CD and check answers. Make sure SS know what all the phrases mean. Model the phrases for SS to repeat, encouraging them to use the right rhythm.

🔘 **1.33**   CD1 Track 34

What's (*bonjour*) **in** English?
How do you spell it?
Where's the stress?
Can **you** repeat it?
I **don't** know.
I **don't** remember.
I **don't** understand.

---

d • This is a revision game to recycle classroom phrases and revise vocabulary.

• Divide the class into two teams. The teams take it in turns to ask each other the first three questions in **c**:
  What's _____ in English? (SS supply a word in their own language)
  How do you spell it?
  Where's the stress?

GAME RULES
– The words SS choose to ask the other team must be words that have already come up in the course. Give the teams a few moments to choose, e.g. six words that they're going to ask the other team.
– Make sure different SS ask a question each time.
– Give teams one point for each question answered correctly.
– In a multilingual class SS can point to or show objects for the first question.

5 SONG *Eternal Flame*

🔘 **1.34**

• This song was originally recorded by the Bangles and later by Atomic Kitten. For SS of this level all song lyrics will include language that they don't know. Nevertheless SS are usually motivated to try to understand song lyrics. The activity for this song focuses on words and phrases SS know and uses pictures to teach new vocabulary.
• If you want to do this song in class use the photocopiable activity on *p.222*.

🔘 **1.34**   CD1 Track 35

Close your eyes, give me your hand, darling
Do you feel my heart beating, do you understand?

Do you feel the same, am I only dreaming?
Is this burning an eternal flame?

I believe it's meant to be, darling
I watch you when you are sleeping,
You belong with me

Do you feel the same, am I only dreaming?
Is this burning an eternal flame?

Say my name, sun shines through the rain
A whole life so lonely
and then you come and ease the pain
I don't want to lose this feeling, oh…

Extra photocopiable activities

Grammar
a/an, the, this, that, these, those p.143.
Communicative
Mystery objects *p.188* (instructions *p.175*).
Song
Eternal Flame p.222 (instructions *p.220*).

HOMEWORK

Study Link **Workbook** *pp. 10–11*.

Vocabulary drinks: *coffee, tea*, etc.
Function Offering and accepting drinks
Language *Would you like…? Yes please./No thanks.*

Lesson plan

This is the first in a series of eight Practical English lessons (one per File) which teach SS language to help them 'survive' in English in travel and social situations. There is a story line based on two characters, Mark Ryder, an American who works for MTC, a music company, and Allie, his British counterpart. SS meet them for the first time in this lesson, where Mark arrives in the UK and is met by Allie at the airport. SS learn vocabulary for drinks and how to offer and accept them.

StudyLink These lessons are also on the *New English File Elementary* Video, which can be used **instead of** the Class Cassette/CD (see introduction *p.9*).
The first section of the Video is also on the MultiROM, with additional activities.

Optional lead-in (books closed)

- Introduce this lesson (in SS' L1 if you prefer) by giving the information above.

VOCABULARY   drinks

a • Focus on the pictures. Give SS in pairs a few moments to match the words and pictures.
  • Check answers. Drill pronunciation. You could also elicit other kinds of juice, e.g. *tomato*, *apple*, etc.

1 (diet) Coke	4 mineral water	7 lemon
2 coffee	5 (orange) juice	8 milk
3 tea	6 ice	9 sugar

b • Tell SS to cover the words and test each other in pairs.
  A *What's this?* (pointing at a picture).
  B *Milk. What's this?*
  • Ask SS *What's your favourite drink when you're on a plane?* and elicit/teach any other drinks, e.g. *beer, wine*.

ASKING FOR A DRINK

a **1.35**
  • Tell SS to cover the dialogue with their hand or a piece of paper. Focus on the picture and the caption, and check comprehension. Ask *What's his name?* (Mark) *Where's he from?* (He's American) *Is he a student?* (No, he works for a music company) *Where is he?* (On a plane to the UK).
  ⚠ If you think that SS won't cover it, you could always get them to close their books at this stage and write the first, usually very simple task on the board.
  • Play the tape/CD once. Check answers.

> Mark has a diet Coke, and a coffee with milk but no sugar.

b • Now tell SS to uncover the dialogue (or open their books). Explain that the **YOU HEAR** part is what they need to understand, and the **YOU SAY** part is the phrases they need to be able to say.
  • Give SS a minute to read through the dialogue and remember or guess the missing words. Then play the tape/CD again, for them to complete the dialogue.
  • Check answers.

1.35   CD1 Track 36
F = flight attendant, M = Mark
F   Would you like a **drink**, sir?
M   Yes, a Diet Coke, please.
F   **Ice** and lemon?
M   Just lemon.
F   Here you **are**.
M   Thank you.

F   Coffee? **Tea**?
M   Coffee, please.
F   **Milk**?
M   Yes, please.
F   **Sugar**?
M   No, thanks.
F   Here you are.
M   Thanks.

- Go through the dialogue line by line with SS. Highlight that *Would you like* (…) is a common way of offering things. SS will study this in more detail in **8C**.

c **1.36**
  • Now focus on the **YOU SAY** phrases. Tell SS they're going to hear the dialogue again. They repeat the **YOU SAY** phrases when they hear the beep. Encourage them to copy the rhythm.
  • Play the tape/CD, pausing if necessary for SS to repeat the phrases.

1.36   CD1 Track 37
F   Would you like a drink, sir?
M   Yes, a Diet Coke, please.
    repeat
F   Ice and lemon?
M   Just lemon.
    repeat
F   Here you are.
M   Thank you.
    repeat
F   Coffee? Tea?
M   Coffee, please.
    repeat
F   Milk?
M   Yes, please.
    repeat
F   Sugar?
M   No, thanks.
    repeat
F   Here you are.
M   Thanks.
    repeat

---

d • Put SS in pairs, **A** and **B**. **A** is the flight attendant. Tell **B** to close his/her book and try to remember the phrases. Then **A** and **B** swap roles.
  ⚠ Teach SS *madam* (instead of *sir*) for the first line of the dialogue if they're talking to a woman.

SOCIAL ENGLISH

a 🔊 **1.37**

- Now focus on the next picture. Ask SS *Where is it?* (an airport) *Who is she?* (You may want to teach/revise *maybe* and *I think* to encourage speculation.)
- Focus on the instructions and get SS to read through the alternatives. Play the tape/CD at least twice.
- Check answers.

> 1 Ryder
> 2 in the city centre
> 3 no
> 4 by car

> **1.37**   CD1 Track 38
>
> (tapescript in Student's Book on *p.114*.)
> **A = Allie, M = Mark**
> A Hello. Are you Mark Ryder?
> M Yes. Are you Allie?
> A Yes, I am.
> M Nice to meet you.
> A And you. **Welcome to the UK**. Your hotel's in the city centre.
> M **How far is it?**
> A It's about 30 minutes if the traffic's OK.
> M **Great!**
> A Would you like a coffee first?
> M No, I'm fine, thanks.
> A **All right. Let's go.** My car's in the car park. **Can I help you with your bags?**
> M **No, it's OK, thanks.**

Extra support

Let SS listen again with the tapescript on *p. 114*. Deal with any problematic vocabulary.

b
- Focus on the questions. Tell SS to listen again and see if they can hear a difference in their accents, and if they sound like friends or not. Play the tape/CD again.
- Feedback SS' ideas. Allie is not American, she's English. They are meeting here for the first time so they are not friends (yet).

c
- Focus on the **USEFUL PHRASES**. For each phrase, drill the pronunciation. Ask SS *Who says it, Mark or Allie?* Highlight that *all right* and *OK* have the same meaning.
- Play the tape/CD again for SS to check. Pause after each phrase for SS to repeat (see tapescript above).

> Welcome to the UK. – Allie
> How far is it? – Mark
> Great! = very good – Mark
> All right. Let's go. – Allie
> Can I help you with your bags? – Allie
> No, it's OK, thanks. – Mark

Extra challenge

Get SS in pairs to roleplay the second conversation using the tapescript on *p. 114*. Let SS read their parts first and then try to act it from memory.

HOMEWORK

Study Link Workbook *p. 12*.

WRITING
COMPLETING A FORM

Lesson plan

This is the first of eight Writing lessons, one at the end of each File. In today's world of e-mail communication, being able to write in English is an important skill for many SS. We suggest that you go through the exercises in class, but set the actual writing (the last activity) for homework.

a
- Focus on the registration form. Go through the different sections with SS. Highlight:
  - *Mr* is for a man, *Mrs* for a married woman, and *Ms* for a woman, without saying if she is married or not.
  - the meaning and pronunciation of <u>mar</u>ried, <u>sin</u>gle, <u>sep</u>arated, di<u>vor</u>ced.
- Give SS a few minutes to complete the form.
- Go round checking SS are completing it correctly. Then elicit answers from individual SS for each section.

Extra idea

If you want to give extra practice with personal information questions, get SS to use the forms to interview each other.

b
- Focus on the rules and go through them with SS. Tell them to highlight any rules which are different from their L1, e.g. days of the week and languages, which are not written with a capital letter in several languages.

c
- Get SS to copy the whole text out again, using capital letters where necessary.
- Check answers by eliciting from SS the words which need capital letters and writing the text on the board.

Extra support

Quickly revise how to say the alphabet in English before SS try to correct the text.

> My name's Marta. I'm from Rio in Brazil, and I speak Portuguese. My teacher is American. His name 's Gerry. My English classes are on Tuesdays and Thursdays.

Write a similar text about you

As this writing task is very short, you may like to get SS to do it in class. Get them to write their own texts on a piece of paper, check for capital letters, and then swap the text with another S to read and check for mistakes.

The File finishes with two pages of revision and consolidation. The first page, **What do you remember?** revises the grammar, vocabulary, and pronunciation. These exercises can be done individually or in pairs, in class or at home, depending on the needs of your SS and the class time available. If SS do them in class, use the scoring system to check which SS are still having problems, or any areas which need further revision. The second page, **What can you do?** presents SS with a series of skills-based challenges. First there is a reading text which is of a slightly higher level than those in the File but which revises grammar and vocabulary SS have already learnt. Then there is a listening exercise which focuses on small differences which can cause confusion. Finally there is a speaking activity which measures SS' ability to use the language of the File orally. We suggest that you use some or all of these activities according to the needs of your class.

What do you remember?

GRAMMAR

1 a   2 b   3 b   4 b   5 b   6 a   7 b   8 a   9 a   10 b

VOCABULARY

a **1** from **2** to **3** in **4** at **5** off
b **1** Read
   2 Work
   3 Listen to
   4 Open
   5 Answer
c **1** file (not a number)
   2 Chinese (not a country)
   3 France (not a nationality/language)
   4 sixteen (not a multiple of ten)
   5 her (not a personal pronoun)
   6 they (not a possessive pronoun)
   7 watch (not a question)
   8 address (not an object)
   9 lipstick (not something you can read)
  10 pen (not a verb)

PRONUNCIATION

b **1** what **2** they **3** table **4** one **5** China
c <u>a</u>ddress   <u>sur</u>name   Argen<u>ti</u>na   Portug<u>ue</u>se um<u>br</u>ella

What can you do?

CAN YOU UNDERSTAND THIS TEXT?

b Old English	Latin	French	Other languages	New words
woman	wine	menu	siesta	Internet
house	family	hotel	judo	e-mail

CAN YOU HEAR THE DIFFERENCE?

1 a   2 b   3 b   4 a   5 b   6 a   7 b   8 a   9 a   10 a

1.38   CD1 Track 39

1 A Niki's a very good student.
   B Yes. Where's he from?
   A Russia.
2 A Is your boss English?
   B No, she's from Italy.
3 A What's her name?
   B Françoise. But she isn't French.
   A Where's she from?
4 A What's his name?
   B I don't remember.
5 A Where are the credit cards?
   B The what?
   A The credit cards.
   B They're on the table.
6 A OK, now go to page 13.
   B Page 30?
   A No, 13.
7 Passengers for the Lufthansa flight to Munich, please proceed immediately to gate number 40.
8 A What's your e-mail address, Mike?
   B It's Mike@info.de.
   A Mike@info.de.
   B That's it.
9 A What's your name, sir?
   B Mr Smith. Mr G. Smith.
   A Mr G. Smith. Ah yes, here it is.
10 A When's your English class?
   B Tuesday.

CAN YOU SAY THIS IN ENGLISH?

b What How Where What What

Extra photocopiable activities

Quicktest 1 *p.231*.

2A

G present simple ⊞ and ⊟ forms
V verb phrases: *live in a flat, play tennis*, etc. irregular plurals: *men, women*, etc.
P consonant sounds: /v/, /d/, /s/, /z/, /l/, /w/, third person -s

Cappuccino and chips

Lesson plan

The lesson is based on real interviews with foreigners living in Britain who talk about the way British people live. Their comments are not the typical stereotypes and some things may surprise your SS.

SS learn or revise the present simple in positive and negative sentences. Question formation is dealt with in the next lesson. They also learn a group of common verb phrases.

The lesson finishes with SS talking about a typical family in their country.

Optional lead-in (books closed)

- Write up on the board WHAT'S TYPICALLY BRITISH? Elicit ideas from the class, e.g. *black taxis, red buses, Agatha Christie, tea with milk*, etc.
- Write their ideas on the board.

1 VOCABULARY   verb phrases

a 🔊 **2.1**

- Books open. Focus on the survey about British people (*What % of British people…?*). Elicit/teach the meaning of the verb phrases (*read a newspaper*, etc.) and the time expressions *every day, every night, every weekend*. Use mime or draw pictures on the board.
- Model and drill the pronunciation of the phrases. Then focus on the percentages in the box and get SS in pairs to guess and complete the survey with a number.
- Get feedback from a few SS. Elicit full sentences, e.g. *Sixty percent of British people read a newspaper every day.* Don't tell them if they are right or wrong yet.
- Play the tape/CD once or twice, and then check answers.

> 🔊 **2.1**   CD1 Track 40
> **70%** of British people read a newspaper every day.
> **25%** smoke.
> **90%** watch TV every night.
> **10%** go to the cinema every weekend.
> **45%** have a pet.
> **60%** live in a house with a garden.

b
- Focus on the instructions, and the two example sentences. Highlight the use of *don't* to make a negative. (SS have already seen this used in instructions like *Don't look at the board*). Then demonstrate the activity by making true sentences about yourself using the verbs in **1a**.
- In pairs SS make true sentences about themselves. Get feedback from a few individual students.

Extra idea

In a monolingual class you could ask SS in pairs to guess the statistics for their country. Get feedback from different pairs and see if they agree/disagree.

c
- Tell SS to go to **Vocabulary Bank** *Verb phrases* on p. 143.
- Give SS five minutes to do **a** in pairs. Many of these verbs may already be familiar to them.
- Check answers. Get SS to say the whole phrase. Model and drill pronunciation.

1 live	**8** like	**15** play
2 work	**9** go	**16** have
3 have	**10** watch	**17** drink
4 study	**11** listen	**18** eat
5 speak	**12** play	**19** cook
6 drive	**13** smoke	**20** do
7 read	**14** do	**21** wear

⚠ Make sure SS are clear about the difference between *have* and *eat*. *Have* can be used with both food and drink (*have a sandwich, have a coffee*) and is more common when we talk about specific meals, e.g. *have breakfast/lunch*. *Eat*, e.g. *eat fast food* can only be used for food and expresses the general action.

- Focus on **b**. Get SS to cover the words and use the pictures to test themselves or their partner.

Study Link SS can find more practice of these words on the MultiROM and on the *New English File Elementary* website.

- Tell SS to go back to the main lesson on *p. 16*.

2 READING

a
- Focus on the photos. Go through them, eliciting/teaching any vocabulary, e.g. *a newspaper, a garden, fish (fingers) and chips, pizza, beer, cappuccino, a sign, a non-smoking restaurant.*
- Get SS in pairs to decide which of the pictures show something which they think is 'typically British.'
- Get some feedback from the class, but don't tell them yet if they are right or wrong.

b
- Focus on the text. This is the first real reading text that SS have been faced with. Emphasize that when they read they should try to focus on the words they know, and try to guess the meaning of new words.
- Tell SS to read the text once to check their answers to **a**.
- Check answers.

> According to the four people, *all* the things in the photos are 'typically British.'

Extra challenge

With a strong class, use the photos as prompts to get SS to tell you about the British, e.g. *They read big newspapers.*

- Tell SS to read the text again, underlining any new words. In pairs they should try and guess the meaning.
- Now read the text aloud to the class, paragraph by paragraph, checking and explaining the meaning of any words they don't know. These will depend on SS' L1 and their previous knowledge of English.

c • Ask SS *How do you make plurals?* (Adding -*s* or -*es*). Then tell them that a very small number of English words have an irregular plural form. Get SS to find the four irregular plurals in the first paragraph.
  • Check answers and model and drill pronunciation, focusing especially on the different vowel sounds in *woman/women* and *child/children*.

> man – men
> woman – women
> child – children
> person – people

⚠ Emphasize that as these words are plural you must use a plural verb with them, e.g. British people *are*... NOT ~~British people is~~...

d • Focus on the instructions. Get SS to do this individually.
  • Tell to SS to compare with a partner, and then get feedback from the class.

3 GRAMMAR   present simple ⊞ and ⊟

a • Focus on the instructions, and get SS to answer the questions in pairs.
  • Check answers.

> **1** The verbs in paragraph 4 end in *s* because they are all third person singular (he, she).
> **2** cooks, makes, goes, watches, has
> **3** they don't smoke, cars don't stop, the woman doesn't cook. The last one is different because it is third person singular.

Extra support

If you have a monolingual class, don't be afraid of using your SS's L1 to talk about the grammar here. At this level it is unrealistic to expect SS to talk about grammar in English.

b • Tell SS to go to **Grammar Bank 2A** on *p. 124*.
  • Go through the rules with the class. Model and drill the example sentences.

Grammar notes

  • There is only one different verb ending in the present simple (third person singular verbs add an *s* or *es*). All other forms are the same as the infinitive. For this reason the use of the pronoun (*I, you*, etc.) is not optional as it is in many languages. It is essential as it identifies which person is being used.
  • In the negative, *don't* and *doesn't* go before the infinitive. These contracted forms (of *do not* and *does not*) are almost always used in spoken English and in informal writing.
  • *goes* /gəʊz/ and *does* /dʌz/ are pronounced differently.

  • Focus on the exercises for **2A** on *p. 125*. SS do the exercises individually or in pairs.
  • Check answers. Get SS to read the sentences out loud and help them with the rhythm of ⊞ and ⊟ sentences, e.g. We <u>live</u> in a <u>flat</u>. They <u>don't</u> <u>drink</u> <u>coffee</u>.

> **a 1** She listens to the radio.
>   **2** We live in a flat.
>   **3** He has two children.
>   **4** They don't drink coffee.
>   **5** My father doesn't smoke.
>   **6** The shops close at 5.00.
>   **7** He goes to the pub.
>   **8** She does housework.
> **b 1** reads   **5** drives
>   **2** doesn't have   **6** don't play
>   **3** speak   **7** doesn't do
>   **4** don't eat   **8** studies

  • Tell SS to go back to the main lesson on *p. 17*.

4 PRONUNCIATION   consonant sounds, -s

a 2.2
  • Before starting on the consonant sounds, test SS on the vowel sounds either using the **Sound Bank** on *p. 156* (or the *New English File* pronunciation wall chart if you have it).
  • Tell SS that in this File they are going to learn the consonant sounds (there are 24). Here they learn the first six sounds.
  • Focus on the six sound pictures (*vase, dog*, etc.) and play the tape/CD once for SS just to listen to the words and sounds.
  • Play the tape/CD again, pausing after each word and sound for SS to listen and repeat.
  • Focus attention especially on sounds which are difficult for your SS and model them yourself so that SS can see your mouth position. Get SS to repeat these sounds a few more times.

> **2.2**   CD1 Track 41
> vase   /v/   zebra   /z/
> dog   /d/   leg   /l/
> snake   /s/   witch   /w/

Pronunciation notes

  • Highlight that the phonetic symbols for these sounds are the same as the letters of the alphabet that produce them. There are also some clear sound–spelling patterns:
    /d/ the letter *d* is always pronounced /d/, e.g. *do*.
    /v/ the letter *v* is always pronounced /v/, e.g. *live*.
    /l/ the letter *l* is always pronounced /l/, e.g. *like*.
    /w/ the letter *w* at the beginning of a word is pronounced /w/, e.g. *women*.
    /z/ the letter *z* is always pronounced /z/, e.g. *zero*; the letter *s* can be pronounced /z/, e.g. *plays, watches, music*, but not at the beginning of a word.
    /s/ the letter *s* at the beginning of a word is nearly always pronounced /s/, e.g. *smoke*; *s* at the end of a word is sometimes /s/, e.g. *cooks*.
  • As with the plurals, if SS want to know when the final *s* is pronounced /s/ and when it is pronounced /z/, you could give them further rules by explain that it is pronounced /s/ after verbs ending with these unvoiced sounds: /k/, /p/, /f/, /t/, e.g. *smokes, hopes, laughs, eats*. After all other endings the *s* is pronounced /z/.

b ● Model and drill the sentences with the whole class, paying particular attention to consonant sounds which are difficult for your SS. Then get SS to practise the sentences in pairs.

⚠ SS may have problems distinguishing between the /s/ and the /z/ sounds. Tell them that the /s/ is like the sound made by a snake, and the /z/ is like the sound made by a bee or a fly.

c 🔊 **2.3**

● Focus on the sentences, which are all third person singular in the present simple. SS have already practised these pronunciation rules with plural nouns. Tell them that the pronunciation of the third person singular ending (*he*, *she*, and *it*) is the same as for plurals.

● Play the tape/CD, pausing after each sentence for SS to repeat. If they are having difficulties, tell them that the difference between the /s/ and the /z/ endings is small and reassure them that it will come with practice.

> 🔊 **2.3**   **CD1 Track 42**
>
> /s/   She smokes a lot. She drinks coffee. He eats chips.
> /z/   She lives in a flat. He has a cat. She does exercise.
> /ɪz/ He watches TV. It finishes in a minute.

Study Link SS can find more practice of English sounds on the MultiROM or on the *New English File Elementary* website.

5 WRITING & SPEAKING

a ● Focus on the instructions and go through them with the SS, showing them what to do. Elicit the type of words they should use to fill the gaps, e.g. They have *two* children. They go to *Brighton* for their holiday.

Extra idea

If you are not the same nationality as your SS demonstrate the activity first, telling them about a typical family in your country.

● Give SS at least five minutes to complete the sentences. Monitor and help them with vocabulary as required.

b ● In pairs, get SS to read their sentences to each other. In a monolingual class, get them to see if they agree or not. In a multinational class, get them to see what is the same and what is different about their countries.

● Get some feedback from individual SS.

Extra photocopiable activities

Grammar
present simple ⊞ and ⊟ *p. 144.*
Communicative
They're brothers but they're different *p.189* (instructions *p.176*).

HOMEWORK

Study Link **Workbook** *pp. 13–14.*

2
B

G present simple questions and short answers
V common verb phrases
P consonant sounds: /k/, /g/, /ð/, /ʃ/, /ʒ/, /r/

When Natasha meets Darren...

Lesson plan

In recent years Internet dating , i.e. meeting a possible partner through website agencies has become increasingly common. This lesson introduces present simple questions (*Do you...? Does she...? Where do you...?*) through the context of an unsuccessful date between two people, Darren and Natasha, who have met through an Internet dating agency.

Optional lead-in (books closed)

- Ask SS where people in their country usually meet new friends or partners and elicit ideas, e.g. *at school, at work*, etc.

1 READING

a • Focus on the pictures of Natasha and Darren and establish that they want to meet a partner on the Internet. Ask SS *How old do you think Natasha is?* and elicit answers. Do the same for Darren.

b • Establish that Natasha e-mails Darren and he answers. Put SS in pairs. Tell them to read the e-mails. You could read them aloud to the SS now or after they have finished.

- Tell SS to cover the e-mails (with their hand or a piece of paper). Focus on the sentences 1–8. Get them to look at number 1 and ask *Do you remember? Who is 30, Darren or Natasha?* Elicit that the answer is *Darren* and get SS to write his name. Then tell them to do 2–8 together.

- Elicit answers from SS or get them to uncover the e-mails and check.

2 Natasha	**6** Natasha
3 Natasha	**7** Natasha
4 Darren	**8** Natasha
5 Darren	

2 GRAMMAR   present simple ?

a 2.4

- Focus on the photos. Ask *Where are they?* (in a Japanese restaurant) *What's the food?* (sushi) *Do you think they like it?*
- Write on the board:
  alcohol
  sushi
  his mother
- Get SS to cover the conversation (or close their books). Tell them just to listen to the conversation between Darren and Natasha and to listen for what Darren says about the three things on the board.
- Play the tape/CD once. Elicit answers in the third person, e.g. ask *What does Darren say about alcohol?* (He doesn't drink alcohol.)

alcohol	He doesn't drink alcohol.
sushi	He doesn't like it.
his mother	She's a good cook. He lives with his mother. She works in a supermarket.

b • Now get SS to look at the conversation. Play the tape/CD again (once or twice) and tell them to write in the missing words.

Extra support

Get SS to read the conversation once (silently) before they listen.

- Check answers.

> **2.4** CD1 Track 43
>
> **D = Darren, N = Natasha**
> D Hi. Are you Natasha?
> N Yes, and you're Darren. Nice to **meet** you.
> D Sorry I'm late.
> N No problem. Would you like a glass of wine?
> D No, thanks. I don't **drink** alcohol. Mineral water for me.
>
> D What's this?
> N Sushi. It's fantastic. Don't you **like** it?
> D No, I **don't**. Sorry.
> N **What** food do you like?
> D I usually **eat** at home. My mother's a very good cook.
> N Do you **live** with your mother?
> D Yes, I do.
> N Oh. Does your mother work?
> D Yes, she **does**.
> N Where does she **work**?
> D She **works** in a supermarket.

c • Give SS a few minutes to complete the questions and answers. Tell them to try to do it *without* looking back at the dialogue.

- Check answers. Ask why it's *do/don't* in the first extract and *does* in the second (the second extract is third person).

Do you like sushi?	**Does** your mother work?
No, I **don't**.	Yes, she **does**.
What food **do** you like?	Where **does** she work?

- Get SS to repeat the extracts after the tape/CD. Use the pause button. Highlight that *do* is pronounced /duː/ and *does* is pronounced /dʌz/, and that when a question starts with a question word (e.g. *What, Where*) *do/does* is not stressed, e.g. <u>Where</u> do you <u>work</u>? Get them to copy the rhythm, stressing the 'information' words.

Extra idea

In pairs get SS to roleplay the conversation between Darren and Natasha. Monitor the pairs correcting incorrect rhythm.

d • Tell SS to go to **Grammar Bank 2B** on *p. 124*.

- Go through the rules with the class. Model and drill the example sentences.

Grammar notes

do and *does*

- The auxiliary *do* (and *does*) can puzzle SS if they try to translate questions word for word. Explain (in SS' L1 if you prefer) that *auxiliary* means 'helper', and that the auxiliaries *do* and *does* 'help' to form questions and negatives. They do not have a separate meaning. The auxiliaries *do* and *does* are also often used to 'soften' a yes/no answer, e.g. *Do you smoke? No, I don't.*

Word order in questions

- The acronyms **ASI** (auxiliary, subject, infinitive) and **QUASI** (question word, auxiliary, subject, infinitive) will help your SS remember to use the correct word order in questions. Use the acronyms as a quick way of reminding them, if they make mistakes.

- Focus on the exercises for **2B** on *p. 125*. SS do the exercises individually or in pairs.
- Check answers.

> **a 1** Do **2** Does **3** Does **4** Do **5** Do **6** Do **7** Does **8** Do
> **b 1** Do you drink coffee?
>   **2** Does your brother work?
>   **3** Where do you work?
>   **4** What music does she like?
>   **5** What newspaper do you read?
>   **6** Do you go to the cinema?
>   **7** Does your father watch sport on TV?
>   **8** Does your mother wear glasses?

Extra challenge

Get SS to ask and answer the questions in **a** orally.

- Tell SS to go back to the main lesson on *p.19*.

3 LISTENING

a 2.5

- Focus on the picture of Darren and Natasha, and go through the instructions. Elicit the meaning and pronunciation of *success* and *disaster*.
- Play the tape/CD once. Get feedback from SS. (The lunch is clearly a disaster!)

b • Focus on the instructions and go through them with SS. Then play the tape/CD again. SS complete the chart. Don't check answers yet.

c • Tell SS they are going to compare their answers. Focus on the examples in the speech bubbles. Elicit the first question for Natasha (*Does Natasha like computers?*), reminding SS to use the infinitive (*like*) after *does*, and to use short answers *Yes, (she does.)* or *No, (she doesn't)*.
- Put SS in pairs, **A** and **B**. **A** asks all four questions about Natasha and then **B** asks about Darren. Demonstrate yourself with a student, or get one pair to demonstrate.
- When SS have finished, check answers.

	Natasha	Darren
likes computers	✗	✓
watches TV	✗	✓
goes to the cinema	✓	✗
smokes	✓	✗

> **2.5**   CD1 Track 44
> (tapescript in Student's Book on *p.114*.)
> **D = Darren, N = Natasha**
> **N** You work with computers Darren, is that right?
> **D** Yes, that's right.
> **N** Do you like your job?
> **D** Yes, I do. I love it. Computers are very interesting, don't you think?
> **N** Um, not really. I don't like computers. Er, what do you do in the evenings?
> **D** I play computer games, or I watch television.
> **N** What do you do at the weekend?
> **D** I… play computer games and watch television.
> **N** Do you go to the cinema?
> **D** No, I don't. I watch films on television or DVD. Do you watch TV?
> **N** No, I don't have a television.
> **D** What do you do at the weekend?
> **N** I go to the cinema.
> **D** Oh.
>
> **N** Ah, coffee, great. Cigarette, Darren?
> **D** No, thanks. I don't smoke. Er, Natasha, can I ask you a question?
> **N** Yes, OK.
> **D** How old are you? 28?
> **N** Yes, that's right.
> **D** And, er, how old are you in the photo – the photo on the Internet? 19? 20?
> **N** Look, Darren, it's two o'clock – time to go back to work. Bye.
> **D** Natasha, wait, wait… Natasha!

Extra idea

Get SS to roleplay the conversation using tapescript 2.5 on *p. 114*.

4 SPEAKING

a • Go through the instructions with the class.
- Elicit the questions from the SS. You may want to write some or all of them on the board. If SS want to copy the completed questions off the board, get them to do it in their notebooks, not in their books.

b 2.6
- Play the tape/CD. Use the pause button and get SS to repeat each question.

> **2.6**   CD1 Track 45
> What's your name?
> How old are you?
> Do you work or study?
> Where do you live?
> Do you have a car?
> What languages do you speak?
> Do you smoke?
> What music do you like?
> What TV programmes do you like?
> What food do you like?
> What newspaper do you read?
> What sports do you play?

c • Put SS in pairs, **A** and **B**. SS interview each other with the *Meeting People* form. **B** asks the questions using the prompts, and writes **A**'s answers in the form.

A If you have an odd number of SS in the class have one group of three. Choose strong students who will have time to do the interview three times.

d • A and B swap roles.

Extra challenge

- Encourage the SS who are asking the questions to ask extra questions if they can, e.g.
  A *Do you work or study?* **B** *I study economics.*
  A *Where?* (Extra question)
- Encourage the SS who are answering the questions to give extra information, e.g.
  A *Do you have a car?* **B** *Yes. I have a VW Golf.*
- With a strong class you could also get the SS who are asking the questions to cover the question prompts (e.g. *What/name?*) and produce the questions from memory.
- Round off the activity by asking pairs of SS what they have in common.

5 PRONUNCIATION consonant sounds

- Quickly revise the previous six consonant words and sounds on *p. 17* or using the *New English File* wall chart if you have it.

a 2.7

- Tell SS they are now going to learn the next six consonant sounds.
- Focus on the six sound pictures (*key, girl*, etc) and play the tape/CD once for SS just to listen.
- Play the tape/CD again, pausing after each word and sound for SS to listen and repeat.
- Focus attention especially on sounds which are difficult for your SS and model them yourself so that SS can see your mouth position. Get SS to repeat these sounds a few more times.

2.7			CD1 Track 46
keys	/k/	shower	/ʃ/
girl	/g/	television	/ʒ/
tie	/t/	right	/r/

Pronunciation notes

- Highlight that the phonetic symbols for /k/, /g/, /t/ and /r/ are the same as the letters of the alphabet that produce them. There are also some clear sound–spelling patterns:
  /k/ the letters *k* and *ck* are always pronounced /k/, e.g. *lipstick, kilo.* Also some words which begin with *c*, e.g. *car.* The only exception is when *k* is silent, e.g. *know.*
  /g/ The letter *g* is always pronounced /g/ at the end of a word, e.g. *bag, dog,* and often at the beginning, e.g. *glasses, good* – <u>but</u> it can also be pronounced /dʒ/, e.g. *Germany.*
  /t/ The letter *t* is always pronounced /t/, e.g. *tea.*
  /ʃ/ The letters *sh* are always pronounced /ʃ/, e.g. *she, shop.* The ending *-ation* also has this sound, e.g. *station, information.*
  /ʒ/ is a very unusual sound in English. It never occurs at the beginning of a word.

/r/ The letter *r* at the beginning or in the middle of a word, and *rr*, are always pronounced /r/, *right, Russia, sorry*, etc. In British English *r* at the end of a word is often silent, e.g. *actor.*

b • Model and drill the sentences with the whole class, paying particular attention to consonant sounds which are difficult for your SS. Then get SS to practise the sentences in pairs.

Study Link SS can find more practice of English sounds on the MultiROM or on the *New English File Elementary* website.

Extra idea

Get SS to memorize the sentences for the sounds which are difficult for them.

6 SONG *Something stupid*

 2.8

- This song was a hit for Frank and Nancy Sinatra and more recently for Robbie Williams and Nicole Kidman.
- If you want to do this song with your SS, there is a photocopiable activity on *p. 223*.

2.8	CD1 Track 47

I know I stand in line, until you think you have the time
To spend an evening with me
And if we find someplace to dance, I know that there's a chance
You won't be leaving with me
And afterwards we drop into a quiet little place
And have a drink or two
And then I go and spoil it all, by saying something stupid
Like: I love you

I can see it in your eyes you still despise the same old lies
You heard the night before
And though it's just a line to you, for me it's true
It never seemed so right before

I practise every day to find some clever lines to say
To make the meaning come through
But then I think I'll wait until the evening gets late
And I'm alone with you
The time is right your perfume fills my head, the stars get red
And oh the night's so blue
And then I go and spoil it all, by saying something stupid
Like: I love you

The time is right, etc.

Extra photocopiable activities

Grammar
present simple ? *p. 145.*
Communicative
Somebody like you *p. 190* (instructions *p. 176*).
Song
Something Stupid p. 223 (instructions *p. 220*).

HOMEWORK

Study Link Workbook *pp. 15–16.*

2
C

G *a*/*an* + jobs
V jobs: *journalist, doctor,* etc.
P consonant sounds: /p/, /f/, /tʃ/, /dʒ/, /j/, /ŋ/

An artist and a musician

Lesson plan

The topic of jobs is introduced through an interview with an illustrator, Annabel Wright (who has done several of the illustrations for the Student's Book), and later practised through a jobs quiz. SS get further practice with the present simple, especially questions, and learn the vocabulary and grammar for talking about their and other people's jobs.

Optional lead-in (books closed)

- Write the following answers on the board. Make them true for you.
  1 I'm a teacher.
  2 I work in ( ) school.
  3 I work ( ) hours a day.
  4 Yes, I do. I like it very much.
- Tell SS that these are your answers to four questions. Give SS in pairs one minute to try to write the questions.
- Elicit their ideas and then write the correct questions on the board. Elicit/explain that *What's your job?* is also a correct question for 1, but that we usually ask *What do you do?* because the other person may not have a job or may be a student, etc.
  1 What do you do?
  2 Where do you work?
  3 How many hours do you work (a day)?
  4 Do you like your job?
- Drill the questions, encouraging SS to get the right rhythm. Then rub the questions out and see if SS can remember them.

1 READING

a • Books open. Focus on the photos of Annabel and on the question. Elicit ideas from SS and then get them to read the first question and answer in the interview. (She's an artist.) Tell SS that in fact she has done all the illustrations on this page, and also in several other lessons, e.g. on *pp.29* and *82*.

⚠ Point out that in English *an artist* normally means a person who paints or draws, not somebody in show business, as in some other languages.

b • Now focus on the interview. Explain that the interviewer's questions are missing from the article, and SS are going to put them in the right place. Go through the questions to make sure SS understand them all, and teach/elicit the meaning of *Why?* and *because*.

- Tell SS to read the interview once and to try to match the questions to her answers.

⚠ Tell SS not to worry about new words/phrases at this point. They will focus on them when they re-read the article.

- Get SS to compare their answers and then check.

2 Where do you work?
3 How many hours do you work?
4 Do you earn a lot of money?
5 Do you like your job? Why?
6 What *don't* you like about your job?
7 How do you relax after work?

c • Tell SS in pairs to look at the highlighted words and expressions, and try to guess their meaning from the context.

- Check answers, either translating into SS' L1 if you prefer, using the glossary below, or getting SS to check in their dictionaries.

> **Glossary**
> **draw** = make a picture with a pencil
> **just** = only
> **I'm in a hurry** = I need to do something quickly
> **paid holidays** = holidays when they pay you
> **I love it** = I like it very much
> **stressful** = produces stress
> **lonely** = a feeling when you are alone and you need other people
> **band** = a pop group

d • Now tell them to read the interview again. Tell them how much £250 and £3,000 are in SS' currency.

- Go through all the answers with the class. Deal with any vocabulary problems if they arise and check their understanding.
- In pairs SS decide what they think is good or bad about her job.
- Get feedback, and then ask individual SS if they would like her job.

> (Possible answers)
>
> | Good things | Bad things |
> | --- | --- |
> | She works at home. | Sometimes she works in the evenings/weekends. |
> | Every day is different. | She doesn't always have a lot of work. |
> | She likes using her imagination. | She doesn't have paid holidays. It's sometimes stressful or lonely. |

Extra idea

Get SS to read the interview aloud in pairs for extra pronunciation practice.

2 VOCABULARY jobs

a • Focus on the pictures and either get SS in pairs to try to write the names of the jobs, or elicit them from the class. Get them to spell the words and write them on the board, with *a*/*an*.

1 a <u>pi</u>lot
2 a mu<u>si</u>cian
3 a <u>doc</u>tor
4 a <u>hair</u>dresser
5 a po<u>lice</u> officer
6 a <u>foot</u>baller

- Model and drill the pronunciation and underline the stress.

b Rub the words off the board. Focus on the instructions and the speech bubbles, and then get SS to ask and answer in pairs.

c • Tell SS to go to **Vocabulary Bank** *Jobs* on *p. 144*.
- Give SS five minutes to do exercise **a** in pairs. Check answers, and go through notes 1–3 under the jobs. It is also common to hear *policeman* for a man and *policewoman*, *actress*, and *waitress* for a woman.

1 a student	12 a lawyer
2 a (bank) manager	13 a musician
3 a hairdresser	14 an actor
4 a shop assistant	15 a police officer
5 a footballer	16 a receptionist
6 a nurse	17 a waiter
7 a doctor	18 a secretary
8 an engineer	19 a housewife
9 a politician	20 a journalist
10 a builder	a retired person
11 a pilot	

- Model and drill the pronunciation. Elicit the answer to question **b** (engi<u>neer</u>, poli<u>ti</u>cian, mu<u>si</u>cian, po<u>lice</u> officer, re<u>cep</u>tionist, re<u>tired</u>.)
- Focus on the instruction **c**, and the example exchange. Get SS to cover the words and practise in pairs.

Study Link SS can find more practice of these words on the MultiROM and on the *New English File Elementary* website.

- Tell SS to go back to the main lesson on *p. 20*.

d • Focus on the flow chart and go through the possible answers to the question *What do you do?* Highlight the use of the prepositions *for, in, at*, and the article *a/an*. Give SS a minute to decide how to say in English what they do, and go round helping with any jobs they don't know how to express.

e • Get SS to stand up and ask at least five other SS what they do.
- Get feedback from as many SS as possible.

3 GRAMMAR   *a/an* + jobs

- Focus on the grammar rule, and stress that you *must* use an article (*a* or *an*) with a singular job. Then give SS a couple of minutes to do the exercise.

1 an	6 an
2 a	7 a
3 –	8 a
4 –	9 a
5 a	

4 PRONUNCIATION   consonant sounds

a 2.9
- Focus on the instructions. Play the tape/CD once for SS to listen to the rhythm. Elicit that *er/or* at the end of a word is pronounced /ə/. Then play it again pausing after each sentence. Get SS to repeat, copying the rhythm.

2.9	CD1 Track 48
1 He's **an** actor.	
2 She's **a** politician.	
3 They're nurses.	
4 We're lawyers.	
5 He's **a** teacher.	
6 She's **an** actress.	
7 Are you **a** journalist?	
8 I'm **a** pilot.	
9 He's **a** builder.	

b 2.10
- Quickly revise the previous six consonant words and sounds on *p. 19* or using the *New English File* wall chart if you have it.
- Focus on the sound pictures. Play the tape/CD once for SS to hear all the words and sounds.
- Now play the tape/CD again pausing after each word and sound for SS to listen and repeat.
- Focus especially on sounds which are difficult for your SS and model them yourself so that SS can see your mouth position. Get SS to repeat these sounds a few more times.

2.10			CD1 Track 49
parrot	/p/	jazz	/dʒ/
flower	/f/	yacht	/j/
chess	/tʃ/	singer	/ŋ/

Pronunciation notes

/p/ *p* and *pp* are always pronounced /p/, e.g. *politician*.

/f/ *f* and *ph* are always pronounced /f/, e.g. *five*, and *photo*.

/tʃ/ *ch* and *tch* are usually pronounced /tʃ/, e.g. *children, watch*.

/dʒ/ *j* is always pronounced /dʒ/, e.g. *job*. Also *g* can sometimes be /dʒ/, e.g. *German*.

/j/ *y* at the beginning of a word is pronounced /j/, e.g. *yes*. The letter *u* is sometimes pronounced /juː/, e.g. *music, student*.

⚠ SS must be careful with this symbol, because it is not the same as the letter *j*.

/ŋ/ The letters *ng* are usually pronounced /ŋ/, e.g. *song*. This sound never occurs at the beginning of a word. The letter *n* (before *k*) is also pronounced /ŋ/, e.g. *think, bank*.

c • Model and drill the sentences with the whole class, paying particular attention to consonant sounds which are difficult for your SS. Then get SS to practise the sentences in pairs.

Extra idea

Get SS to memorize the sentences for the sounds which are difficult for them.

Study Link SS can find more practice of English sounds on the MultiROM or on the *New English File Elementary* website.

5 LISTENING & SPEAKING

a 2.11

- Focus on the cartoon and caption. Explain that in English, when people speak fast they don't pronounce each word separately. They tend to run them together and this can make it difficult for SS to hear what has been said.
- Get SS to separate out the words in the speech bubble (Do you work in an office?) In the next activity the aim is for SS to hear ten questions said at normal speed and relate them to the written form.
- Tell SS they're going to hear a radio quiz programme called 'Guess my job'. There are three contestants who can ask (between them) ten questions, and then have to guess the mystery guest's job.
- Focus on the questions. Go through them, and use the drawings to elicit/teach any new words.
- Play the tape/CD once. SS underline the questions they hear. If most SS have not got the ten questions, play the tape/CD again. Check the ten questions.

2.11 CD1 Track 50

(tapescript in Student's Book on *p.115.*)
C = Compère, P = Phil, B = Brian, L = Liz, M = Marylin
And now on Radio 4, *Guess my job.*
C Good evening and welcome again to the jobs quiz, *Guess my job.* And our team tonight are Brian, a teacher (Hello), Liz, who's unemployed (Hi), and Marylin, who's a writer (Good evening). And our first guest tonight is…
P Phil.
C OK, team, you have *two* minutes and *ten* questions to guess Phil's job, starting now. Let's have your first question.
B Hi, Phil. **Do you work in an office?**
P **No**, I don't.
L **Do you work in the evening?**
P **It depends.** Yes, sometimes.
M **Do you work with your hands?**
P **No**, I don't. Not with my hands.
L **Do you wear a uniform?**
P Er **yes** – well, a kind of uniform.
M **Do you drive?**
P **No**, I don't. Not in my job.
B **Do you write letters or e-mails?**
P **No**, I don't.
L **Do you work with other people?**
P **Yes**, I do.
B **Do you speak any languages?**
P **No**, only English.
M **Do you have special qualifications?**
P **No**, I don't.
C You have *one more question.*
B Er, **do you earn a lot of money?**
P **Yes**, I do.

---

b
- Now ask SS *What does Phil answer?* and elicit that he can only answer *yes, no,* or *it depends.* Play the tape/CD again. SS write Y, N, or D after each question.
- Check answers.

c
- Tell SS in pairs to focus on Phil's answers, and give them one minute to guess his job. Tell them that it's one of the jobs from the **Vocabulary Bank**. Get feedback, but don't tell them if they're right or wrong.

d 2.12
- Play the end of the show on the tape/CD. Pause after they ask *Are you an actor?* and ask SS what they think, before letting them hear his job.

2.12 CD1 Track 51

(tapescript in Student's Book on *p.115.*)
C That's ten questions! So, Brian, Liz, and Marylin – *what's his job?*
M OK Phil. We think you're… an actor.
C Are you an actor, Phil?
F No, I'm not. I'm a professional footballer.

---

e
- Divide the class into groups of four (with a group of three if you have uneven numbers). Tell SS to go to **Vocabulary Bank** *Jobs* on *p. 144* and choose a job. Remind them of the rules of the game (you could write them on the board) and tell them they can use any of the questions in **a**.
- Stop the activity when all SS have had a turn at being the guest.

Extra photocopiable activities

Grammar
a/an + jobs *p. 146.*
Communicative
What do they do? *p. 191* (instructions *p.176*).

HOMEWORK

Study Link Workbook *pp. 17–18.*

2

D

G possessive *s*
V family: *sister*, *aunt*, etc.
P consonant sounds: /b/, /θ/, /ð/, /m/, /n/, /h/

Relatively famous

Lesson plan

The idea for this lesson comes from magazines like *Hello!* or *OK!* which frequently include photographs of people who are not famous in their own right, but simply because they are the relatives of famous people. SS learn family vocabulary and the possessive *s* in the context of famous people's relatives, and then talk about their own family.

Optional lead-in (books closed)

● Draw a simple family tree on the board, preferably of your family, or a well-known family, showing two generations: mother/father + children, e.g.

ALAN = MARIAN
ROBERT   ME   SUSAN

● Ask *Who's Alan?* to elicit *He's your father* and do the same with the other names to elicit *mother/brother/sister*.
● Get SS to spell the words to you and write them on the board. Model and drill the pronunciation.

1 GRAMMAR   possessive *s*

a ● Books open. Ask SS *Do you read magazines like* Hello! *or* OK!*? What kind of people are in them?* (Famous people and their families.) Then focus on the title of the article and elicit/teach relatives (= family members).
● Focus on the photo of Sylvester Stallone's mother, and the caption. Elicit that *'s = of*, i.e. of Sylvester Stallone.

b ● Now focus on the other photos and tell SS that the people in 1–6 are all relatives of the famous people a–f.
⚠ Tell SS not to shout out answers if they already know who some of the people are.

Extra idea

Ask what the famous people a–f do and where they're from.

a JK Rowling, British writer, author of the *Harry Potter* books
b Hugh Grant, British actor
c Will Smith, American actor
d Kate Winslet, British actress
e Naomi Campbell, British model
f Antonio Banderas, Spanish actor

● Focus on the instructions, the speech bubbles, and the words in the box.
● In pairs SS try to match people 1–6 with famous people a–f, either orally or writing sentences. Get feedback but don't tell SS the answers yet.

c 2.13
● Play the tape/CD once for SS to listen and check.

2.13   CD1 Track 52
(tapescript in Student's Book on *p.115*)
1 He's Hugh Grant's brother.
2 She's Naomi Campbell's mother.
3 He's JK Rowling's husband.
4 She's Antonio Banderas's ex-wife.
5 He's Will Smith's father.
6 She's Kate Winslet's sister.

---

d ● Play the tape/CD again and get SS to repeat each sentence. Show how the pronunciation of the *s* is the same as for the third person/plurals, and that the pronunciation is /ɪz/ when a name ends in *s*, e.g. Banderas's = /bænˈdeərəsɪz/.

Extra idea

Try to find some pictures from recent celebrity magazines of famous people's relatives. Use them as flashcards to give SS more practice.

e ● Tell SS to go to **Grammar Bank 2D** on *p. 124*.
● Go through the rules with the class. Model and drill the example sentences.

Grammar notes

Names that end in *s*
● James's or James'. After names ending in *s* you can add either *'s* or just an apostrophe. We teach the first form as it is more common and follows the basic rule.
Whose?
Tell SS to be careful not to confuse *Whose…?* and *Who's…?* (Who is) as the pronunciation is the same.

● Focus on the exercises for **2D** on *p. 125*. SS do the exercises individually or in pairs.
● Check answers. With **b**, go through the instructions with the SS first to make sure they understand exactly what they have to do. Ask SS for the answers and then write the sentences on the board so they can see where they have to put the apostrophes. Elicit each time whether the *'s* is the contraction of *is* or the possessive *s*.

a 1 Jane's cats
  2 my mother's car
  3 my wife's sister
  4 my friend's flat
  5 Daniel's brother
  6 his father's company
  7 the policeman's wife
  8 your sister's homework
b 1 My brother's a lawyer. He's 24. He works for BP.
  2 He lives in Paris with his three children. He has two boys and a girl.
  3 My brother's wife's name is Pauline. She's a teacher.
  4 Pauline's parents live in Paris too. My brother likes Pauline's mother but not her father.

Study Link SS can find an end-of-File grammar quiz on the MultiROM, and more grammar activities on the *New English File Elementary* website.

- Tell SS to go back to the main lesson on *p. 22.*

f • Focus on the pictures of the objects and model and drill pronunciation. Then tell SS that they belong to the famous people in **a**.
- Give SS in pairs a few minutes to match the objects and the people. Check answers, encouraging SS to use *I think… .*

> JK Rowling's pen.
> Hugh Grant's tie.
> Kate Winslet's bag.
> Antonio Banderas's hat.
> Naomi Campbell's shoes.
> Will Smith's cap.

Extra challenge

Teach SS the question *Whose (pen) is it?* Get SS to practise with both the question and the answer.

2 VOCABULARY family

a • Tell SS to go to **Vocabulary Bank** *The family* on *p. 145.*
- Focus on the instructions to **a** and the first family tree. Ask SS *Who is Robert's sister?* (Jill). Then show them how to find the word *sister* and write the number (8) in the box next to Jill.
- Give SS five minutes to write the numbers on the two family trees in pairs.
⚠ Tell SS they will need to use one of the words twice.
- Check answers. Model and drill pronunciation.

1	aunt	Sandra
2	brother	James
3	cousin	David, Vanessa
4	father	Tom
5	grandfather	Bill
6	grandmother	Martha
7	mother	Caroline
8	sister	Jill
9	uncle	Alan
10	daughter	Lucy
11	nephew	Peter
12	niece	Deborah
13	son	Harry
14	wife	Anna

- Demonstrate **b** by asking individual SS, e.g. *Who's Martha?* (She's Robert's grandmother.) Then get SS to continue in pairs, covering the words in the two lists.
- Focus on **c**. Give SS a few moments to complete the gaps. Check answers and model and drill all the new words.

> **1** parents **2** grandparents **3** children

Study Link SS can find more practice of these words on the MultiROM and on the *New English File Elementary* website.
- Tell SS to go back to the main lesson on *p. 23.*

b • Demonstrate the activity first, getting SS to ask you the questions, and telling them a bit about your family. Don't go into too much detail, as this will pre-empt the speaking later on.
- Give SS five minutes to talk in pairs.
- Get feedback, focusing on the numbers of relatives people have rather than any details about them.

Extra challenge

You may also want to teach SS the following to help them describe their families: *stepmother, stepfather, partner* (the most common word used these days to describe people who live together but are not necessarily married), *girlfriend, boyfriend.*

3 PRONUNCIATION consonant sounds

a **2.14**
- Quickly revise the previous six consonant words and sounds on *p. 21* or using the *New English File* wall chart if you have it.
- Tell SS that they are now going to do the last six consonant sounds. Focus on the six sound pictures (*bag, thumb,* etc.) and play the tape/CD once for SS just to listen to the words and sounds.
- Then play the tape/CD again pausing after each word and sound for SS to repeat.

2.14			CD1 Track 53
bag	/b/	monkey	/m/
thumb	/θ/	nose	/n/
mother	/ð/	house	/h/

- Focus especially on sounds which are difficult for your SS and model them yourself so that SS can see your mouth position. Get SS to repeat these sounds a few more times.

Pronunciation notes

- Highlight that the phonetic symbols for /b/, /m/, /n/, and /h/ are the same as the letters of the alphabet that produce them. There are also some clear sound–spelling patterns.
- /b/ the letters *b* and *bb* are always pronounced /b/, e.g. *board.*
- /m/ the letters *m* and *mm* are always pronounced /m/, e.g. *make, summer.*
- /n/ the letters *n* and *nn* are always pronounced /n/, e.g. *name, sunny.*
- /h/ the letter *h* is nearly always pronounced /h/ with a few exceptions. The only one they need to know at this level is *hour* where the *h* is silent.
- /θ/ and /ð/ the letters *th* are pronounced either /ð/, e.g. *this,* or /θ/, e.g. *three.* There is no rule here so SS need to learn words individually. The difference between the two sounds is quite small and does not usually impede communication.

Study Link SS can find more practice of English sounds on the MultiROM or on the *New English File Elementary* website.

b • Drill the sentences with the whole class. Then get SS to practise the sentences in pairs.

4 LISTENING

a 🔊 **2.15**

- Focus on the instructions and on the family photos.

Extra support

Give SS in pairs a minute to look at the photos and guess who the other people are before they listen.

- Play the tape/CD once or twice. Check answers.

> Photo 1: Sarah's mother
> Photo 2: Sarah's sister
> Photo 3: Sarah's cousin.

b • Now focus on the questions under each photo. Play the tape/CD again, pausing after each photo has been described to give SS time to write.

- Get SS to compare with a partner, then check answers. Get more information from SS, e.g. *What does her mother do?* (She's a nurse).

> Photo 1: Martin is her mother's partner. He works at a hospital – the same hospital where her mother works.
> Photo 2: Philip is Lisa's husband, Sarah's brother-in-law. Sophie is three.
> Photo 3: They are at Sarah's grandparents' house. Adam, Sarah's cousin, is a singer.

2.15   CD1 Track 54

(tapescript in Student's Book on *p.115*.)
S = Sarah, G = Guy
S This is my mother, in our garden at home.
G Let's see. Is that your father?
S No, it's Martin, her partner. My mum's divorced.
G Does your mother work?
S Yes, she's a nurse. And Martin's a doctor at the same hospital. I don't like him very much. This is my sister Lisa and her husband Philip. And their daughter, Sophie.
G Ah – she's really sweet. How old is she?
S She's three.
G Do you have any more nieces or nephews?
S No, just Sophie for the moment.
G Is that you?
S Don't laugh! Yes, that's from last Christmas, at my grandparents' house.
G Who's that?
S That's my cousin Adam. Adam and I are really good friends. He's a singer in a band. They play in local pubs and clubs…

---

5 SPEAKING

a • Demonstrate the activity first. Write the first names of five people in your family (or their partners, etc.) on the board, and tell SS that they're people in your family. Then elicit the four questions from **b** from SS for one of the people:

   Who is (Brenda)? How old is she? What does she do? Where does she live?

- Answer the questions, and then repeat for some or all of the other people.

- Now get SS to write the names of five people on a piece of paper, and swap papers with a partner.

b • In pairs SS ask the four questions about each person on their partner's list. Get SS to ask all four questions about one person and then swap roles, until they have talked about all the people. Monitor and correct, encouraging SS to give as much information as they can.

Extra idea

Tell SS to bring in some family photos (for the next class). They can then show them to each other and get more practice with family vocabulary.

Extra photocopiable activities

Grammar
possessive *s* p. 147.
Communicative
Who's who? *p. 192* (instructions *p.177*).

HOMEWORK

Study Link **Workbook** *pp. 19–20.*

Vocabulary hotel words: *double room*, etc.
Function Checking into a hotel
Language *Hello, I have a reservation*, etc.

Lesson plan

In this lesson SS get practice in checking into a hotel. In the Social English section, the Mark and Allie story develops. They have a drink in the hotel bar and find out a bit about each other.

Study Link These lessons are also on the *New English File Elementary* Video, which can be used **instead of** the Class Cassette/CD (see introduction *p.9*).
The first section of the Video is also on the MultiROM, with additional activities.

Optional lead-in (books closed)

- Ask SS what they remember from the previous Practical English lesson, e.g. *Where is Mark from?* (the USA) *What does he do?* (He works for a music company) *Where is he now?* (In the UK) *Who meets him at the airport?* (Allie), etc.

VOCABULARY   hotel words

a • Focus on the symbols. Give SS in pairs a few moments to match the words and pictures.
- Check answers. Drill pronunciation.

> 1 the lift   2 reception   3 a single room
> 4 a double room   5 the ground floor   6 the bar

- Check that SS understand (*ground*) floor, and elicit/teach *first*, *second*, *third*, *fourth*. Tell SS they will be learning all the ordinal numbers in the next File.

b • Tell SS to cover the words and test each other in pairs.

CHECKING IN

a 2.16
- Focus on the picture and ask SS *Who are they?* (Mark and the hotel receptionist.)
- Now either tell SS to close their books, and write questions 1 and 2 on the board, or get SS to cover the conversation.
- Play the tape/CD once. Check answers.

> 1 For five nights   2 425

b • Now focus on the dialogue. Give SS a minute to read through the dialogue and guess the missing words. Then play the tape/CD again, for them to fill the gaps.
- Check answers.

2.16   CD1 Track 55

R = receptionist, M = Mark
R Good evening, sir.
M Hello. I have a reservation. My name's Mark Ryder.
R Can you **spell** that, please?
M R-Y-D-E-R.

R For five nights.
M Yes, that's right.
R Can I **have** your passport, please?
M Just a moment. Here you are.
R Can you sign here, **please**? Do you want a smoking or non-smoking room?
M Non-smoking, please.
R Here's your **key**. It's room 425, on the fourth floor.
M Thank you. Where's the lift?
R It's over there. Do you need help with your **bags**?
M No, it's OK, thanks.
R Enjoy your stay, Mr Ryder.
M Thank you.

- Go through the dialogue line by line with SS, helping them with any expressions they don't understand.

c 2.17
- Now focus on the **YOU SAY** phrases. Tell SS they're going to hear the dialogue again. They repeat the **YOU SAY** phrases when they hear the beep. Encourage them to copy the rhythm and intonation.
- Play the tape/CD, pausing if necessary for SS to repeat the phrases.

2.17   CD1 Track 56

R Good evening, sir.
M Hello. I have a reservation. My name's Mark Ryder.
repeat
R Can you spell that, please?
M R-Y-D-E-R.
repeat
R For five nights.
M Yes, that's right.
repeat
R Can I have your passport, please?
M Just a moment. Here you are.
repeat
R Can you sign here, please? Do you want a smoking or non-smoking room?
M Non-smoking, please.
repeat
R Here's your key. It's room 425, on the fourth floor.
M Thank you. Where's the lift?
repeat
R It's over there. Do you need help with your bags?
M No, it's OK, thanks.
repeat
R Enjoy your stay, Mr Ryder.
M Thank you.
repeat

---

d • Put SS in pairs, A and B. A is the receptionist. Get SS to read the dialogue aloud first. Then tell B to close his/her book and try to respond from memory. Then A and B swap roles.

Extra challenge

Get SS to roleplay in pairs, the person being the guest with book closed. Tell them to use their real names, and to ask for the kind of room they would really like.

3 SOCIAL ENGLISH

a 2.18
- Now focus on the next picture. Ask SS *Where are they?* (in the bar).

- Focus on the chart. Play the tape/CD at least twice, and then give SS time to compare answers before checking.

	Mark	**Allie**
Where are they from?	The USA (San Francisco)	Britain (Cambridge)
Are they married?	no, divorced	no
Do they have children?	yes, a daughter	she doesn't say but we assume not
How old are they?	34	27

b • Focus on the question, and elicit ideas (e.g. because he says *darling*, *I love you*, etc.).

Extra support

Let SS listen again with the tapescript on *p.115*. Deal with any problematic vocabulary.

2.18   CD1 Track 57

(tapescript in Student's Book on *p.115*.)

A = Allie, M = Mark

A Where are you from in the United States, Mark?
M The West Coast. San Francisco.
A Is it nice?
M Oh yeah. It's a great city. Are you from London?
A No, I'm from Cambridge. My family live there but I live here in London.
M **Sorry**. Hello darling, how are you? ……… I'm fine, yeah. ……… Don't worry. ……… Fine, fine. ………. That's great. ………. Bye, darling. I love you. ………. **Sorry**.
A **That's OK**. Your wife?
M No, no, my daughter. She always phones me when I'm travelling.
A How old is she?
M She's nine. She lives with her mother in Los Angeles. We're divorced. Are you married?
A No, I'm not.
M How old are you?
A That's very personal! **What do you think?**
M 25? 26?
A Thanks, I'm 27. How old are you?
M I'm 34. **Would you like another drink?**
A No, thanks. **I have to go now**, Mark. Our first meeting's at 10.00. See you tomorrow.
M See you tomorrow, Allie. Goodnight.
A Goodnight.

---

c • Focus on the **USEFUL PHRASES**. For each phrase ask SS *Who says it, Mark or Allie?* Clarify the meaning if necessary.

⚠ Remind SS that *goodnight* = goodbye (in the evening).

• Play the tape/CD again for SS to check. Pause after each phrase and get SS to repeat it. (See the tapescript above.)

Sorry. – Mark
That's OK. – Allie
What do you think? – Allie
Would you like another drink? – Mark
I have to go now. – Allie

HOMEWORK

Study Link **Workbook** *p. 21.*

---

2 WRITING AN INFORMAL E-MAIL / LETTER

Lesson plan

Here SS consolidate some of the language they have learned in File 2 through writing about themselves, and learn the conventions for writing an informal e-mail and an informal letter. We suggest you do the exercises in class and set the letter for homework. SS will learn how to write a more formal e-mail in File 8.

- Go through the introductory text with SS. Explain what a penfriend is, and tell SS that there are many websites on the Internet where learners of English can find penfriends to practise their English.

a • Focus on the beginning of the e-mail. Elicit/teach the meaning of the headings **To/From** and **Subject**. Tell SS that Rosa is writing her first e-mail to Stefan, a penfriend she has found on the Internet.

- Focus on the instructions and the example. Then give SS five minutes to read the e-mail and match the questions to the information.

- Check answers.

---

1 What's your name?
2 Where are you from?
3 What do you do?
4 What languages do you speak?
5 Why do you want to learn English?
6 Do you have a big family?
7 What do the people in your family do?
8 How old are your brothers and sisters?
9 How old are you?
10 What are your interests?

- Finally focus on the end of the e-mail. Elicit/teach the meaning of *Please write soon* and *Best wishes*, and tell SS they are useful expressions to put at the end of a letter to a friend.

b • Focus on the instructions, and get SS to discuss the question in pairs.

- Check answers. The main difference is that in an informal letter, you usually write your address and the date in the top right hand corner, and start with *Dear* + name, not *Hi*.

- Tell SS that you can also begin an e-mail with *Dear* but *Hi* is more informal.

Write a similar e-mail or letter

Either give SS at least fifteen minutes to write the e-mail or letter in class, or set it for homework.

- If SS do the writing in class, get them to swap and read each other's e-mails/letters and correct any mistakes they find, before you collect them all in.

⚠ Tell SS to set their e-mail/letter out in paragraphs like in the model e-mail.

For instructions on how to use these pages, see *p.28.*

What do you remember?

GRAMMAR

1 b   2 a   3 a   4 b   5 a   6 a   7 a   8 a   9 a   10 b

VOCABULARY

a 1 at   2 for   3 to   4 in   5 to
b 1 do   2 speak   3 watch   4 play   5 have
c 1 job (not a verb)
   2 woman (not plural)
   3 football (not a job)
   4 student (not a place)
   5 niece (not masculine)
d 1 Where   2 What   3 Who   4 How many   5 Why

PRONUNCIATION

b 1 nice   2 garden   3 who   4 watches   5 stops
c po<u>li</u>ceman
   <u>grand</u>mother
   re<u>cep</u>tionist
   <u>ne</u>phew
   <u>art</u>ist

What can you do?

CAN YOU **UNDERSTAND THIS TEXT?**

b 1 F   2 T   3 F   4 F   5 T

CAN YOU **HEAR THE DIFFERENCE?**

1 a   2 b   3 b   4 b   5 a   6 b   7 b   8 a   9 b   10 a

2.19   CD1 Track 58
1 What does your brother do?
2 Do you like spaghetti?
3 Where does she live?
4 How old is your mother?
5 What do you do in the evening?
6 Who is he?
7 Do you speak French?
8 Are they Jane's books?
9 Do they have a car?
10 Where do you go to English classes?

Extra photocopiable activities

Quicktest 2 *p.232.*

3A

G adjectives and modifiers
V adjectives: *big*, *cheap*, etc. modifiers: *quite*/*very*
P vowel sounds: /iː/, /uː/, /aɪ/, /əʊ/, /e/

Pretty woman

Lesson plan

In this lesson SS learn, or revise, common adjectives and the two basic rules governing the position of adjectives. The context is a quiz about the USA which includes common adjective/noun phrases such as *The White House* and *New York* which should be familiar to SS in English or in their own language. These provide clear and easy to remember examples of adjective/noun word order. In the second half of the lesson SS practise writing simple descriptions through the context of a 'Guess the Mystery Person' activity.

Optional lead-in (books closed)

● Write *the USA* on the board and ask SS to tell you things which they think are typically American, e.g. *Hollywood films*, *hamburgers*, etc.
● Feedback their suggestions onto the board.

1 VOCABULARY adjectives

a ● Books open. Put SS in pairs. Focus on the quiz and on the adjectives and nouns. Focus on the example and make sure SS know what they have to do. Set a time limit, e.g. two or three minutes for SS to do the quiz. Check answers.

> **2** New York
> **3** American Airlines
> **4** fast food
> **5** Pretty Woman
> **6** blue jeans
> **7** Big Apple
> **8** yellow taxis

b ● Tell SS to go to **Vocabulary Bank** *Common adjectives* **Part 1** on *p. 146*. SS do the exercises in pairs. Check answers then model and drill pronunciation.

> **a** **1** red   **6** white
> **2** blue   **7** pink
> **3** yellow   **8** green
> **4** orange   **9** brown
> **5** black   **10** grey
>
> **b+c** **1** big small   **8** fast slow
> **2** expensive cheap   **9** dirty clean
> **3** bad good   **10** empty full
> **4** old new   **11** high low
> **5** easy difficult   **12** beautiful ugly
> **6** wet dry   **13** dangerous safe
> **7** rich poor

● Tell SS to go back to the main lesson on *p.28*.

2 PRONUNCIATION vowel sounds

a ● Focus on the five sound pictures and elicit the pronunciation of the words, e.g. *tree*. Give SS two minutes to put the words in the box in the right columns and then check their answers in pairs.

/iː/	/uː/	/aɪ/	/əʊ/	/e/
cheap	blue	white	slow	expensive
easy	new	dry	old	wet
clean	beautiful	high	low	empty

b **3.1**
● Play the tape/CD for SS to check their answers. Then play the tape/CD again pausing after each group for SS to repeat.

> **3.1**   CD1 Track 59
> tree   cheap, easy, clean
> boot   blue, new, beautiful
> bike   white, dry, high
> phone   slow, old, low
> egg   expensive, wet, empty

c ● Tell SS to go the **Sound Bank** on *p. 157*. Go through the typical and less common spellings for each of the six sounds.
● Tell SS to go back to the main lesson on *p. 29*.

3 GRAMMAR adjectives

a ● Focus on the answers to the USA quiz and ask SS first to tell you what the **adjectives** are (e.g. *White*, *New*, *American*, *fast*, etc.). Now ask where the adjective is, *before* or *after* the noun. Demonstrate *before*/*after* on the board if necessary. Elicit the answer *before*.
● Now focus on the answers to questions 3, 6, and 8 only. Ask if the adjective changes when the noun is plural. Elicit that the adjective *doesn't* change.
● Now focus on the two rules in **a** and get SS to circle the correct answers. Check answers.

> before   don't change

b ● Tell SS to go to **Grammar Bank 3A** on *p. 126*.
● Go through the rules and example sentences.

Grammar notes

● The grammar of adjectives in English is very simple. There is only *one* possible form which never changes. When an adjective is together with a noun there is only *one* possible position: *before* the noun.

● Focus on the exercises for **3A** on *p. 127*. SS do the exercises in pairs, or individually and check in pairs. Check answers and model and drill pronunciation.

a 1 **Nice** to meet you.
 2 Do you like **Japanese** food?
 3 It's an **international** school.
 4 They're a **typical British** family.
 5 My father makes **fantastic** pasta.
 6 Do you work with **other** people?
 7 I'm a **professional** footballer.
 8 We're **good** friends.
b 1 ✓
 2 ✓
 3 ✗ I have a big family.
 4 ✓
 5 ✗ They're new boots.
 6 ✗ It's an expensive flat.

- Tell SS to go back to the main lesson on *p. 29.*

c - Put SS in pairs. Focus on the picture and the example, and explain the activity. Make it clear that it is a race and set the time limit of three minutes (later you can extend it if you think your class needs more time).

- When the time limit is up find out if any pairs have made eight correct phrases. Feedback answers on to the board.

(Suggested answers)
a full moon   a red dress   old men   a high mountain
a rich woman   a dirty window   a black cat
an empty bag   a poor man   blue boots
a wet umbrella

Extra idea

Get SS to make adjective + noun phrases about things in the classroom, e.g. a dirty board, big windows, a brown bag, etc.

4 LISTENING

- Focus on the **REMEMBER!** instruction and then on the example sentence *It's an easy exercise.* First say the sentence slowly separating the words and then say it fast, running the words together (or play the first sentence on the tape/CD).

- Point out that the words you can hear most clearly are the two stressed words (*easy* and *exercise*). The unstressed words (*It's* and *an*) are said very quickly and almost disappear.

3.2

- Tell SS they are going to hear (and try to write down) six sentences where people are speaking quite fast and not separating all the words.

- Now play sentences 1–6 pausing to let SS write what they hear. Play the tape/CD again for them to check their answers. Then get them to compare answers in pairs. Play the tape/CD again if necessary.

Extra support

Read out the sentences slowly to give SS one more chance to check their answers.

3.2   CD1 Track 60
(tapescript in Student's Book on *p.115.*)
1 It's an easy exercise.
2 I live in an old house.
3 She's an American actress.
4 She has an expensive flat.
5 It's a nice evening.
6 I have a black and white cat.

5 VOCABULARY & SPEAKING

a - Focus on the two pictures (which show the features of two famous people) and the accompanying texts. Give SS two minutes, in pairs, to guess the identity of the two people. If necessary, elicit/teach the meaning of *adopted* (*adopt* = take a child into your family and become the legal parents).
  ⚠ Tell SS not to shout out the answers!
- Feedback SS' guesses and then give the right answers.

Enrique Iglesias   Nicole Kidman

b - Tell SS to go to **Vocabulary Bank** *Common adjectives* **Part 2** on *p. 146.* Here SS learn adjectives to describe a person.
- SS do the exercises in pairs. Check answers then model and drill pronunciation.

a 1 old - young   2 tall - short   3 fat - thin
 4 long - short (hair)   5 fair - dark
c 1 very tall   2 quite tall   3 not very tall

Study Link SS can find more practice of these words on the MultiROM and on the *New English File Elementary* website.

- Tell SS to go back to the main lesson on *p. 29.*

c - Now SS in pairs think of their own mystery person and write five clues on a piece of paper. They could also draw a quick sketch. Then they give the piece of paper to another pair who tries to guess the identity of the famous person.

Extra challenge

Get SS to do this individually, and then read their sentences to a partner for him/her to guess the person.

d - Here SS learn some more common adjectives to describe simple states and feelings.
  ⚠ In your SS' language some of these concepts may also be expressed using the verb *have* + a noun.
- Set the SS, in pairs, a time limit to match the faces to the words.

e **3.3**
- Play the tape/CD for SS to listen and check their answers.

3.3   CD1 Track 61
1 I'm happy.
2 I'm sad.
3 I'm angry.
4 I'm cold.
5 I'm tired.
6 I'm hot.
7 I'm thirsty.
8 I'm hungry.

- Play the tape/CD again pausing after each adjective for SS to repeat. Model and drill any phrases which are difficult for your SS, e.g. *thirsty*. Make sure SS can hear and pronounce the difference between *angry* /ˈæŋgri/ and *hungry* /ˈhʌŋgri/.

f • Demonstrate the activity by telling SS about yourself and making sentences using the phrases in **d**. Remind SS of the modifiers *very* and *quite*. You could also teach here *a bit* = a little, e.g. *I'm a bit cold*.

- In pairs, SS cover the words and make true sentences about themselves. Get some quick feedback asking the class about a few of the adjectives, e.g. *Who's thirsty?* and getting a show of hands.

6 SONG *Oh Pretty Woman*

3.4

- Here SS listen to a popular 1960s song by Roy Orbison which inspired the title of the film *Pretty Woman* referred to in the USA quiz in **1a**. If you want to do this song with your SS there is a photocopiable activity on *p. 224*.

3.4   CD1 Track 62

Pretty woman, walking down the street
Pretty woman, the kind I like to meet
Pretty woman
I don't believe you, you're not the truth
No one could look as good as you
Mercy

Pretty woman, won't you pardon me
Pretty woman, I couldn't help but see
Pretty woman
That you look lovely as can be
Are you lonely just like me
Wow

Pretty woman, stop a while
Pretty woman, talk a while
Pretty woman, give your smile to me
Pretty woman, yeah yeah yeah
Pretty woman, look my way
Pretty woman, say you'll stay with me
'Cause I need you, I'll treat you right
Come with me baby, be mine tonight

Pretty woman, don't walk on by
Pretty woman, don't make me cry
Pretty woman, don't walk away, hey ... okay
If that's the way it must be, okay
I guess I'll go on home, it's late
There'll be tomorrow night, but wait
What do I see?
Is she walking back to me?
Yeah, she's walking back to me
Oh, oh, Pretty woman

Extra photocopiable activities

Grammar
adjectives *p. 148*.
Communicative
The same or different? *p. 193* (instructions *p.177*).
Song
Oh Pretty Woman p. 224 (instructions *p.220*).

HOMEWORK

Study Link Workbook *pp. 22–23*.

3
B

G telling the time, present simple
V daily routine verbs: *get up, get dressed*, etc.
P the letter *o*

Wake up, get out of bed...

Lesson plan

This lesson is based on an article which looks at the daily routine of two real people – a single mother and a commuter. A stress expert assesses their stress levels and gives advice on how they could improve their daily lives. This provides the context for SS to learn/revise telling the time (non-digitally) and describing their own day using the present simple.

Optional lead-in (books closed)

- Revise numbers. Get SS to count round the class in 5s, i.e. 5, 10, 15, up to 60.
- If you have a teaching clock you could use this to teach SS the time before going to the **Grammar Bank** in **1**.

1 GRAMMAR   telling the time

a • Focus on the question and elicit answers. SS will probably be able to say the time their class starts/finishes 'digitally' (e.g. seven thirty, etc.) and may also know how to say it in 'non-digital' time (e.g. half past seven and nine o'clock). Explain that, in conversation, it is normal to use non-digital time and this is what SS learn/revise here.
b • Tell SS to go to **Grammar Bank 3B** on *p. 126*. Go through the rules with the class. Model and drill the example sentences.

Grammar notes

- When answering the question *What's the time?* you can leave out *It's*.
- With *quarter past/to*, some people say *a quarter past/to*, but it is optional.
- To say the time when the minutes are not a multiple of five, add the word *minutes*, e.g. *It's three minutes past one* NOT ~~It's three past one~~.
- Digital time, i.e. ten twenty, is normally used for train/bus/plane times, where the 24-hour clock is used. SS may like to know that the *o'* in *o'clock* comes from the old way of saying the time, e.g. *It's six of the clock*.

- Focus on the exercise for **3B** on *p. 127*. SS do the exercises individually or in pairs. Check answers.

> 1 b   2 d   3 h   4 f   5 a   6 c   7 e

c • Put SS in pairs A and B and get them to sit face to face if possible. Then tell them to go to **Communication** *What's the time?* A on *p. 108*, B on *p. 111*.
- Go through the instructions with them, and drill the question *What time is it?* or *What's the time?* Explain that the two expressions are equally common, but it's best to choose one expression to practise.
- At the end of the activity get SS to compare their clocks to check they've drawn the times in correctly.
- Tell SS to go back to the main lesson on *p. 30*.

d ● **3.5**

- Tell SS they're going to hear a woman called Vicky getting up and going to work in the morning.
- Play the tape/CD. SS listen and write down the seven times they hear. Play the tape/CD again pausing after each part to give SS time to write. Let SS compare answers, and repeat the tape/CD if necessary.
- Check answers. Get SS to say the times non-digitally. Ask what her job is (She's a TV newsreader/presenter).

> **2** 7.15 (quarter past seven)
> **3** 7.25 (twenty-five past seven)
> **4** 7.30 (half past seven)
> **5** 7.45 (quarter to eight)
> **6** 7.55 (five to eight)
> **7** 8.00 (eight o'clock)

> **3.5**   CD1 Track 63
> (tapescript in Student's Book on *p.115*.)
> H = Husband, V = Vicky, D = DJ, T= Taxi driver,
> A = Assistant, M = Man
> 1 H Vicky, it's **seven o'clock**. Wake up.
> 2 H Vicky, wake up!
>   V Oh no! It's **quarter past seven**! I'm late again.
> 3 D This is Dave Martin on Breakfast Special and the time now on Radio 1 is **twenty-five past seven**.
>   V Oh where's my bag?
> 4 V Taxi! Do you have the right time?
>   T Yes, love. It's **half past seven**.
>   V Half past seven! Oh no, I'm late. Please hurry!
> 5 V A white coffee, please.
>   A Here you are. That's 1.80.
>   V Oh no, is that clock right?
>   A Yes, it's **quarter to eight**.
>   V Help!
>   A Careful with your coffee.
> 6 M Hurry up Vicky, you're late. It's **five to eight**.
> 7 V Good morning. It's **eight o'clock** and this is Vicky McGuire with the news on CTV.

2 VOCABULARY   daily routine

a • Focus on the pictures. Tell SS that they show Vicky on a typical morning (i.e. when she's not late/stressed).
- Give SS a minute or two to match the phrases and pictures. Check answers. Model and drill pronunciation. Make sure SS are clear about the difference between *wake up* (= open your eyes) and *get up* (= get out of bed).

> 1 wake up   4 get dressed
> 2 get up   5 have breakfast
> 3 have a shower   6 go to work

b • SS use the pictures in **a** to describe Vicky's morning.

> She wakes up at 7.00. She gets up. She has a shower.
> She gets dressed. She has breakfast. She goes to work.

c • Demonstrate the task yourself. Use the pictures 1–6 to tell the class your typical morning.

• In pairs, SS describe their typical morning. They should listen to each other to see if they do things in the same order. Get two or three SS to tell their mornings to the class.

d • Tell SS to go to **Vocabulary Bank** *Daily routine* on *p. 147*.

• Give SS five to ten minutes to do **a** in pairs.

• Check answers. Model and drill pronunciation. Make sure SS know the difference between *go to work* (= leave the house), *get to work* (= arrive at work), *go home* (= leave work), and *get home* (= arrive home).

1 wake up (*early/late*)	13 go home
2 get up	14 go to her Italian class
3 have a shower/a bath	15 go to the gym
4 get dressed	16 get home
5 have breakfast	17 make the dinner
6 go to work/school	18 have dinner
7 get to work/school	19 take (*the dog for a walk*)
8 have a coffee	20 watch TV
9 start work/school	21 do her Italian homework
10 have lunch	22 go to bed
11 go shopping	23 sleep (*for seven hours*)
12 finish work/school	

• Focus on **b**. Get SS to cover the words and use the pictures to test themselves or each other. Encourage them to say the complete phrase, i.e. *She gets up.*

Study Link SS can find more practice of these words on the MultiROM and on the *New English File Elementary* website.

• Tell SS to go back to the main lesson on *p. 30.*

3 READING & LISTENING

a • Focus on the title of the text and the two photos of Louisa and Simon. Explain that this is based on an article from a British newspaper. These two people talk about a typical (working) day in their lives and a stress expert gives them advice.

• Focus on the caption to the photo of Louisa and elicit the meaning of *a single mother* (= a woman who looks after her child/children alone i.e. without a partner).

• Set SS a time limit, e.g. three or four minutes, and tell them that all they have to do is find out how stressed Louisa is (i.e. very, quite, or not very stressed).

• Get feedback from a few SS.

> Louisa seems **quite stressed** or **very stressed**. She has to look after her son and work all day. She gets up early and is always in a hurry. She has very little free time.

b • Focus on the first highlighted word (*guide*) and elicit the meaning. Then get SS in pairs to guess the meaning of the other highlighted words in the text. Tell them to read the whole sentence as the context will help them guess.

• Check answers, either translating into SS' L1 if you prefer, using the glossary below, or getting SS to check in their dictionaries.

> **a guide** = a person who helps visitors in a museum
> **Then** = after that, e.g. *I get up, then I have shower*
> **always** = every time, e.g. *nurses always wear a uniform*

> **at home** = in your house or flat
> **cycle** = (verb) to go by bicycle ('bike')
> **canteen** = a kind of restaurant at work/school
> **pick up** = go and collect, e.g. pick up children from school, tickets from the travel agency
> **After** = the opposite of before
> **until** = up to a time
> **babysitter** = a person who comes to your house to look after your baby/child
> **a story** = something you read to children at night

c • Set a time limit for SS to read the article again and tell SS to try to remember the information in the text.

d • Put SS in pairs. Tell SS to go to **Communication** *Louisa's day*, A on *p. 108*, B on *p. 111.*

• Go through the instructions. SS take it in turns to test their partner's memory of the text by asking the questions they have been given.

• Tell SS to go back to the main lesson on *p. 31.*

e 3.6

• Focus on the photo of Simon and the caption. Ask the class what he does (he works for a computer company), where he is (on a train) and where he lives and works (Brighton and London). Tell SS that Brighton is about 55 miles (88 kilometres) from London. It is quite common in the UK for people to travel this distance to work.

• Tell SS that they are going to hear an interview with Simon. But first they are just going to hear some extracts. This is to help SS 'tune in' to Simon's voice and to help them understand more of the interview.

• Focus on the five drawings and tell SS to listen to five sentences that Simon says and to match them to the drawings by writing numbers 1–5.

• Play the tape/CD once or twice and SS number the pictures. Check answers.

> 1 London–Brighton 55 miles
> 2 daughters in bed
> 3 man walking in the street
> 4 contract
> 5 man asleep in front of TV

> **3.6** CD1 Track 64
> (tapescript in Student's Book on *p.115.*)
> 1 I travel 55 miles to work!
> 2 I don't see my daughters – they're in bed.
> 3 I walk from the station to work.
> 4 I'm very worried about my contract.
> 5 I usually go to sleep in front of the TV.

f • Play the tape/CD again and this time tell SS to write any words they hear. Pause the tape/CD after each sentence and give SS time to write and compare in pairs.

Extra support

Write the following gapped sentences on the board, and get SS to listen just for the missing words instead of for the whole sentences.

1 I travel _____ miles to _____.
2 I don't see my _____. They're in _____.
3 I _____ from the station to _____.
4 I'm _____ _____ about my contract.
5 I usually go to _____ in front of the _____.

- Play the tape/CD again for SS to check their answers.

g 3.7

- Now SS hear the whole interview and answer the questions. Go through the questions first with the class.
- Play the tape/CD twice. Get SS to compare their answers with their partners. Tell SS they don't have to write full sentences.
- Check answers, accepting as correct any answer which shows that SS have understood what they heard, e.g. for number 3 'no time' would be correct.

1	three	6	a sandwich
2	six o'clock	7	5.30
3	He doesn't have time.	8	Because he's on the train.
4	9.00	9	7.45
5	six a day	10	He goes to sleep in front of the TV.

3.7 CD1 Track 65

(tapescript in Student's Book on *p.116*.)
P = Professor Parker, S = Simon
P Where do you do work, Simon?
S I work for a computer company in London – but I live in Brighton.
P Are you married?
S Yes, I have three daughters.
P So you travel from Brighton to London every day?
S Yes. **I travel 55 miles to work!**
P Tell me about a typical day.
S Well, I get up at six o'clock and I have a shower and get dressed. **I don't see my daughters – they're in bed.**
P Do you have breakfast?
S No, I don't have time. I have to get the train to London at half past seven.
P What time do you get to London?
S The train usually arrives at half past eight. Then **I walk from the station to work**. That's about half an hour.
P What time do you start work?
S At 9.00. I start work and I have a coffee. I drink about six cups of coffee a day.
P Do you go out for lunch?
S No, I'm very busy. I have a sandwich in the office.
P Do you like your job?
S It's OK, but **I'm very worried about my contract**. It finishes in six months.
P What time do you finish work?
S I finish work at half past five. Then I walk to the station again to get the train.
P Do you have dinner with your family?
S No, I don't. My family have dinner at six – but I'm on the train then. I don't get home until quarter to eight.
P What do you do after dinner?
S After dinner I sit and watch TV. I'm very tired. **I usually go to sleep in front of the TV**.
P What time do you go to bed?
S About 11.00.

---

h 3.8

- Ask SS if they think Simon is stressed, and to guess what advice they think the professor will give him. Play the tape/CD twice to see if they were right.

3.8 CD1 Track 66

(tapescript in Student's Book on *p.116*)
P Have breakfast in the morning, Simon, it's very important. But don't drink six cups of coffee – that's

---

too much. Don't have lunch in the office, go out to a sandwich bar or restaurant. And finally, if possible find a new job in Brighton, not in London.

i • Finally ask SS who they think is more stressed, Louisa or Simon. Encourage them to try to say why (even if they make mistakes).

4 PRONUNCIATION   the letter *o*

- Remind SS that in English the vowels can be pronounced in different ways. This exercise focuses on the two most common pronunciations of the letter *o*, /ɒ/ and /əʊ/ and two less common ones, /ʌ/ and /uː/.

a • Focus on the sound pictures and elicit the four words and sounds, e.g. *clock* /klɒk/.
  • Give SS, in pairs, two or three minutes to put the twelve words into the correct columns according to their pronunciation. Encourage SS to say the words out loud to help them decide where to put them.

b 3.9

- Play the tape/CD for SS to check their answers. Then feedback the correct answers onto the board.

3.9 CD1 Track 67

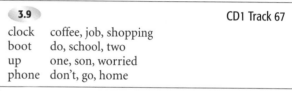

clock	coffee, job, shopping
boot	do, school, two
up	one, son, worried
phone	don't, go, home

⚠ If SS ask if there are other ways of pronouncing *o*, tell them that *or* is usually /ɔː/, e.g. *story*, and *oo* can also be /ʊ/, e.g. *good*.

5 SPEAKING

- Focus on the two circles, and ask SS what two words are missing from the questions (*do you*).
- Demonstrate the activity by getting SS to ask you two or three questions. Remind SS of the typical rhythm of questions and encourage them not to stress *do you*, e.g. <u>What</u> <u>time</u> do you <u>wake</u> <u>up</u>?
- Focus on the speech bubbles and teach the expression *It depends*. Model and drill pronunciation. Teach also the meaning of *about* (= approximately, more or less).
- SS ask and answer the questions in pairs. Monitor and help, correcting especially any mistakes with the time.
- Get feedback asking as many pairs as possible who is more stressed.

Extra photocopiable activities

Grammar
telling the time, present simple *p. 149.*
Communicative
A day in the life of an English teacher *p. 194* (instructions *p.177*).

HOMEWORK

Study Link Workbook *pp. 24–25*.

3 C

G adverbs of frequency
V time words and expressions: *minute, hour,* etc.
P the letter *h*

The island with a secret

Lesson plan

A study carried out over several years has investigated why inhabitants of the Japanese island of Okinawa (population 1.2 million) have the highest life expectancy in the world. The results have been published in a book *The Okinawa Way*, which highlights the aspects of the Okinawans' life style which help them to live long lives. Information from the Okinawa study provides the context for SS to learn and practise *How often…?* and adverbs and expressions of frequency. At the end of the lesson they find out if they and other SS live 'the Okinawa way.'

Optional lead-in (books closed)

- Write on the board the name and age of your oldest living relative. Ask SS if they have a living relative who is older.
- Get feedback to find who has the oldest relative.

1 GRAMMAR adverbs of frequency

a • Focus on the photo of the old man and elicit ideas from the class about his nationality and age. (His age has been blanked out in the text).

- Tell SS the answers to the two questions.

> He's Japanese.   He's 103 years old.

b • Get SS to read the first paragraph of the text focusing on the highlighted words which all express frequency.

- Focus on the chart and establish the meaning of *always*. Tell SS to write the expressions from the text in the chart in the correct place according to relative frequency. (The gradings 0–100 are given as a rough guide.) SS can help each other, use a dictionary or ask you for help to complete the task.
- Check answers and make sure SS are clear about the difference in meaning between the six adverbs. Model and drill pronunciation.

> always /ˈɔːlweɪz/
> usually /ˈjuːʒuəli/
> often /ˈɒfn///ˈɒftən/
> sometimes /ˈsʌmtaɪmz/
> hardly ever /ˈhɑːdli ˈevə/
> never /ˈnevə/

c • Tell SS to go to **Grammar Bank 3C** on *p. 126.*

- Go through the rules and model and drill the example sentences.

Grammar notes

- With all verbs except *be* adverbs of frequency go *before* the main verb.
  – In ⊕ sentences they go *between* the pronoun and the verb, e.g. I *never eat meat.*
  – In ⊖ sentences they go between the negative and the verb, e.g. *I don't usually work on Saturday.*

- With the verb *be* adverbs of frequency go *after* the verb, e.g. *I'm always late.*
- You could also point out that *usually* and *sometimes* can be used at the beginning of the sentence.

- Focus on the exercises for **3C** on *p. 127.* SS do the exercises individually or in pairs.
- Check answers.

> **a 1** hardly ever **2** never **3** always
>   **4** usually **5** sometimes
> **b 1** I'm always late for class.
>   **2** We hardly ever meet.
>   **3** What time do you usually finish work?
>   **4** I'm never hungry in the morning.
>   **5** I don't often read the newspaper.
>   **6** We sometimes go to expensive restaurants.
>   **7** This wine is usually very good.

- Tell SS to go back to the main lesson on *p. 32.*

d • Demonstrate the activity first by making true sentences about yourself.

- In pairs SS add an adverb to each sentence to make it true for them and compare their sentences with a partner. Feedback, asking two or three pairs if they were similar or different.

2 READING

a • Focus on the other photos and ask SS to read the introduction to the text **The mystery of Okinawa**. Then ask them the two questions. Elicit the answer to the first question (the people there live a long time) and possible answers to the second (e.g. their life style/the food, etc.).

b • Explain the task. SS have to put the four headings (*Always active*, etc.) into the text in the right place.

- Set SS a time limit to read the text, e.g. four minutes. Tell them to read the text once *before* trying to put in the headings. Then give them more time to put in the headings and to check their answers with a partner.
- Check answers.

> **1** A healthy diet **2** Exercise **3** Low stress
> **4** Always active

c • Tell SS to read the text again and in pairs try to guess the meaning of the highlighted words and phrases.

- Check answers, either translating into SS' L1 if you prefer, using the glossary below, or getting SS to check in their dictionaries.

> **rice** = a type of food, very popular in China and Japan
> **meat** = a type of food which comes from animals
> **popular** (adj) = something which a lot of people like
> **unusual** (adj) = not usual or common
> **take their time** = do things slowly, not in a hurry

50

beach = the land next to the sea. It is often yellow or white.
sunset = the time of day when the sun goes down
busy (adj) = with a lot of things to do, e.g. *I'm very busy this week*
stay at home = not go out

d • Ask the class if people in their country live like the Okinawans. Elicit things which are similar or different on the board.

Extra challenge

With a strong class you could write down the four headings from the article on the board. SS, in pairs, try to remember all the information they can from the four paragraphs.

3 VOCABULARY   time words and expressions

a • In pairs SS complete the quiz. Check answers. Model and drill pronunciation, especially *second* /ˈsekənd/, *minute* /ˈmɪnɪt/, *hour* /ˈaʊə/, and *month* /mʌnθ/.

a minute   an hour   a day   a week   a month   a year

Extra support

Write the time words in random order for SS to match with the definitions.

b • Tell SS to go to **Vocabulary Bank *Times and dates Part 1*** on *p. 148*.
  • Give SS two minutes to do exercise **a** in pairs.
  • Check answers and model and drill pronunciation. Highlight *once a* /ˈwʌnsə/ and *twice a* /ˈtwaɪsə/.
  • Make sure SS are clear about the meaning and pronunciation of *How often…?* (which is used when you want to ask someone about the frequency with which they do an activity) and *every* (= all, without exception).
  • Highlight that *once* and *twice* are irregular forms (you can't say *one time* or *two times*). For all other numbers we use a number + *times*, e.g. *five times, ten times*.

week   month   year   week   week   week   year

  • Now get SS to cover the right-hand column and try to remember the expressions.
  • Tell SS to go back to the main lesson on *p. 33*.

4 SPEAKING

a • Tell the class that they are going to find out if they live the Okinawa way by answering the questionnaire.
  • You could demonstrate the activity by getting the class to interview you first and show how you can give extra information in your answers.
  • Put SS in pairs. Give the As time to interview the Bs and to circle their partners' answers.
  • Now the pairs change roles and the Bs interview the As and circle their answers.
b • Tell SS to go to **Communication *The Okinawa Way*** on *p. 108* and to calculate their partner's score.
  • SS take turns to tell their partner his/her score and to read him/her the results.

  • Get feedback from the class and find out how many people live the Okinawa way or the complete opposite!
  • Tell SS to go back to the main lesson on *p. 33*.

5 PRONUNCIATION the letter *h*

a 🔊 **3.10**
  • Focus on the task (practising the /h/ sound) and on words in the box.

Pronunciation notes

  • How difficult this sound is will depend on your SS' first language and you should spend more or less time here accordingly.
  • Highlight that the letter /h/ is almost always pronounced like the /h/ in *hotel* and *How?* There are very few exceptions. The only one which is relevant at this level is *hour*, but don't mention this until after SS have done **b**.
  • Play the tape/CD once or twice and SS listen and repeat the words.

🔊 3.10	CD1 Track 68
house /h/ how, hardly, heavy, high, have, half, hungry, happy	

b • In pairs, SS read the sentences aloud and try to find in which word the letter *h* is not pronounced. Don't check answers yet.

c 🔊 **3.11**
  • Play the tape/CD and SS listen and check. Confirm that in the word *hour* the *h* is not pronounced.
  • Play the tape/CD again pausing after each sentence for SS to repeat.

Extra support

If this sound is difficult for your SS you could get them to practise the sentences further in pairs and then ask three or four pairs to say the sentences to the class.

🔊 3.11	CD1 Track 69
Harry's unhealthy. He hardly ever has breakfast. He usually eats hamburgers. He's always in a hurry. He's often half an hour late for work.	

Extra photocopiable activities

Grammar
adverbs of frequency *p. 150*.
Communicative
How often …? *p. 195* (instructions *p.177*).

HOMEWORK

Study Link Workbook *pp. 26–27*.

3 **G** prepositions of time: *in*, *on*, or *at*.
V the date
P word stress, /ð/ and /θ/

D

On the last Wednesday in August

Lesson plan

The main focus in this lesson is expressing time: how to say what the date is and how to use common prepositions of time correctly. Although the date can be said in two ways, e.g. *the sixth of April* or *April the sixth*, we have focused on the former, which is more common, as it is easier for SS just to learn one form. The context is three unusual 'throwing' festivals which are held in different countries around the world and, later in the lesson, an interview with a Chilean novelist who talks about her favourite times of day, year, etc.

Optional lead-in (books closed)

- Write the question WHAT'S THE DATE TODAY? on the board. Elicit/teach the answer and write it on the board like this: *6th April 2009*. Elicit/teach that *th* indicates an ordinal number (here six**th**). SS will practise this in more detail in **VOCABULARY**. You may want to explain that the date can also be written *6 April 2009* (without *th*).
- Draw a face and a speech bubble on the board and write in the bubble: *The sixth of April two thousand and nine.* Explain that this is the way the date is said in English.
- Highlight the use of *the* /ðə/ and *of* /əv/ and model and drill pronunciation.

1 READING

a • Books open. Focus on the photos and ask SS what people do in the three festivals. Elicit/teach the verb *throw* (They throw tomatoes/oranges/water).
- Give SS a couple of minutes to read the texts and match the three photos to the paragraphs.
- Now read the text with the class and deal with any vocabulary which is new or problematic for your SS.

> 1 Water Festival (Songkran)
> 2 Carnevale d'Ivrea
> 3 Tomatina

b • SS read the text again and try to remember the details. Then they cover the text and in pairs ask and answer the three questions.

> **Picture 1:** 1 Thailand. 2 It's from the 13th to the 15th of April. 3 Water.
> **Picture 2:** 1 Italy. 2 It's in January. 3 Oranges.
> **Picture 3:** 1 Spain. 2 It's on the last Wednesday in August. 3 Tomatoes.

c • Ask this question to the whole class and get several answers. Get a show of hands to see which of the festivals is the most popular.

2 VOCABULARY the date

a • Tell SS to go to **Vocabulary Bank** *Times and dates* p. 148.

- In pairs SS do part 2.
- Check answers and model and drill pronunciation.

> **a** 1 autumn   5 winter
>   2 New Year   6 Easter
>   3 summer   7 spring
>   4 Christmas
> **b** January, February, March, April, May, June, July August, September, October, November, December
> **c** second 3rd fourth 5th sixth seventh 8th 9th tenth eleventh 12th thirteenth fourteenth 20th twenty-first 22nd twenty-third 24th thirtieth 31st

- Now get SS to cover the words in **a** and use the pictures to test themselves or each other.

> **Study Link** SS can find more practice of these words
on the MultiROM and on the *New English File Elementary* website.

- Tell SS to go back to the main lesson on *p. 34*.

b • Do this as an open-class question if SS are from the same place. If they are from different countries, do it in pairs and get feedback.

3 PRONUNCIATION word stress, /ð/ and /θ/

a ◖ **3.12** ◗
- Focus on the months and play the tape/CD for SS to listen and repeat.

> | **3.12** ◗ | | CD1 Track 70 |
> |---|---|---|
> | January | May | September |
> | February | June | October |
> | March | July | November |
> | April | August | December |

- Play the tape/CD again, pausing for SS to underline the stressed syllable. Ask which five months have the stress on the second syllable.

> Ju<u>ly</u> Sep<u>tem</u>ber Oc<u>to</u>ber No<u>vem</u>ber De<u>cem</u>ber

- Ask where the stress is on all the other months (the first syllable).

b ◖ **3.13** ◗
- Focus on the activity. Play the tape/CD and SS repeat after it. Play the tape/CD again or model the pronunciation yourself for SS to repeat again.

> | **3.13** ◗ | | CD1 Track 71 |
> |---|---|---|
> | mother | /ð/ | this, the, other, their, they, with |
> | thumb | /θ/ | Thursday, thirteenth, third, birthday, think, throw |

52

Pronunciation notes

- *th* can only be pronounced in two ways, /ð/ or /θ/, and there are no easy rules to give SS. Many nationalities tend to pronounce all *th* like *thumb*. In fact the difference between these two sounds is a small one, and doesn't usually cause communication problems.
- If your SS have difficulty distinguishing and making the two sounds, and you want to focus on the difference, try to show that the /θ/ is made in the mouth without using the voice (an unvoiced sound) and the /ð/ sound is made lower down in the chest using the voice (a voiced sound).

c 3.14

- Focus on some other ways of writing the dates on the left and highlight that what is written on the right is the way that you say the date.
- Highlight that:
- The words *the* and *of* are <u>said</u> but not written. Don't say *of* before the year. NOT The sixth of May ~~of~~ 1985.
- Years up to 2000 are said like this: 1950 = *nineteen fifty* 2000 is said like this: *two thousand*.
- From 2000 the most common way of saying the years is like this:
- 2008 = *two thousand and eight*.
- Play the tape/CD and SS listen and repeat, trying to copy the rhythm.

3.14   CD1 Track 72

Thursday the thirteenth
the twelfth of May
the twenty-third of September
the fifteenth of April, nineteen ninety-nine
the thirtieth of January, two thousand and eight

Extra support

Write other dates on the board for SS to practise saying, e.g. 11/6/53 22nd March 1854 3/3 12th July 31/12/2010

d • Model and drill the question *When's your birthday?* Get SS to stand up and move around the class. If this is not practical get them to ask all the students around them. Ask SS to put their hands up if they have a birthday in January. Write the number on the board and repeat for other months to find out which month has the most birthdays.

4 GRAMMAR prepositions of time

a • Put SS in pairs. Tell them not to look back at the reading text on *p. 34* but to try to complete the sentences from memory. After a minute or so get SS to check their answers by looking at the text again. Check answers.

1 at in **2** In **3** on **4** at

b • Tell SS to go to **Grammar Bank 3D** on *p. 126*. Go through the rules with the class. Model and drill the example sentences.
- Go through the rules and the chart.

Grammar notes

- There are three main prepositions of time: *in, on, at*.
- There are simple rules for *in* and *on*. The rules for *at* require a little bit more effort to remember, because these include the exceptions *at night, at the weekend*.

- Now focus on the exercises for **3D** on *p. 127*. SS do them individually or in pairs. Check answers.

---

a 1 at **2** in **3** at **4** on **5** in **6** in **7** at
8 in **9** at **10** on **11** at **12** on
b 1 at midnight   **5** on Sundays
   2 on July 4th   **6** in the afternoon
   3 at Christmas   **7** at five o'clock
   4 in the summer

Study Link SS can find an end-of-File grammar quiz on the MultiROM, and more grammar activities on the *New English File Elementary* website.

c • Now put SS in pairs, A and B. Tell SS to go to **Communication When...?** (A to *p. 108* and B to *p. 111*).
- SS take turns to ask questions with *When...?* and to answer with a preposition of time, *in, on,* or *at* and a time word. Monitor and help, correcting any mistakes with prepositions.
- Get feedback from different SS asking a few of the *when* questions.
- Tell SS to go back to the main lesson on *p. 35*.

5 READING & LISTENING

a • Focus on the photo of Carla, a novelist from Chile, and on the interview **Times you love**. Make sure SS understand the word *favourite*. Model and drill the pronunciation /ˈfeɪvərɪt/.
- Give SS a time limit, e.g. two minutes to read the text.
- Now focus on sentences A–E. Tell SS that these five sentences have been cut from Carla's answers. They have to try to match the sentences to her answers. Again, set a time limit.
- Check answers and elicit/teach any new words/phrases.

C E A D B

b 3.15

- Explain the task. Before SS hear the two interviews they hear four extracts from them (two from each). This will later help them understand the interviews.
- Play the tape/CD once or twice. Check SS understand the highlighted words, either translating into SS' L1 if you prefer, using the glossary below, or getting SS to check in their dictionaries. Model and drill pronunciation.

---

enjoy = like a lot
far away = another way of saying far, the opposite of very near
energy = when you have a lot of energy you don't feel tired
temperature = e.g. 40 degrees C
comfortable /ˈkʌmftəbl/ = in this context physically well, e.g. not too hot, but also a comfortable bed, sofa, etc.

> **3.15** CD1 Track 73
>
> 1 I can start to relax and enjoy the evening.
> 2 My family live very far away…
> 3 I get up early and feel full of energy.
> 4 …in winter it's a nice temperature and it's when I feel comfortable.

c **3.16**

- Focus on the chart and instructions. Play the tape/CD once.
- SS complete the chart and compare with a partner. Play the tape/CD again for them to check their answers.

Cristina	Udom
1 10 p.m.	the morning
2 Thursday	Friday
3 July	December
4 spring	winter
5 Christmas	New Year

d • Now SS listen again for more detail, i.e. for why these are their favourite times. Get SS to write 1–5 on a piece of paper. Play the tape/CD again pausing to give SS time to write down their answers. Get them to compare with a partner and then play the tape/CD again to see if they can add more detail.

Extra support

Tell SS not to write anything but just to listen and try to understand their reasons. Pause the tape/CD after each section, e.g. in the first interview after the evening, and ask comprehension questions *Why is this her favourite time? What can she start to do?* Finally let SS listen with the tapescript on *p. 116.*

> **3.16** CD1 Track 74
>
> (tapescript in Student's Book on *p.116.*)
> **Cristina**
> My favourite time of day is 10 o'clock at night, **because it's when I finish training and I can start to relax and enjoy the evening.** My favourite day of the week is Thursday, **because I don't work on Friday**, so for me the weekend begins on Thursday night. My favourite month is July **because it's the month when I have my holiday.** My favourite season is the spring. One of my hobbies is gardening and **my garden is really beautiful in the spring.** My favourite public holiday is Christmas. **My family live very far away, and it's the only time when I can see them.**
>
> **Udom**
> My favourite time of the day is the morning **because I get up early and feel full of energy.** My favourite day of the week is Friday **because it's the end of the week and I can go home for the weekend.** My favourite month is December because here in Thailand **it's when you can see a lot of flowers.** My favourite season is winter, **because in winter it's a nice temperature and it's when I feel comfortable. The summer here is very hot.** My favourite public holiday is the Thai New Year in April. **It's a water festival, and people throw water at each other and everyone is very happy.**

6 SPEAKING

- SS now take turns to interview each other using the questions in Carla's interview. SS will not find it easy to say *why*. Encourage them to communicate in any way they can (single words, etc.).
- Get feedback, asking a few SS about their favourite times.

Extra photocopiable activities

Grammar
prepositions of time *p. 151.*
Communicative
Dates and times survey *p. 196* (instructions *p.178*).

HOMEWORK

Study Link **Workbook** *pp. 28–29.*

<table>
<tr><td>

3 PRACTICAL ENGLISH IN A COFFEE SHOP

Vocabulary snacks: *cappuccino, brownie*, etc.
Function Buying a coffee
Language *Can I have an espresso please?* etc.

Lesson plan

In this lesson SS get practice in ordering coffee and snacks in a coffee shop and in saying prices. In the story Mark invites Allie for a coffee to kill time before their next meeting. Unfortunately he spills coffee on Allie's white shirt and takes her shopping to buy her a new one before the meeting.

Study Link These lessons are also on the *New English File Elementary* Video, which can be used **instead of** the Class Cassette/CD (see introduction *p.9*).
The first section of the Video is also on the MultiROM, with additional activities.

VOCABULARY coffee and snacks

a • Focus on the coffee shop menu and get SS to match the pictures to the items in the menu by writing the correct number.
  • Check answers and model and drill pronunciation. Make sure SS pronounce the words with the correct word stress.
  • Give SS practice in saying the prices by asking them, e.g. *How much is a filter coffee? How much is a brownie?* Explain that prices are said like this: 1.45 = one forty five.

⚠ In the Practical English lessons the actual currency is not referred to. SS can use the expressions, e.g. one forty five, for most major currencies, e.g. pounds, dollars, and euros. If you wish to teach a particular currency, now would be a good time to do so.

> 1 Cappuccino
> 2 Filter coffee
> 3 Espresso
> 4 Brownies
> 5 Chocolate chip cookies

b • Get SS in pairs to cover the menu and try to remember all the items by looking at the pictures and saying the words.

Extra idea

In pairs SS take turns to ask and answer using the menu, e.g. **A** *How much is an espresso?* **B** *A regular is 1.65 and a large is 2.85.* Make sure SS use the indefinite article *a/an* for the drinks.

BUYING A COFFEE

a 3.17
  • Focus on the picture of Mark and Allie. Ask *Where are they?* (in a coffee shop).
  • Now either tell SS to close their books, and write questions **1** and **2** on the board, or get SS to cover the conversation.

</td><td>

  • Play the tape/CD once or twice. Check answers.

Extra support

As they listen get SS to look at the menu and tick the things they hear being ordered.

> **1** Mark has an espresso and a brownie.
>   Allie has a large cappuccino.
> **2** It costs 6.45.

b • Now focus on the dialogue and the gaps. Give SS a minute to read through the dialogue and guess the missing words. Then play the tape/CD again once or twice as necessary. Check answers.
  • Get SS to compare answers in pairs. Check answers.

> **3.17**   CD2 Track 2
> **As = assistant, M = Mark, A = Allie**
> AS Can I help you?
> M   What would you like?
> A   A cappuccino, please.
> AS **Regular** or large?
> A   Large, please.
> M   And can I have an espresso, please?
> AS To have here or **take away**?
> M   To have here.
> AS **Anything** else?
> A   No, thanks.
> M   A brownie for me, please.
> AS OK.
> M   How much is that?
> AS Together or **separate**?
> M   Together.
> AS That's **6.45**, please.
> M   Sorry, how much?
> AS **6.45**. Thank you.

  • Go through the dialogue line by line with SS, helping them with any expressions they don't understand.

c 3.18
  • Focus on the **YOU SAY** column of the conversation.
  • Focus on the instructions. Before you play the tape/CD, emphasize that you want SS to try to copy the rhythm of the phrases they hear. Play the tape/CD again if you think the SS need more practice.

> **3.18**   CD2 Track 3
> AS Can I help you?
> M   What would you like?
> *repeat*
> A   A cappuccino, please.
> *repeat*
> AS Regular or large?
> A   Large, please.
> *repeat*
> M   And can I have an espresso, please?
> *repeat*
> AS To have here or take away?
> M   To have here.
> *repeat*
> AS Anything else?
> A   No, thanks.
> M   A brownie for me, please.
> *repeat*
> AS OK.
> M   How much is that?
> *repeat*

</td></tr>
</table>

AS Together or separate?
M   Together.
repeat
AS That's 6.45, please.
M   Sorry, how much?
repeat
AS 6.45. Thank you.

d • Put SS in threes, A, B, and C. A is Mark, B is Allie, and C is the coffee shop assistant. If you finish with only two SS in one group then just have Mark and the coffee shop assistant and don't say Allie's lines.

• Tell A and B to use the menu and to choose two things, a drink and a snack. C should add up all the things and say the total price. Then SS change roles.

SOCIAL ENGLISH

a **3.19**

• Tell SS that they are going to listen to the rest of the conversation between Allie and Mark in the coffee shop.

• Focus on the four questions and make sure SS understand them. Demonstrate the meaning of *spill*.

• Play the tape/CD once or twice and SS circle the correct answer and then compare with their partner. Play the tape/CD again if necessary and check answers.

1 There **is** a free table.
2 **Mark** spills the coffee.
3 Their next meeting is at **12.30.**
4 Allie **agrees** to go shopping for a new shirt.

3.19   CD2 Track 4

(tapescript in Student's Book on *p.116*.)
A **Thanks**, Mark.
M **You're welcome.** Look, **there's a free table over there**.
M **Here you are.** Oh, **I'm really sorry**!
A **Don't worry.** It's always the same. When I wear white something like this always happens.
M Look, first I'll get you another coffee, then we can go shopping.
A Shopping?
M Yeah. I want to buy you a new shirt. You can't go to a meeting like that.
A But we don't have time – the next meeting's at 12.30.
M We have time. It's only 11.00.
A Are you sure?
M Yes. Sit down and relax. Let's have coffee and then go.
A Well, OK.

b • Ask the question to the class. SS need to listen to the 'tone' of Allie's voice to decide if she is angry or not.

No, not really.

c • Focus on the **USEFUL PHRASES**. For each phrase, ask SS *Who says it, Mark or Allie?*

• Play the tape/CD again for SS to check. Pause after each phrase and get SS to repeat it. (See the tapescript above). In a monolingual class, tell them to decide together what the equivalent phrase is in their language.

Thanks. – Allie
You're welcome. – Mark
There's a free table over there. – Mark
Here you are. – Mark
I'm really sorry. – Mark
Don't worry. – Allie

• Give SS practice in the **USEFUL PHRASES** by saying *Thanks* and *Sorry* and getting them to respond. Elicit *Over there* by asking where things are in the class which are out of their reach.

Extra support

If there's time, you could get SS to listen to the tape/CD for a final time with the tapescript on *p. 116* so they can see exactly what Mark and Allie said and see how much they understood. Translate/explain any new words or phrases.

Extra challenge

Get SS in pairs to roleplay the second conversation using the tapescript on *p. 116*.

HOMEWORK

Study Link **Workbook** *p. 30.*

Lesson plan

The aim here is to give SS practice describing habitual actions. SS learn to recognize and use common connectors and common sequencers.

a • Focus on the task. Set SS a time limit to read the article, e.g. three minutes. Tell them to read all the article first before trying to order the paragraphs.
  • Give SS another minute to order the paragraphs and to compare with their partner. Check answers.

> 3 1 4 2

b • SS read the article again, this time focusing on the highlighted words. They should try to guess the meaning of the words in their own language.
  • Focus on **Connectors**. With a partner SS complete the five sentences. Check answers

> 1 and 2 but 3 because 4 or 5 or

  • Make sure SS are clear about the meaning of the four connectors. Highlight that:
  – *and* is used to join two similar ideas: *I like coffee **and** tea.*
  – *but* is used to contrast two ideas: *I like coffee, **but** not tea.*
  – *or* is used in two ways:
    1 To join two alternative ideas: *I don't like tea **or** coffee.*
    2 To express two possible ideas: *You can have tea **or** coffee.*
  – *because* is used to give a reason: *I want to learn English **because** it's an important language.*
  • Focus on **Sequencers**. With the same partner SS complete the three sentences. Check answers.

> 6 Then 7 After 8 before

  • Make sure SS are clear about the meaning of the three sequencers. Highlight that:
  – *Then* is used with a verb phrase. It can be used at the beginning or in the middle of a sentence: *I have a shower. **Then** I go to bed. I have a shower and **then** I go to bed.*
    You may want to teach **after that** as an alternative to **then**.
  – *after* and *before* are prepositions and opposites. They are used with a noun or a verb phrase: *I always have a cup of coffee **after** lunch / **after** I have lunch.*

c • Put SS in pairs to do this final check exercise. Set a time limit, e.g. two minutes.

> 1 or 2 but 3 After 4 or 5 then 6 and 7 because

Write an article for a magazine

  • Focus on the task and the instructions. Make sure SS know what a paragraph is. Elicit/explain that the article has four paragraphs and each one describes one main idea.
  • SS can write their article in class if there is time or for homework. In either case give them two or three minutes to check their work before they give it you to be marked.

For instructions on how to use these pages see *p.28*.

What do you remember?

GRAMMAR

> **a** 1 b 2 a 3 a 4 b 5 a 6 b 7 a 8 a 9 b 10 a
> **b** 1 What colour is   4 How often do you eat
>   2 What time is   5 When do…watch
>   3 What time do

VOCABULARY

> **a** 1 bad 2 cheap 3 ugly 4 short 5 full
> **b** 1 get 2 take 3 have 4 do 5 go
> **c** 1 tall 2 seven 3 one 4 nephew 5 Easter
> **d** 1 up 2 until 3 by 4 at 5 for

PRONUNCIATION

> **a** 1 do 2 stop 3 think 4 father 5 hour
> **b** 1 ex<u>pen</u>sive 2 <u>diff</u>icult 3 <u>al</u>ways 4 <u>Ju</u>ly 5 De<u>cem</u>ber

What can you do?

CAN YOU UNDERSTAND THIS TEXT?

> **a** 4 ✓ 5 ✓
> **b** **resolution** = a decision to do something new
>   **happens** = occurs
>   **very enthusiastic** = feel very positive about
>   **a personal trainer** = a person who helps you get fit
>   **cut out** = stop eating
>   **go jogging** = run slowly as a form of exercise
> **c** Because in the winter our bodies need food and sleep not diets and exercise.

CAN YOU HEAR THE DIFFERENCE?

> **a** 1 a 2 b 3 b 4 a 5 b

> **3.20**   CD2 Track 5
> 1 I'm very angry.
> 2 It's quarter past ten.
> 3 She goes home at five.
> 4 It's on the first of May.
> 5 Today's September 20th.

> **b** 1 a 2 a 3 b 4 a 5 b

> **3.21**   CD2 Track 6
> 1 What colour's your car?
> 2 What do you have for breakfast?
> 3 When do you have lunch?
> 4 How often do you go to English classes?
> 5 What's the date today?

Extra photocopiable activities

Quicktest 3 *p.233*.

G *can/can't* (ability and other uses)
V verb phrases: *buy a newspaper*, etc.
P sentence stress

I can't dance

Lesson plan

Can is a very versatile verb in English and is used to express ability, possibility, permission, and to make requests. In your SS' language these concepts might not all be expressed by just one verb. *Can* for ability is presented through the context of an audition for a TV show where young people compete for the chance to be trained as a pop star. In the second half of the lesson other common uses of *can* are presented.

Special attention is given to the pronunciation of *can/can't* which may cause problems of communication.

Optional lead-in (books closed)

- Play a short extract from the tape/CD **4.1**, e.g. the three contestants playing the guitar. Tell SS that this is part of a TV programme. Ask SS what kind of programme they think it is.
- Elicit ideas, then tell SS that they are going to find out.

1 GRAMMAR *can / can't* (ability)

a • Books open. Go through the advertisement with SS, and ask them if there is (or has been) a similar programme in their country.
  - Then focus on the photos of the three people. Explain that these three people want to be on the TV programme.

b **4.1**
  - Tell SS that they are going to hear the three contestants play the guitar, dance, and sing, and then decide who they think wins a place on the programme.
  - Focus on the instructions and on sentences 1–8. Check that SS remember the difference between *very well* and *quite well*, and highlight that sentences 1–3 are about the guitar, 4 and 5 about dancing, and 6–8 about singing.
  - Now tell SS that they are going to hear Jude, Gareth, and Kelly play the guitar. Play the first part of the audition (guitar). Then tell SS in pairs to complete sentences 1–3.
  - Now play the second part of the audition (dancing) and get SS to complete sentences 4–5. Finally, play the last part of the audition (singing) and get SS to complete sentences 6–8.

> **4.1**   CD2 Track 7
> OK, quiet everyone, please. It's time to start. The guitar first. Can you start, Jude?
> *Jude plays quite well*
> Thank you. And now Gareth.
> *Gareth can't play*
> Thank you. OK, your turn, Kelly.
> *Kelly plays very well*
> Thank you very much. OK. Next part now – the dancing. Jude first.
> *Jude dances well*

> Thank you. And Gareth.
> *Gareth can't dance*
> Thank you. And Kelly.
> *Kelly dances well*
> OK. Are you ready with your songs? Jude?
> *Jude sings very well*
> Great. Thank you. OK, Gareth.
> *Gareth sings quite well*
> Thank you, Gareth. And now Kelly.
> *Kelly can't sing*
> Thank you, Kelly, thank you, that's fine.

- Check answers.

2 Kelly	5 Gareth	7 Jude
3 Gareth	6 Gareth	8 Kelly
4 Jude and Kelly		

c **4.2**
  - Now ask SS *Who do you think is the winner?* (Most SS will probably say Jude but there may not be complete agreement.) Ask *Why?* Encourage SS to talk about each of the three candidates using *can* and *can't*.
  - Don't confirm who is the winner yet. Play the tape/CD for SS to hear who the winner is.

> Jude

> **4.2**   CD2 Track 8
> OK! The winner of this morning's audition is… Jude!

d • Now focus on the sentences and get SS to complete them. Check answers.

> [+] I **can** dance.
> [–] She **can't** dance.
> [?] **Can** he dance?   [✓] Yes, he **can**.   [✗] No, he **can't**.

Grammar notes

- *can/can't* in this context = know how to.
- *can* is a modal verb and questions are formed by inverting the subject and verb, not with auxiliaries: *Can you play the guitar?* NOT *Do you can…?*
- There are only two possible forms, *can* or *can't* (there is no change for the third person).
- The negative form *can't* is a contraction of *cannot*. *Can't* is almost always used in both conversation and informal writing.
- The verb after *can* is the infinitive without *to*: *I can play the guitar* NOT *I can to play…* .

⚠ SS do not go to the **Grammar Bank** at this point. They will do so later in the lesson when they practise other uses of *can* in exercise **4**.

e • Focus on the speech bubbles. Highlight the use of *Can you?* to return a question. Drill the questions and short answers, getting SS to copy the rhythm. Then demonstrate the dialogue with a student.
  - SS ask and answer in pairs.

2 PRONUNCIATION sentence stress

a (4.3)

- Focus on the dialogue which gives examples of +, −, and ? forms of *can/can't*. Remind SS that the underlined words in the dialogue are stressed.
- Play the tape/CD once right through for SS just to listen. Then play it again, stopping after each sentence for SS to repeat and to try to copy the rhythm.

Pronunciation notes

- There are two main pronunciation problems related to *can/can't*:
- *Can* is usually unstressed = /kən/ in + sentences like *I can sing*. Your SS may find this difficult to hear and to say. If they stress *can* the listener may think they are saying a − sentence.
- The negative *can't* is always stressed. Not stressing it can cause a communication problem (the listener may understand *can* not *can't*). The pronunciation of this word varies among different groups of native English speakers. In British English it is usually pronounced /kɑ:nt / but there are regional variations. The important thing for SS is to make sure that they stress /kɑ:nt / quite strongly.

⚠ If your own pronunciation of *can/can't* is different from what is on the tape/CD, you may want to model the dialogue yourself.

- Get SS to practise the dialogue in pairs. Encourage them to stress the underlined words more strongly and say the other words more quickly and lightly.

> (4.3)   CD2 Track 9
>
> A <u>Can</u> you <u>sing</u>?
> B <u>Yes</u>. I can <u>sing</u> quite <u>well</u>.
> A <u>Can</u> you <u>play</u> a <u>musical</u> <u>instrument</u>?
> B <u>Yes</u>, I <u>can</u>.
> A <u>What</u> can you <u>play</u>?
> B I can <u>play</u> the <u>guitar</u>.
> A <u>Can</u> you <u>dance</u>?
> B <u>No</u>, I <u>can't</u>. I <u>can't</u> <u>dance</u>.

b
- Now focus on the rules. Give SS a minute to read the dialogue again and complete the rules in pairs.
- Check answers.

> in positive + sentences ✗   in *Wh-* questions ? ✗
> in negative − sentences ✓   in short answers ✓

c (4.4)
- This exercise gives SS practice in distinguishing between positive and negative statements.
- Write a positive and negative sentence on the board and underline the stressed words, e.g. *I can <u>dance</u>. I <u>can't</u> dance.*
- Elicit or model the difference in pronunciation, highlighting the much longer sound in *can't*.
- Focus on the instructions. Play the tape/CD at least twice. Get SS to compare their answers in pairs.
- Check answers by playing the tape/CD again, stopping after each sentence, and asking SS first if it's positive or negative and then what the sentence is.

> 1 − 2 + 3 − 4 − 5 + 6 −

> (4.4)   CD2 Track 10
> (tapescript in Student's Book on *p.116*.)
> 1 I can't sing.
> 2 She can dance very well.
> 3 He can't cook.
> 4 My boyfriend can't speak English.
> 5 Her brother can play the piano.
> 6 I can't drive.

Extra challenge

You could do **c** as a dictation, getting SS to write the complete sentences.

As a follow up, get SS in pairs to write four sentences each (two positive and two negative). They take turns to say their sentences to each other as clearly as possible and decide if their partner has said a positive or negative sentence, e.g. A *I can't cook*. B *Negative.*

3 VOCABULARY verb phrases

a
- Tell SS to go to **Vocabulary Bank** *More verb phrases* on *p. 149*.
- Give SS five minutes to do **a** in pairs. They should be able to do this quite quickly as many of the verbs will be familiar to them.
- Check answers. Model and drill pronunciation.

> | | |
> |---|---|
> | 1 **run** a race | 15 **turn on/off** the TV |
> | 2 **walk** home | 16 **take** photos |
> | 3 **hear** a noise | 17 **swim** every day |
> | 4 **see** a film | 18 **ride** a bike |
> | 5 **come** here | 19 **dance** the tango |
> | 6 **find** some money | 20 **sing** a song |
> | 7 **meet** a friend | 21 **play** chess |
> | 8 **call/phone** a taxi | 22 **draw** a picture |
> | 9 **wait** for a bus | 23 **paint** a picture |
> | 10 **take** your umbrella | 24 **travel** by plane |
> | 11 **give** someone a present | 25 **buy** a newspaper |
> | 12 **tell** someone a secret | 26 **talk** to a friend |
> | 13 **help** someone | 27 **use** a computer |
> | 14 **look for** your keys | |

- Get SS to cover the words and use the pictures to test themselves or each other. Encourage them to say the complete phrase, i.e. verb + collocate. Highlight that it is more useful for SS to remember complete phrases, e.g. *meet a friend* (instead of just *meet*).

> **Study Link** SS can find more practice of these words on the MultiROM and on the *New English File Elementary* website.

- Tell SS to go back to the main lesson on *p. 41*.

b
- Focus on the survey and the instructions. Go through the verbs, making sure SS understand them all. The meaning of *physical*, *creative*, and *practical* should be clear from the illustrations but check that SS understand the meaning of the three adjectives.
- Now focus on the examples in the speech bubbles and highlight that after they've asked a question, if their partner says *Yes* (*I can*) they should ask *How well?* Their partner can answer either *Very well* or *Quite well*.
- Demonstrate the activity yourself. Ask SS to guess if you are physical, creative, or practical. Then get them to ask you the questions and decide if you clearly fall

---

59

into one of the three categories. If not, teach the word *a mixture*.

- Put SS in pairs A and B. A interviews B and completes the form for him/her, and then they swap roles. Monitor, helping and correcting especially the pronunciation of *can't*.

c • Focus on the question. If you haven't already done so above, elicit/teach *a mixture*, and tell SS to decide according to where there are the most ticks (✓).

- Get feedback, asking a few pairs if they are physical, creative, or practical.

4 GRAMMAR *can / can't* (other uses)

a 4.5
- Focus on the pictures and the instructions, and elicit ideas from different SS. Accept all possible ideas, and tell them they're going to hear two conversations.
- Play the tape/CD once and ask SS what the problem is (in the first situation the man can't find the sugar, in the second the woman is having problems with the printer).

b • Play the tape/CD again, stopping after each conversation for SS to write the three sentences. Repeat the tape/CD as many times as SS need.

Extra support

Tell SS that in the first conversation all the three sentences are negative, and in the second they are all questions. Then the second time you play the tape/CD, pause after each *can/can't* sentence.

- Get SS to compare with a partner and then check answers.

1 I can't see it.	1 Can you come here a minute?
2 I can't find it.	2 Can you help me?
3 I can't hear you.	3 Can you wait a minute?

4.5   CD2 Track 11

(tapescript in Student's Book on *p.116*.)
1 A Mandy, where's the sugar?
   B In the cupboard, on the right.
   A I can't see it. It isn't there.
   B Yes, it is. Look for it.
   A I can't find it. It's definitely not there.
   B I *know* it's there. It's on the second shelf.
   A I can't hear you.
   B Turn the radio off then. It's on the second shelf.
   A Well, I'm sorry, but it isn't there.
   B The sugar!
   A Oh.
2 A Tony. Can you come here a minute? Tony!
   B What?
   A Can you help me?
   B What is it?
   A It's the computer. The printer doesn't work.
   B Can you wait a minute?
   A TONY!
   B Coming. What's the problem?
   A It's the printer – it doesn't work.
   B It helps if you turn it on!

---

c • Tell SS to go to **Grammar Bank 4A** on *p. 128*.
- Go through the rules with the class. Focus on the different meanings. Get SS to translate them into their

L1 and ask them if they use the same verb for them (in many languages the equivalent of the verb 'know' is used to express ability).

- Model and drill the example sentences.
- Focus on the exercises for **4A** on *p. 129*. Get SS to do **a** individually.
- Check answers. Get SS to read the sentences out loud, making sure they get the rhythm right (stressing *can't* and trying not to stress *can* in positive sentences).

a 1 can   2 Can   3 can't   4 can   5 Can   6 can't
7 can't   8 can

- Now focus on **b** and the first symbol and example sentence. Explain that here *You* means people in general, and that English doesn't have a separate impersonal pronoun (SS' L1 may have one).
- Elicit a sentence for the second symbol, e.g. *You can have a coffee here.* Then get SS to write sentences for symbols 1–7 in pairs. Check answers.

b (Suggested answers)
1 You can have a coffee here.
2 You can't smoke here.
3 You can't take photographs.
4 You can camp here.
5 You can't drive in this street.
6 You can pay with a credit card.
7 You can't use mobiles here.

- Tell SS to go back to the main lesson on *p. 41*.
d • Focus on the instructions and the pictures. Get SS to write the sentences in pairs.
- Get feedback, accepting all possible sentences and writing them on the board.

(Suggested answers)
1 Can you help me? OR Help! I can't swim.
2 Can you take a photo, please?
3 I can't see. Can you move?/take off your hat, please?
4 Can you tell me the time?

Extra challenge

Teach SS some expressions for responding to requests, e.g. *Yes, of course, sure.* Then get them to roleplay a short conversation using the sentences they have written for each picture.

Extra photocopiable activities

Grammar
can/can't p. 152.
Communicative
Find someone who ... *p. 197* (instructions *p.178*).

HOMEWORK

Study Link **Workbook** *pp. 31–32.*

4

B

G *like, love, hate* + (verb + *-ing*)
V free time activities: *shopping, playing computer games,* etc.
P /ŋ/, sentence stress

Shopping – men love it!

Lesson plan

In this lesson SS learn to talk about activities they *like, love, hate* and how to make the *-ing* form of the verb which follows these three verbs. The presentation context is men and women talking about shopping. SS also read a newspaper article which says that shopping is a popular activity with both men and women, but that they do it in very different ways. The lesson finishes with SS talking about what free time activities they like and dislike.

Optional lead-in (books closed)

- Write on the board: DO MEN LIKE SHOPPING? YES   NO
- Ask the question to the class and get a show of hands for YES and for NO to find out what they think.
- Say what you think without giving too much away about the text.

1 LISTENING

a • Books open. Focus on the title of the lesson to see if your class agree.
  • Now focus on the instructions. Give SS a minute to tick the things they like buying, and then compare with a partner. Make sure they understand the meaning and use of *What about you?* (= *And you?*). It is used to return a question.
  ⚠ Make sure SS understand the difference between *shopping* and *buying*, e.g. that *shopping* = going to the shops, and that *buying* = giving money in exchange for something. We always put a noun (thing) after *buying*, e.g. *I love buying clothes, CDs*, but not after *shopping*, e.g. *I love shopping*.
b • Write on the board:

  Women (total number)   Men (total number)

  clothes
  food
  CDs/DVDs
  books
  presents

  • Now get class statistics, by asking *How many people like buying clothes?* (etc.) and getting a show of hands. Count the women and then the men and write up the figures on the board.
  • Get some feedback, e.g. asking SS if they think their class statistics are typical for men/women in their country.

c ● **4.6**
  • Focus on the pictures and the instructions. Play the tape/CD once for SS to match the conversations and pictures. Get SS to compare and then check answers.

  | A 4 | B 2 | C 3 | D 1 |

d • Focus on the sentences 1–4 and on the four verbs in

the *-ing* form above. Play the tape/CD again. Repeat if necessary for SS to complete the sentences. Elicit/teach the meaning of *try on* here.
  • Check answers. Ask SS to spell the missing verbs and write them on the board.

1	going
2	shopping
3	buying
4	trying on

Extra challenge

Focus on the pictures A–D again. Play the tape/CD again, pausing after each person and asking a few extra comprehension questions, e.g.
1 (Picture D) Why doesn't he like shopping? (It's boring.) Why doesn't he like going to clothes shops with his girlfriend? (They always argue.)
2 (Picture B) What does she like buying? (Food and things for the house.) Why doesn't she like buying clothes? (She can never find anything she likes and clothes are expensive.)
3 (Picture C) What day does he go shopping? (Saturday.)
4 (Picture A) Who *doesn't* she like shopping with? (Her mother.)

4.6   CD2 Track 12

(tapescript in Student's Book on p.116.)
1 A Do you like shopping?
  B No, I don't. I hate it. It's boring. I hate going to clothes shops with my girlfriend. We always argue.
2 A Do you like shopping?
  B It's OK. I like buying food, and things for the house. I don't like shopping for clothes. I can never find things I like, and clothes are very expensive.
3 A Do you like shopping?
  B Yeah! I go shopping every Saturday. I love buying clothes, music, books, food – everything. Shopping's fun. I love it.
4 A Do you like shopping?
  B It depends. I like trying on clothes with my friends. That's fun but I don't like going shopping with my mother, and I hate going to the supermarket.

---

2 GRAMMAR *like* + (verb + *-ing*)

a • Focus on the faces and the four verbs. Give SS a minute to complete the chart in pairs.
  • Check answers.

love
like
don't like
hate

b • Tell SS to go to **Grammar Bank 4B** on *p. 128*.
  • Go through the rules with the class. Model and drill the example sentences.

Grammar notes

like (+ **verb** + -*ing*)

- SS may find it strange that in English we use the same verb to say *I love you* and *I love shopping*.
- When another verb follows *love, like, don't like*, and *hate*, the -*ing* form is normally used, e.g. buy*ing*, go*ing*, not the infinitive, e.g. NOT ~~I love buy clothes~~.
- ⚠ The infinitive with *to* after *like, love*, etc. is also possible in certain circumstances but it may be confusing for SS and it's best to avoid it at this stage.

  Spelling rules
- In the -*ing* form, remind SS that verbs ending in *y* don't change the *y* for an *i* as they do in 3rd person singular (e.g. *study* – studying NOT ~~studing~~).

- Focus on the exercises for **4B** on *p. 129*. SS do **a** individually or in pairs.
- Check answers. When you check the -*ing* forms also check that SS remember the meaning of the verbs.
- SS now do **b**. Remind SS that they have to add -*ing* to the verbs, e.g. *playing* to make the sentences.

a **working**	**living**	**shopping**
talking	writing	running
playing	having	sitting
cooking	making	getting
studying	phoning	swimming

b 1 He loves watching TV.
   2 He likes taking photos.
   3 He likes going to the cinema.
   4 He doesn't like doing exercise.
   5 He doesn't like listening to the radio.
   6 He hates doing housework.
   7 He hates eating fast food.

- Tell SS to go back to the main lesson on *p. 42*.
- **c** • Focus on the list of expressions. Demonstrate the activity by making at least three true sentences about yourself. Add a bit of extra information if you can, e.g. why you like/dislike each activity, etc.
- Get SS to write at least three true sentences (with *like, love*, etc.), and then compare with a partner (or in groups of three).

Extra idea

If SS want to know how to give a 'neutral' answer, teach *I don't mind* (*shopping with my family*).

- Get some feedback to see if SS agree with each other.

3 READING

a • Focus on the article. Go through the instructions and show that *Men* and *Women* have been filled in for the first paragraph.
- Set a time limit for the reading, e.g. three minutes. Encourage SS to try to guess any new words, or ask a partner for help. When they have finished, get them to compare their answers with a partner.
- Check answers.

Paragraph 2: Men Women
Paragraph 3: Women Men
Paragraph 4: Men Women

b • Get SS to read the text again carefully. Go through it paragraph by paragraph, explaining/translating any new words, e.g. *toys* (usually things children play with, e.g. dolls, soldiers, but here referring to things men play with, e.g. electronic devices).
- Now get SS to underline one thing they think is true and one that they think is not true, and compare with a partner. Emphasize that they are talking about men and women in general, not themselves!
- Get feedback from the whole class.
- ⚠ You may like to point out here the omission of the definite article (*the*) when talking in general, i.e. that we say *Men like… Women love…* NOT ~~The men…~~, ~~The women…~~

4 PRONUNCIATION /ŋ/, sentence stress

a 🔊 **4.7**
- Focus on the sound picture and elicit the word and sound (*singer*, /ŋ/).
- Play the tape/CD once for SS just to listen. Then play it again, pausing for SS to repeat the words (*shopping, waiting*, etc.)

🔊 **4.7**	CD2 Track 13

singer /ŋ/ shopping, waiting, think, things, thanks, young

b 🔊 **4.8**
- Play the tape/CD several times with pauses for SS to write the four sentences.

Extra support

Write spaces on the board so that SS know exactly how many words there are in each sentence, e.g.
1 ___ ___ ___ ___ ___ ___

🔊 **4.8**	CD2 Track 14

(tapescript in Student's Book on *p.117*.)
1 I <u>love</u> talking on the <u>phone</u>.
2 I <u>like</u> <u>playing</u> compu<u>ter</u> <u>games</u>.
3 I <u>don't</u> <u>like</u> <u>doing</u> <u>house</u>work.
4 I <u>hate</u> <u>watching</u> football.

c • Play the tape/CD again pausing for SS to listen and repeat. Ask SS which two words have 'extra stress'. Elicit that *love* and *hate* are usually said with extra stress because they convey strong feelings.

Extra challenge

Get SS to underline the stressed words (see tapescript above).

d • Tell SS to go to the **Sound Bank** on *p. 159* and look at the spelling rules for the /ŋ/ sound.
- Tell SS to go back to the main lesson on *p. 43*.

5 VOCABULARY & SPEAKING

a • Focus on the pictures and explain that they all show a free time activity.
- Focus on picture 1 and elicit *reading*. Get SS to spell the -*ing* form. Then focus on picture 2 and elicit *watching football (on TV)*.

- Give SS in pairs a minute to write verbs/expressions for the other ten pictures. Remind them to write the verb in the *-ing* form.
- Check answers.

> 1 reading
> 2 watching football (on TV)
> 3 cooking
> 4 playing computer games
> 5 listening to music
> 6 walking
> 7 going to the cinema
> 8 doing housework
> 9 dancing
> 10 running
> 11 talking on the phone
> 12 going to the gym

b
- Now focus on the flow chart. Highlight the use and intonation of *It's OK* as a neutral answer. Remind SS of the use of **it** in *I love it/I hate it*.
- Demonstrate the activity, by asking *Do you like reading?* to different SS until one answers *Yes, (I do)* or *Yes, I love it.* Then continue with the follow-up questions.
- Get SS to continue in pairs (or threes), asking and answering about the different activities. Monitor, encouraging them to add extra stress to *I love it/I hate it*, and helping them with follow up questions.

Extra challenge

Play 'truth or lie'. Tell SS to include in their answers one lie, i.e. to say 'Yes, I love it' for something they don't really like, and then invent answers to the follow-up questions. At the end of the conversation their partner must decide which answer was a lie.

Extra idea

- Find out what the three favourite free time activities in the class are.
- First elicit everybody's favourite activity (it may be something different from the ones in **b**). Then count up the 'votes' for each activity and see which is the most popular.

Extra photocopiable activities

Grammar
like + (verb + *-ing*) *p. 153.*
Communicative
A partner for the perfect weekend? *p. 198* (instructions *p.178*).

HOMEWORK

Study Link Workbook *pp. 33–34.*

4
C

G object pronouns: *me, you, him*, etc.
V love story phrases: *she falls in love*, etc.
P /ɪ/ and /iː/

Fatal attraction?

Lesson plan

This lesson looks at famous cinema love stories and is based on a newspaper article which says that there are only really *five* basic types of love story. It illustrates them with examples taken from the plots of famous Hollywood films.

The grammar aim is object pronouns (*me, you, him*, etc.). These are presented through film stories which allow SS to see how pronouns work, i.e. to avoid repeating names and nouns.

Optional lead-in (books closed)

- Write up on the board **Romantic films**. Then give SS in pairs one minute to write the names of three famous romantic films.
- Get feedback. If they only know some names in their L1, tell them the names in English (if you can), and write them on the board.
- Find out which film is the class favourite.

1 GRAMMAR object pronouns

a ● Books open. Focus on the photos and text. Tell SS not to shout out the name of the film (if they know it), but to read the text first.
   ● Give SS a minute or two to read the text. Tell them to try to guess any new words, or ask a partner.
   ● Elicit the name of the film (*Ghost*) and ask SS (in their L1 if necessary) if they have seen it. Check SS have guessed the meaning of *die* (opposite of *live*) and *a psychic* /ˈsaɪkɪk/(a person with unusual powers, e.g. who can see the future or communicate with dead people).

b ● Focus on the highlighted words and the example. Explain that we use these words because we don't want to repeat the names of the people. Then give SS a few minutes in pairs to write the names. Then check answers.

   2 Molly   3 Sam   4 Ota   5 Molly

c ● Focus on the chart and get SS to complete it in pairs. Although some of the words may be completely new to them, they should be able to do this by a process of elimination.
   ● Check answers. Highlight that *you* and *it* don't change, and that *her* is the same as the possessive adjective.

subject pronouns	object pronouns
I	**me**
you	**you**
he	**him**
she	**her**
it	**it**
we	**us**
they	**them**

d ● Tell SS to go to **Grammar Bank 4C** on *p. 128*.

- Go through the rules with the class. Model and drill the example sentences.

Grammar notes

- Both subject and object pronouns are used to refer to people and things when we don't want to repeat the noun, e.g. *Sam can see Molly but **she** can't see **him**.*
- *it* is used for things, *him* for masculine, and *her* for feminine. The plural *them* is used both for people and things.
- ⚠ You could point out that the object pronoun *me* is used instead of the subject pronoun *I* to answer the question *Who?*, e.g. **A** *Who wants a cup of coffee?* **B** *Me!* (NOT *I*).

- Focus on the exercises for **4C** on *p. 129*. SS do the exercises individually or in pairs.
- Check answers.

a 1 her him	**4** us
2 it	**5** her me
3 you	**6** them
b 1 her	**4** it
2 him	**5** her
3 them	**6** us

- Tell SS to go back to the main lesson on *p. 44*.

2 SPEAKING

a ● Focus on the four circles. Set a time limit for SS to write four names in each circle.

b ● Focus on the instructions and speech bubbles. Then demonstrate the activity: get four SS to ask you a question (*What do you think of … ?*) , one from each circle. Answer choosing suitable words from the speech bubbles, e.g. S: *What do you think of Keanu Reeves?* T: *I like him. He's great.*

Extra challenge

If you want to extend SS' vocabulary you could elicit/teach a few more adjectives of opinion, e.g.
   + fan*tas*tic, *in*teresting
   − *aw*ful, *bor*ing

- Put SS in pairs or groups of three, to ask and answer about the people/things in their circles. Monitor and help, reminding SS to use extra stress with *love* and *hate*.
- When you think the activity has gone on long enough, stop it and get some feedback from different pairs/threes.

3 READING

a ● Focus on the films. Ask SS if they know if they have happy or sad endings.

b • Now focus on the title of the article, and go through the introduction with the class. Explain/translate *basic* (= simple, elementary), *obsession* (= when somebody can't stop thinking about something), and *sacrifice* (= giving up one thing you like/want).

• Set a time limit of e.g. three minutes. SS read the texts, and write the names of the films. Get them to compare with a partner first, and then check answers.

> 2 An Officer and a Gentleman
> 3 Fatal Attraction
> 4 Romeo and Juliet
> 5 The Bridges of Madison County

c • Now get SS to read the stories again, and work with a partner to decide what the highlighted phrases mean. Encourage SS to use the context, and any part of the expression that they know to help them.

• Check answers, either translating into SS' L1 if you prefer or getting SS to check in their dictionaries.

Extra support

Go through each story line by line with SS, eliciting guesses for the meaning of any vocabulary that they don't know, including the highlighted expressions.

d • Now get SS in pairs to decide what type of love story each film is. Check answers.

> 1 Teacher and pupil
> 2 Rich and poor
> 3 Obsession
> 4 First love
> 5 Sacrifice

Extra challenge

Get SS to cover the texts and look at the photos, and try to retell in pairs the story of each film.

Extra idea

Ask SS if they can think of any other famous films for each of the five types of love story, e.g. *First love* –Titanic.

4 PRONUNCIATION /ɪ/ and /iː/

a 4.9

• Focus on the sound pictures, and elicit the words (*fish* and *tree*). Tell SS that these sounds can seem quite similar, but the main difference is that *fish* is a short sound and *tree* is a long sound. Remind them that the symbols which have two dots are always long sounds.

> **4.9**   CD2 Track 15
> fish /ɪ/   him, it, his, film, kill, live
> tree /iː/   he, she, me, meet, leave

Pronunciation notes

• This pronunciation exercise focuses on a small but significant difference between two similar but very common sounds. Depending on their L1 SS may find this difference difficult to hear and to produce. It is important to encourage elementary SS when they do these kinds of pronunciation exercises. Reassure them that this difference is small and that with time and practice they will be able to differentiate and make these sounds.

b 4.10

• Focus on the story. Play the tape/CD once for SS to listen. Then go through it line by line, asking SS if the highlighted sounds are like *fish* or like *tree*. Encourage SS to see the sound–spelling relationship, i.e. that the *fish* sound here is always the letter *i*, usually between consonants; the *tree* sound here is always *e*, *ee*, or *ea*.

> **4.10**   CD2 Track 16
> They live in a big city.
> She meets him in the gym.
> He works in films, she's a teacher.
> She kisses him and he thinks she loves him.
> But in the end she leaves him.

• Now get SS in pairs to take turns telling the story to each other. (NB It is an invented story, not the story of a particular film, in case SS ask.) Then choose individual SS to say a sentence and re-tell the story round the class.

Extra challenge

SS can try to memorize the whole story and re-tell it to each other from memory.

The student who is listening can look at the book and prompt his/her partner if necessary.

c • Finally get SS to go to the **Sound Bank** on *p. 157* and look at the spelling rules for the /ɪ/ and /iː/ sounds.

Extra photocopiable activities

Grammar
object pronouns *p. 154.*
Communicative
What do you think of …? *p. 199* (instructions *p.178*).

HOMEWORK

Study Link Workbook *pp. 35–36.*

G possessive pronouns: *mine, yours,* etc.
V music: *jazz, classical,* etc.
P rhyming words

4 D Are you still mine?

Lesson plan

The topic of this lesson is music and songs. First, SS talk about their musical tastes. Then possessive pronouns (*mine, yours,* etc.) are introduced through the lines from some well-known songs. The lesson finishes with the song *Unchained Melody,* which links back to the previous lesson as it was the theme song of the film *Ghost.*

Optional lead-in (books closed)

- Give SS in pairs a minute or two to brainstorm English words for different kinds of music, e.g. *pop, rock, classical, blues.* Many of these words will be 'international'. Your SS may well come up with types of music you haven't heard of.
- Feedback their ideas on the board, and model and drill pronunciation.

1 SPEAKING

a • Books open. Ask SS to look at the photos and tell you what they can see (an orchestra, a DJ, a blues guitarist, a group, lyrics).

b **4.11**
- Focus on the list of types of music and tell SS they are going to hear six short excerpts of music. Play the tape/CD once and SS tick the types of music they hear. Then get SS to compare with a partner. Play the tape/CD again if necessary. Check answers.

> **4.11** CD2 Track 17
> *rock, opera, jazz, dance, and classical music*

c • Focus on the questionnaire. Go through it, making sure SS understand all the questions and can pronounce new words, e.g. *orchestra* /ˈɔːkɪstrə/, *download (v)* /daʊnˈləʊd/.
- Put SS into pairs, **A** and **B**. Get SS to sit facing each other if possible. **A** (book open) interviews **B** (book closed). Get **A** to interview **B** first with all the questions. Encourage SS to ask for and give more information where they can.
- SS swap roles.

Extra support

Get SS to interview you first and encourage them to ask you extra questions, so that they know what to ask when they interview each other. Write key words on the board to help SS remember the questions.

- Monitor and help SS with any extra vocabulary they may need. When they have finished get feedback by asking some pairs if they had similar or different tastes in music.

2 GRAMMAR possessive pronouns

a • Focus on the song lyrics. SS, in pairs, try to match them to the correct singer. Check answers.

> 1 Kylie Minogue
> 2 Roy Orbison, *Oh Pretty Woman*
> 3 Joe Cocker
> 4 Elvis Presley, *Love me tender*

- Now focus on the highlighted words, and ask SS in pairs to work out the difference between *my/your* and *mine/yours*. Check answers.

> *My* and *your* are (possessive) adjectives. They always go with a noun, e.g. *head, hat.*
> *Mine* and *yours* are (possessive) pronouns. They are alone, not with a noun.

b • Tell SS to go to **Grammar Bank 4D** on *p. 128.*
- Go through the rules with the class. Model and drill the example sentences. Highlight that apart from *mine,* the possessive pronoun is formed by adding an *s* to the possessive adjective (*his* stays the same as it already ends in *s*).

Grammar notes

- There is a clear difference between possessive adjectives and pronouns. The adjectives (*my, your,* etc.) always go *with* a noun while the possessive pronouns are used *without* a noun.
- A name + *'s* can also be used as a pronoun (i.e. without a noun), e.g. *Whose car is it? It's Mark's.*
- *Whose* is pronounced exactly the same as *Who's* (=*Who is*). For this reason they are sometimes confused.

- Focus on the exercises for **4D** on *p. 129.* SS do the exercises individually or in pairs.
- Check answers.

> **a 2** ours
> **3** his
> **4** theirs
> **5** hers
> **6** yours
> **b 1** your mine
> **2** her Their
> **3** my yours
> **4** ours Our

Study Link SS can find an end-of-File grammar quiz on the MultiROM, and more grammar activities on the *New English File Elementary* website.

- Tell SS to go back to the main lesson on *p. 47.*

3 PRONUNCIATION rhyming words

a • Focus on the instructions. You could give more
examples of rhyming words at the end of song lines
using songs you think your SS will know, e.g. *Every
breath you **take**, every move you **make*** (The Police).

 • Focus on the words in the circles and do one pair with
SS, e.g. *mine – fine*. Then give them a few minutes in
pairs to match the rest.

b **4.12**

 • Play the tape/CD for SS to check answers. Then play it
again, pausing after each pair for SS to listen and repeat.

4.12	CD2 Track 18
mine	fine
yours	doors
his	quiz
hers	Thursday
its	sits
ours	showers
theirs	wears

c • Get SS to do this in pairs, **A** (book open) and **B** (book
closed). **A** says a word from circle B and **B** tries to
remember the rhyming pronoun.

d • Tell SS to choose a single possession (pen, book,
glasses, etc.) and put it in front of them. Tell SS that
they should remember who the things belong to.

 • Quickly collect the possessions. Then pick up one
thing and ask the class *Whose is it?* Get SS to point at
the person who they think it belongs to and say *It's his*
or *It's hers*.

 • Check by asking the student *Is it yours?* and elicit the
answer *Yes, it's mine.*

 • Continue with the other possessions.

4 LISTENING

a **4.13**

 • Focus on the song (originally recorded by the
Righteous Brothers) and ask SS which film it's from
(*Ghost*). Then focus on the instructions.

 • Play the tape/CD once or twice for SS to complete the
song with the missing words. Check answers.

4.13	CD2 Track 19

Oh **my** love, **my** darling,
I hunger for **your** touch,
A long, lonely time.
And time goes by so slowly,
And time can do so much,
Are you still **mine**?
I need **your** love.
I need **your** love.
God speed your love to **me**.
Lonely rivers flow to the sea, to the sea,
To the open arms of the sea.
Lonely rivers sigh, wait for **me**, wait for **me**,
I'll be coming home, wait for **me**.

b • Play the tape/CD again for SS to read the lyrics with
the glossary. Then go through it line by line with
them, and elicit the right summary (2). If your SS like
singing you could play the tape/CD again for SS to
sing along with it.

c • Do this as an open class question.

Extra photocopiable activities

Grammar
possessive pronouns *p. 155.*
Communicative
Vowel sounds dominoes *p. 200* (instructions *p.179*).

HOMEWORK

Study Link Workbook *pp. 37–38.*

Vocabulary clothes: *shirt, shoes*, etc.
Function Buying clothes
Language *What size is this shirt?*, etc ... .

Lesson plan

In this episode, Mark takes Allie shopping to buy her a new shirt (to replace the one he spilt coffee on). After buying the shirt Mark invites Allie to have dinner with him that night to celebrate his birthday. Allie declines the invitation but agrees to go out with Mark on Friday night.

In the lesson SS learn some basic clothes vocabulary and some key phrases for buying clothes in English.

Study Link These lessons are also on the *New English File Elementary* Video, which can be used **instead of** the Class Cassette/CD (see introduction *p.9*).

The first section of the Video is also on the MultiROM, with additional activities.

VOCABULARY clothes

a • Focus on the pictures. Give SS in pairs a few moments to match them to the words.
   • Check answers. Model and drill pronunciation.

1 a shirt	4 a jacket
2 trousers	5 jeans
3 shoes	6 a sweater

   • Ask SS why they think it's *a shirt, a sweater, a jacket* (with article) and *jeans, shoes, trousers* (no article) and elicit that it's because the latter are plural.

b • Tell SS to cover the words and test each other in pairs.

Extra idea

SS are often interested in clothes vocabulary and you may want to expand their vocabulary in this area, but be careful not to overload them.

   • Use what you or SS are wearing to elicit/teach, e.g. *skirt, dress, suit, trainers, T-shirt, coat, socks*, etc. Model and drill the words and then write them on the board and get SS to copy them into their vocabulary notebooks.
   • Get SS in pairs to say what they usually wear during the week and at the weekend.

BUYING CLOTHES

a 4.14
   • Focus on the picture and ask SS *Where are Mark and Allie?* (in a clothes shop). *Why?* (because Mark wants to buy Allie a new shirt).
   • Now either tell SS to close their books, and write questions 1–3 on the board, or get SS to cover the conversation.
   • Play the tape/CD once. Check answers.

1 A medium	**2** 34.99	**3** American Express

b • Focus on the conversation and the gaps. Give SS a minute to read through the dialogue and guess the missing words. Then play the tape/CD again once or twice as necessary.
   • Get SS to compare answers in pairs. Check answers.

4.14 CD2 Track 20

S = shop assistant, A = Allie, M = Mark
S **Can** I help you?
A Yes, what size is this shirt?
S Let's see. A small. What **size** do you want?
A A medium.
S **This** is a medium.
A Thanks. Where can I try it on?
S The changing rooms are **over** there.
A Thank you.

S **How** is it?
A It's fine. How much is it?
S 34.99.
M Do you take American Express?
S Yes, sir.

   • Go through the dialogue line by line, helping SS with any expressions they don't understand.

c 4.15
   • Now focus on the **YOU SAY** phrases. Tell SS they're going to hear the dialogue again. They repeat the **YOU SAY** phrases when they hear the beep. Encourage them to copy the rhythm and intonation.
   • Play the tape/CD, pausing if necessary for SS to repeat the phrases.

4.15 CD2 Track 21

S Can I help you?
A Yes, what size is this shirt?
repeat
S Let's see. A small. What size do you want?
A A medium.
repeat
S This is a medium.
A Thanks. Where can I try it on?
repeat
S The changing rooms are over there.
A Thank you.
S How is it?
A It's fine. How much is it?
repeat
S 34.99.
M Do you take American Express?
repeat
S Yes, sir.

---

d • Put SS in pairs, A and B. A is the shop assistant. Get SS to read the dialogue first. Then tell B to close his/her book and try to respond from memory. Then A and B swap roles.
   • ⚠ It's not necessary to roleplay this dialogue in threes. The SS taking the role of the customer should say Allie's lines and also Mark's line at the end (*Do you take American Express?*).

SOCIAL ENGLISH

a 4.16

- Write these questions on the board: *Does Mark like Allie's new shirt? What day is it today? What does Mark ask Allie?* Then play the tape/CD once. Check answers.

> He thinks it the same as the other one. It's his birthday. He asks her to have dinner with him.

- Focus on the five sentences. Play the tape/CD once and get SS to try and fill the gaps with one word. Play the tape/CD again and then get SS to compare their answers in pairs. Check answers.

> 1 coffee   4 dinner
> 2 taxi   5 restaurant
> 3 same

b • Focus on the question and if necessary play the last part of the conversation again (where Mark invites Allie to dinner). Get SS to focus on Allie's intonation (and body language if you're using the video). Feedback SS' ideas.

> This is a matter of opinion, but probably yes.

4.16   CD2 Track 22

(tapescript in Student's Book on *p.117*.)

A Thank you very much, Mark.
M You're welcome. I'm really sorry about the coffee.
A That's OK. It's late. Our meeting's at 12.30.
M We can take a taxi.
A OK. Do you like the shirt?
M Well, yeah, it's exactly the same as the other one.
A The same? It's completely different!
M Sorry!
A Typical man!
M Allie, can I ask you something?
A Yes. What?
M **Would you like to have dinner with me tonight?**
A Tonight?
M Yeah. You see, it's my birthday.
A Oh! **Happy birthday!** I'm sorry, but I can't have dinner tonight. **I'm busy.**
M Oh. **How about Friday night?**
A Friday? Well ... OK.
M Do you know a good restaurant?
A **Let me think**. Do you like Italian food?
M I love it.
A Well, there's a new Italian restaurant. We can go there.
M **Good idea**. Taxi!

---

c • Focus on the **USEFUL PHRASES**. For each phrase, ask SS *Who says it, Mark or Allie?*

- Play the tape/CD again for SS to check. Pause after each phrase and get SS to repeat it. In a monolingual class, tell them to decide together what the equivalent phrase is in their language.

> Would you like to have dinner with me tonight? – Mark
> Happy birthday! – Allie
> I'm busy. – Allie
> How about Friday night? – Mark
> Let me think. – Allie
> Good idea. – Mark

- Highlight that:
  Would you like... ? is a useful phrase for inviting somebody to do something. SS will have seen this in *File 1 Practical English*.

  How about... ? is very useful for making a suggestion, e.g. when you are trying to decide on a day to meet. *How about Friday?* (= *Is Friday OK for you?*); You could also teach the alternative *What about...?*

Extra support

If there's time, you could get SS to listen to the tape/CD for a final time with the tapescript on *p. 117* so they can see exactly what Mark and Allie said and see how much they understood. Translate/explain any new words or phrases.

Extra challenge

Get SS in pairs to roleplay the second conversation using the tapescript on *p. 117*.

HOMEWORK

Study Link **Workbook** *p. 39.*

Lesson plan

In this writing lesson, SS revise adjectives from File 3, and consolidate language to express free time activities from File 4 in the context of describing a person. The writing skills focus is on correcting spelling, and organizing a text into paragraphs. We suggest you do the exercises in class and set the description for homework.

- Focus on the photograph. Tell SS that her name is Stephanie, and ask SS a few questions about her appearance, e.g. *Is her hair long or short?* (quite short) *Is she fair or dark?* (dark), etc.

a
- Now focus on the instructions and on the highlighted words. Tell SS that these are typical spelling mistakes. Give them a minute to write the words correctly.
- Check answers.

1 friend	4 writing
2 studies	5 beautiful
3 intelligent	6 always

b
- SS now read the description and match the paragraphs and questions. Set a time limit, e.g. three minutes.
- Check answers.

1 Who is the person in the photo?
2 How old is he/she? etc.
3 Describe him/her.
4 What does he/she like doing? etc.
5 Why is your friend special?

c
- Now get SS to read the description carefully and try to remember the information. Help SS with any words they don't understand/remember.
- Put SS in pairs. Get them to cover the text, and then ask each other the questions in order, beginning with *Who is the person in the photo?*. They should try to answer from memory.
- Then test their memories by getting SS to close their books and asking questions round the class.

Write a description

- Go through the instructions with SS. Stress the importance of checking writing after they've done it, and remind them that if they write on a computer, they could run a spell check when they've finished.
- Either give SS at least fifteen minutes to write the description in class, or set it for homework. Encourage SS to attach a photo, or scan one in if they write on a computer.
- If SS do the writing in class, get them to swap and read each others' descriptions and correct any mistakes they find, before you collect them all in.

Extra idea

Give SS more oral practice by telling them to think of a friend and then getting them in pairs to interview each other about their friend using the questions in **b**.

---

4   REVISE & CHECK

For instructions on how to use these pages, see *p.28.*

What do you remember?

GRAMMAR

1 a   2 b   3 b   4 b   5 b   6 a   7 b   8 a   9 a   10 a

VOCABULARY

a 1 for   2 in   with   3 for   4 to
b 1 turn on   2 ride   3 tell   4 play   5 take
    6 use   7 get   8 run   9 go   10 draw

PRONUNCIATION

a 1 find   2 die   3 wait   4 turn   5 cook
b to<u>ge</u>ther   <u>follow</u>   in<u>stru</u>ction   <u>cla</u>ssical
    be<u>cause</u>

What can you do?

CAN YOU UNDERSTAND THIS TEXT?

a 1   a
    2   e.g. *Cooking is a waste of time; A lot of adults don't cook; if a mother hates cooking she doesn't teach her children to cook; many schools don't teach cooking*

b
1 boil	5 a waste of time
2 teenager	6 delicious
3 a spectator sport	7 take-away food
4 it doesn't matter	

CAN YOU HEAR THE DIFFERENCE?

a 1 b   2 a   3 a   4 b   5 b

4.17	CD2 Track 23
1 You can't park here.	4 She doesn't like them.
2 Is the house theirs?	5 Who is it?
3 Can you turn on the TV?	

b 1 a   2 b   3 a   4 b   5 a

4.18	CD2 Track 24
1 What do you think of his new film?	
2 Do you like driving?	
3 Excuse me? Can I smoke here?	
4 Can you play chess?	
5 Do you like him?	

Extra photocopiable activities

Quicktest 4 *p.234.*

G past simple of *be*: *was / were*
V word formation: *paint → painter*
P sentence stress

Who were they?

Lesson plan

This lesson uses the context of historical figures to introduce and practise the past simple of the verb *be* (*was/were*). The first context is tourists asking about famous statues, a situation which SS later roleplay. The speaking involves SS deciding who are the top three people of all time in their country. This idea is based on a BBC radio and TV survey in the UK where listeners and viewers chose the Top Ten British people of all time.

Optional lead-in (books closed)

- Write on the board the names of a President, a Prime Minister, a King, and a Queen (all presently in power) who you think your SS will know. Ask *Who is (x)?* to elicit the words *President, Prime Minister, King,* and *Queen.*
- Model and drill the pronunciation and get SS to underline the stress.

1 LISTENING

a • Books open. Focus on the photo of Mount Rushmore with the heads of four famous US presidents. Elicit that they are all presidents of the USA.
- Now get SS in pairs to try to match the names and surnames and say which head is which. (You could get SS to cover the dialogue below as this will give them one of the answers.) Don't check answers at this point.

b **5.1**
- Play the tape/CD once or twice. Then check answers to **a**.

George Washington
Thomas Jefferson
Theodore Roosevelt
Abraham Lincoln

> **5.1**   CD2 Track 25
> (tapescript in Student's Book on p.117.)
> **Guide** We are now at Mount Rushmore, in South Dakota, and you can see in front of you, from left to right, the heads of George Washington, Thomas Jefferson, Theodore Roosevelt, and Abraham Lincoln. As you know, all four men were presidents of the United States of America. George Washington was the first president...

c **5.2**
- Now focus on the dialogue. Stress that the missing words are either numbers or dates. Give SS a few moments to go through the dialogue before they listen. If they ask, explain that *was* (*He was President of the United States*) is the past simple of *is* and that *were* (*His parents were very rich*) is the past simple of *are*. Reassure SS that they will look at this more closely later in the lesson.

⚠ *When was he born?* SS may find it confusing that this concept is expressed by a passive construction in English. If you know your SS' L1, a literal translation (i.e. *born* is the past participle of *bear*) may help here.

Extra support

Give SS time to read the dialogue and work out what kind of number is missing before they listen, and remind them how to say years, e.g. 1801, 1842, etc.

- Play the tape/CD once. Get SS to compare their answers, and then play it again. Check answers.

> **5.2**   CD2 Track 26
> **G = guide, T = tourist**
> **G** The second head is of Thomas Jefferson. He was President of the United States from **1801** to **1809**.
> **T1** When was he born?
> **G** He was born in **1743**, in Virginia. His parents were very rich.
> **T1** Was he President after Washington?
> **G** No, he was the **third** President.
> **T2** What's Jefferson famous for?
> **G** Well, he's famous for writing the Declaration of Independence – that was when he was **33**, before he was President – and for buying the state of Louisiana from Napoleon in **1803**.

- Go through the dialogue line by line. Elicit/teach the meaning of *was born* and help SS with any other vocabulary problems.

2 GRAMMAR *was / were*

a • Focus on the chart and the instructions. Tell SS to look at the examples of *was/were* in the dialogue if they are not sure of the difference between them. Check answers.

> They **were** all Presidents of the USA.
> He **was** the first American President.

b • Tell SS to go to **Grammar Bank 5A** on *p. 130.* Go through the rules with the class. Model and drill the example sentences.

Grammar notes

- *was* is the past of *am* and *is* and *were* is the past of *are*.
- *was* and *were* are used exactly like *is* and *are*, i.e. they are inverted to make questions (*he was → was he?*) and *not* (*n't*) is added to make negatives (*wasn't, weren't*).
- Some SS have a tendency to remember *was* and forget *were*.

- Focus on the exercises for **5A** on *p. 131.* SS do the exercises individually or in pairs.
- Check answers, getting SS to read out the full sentences, not just say the verbs.

71

a	1 was	5 was
	2 were	6 was
	3 were	7 weren't
	4 was	
b	1 were	7 were
	2 Was	8 was
	3 wasn't	9 Were
	4 was	10 weren't
	5 were	11 was
	6 was	12 was

- Tell SS to go back to the main lesson on *p. 52*.

3 PRONUNCIATION sentence stress

a 5.3

- Focus on the sentences and play the tape/CD once for SS to listen. Then play it again pausing after each sentence for SS to repeat.

5.3 CD2 Track 27

He was <u>born</u> in <u>Virginia</u>. His <u>parents</u> were <u>very</u> <u>rich</u>.
He <u>wasn't</u> the <u>second</u> <u>President</u>. They <u>weren't</u> <u>all</u> <u>famous</u>.
<u>Where</u> was he <u>born</u>? <u>When</u> was he <u>born</u>?
<u>Was</u> he <u>famous</u>? <u>No</u>, he <u>wasn't</u>.
<u>Were</u> they <u>good</u> <u>Presidents</u>? <u>Yes</u>, they <u>were</u>.

Pronunciation notes

- *was* and *were* have two different pronunciations depending on whether they are stressed or not (i.e. they can have either a strong or weak pronunciation).
- *was* and *were* tend to have a weak pronunciation in ⊞ sentences: *I was* /wəz/ *born in 1990. They were* /wə/ *famous.*
- *was/wasn't* and *were/weren't* have a strong pronunciation in short answers and ⊟ sentences: *Yes, I was* /wɒz/, *No, I wasn't* /wɒznt/ *Yes we were* /wɜː/ *No we weren't* /wɜːnt/.
- As pronunciation of strong and weak forms tends to occur quite naturally when there is good sentence stress and rhythm, it is best to concentrate your efforts on this (as in **3a**).

b • Divide SS into pairs, **A** and **B**. Tell them to go to **Communication** *Three Presidents* **A** *p. 109*, **B** *p. 112*.
- Go through the instructions with them and elicit and drill the questions, e.g. *What was (Washington's) first name? Which president was he? When was he born? Where was he born? Where were his parents from?*

Extra support

When you have elicited and drilled the questions, write them on the board.

- SS ask and answer questions to complete the chart. Remind them to ask *How do you spell it?* for first names and place names they don't know.
- Monitor, encouraging SS to get the right rhythm.
- If necessary, when they have finished the activity, let SS check their answers by looking at each other's books.
- Tell SS to go back to the main lesson on *p. 52*.

c • Focus on the questions. Model and drill them for SS to get the right rhythm. SS ask the questions in pairs.

- Get some feedback by asking individual SS about their partner in the third person, e.g. *Where was David born?*

4 READING

a • Focus on the photos, names, and cities. Set a time limit for SS in pairs or small groups to match the names, places, and photos. Check answers.

---

1 Chopin Warsaw
2 Joan of Arc Paris
3 Nelson London
4 Garibaldi Rome

- You could ask SS if they know who the four people were, encouraging them to use *was* in their answers.

b • Now focus on the biographies, and set a time limit again for SS to read them and complete the missing information.

---

1 Chopin Poland
2 Joan of Arc France
3 Nelson England
4 Garibaldi Italy

---

c 5.4

- Play the tape/CD for SS to check their answers, and to hear how to pronounce the names and place names.

5.4 CD2 Track 28

Chopin was born in Mazovia in Poland in 1810. When he was seven years old he was already a brilliant pianist. He was a great composer and his piano music is world-famous and very popular.
Joan of Arc was born in 1412 in the village of Domrémy in France. She was only a young girl but she was also a soldier and a famous leader in the war against the English.
Nelson was born in Norfolk, England, in 1758. He was a great sailor. He was famous for his victory against the French at the battle of Trafalgar in 1805. His statue is in Trafalgar Square.
Garibaldi was born in 1807. His family were from Genoa, in Italy. He was a famous politician and soldier, and a great leader.

- Read the texts aloud to the class and clarify meaning of any new words.

Extra idea

You could also get SS to read the texts aloud in pairs, to get more practice with the rhythm of *was* and *were*, i.e. not stressing them in ⊞ sentences.

- Now get SS to cover the texts and to try and remember what they have read. In pairs, **A** says anything he/she can remember about the first statue. **B** checks and prompts. Then they swap roles for the second statue.

5 VOCABULARY word formation

a • Focus on the explanation about making the word for a person (e.g. *painter*) and ask them what letters you add to a verb or noun. Give SS time to look at the examples and find the answers.

-er or *-or* to a verb, *-ist* or *-ian* to a noun

- Point out to SS that sometimes with nouns you have

to make more changes, e.g. *science – scientist* (the *ce* disappears and a *t* is added).

- Model and drill pronunciation of the words. Then test SS' memory by getting them to cover the words and then saying the noun/verb as a prompt, e.g. T: *art* SS: *artist.*

b • Give SS a few minutes to find the words in the texts, or get them to guess first and then check with the texts.

c • Check answers, modelling the pronunciation and getting SS to underline the stress.

1 pianist	4 sailor
2 composer	5 politician
3 leader	

Extra challenge

Elicit a famous name(s) for each of the professions in **a** and **b** (preferably a dead person). Then get SS to say a full sentence, e.g. (*X*) *was a famous pianist.*

d • Demonstrate by telling SS about a famous statue in your town or city. If you can show SS a photo of it, even better. In a monolingual class you could get SS to write their text in pairs.

Extra idea

You could set this for homework, and get SS to do some research to prepare their texts, e.g. from the Internet, and include photos of the statues.

6 SPEAKING

a • Focus on the photo and ask SS who he is and what he was (Winston Churchill, a politician). Then go through the short text with them, clarifying meaning.

- If SS want to know who the top ten were and in what order, they were 1 Churchill, 2 Brunel (engineer), 3 Princess Diana, 4 Charles Darwin (scientist), 5 Shakespeare, 6 Isaac Newton (scientist) 7 Queen Elizabeth I, 8 John Lennon, 9 Lord Nelson, and 10 Oliver Cromwell (17th century leader of the English Revolution who executed King Charles I).

- Put SS in groups of three and get them to agree on their top three. Monitor and help with vocabulary as necessary.

⚠ In a multilingual class, put SS in groups and get them to think of a world top three. You may want to exclude people from their own countries.

b • Get SS to tell the class about their choices. Each student could describe one person.

Extra photocopiable activities

Grammar
was / were p. 156.
Communicative
Where was James? *p. 201* (instructions *p.179*).

HOMEWORK

Study Link Workbook *pp. 40–41.*

G past simple regular verbs
V past time expressions: *three years ago, last week*, etc.
P pronunciation of *-ed* endings

5B Sydney, here we come!

Lesson plan

Past simple regular verbs are introduced in this lesson. The context is provided by the true story of two young people (from Sidcup in south-east England) who booked tickets to what they thought was Sydney, Australia but which turned out to be a remote town in Canada also called Sydney.

Although SS learn all forms (⊞, ⊟, and ⸱?⸱) of the past simple, the focus in this lesson is mainly on the ⊞ form and SS are given thorough practice of the *-ed* ending. Irregular verbs will be introduced in the next lesson where the focus will move to question forms.

Optional lead-in (books closed)

- Play 'Hangman' (see *p. 20*) with the word **AUSTRALIA**. Then ask SS *What's the capital of Australia?* (Canberra) *What other big cities are there?* (Sydney, Melbourne, Perth, etc.).
- Ask *What's Australia famous for?* and elicit some ideas on the board (e.g. Sydney Opera House, Ayers Rock (Uluru), kangaroos, koalas, the 2000 Olympic games, beaches, beer, dangerous spiders and snakes, etc.).

1 READING

a ◗ 5.5 ◗

- Books open. Focus on the photo and elicit that it's of Sydney and shows Sydney Opera House. Ask SS if they'd like to go there for a holiday or not and why.
- Focus on the text, and tell SS they're going to read and listen to a true story which was in the news all over the world. Explain that the story will be in the past simple (the first time in the book that SS have seen this form of the verb).
- Play the tape/CD once and SS read and listen. Then focus on the final question and elicit ideas. If SS say no, ask *Why?* (e.g. very small airport, Sydney is a major city). **Don't tell them the answer at this stage.**

◗ 5.5 ◗   CD2 Track 29
A tale of two Sydneys
Last April two British teenagers wanted to go to Australia for their summer holiday. But it was a 24-hour journey by plane and tickets were very expensive. So, Raoul Sebastian and Emma Nunn, aged 19, looked for cheap tickets on the Internet. They were lucky, and they booked two tickets to Sydney.
On August 4th they arrived at Heathrow airport. They checked in and waited for the plane to leave. Six hours later they landed at a big airport and changed planes.

Emma	I was a bit worried because the second plane was very small, but I didn't want to say anything to Raoul.
Raoul	After only an hour the plane landed. We looked out of the window. It was a very small airport. We walked to the information desk and I showed our tickets to the woman. 'When is our next flight?' I asked. She looked

---

at our tickets. 'The next flight? This is the end of your journey. Where did you want to go?' 'Where are we?' I asked.

b
- Now focus on the pictures. Tell SS to read the story again and number the pictures in order. Encourage them to use the pictures to help them guess any new vocabulary.
- Get SS to compare their order with a partner, before checking answers.

1 I	6 C
2 G	7 E
3 B	8 A
4 F	9 H
5 D	

- Tell SS to read the text again quickly and underline all the words and phrases they don't know, e.g. *teenagers, journey, lucky*, etc. Then with their partner they try to guess the meaning or use their dictionaries to check.
- Get feedback to find out which words they didn't know, and model and drill pronunciation.

c ◗ 5.6 ◗

- Now play the end of the story where SS discover that Emma and Raoul were in Sydney, Canada, not Sydney, Australia.

◗ 5.6 ◗   CD2 Track 30
(tapescript in Student's Book on *p.117*.)
N = narrator, R = Raoul, W = information
N They walked to the information desk and they showed their tickets to the woman.
R When is our next flight?
W The next flight? This is the end of your journey. Where did you want to go?
R Where are we?
W You're in Sydney.
R We're in Australia?
W Australia? No, you're in Canada!
R Canada!

---

d
- Tell SS to go to **Communication** *Sydney* on *p. 112* to read about what happened next. Ask a few comprehension questions, e.g. *Do you think Sydney Nova Scotia is exciting?* (not very) *How many days did they stay there?* (four days) *Where did they go next?* (back to London – they never went to Australia).
- Then ask the whole class if they think it is easy to make a mistake like this.
- Tell SS to go back to the main lesson on *p. 55*.

2 GRAMMAR past simple regular verbs

a
- Focus on the chart, and tell SS to complete the past simple column with the highlighted verbs from the story. Check answers.

They **wanted** to go to Australia.
I **didn't want** to say anything.
Where **did you want** to go?

b • Tell SS to go to **Grammar Bank 5B** on *p. 130.*
   • Go through the rules with the class. Model and drill the example sentences.

Grammar notes

past simple (regular verbs)

• The past simple is used for completed actions in the past however distant or recent.
• The past simple of regular verbs is very easy. There is no third person change, ⊞ verbs all end in *-ed, didn't* is used instead of *don't/doesn't* for ⊟ sentences, and *Did...?* instead of *Do/Does...?* for ⁇.
• The infinitive is used after *did/didn't*, not the past.
• The word order in questions is the same as in the present simple, i.e. **ASI** (**A**uxiliary, **S**ubject, **I**nfinitive) and **QUASI** (**Qu**estion **A**uxiliary, **S**ubject, **I**nfinitive).

• Focus on the exercises for **5B** on *p. 131.* SS do the exercises individually or in pairs.
• Check answers. Get SS to read the sentences aloud and correct any mispronunciation of the *-ed* ending. Get SS to spell the verbs to you and write them on the board.

a 1 I watched TV yesterday.
   2 Did you listen to the radio yesterday?
   3 We studied English yesterday.
   4 He didn't work yesterday.
   5 The film finished at 7.00 yesterday.
   6 I didn't like the film yesterday.
   7 Did she smoke yesterday?.
   8 They played tennis yesterday.
b 1 stayed
   2 didn't book
   3 Did   watch
   4 didn't remember
   5 lived
   6 did want
   7 arrived
   8 landed turned on

• Tell SS to go back to the main lesson on *p. 55.*
c • Focus on the questions, and give SS, in pairs, two minutes to complete them.

d 🔊 **5.7**
   • Play the tape/CD for SS to listen and check.

🔊 **5.7**	CD2 Track 31

1 Did they want to go to Australia?
2 Was it a long journey?
3 Did they book their tickets at a travel agent's?
4 Were the tickets expensive?
5 Did they check in at Heathrow airport?
6 Did they change planes three times?
7 Was the second plane big?
8 Was Emma worried?
9 Did the plane land in Australia?
10 Did they stay in Nova Scotia for a long time?

• Play the tape/CD again pausing after each sentence for SS to repeat and copy the rhythm.

e • Focus on the speech bubbles and get SS to ask and answer the questions in pairs. They should be able to remember the answer. Although it isn't necessary to always answer *yes/no* questions with a short answer using the auxiliary verb, i.e. *Yes, they did*, get SS to use them here as it will help to reinforce the difference between *was* and *did*.

3 PRONUNCIATION *-ed* endings

a 🔊 **5.8**
   • Get SS to underline the regular verbs in the first paragraph of the story. Focus on the ⚠ box and give SS time to read through it.
   • Focus on the verbs in the three columns and play the tape/CD once. Tell SS to listen and concentrate on how the *-ed* is pronounced.
   • Elicit/explain that there are three different ways of pronouncing *-ed*. Two are similar (the first two columns) but the third column is very different.

Pronunciation notes

• The regular past simple ending (*-ed*) can be pronounced in three different ways:
   1 *-ed* is pronounced /t/ after verbs ending in these unvoiced sounds: /k/, /p/, /f/, /s/, /ʃ/, /tʃ/, e.g. *booked, hoped, laughed, passed, washed, watched.*
   2 After voiced endings *-ed* is pronounced /d/, e.g. *arrived, changed, showed.*
   3 After verbs ending in /d/ or /t/ the pronunciation of *-ed* is /ɪd/, e.g. *wanted, needed, decided.*
• In practice, the difference between 1 and 2 is very small and can only be appreciated when a verb is said in isolation or is followed by a word beginning with a vowel (e.g. *I liked it*).
• However the difference between 3 and the other two is significant (it is an extra syllable) and SS tend to transfer this ending to verbs from groups 1 and 2 by mistake.
• If SS want more information about when the *-ed* is pronounced /t/ and when it is pronounced /d/, you could explain that *-ed* is pronounced /t/ after verbs ending with unvoiced sounds (made in the mouth without using the voice, see above). After all other endings (except /d/ and /t/) it is pronounced /d/.

• Focus on the phonetics which show the three different pronunciations of *-ed* (/t/, /d/ and /ɪd/). Then play the tape/CD again, pausing after each verb for SS to repeat it.

🔊 **5.8**	CD2 Track 32

1 /d/   arrived, changed, showed, tried
2 /t/   booked, checked, looked, walked, asked
3 /ɪd/   wanted, landed, waited

• Now ask SS the question *In which group do you pronounce the* e *in* -ed? (column 3).
• Tell SS to look at the spelling of the verbs, and see what letters come before the *-ed.* (*d* or *t*). Explain/demonstrate that it would be impossible to pronounce another /d/ or /t/ after a *d* or a *t*. For that reason an extra syllable is added, which is why the

pronunciation here is /ɪd/. Emphasize that this group of verbs is very small.

- Highlight that the most important rule to remember is not to pronounce the e in -ed (unless it comes after a t or d.)

b 5.9

- Now focus on the sentences telling Raoul and Emma's story. Play the tape/CD and SS repeat the sentences. Give more practice modelling the sentences yourself or playing the tape/CD again. Encourage SS to 'link' the past simple verbs with the words following them, e.g. *They␣arrived␣at Heathrow␣airport.*

▲ SS may find it difficult to pronounce sentences 1, 2, and 8 because the -ed ending is followed by a word beginning with t. At this level SS will find it easier in these cases if they pronounce each word separately.

- Get SS to quickly match the nine sentences to the pictures in **1b** and tell them to try and memorize the story.

c
- Now get SS to cover the sentences and focus on pictures A–I in **1b**. Elicit the sentence for picture **I** (they wanted to go to Australia), and continue until the class have told the whole story from memory.

5.9   CD2 Track 33

They wanted to go to Australia.
They booked two tickets on the Internet.
They arrived at Heathrow airport.
They checked in.
They landed at a big airport.
They changed planes.
They looked out of the window.
They walked to the information desk.
They showed their tickets to a woman.

Extra idea

- Now put SS in pairs to re-tell the story. They can either say alternate sentences, or **A** can tell the whole story while **B** helps and prompts, and they then swap roles.

- Monitor and correct any pronunciation errors, focusing on where SS pronounce the e in the -ed and where they shouldn't, e.g. /bʊkt/ NOT /bʊkɪd/ for *booked.*

4 VOCABULARY & SPEAKING

a
- Write a true ⊞ sentence about yourself in the past with a regular verb, e.g. *I started teaching English in 1999.* Then write underneath it *I started teaching English (x) years ago*, and elicit the meaning of *ago*. Model and drill pronunciation.

- Focus on the past time expressions, and explain that SS must number them from the most recent (*five minutes ago*) to the most distant (*a year ago*).

- Check answers, getting SS to read the whole sentence, e.g. *I booked the tickets five minutes ago.*

- Go through the ▲ rule and highlight that in time expressions with *last* (e.g. *last week*) the definite article *the* is not used. Also explain that we say *last night* NOT *yesterday night.*

---

2 last night
3 yesterday morning
4 three days ago
5 last week
6 last November
7 a year ago

▲ If you are teaching this lesson in November, *last November* will be the same as *a year ago.*

b
- Focus on the instructions and explain the activity. Elicit the first two questions that the SS have to ask, *Did you travel by plane last year? Did you start learning English a long time ago?* Then focus on the follow-up questions, *Where to? When?* and emphasize that SS should just use these words (not full questions) to get more information.

- Set a time limit. SS move around the class (or if this is not possible, talk to SS sitting near them) asking the questions. When they get a 'yes' answer, they write the name of the person and ask the 'follow-up' question.

Extra photocopiable activities

Grammar
past simple regular verbs *p. 157.*
Communicative
Where's the match? *p. 202* (instructions *p.179*).

HOMEWORK

Study Link **Workbook** *pp. 42–43.*

5 C

G past simple irregular verbs: *went, got*, etc.
V expressions with *go, have, get*, e.g. *go out*
P sentence stress

Girls' night out

Lesson plan

This lesson is based on an article from the magazine *Marie Claire*. The magazine asked women members of staff in different offices round the world to have a 'girls' night out' and then to write a report about it. The reports from Moscow, Beijing, and Rio de Janeiro provide the context for the introduction of common past simple irregular verbs. The main focus of the lesson is question formation to prepare SS to ask each other about their last night out. The vocabulary focus is common collocations of the key verbs *go, have*, and *get* (e.g. *go out, get home*, etc.).

Optional lead-in (books closed)

- Revise some of the verbs and expressions from **Vocabulary Bank** *Daily routine* on *p. 147*. Say the collocate, and elicit the verbs from SS, e.g.

  T: *breakfast*   SS: *have*
  T: *shopping*   SS: *go*

- Skip **1a** and go straight to **Vocabulary Bank** *Go, have, get* on *p. 150*. (See **1b** below.)

1 VOCABULARY *go, have, get*

a • Books open. Focus on the three collocates and give SS a moment to decide if they are *go, have*, or *get*. Check answers.

> **have** lunch   **go** shopping   **get** up

b • Tell SS to go to **Vocabulary Bank** *Go, have, get* on *p. 150*.
- Give SS five minutes to do **a** in pairs. They should be able to do this quite quickly as many of the words will be familiar to them.
- Check answers. Model and drill pronunciation.

1 go shopping	13 have a shower
2 go to bed	14 have a good time
3 go out	15 have breakfast/lunch/
4 go to the beach	dinner
5 go by bus	16 have a car
6 go to church/to mosque	17 get a taxi/bus/train
7 go for a walk	18 get home
8 go home	19 get to a restaurant
9 go away	20 get dressed
10 go to a restaurant	21 get a newspaper
11 have a sandwich	22 get an e-mail/letter
12 have a drink	23 get up

- Focus on **b** and elicit that *go home* = go to your house, *get home* = arrive at your house.
- Focus on **c**. Get SS to cover the words and use the pictures to test themselves or each other. Encourage them to say the complete phrase.

> **Study Link** SS can find more practice of these words on the MultiROM and on the *New English File Elementary* website.

- Tell SS to go back to the main lesson on *p. 56*.

2 READING

a • Do this as an open class question and elicit ideas.
b • Focus on the photo and the introduction to the article Make sure the SS understand that the women went out for the night and then wrote a report about it.
- Tell SS that they are only going to read *two* of the reports, and must decide which two cities the women are from, choosing from Rio, Beijing, and Moscow.
- You may want to pre-teach the past of *go* = *went* to help SS understand the text. Give SS four or five minutes to read the text and then discuss with a partner where Sabina and Sharon live. Encourage them to use the photos to help them. Check answers.

> Sabina lives in Moscow. Sharon lives in Beijing.

c • Focus on the questions, and ask SS if they are in the present or in the past (the past). Ask how they know (because of the auxiliary *did*). Then get SS to match the questions and the answers. Check answers.

> 1 What did you wear?
> 2 What did you do?
> 3 What did you have to eat and drink?
> 4 What did you talk about?
> 5 How did you go home?
> 6 What time did you get home?
> 7 Did you have a good time?

d • SS quickly read the text again and complete the chart.

Extra idea

Get SS to complete the chart first from memory and then read the text again to check.

e • Focus on the instructions. SS ask and answer questions in pairs, answering with short answers.
- Finally check answers with the whole class.

	Sabina	Sharon
wear a dress	✗	✓
go to a bar	✓	✗
drink alcohol	✓	✗
talk about men	✓	✓
talk about clothes	✗	✓
go home by taxi	✓	✗
get home after 1.30	✓	✗

- Tell SS to go through the text again quickly and underline any words and phrases they don't know, e.g. *dress, traditional, fashions*, etc. Then with their partner they try to guess the meaning or use their dictionaries to check.
- Get feedback to find out which words were new and model and drill pronunciation.

3 GRAMMAR past simple irregular verbs

a • Focus on the ten infinitives and check SS remember their meaning. Then give them a few minutes to find the past simple verbs in the text. Encourage them to use the phonetics to help them.

Grammar notes

• The vast majority of verbs in the past are regular. However a small number of verbs (several of which are very common) are irregular in the past simple. These verbs don't add *-ed* in the past, they change their form. This change can be just one or two letters, e.g. *wear* → *wore*, or can be a completely new word, e.g. *go* → *went*.

• Irregular verbs are only irregular in the affirmative. In questions and negatives, as with regular verbs, the infinitive is used after *did / didn't*.

• There is a list of the most common irregular verbs on *pp. 154–155* of the Student's Book.

b 5.10

• Write the ten infinitives on the board. Play the tape/CD, pausing after each verb to check answers. Get SS to spell the verbs to you and write the past simples on the board next to the infinitives.

5.10		CD2 Track 34
wear	**wore**	
go	**went**	
see	**saw**	
have	**had**	
buy	**bought**	
get	**got**	
leave	**left**	
drive	**drove**	
meet	**met**	
can	**could**	

• Focus on the phonetics and tell SS to listen to the pronunciation. Play the tape/CD again.

Extra challenge

Focus on the phonetics and elicit the pronunciation of the verbs *before* playing the tape/CD.

• Play the tape/CD again, pausing after each pair of verbs for SS to repeat them. Give more practice as necessary, getting SS to repeat after you or after the tape/CD.

• Get SS to cover the past simple and see if they can remember it, uncovering them one by one to check their answers.

c • Tell SS to go to **Grammar Bank 5C** on *p. 130*. Go through the rules with the class. Model and drill the example sentences.

• Now focus on the exercises for **5C** on *p. 131*. SS do them individually or in pairs. Highlight in **a** that if the verb is not an irregular one they just learned, then it is regular.

⚠ Monitor while SS are doing the exercises. If you see they are having problems with word order in **b**, remind them of **QUASI** and **ASI** (see *p. 33* of this book).

• Check answers. Get SS to read the sentences and questions aloud, helping them with the rhythm, and correcting any mispronunciation of the *-ed*.

---

a 1 bought	7 saw
2 went	8 met
3 wore	9 danced
4 looked	10 didn't get
5 couldn't	11 was
6 had	12 went

b 1 What did you wear?
2 Where did you go?
3 What did you do?
4 Did your sister go with you?
5 What did you have to eat?
6 What time did the party finish?
7 What time did you get home?
8 Did you have a good time?

Study Link SS can find an end-of-File grammar quiz on the MultiROM, and more grammar activities on the *New English File Elementary* website.

• Tell SS to go back to the main lesson on *p. 57*.

4 LISTENING

a • Focus on the third photo with the *Girl's Night Out* article and ask where the women are (Rio de Janeiro in Brazil).

• Get SS to cover the questions from **2c**, and see if they can remember them. Elicit them from the class and write them on the board.

⚠ Leave the questions up on the board for when SS practise the pronunciation later.

b 5.11

• Now tell SS they're going to listen to Sílvia from Rio answering the questions. Tell them to relax and listen, and just focus on the answer to the two questions: *Did they have a good time?* and *How many points out of 10?*

• Play the tape/CD once, and elicit the answers to the two questions.

They had quite a good time – 7 out of 10.

c • Now tell SS to listen for the answers to questions 1–6, and play the tape/CD again. SS compare their answers in pairs and then listen again if necessary.

5.11	CD2 Track 35

(tapescript in Student's Book on *p.117*.)
I = interviewer, S = Sílvia
I Sílvia, from Rio de Janeiro, went out with four friends, Karina, Mônica, Ana, and Thelma. Sílvia, can you tell us about your girls' night out?
S Sure.
I What did you wear?
S I wore jeans and a jacket – and two friends wore the same!
I And what did you do?
S Well, first we went to a restaurant in Ipanema. It's a place where a lot of famous people go and we saw an actor there, called Fernando Pinto. Karina really likes him – in fact she's crazy about him! Then we went to a beach bar and we had some drinks. And then later we went to a party.
I What did you have to eat and drink?
S At the restaurant we had beer and we had some French fries. And at the beach bar we had beer and coconut water.

I What did you talk about?
S About men, of course! What else?
I How did you go home?
S By taxi. I have a car, but I don't like driving at night.
I What time did you get home?
S Very, very late – I don't remember exactly what time.
I So, did you have a good time?
S Yes, it was good. Not fantastic, but good – seven out of ten!

● Check answers. SS may not have understood *French fries* (US English for *chips*).

> 1 jeans and jackets
> 2 They went to a restaurant (in Ipanema) and saw a famous actor. Then they went to a beach bar and a party.
> 3 beer, French fries, and coconut water
> 4 men
> 5 by taxi
> 6 very late – she doesn't remember

Extra support

Get SS to listen to the tape/CD for a final time with the tapescript on *p. 117* so they can see exactly what Sílvia said and see how much they understood.
Translate/explain any new words or phrases.

● Finally ask SS which 'Girls' night out' they think was the most fun, in Moscow, in Rio, or in Beijing.

5 SPEAKING & PRONUNCIATION

a ● Go through the instructions and focus on the questions. Elicit that the missing words are *did you*.

b **5.12**
● Play the tape/CD once for SS just to listen and focus on the rhythm. Then play it again pausing after each question for SS to repeat, trying to copy the rhythm. Make sure they don't stress *did you*.

> **5.12**   CD2 Track 36
> Who did you go with?
> What did you wear?
> Where did you go?
> What did you do?
> What did you have to eat and drink?
> Did you meet anyone?
> How did you go home?
> What time did you get home?
> Did you have a good time?

Extra idea

Get SS to interview you about a night out.

c ● Now give SS a few minutes to plan their own answers individually. Help with any new vocabulary SS might need.

d ● Put SS in pairs. Get A to give B a complete 'interview' and then they swap roles. Monitor the conversations again helping with any new vocabulary that they need and correcting (especially incorrect questions). SS should score their evening out of 10.

● Get feedback, asking a few pairs how many points they gave their evening out of 10.

6 SONG *Dancing Queen*

5.13

● Here SS listen to a song by the Swedish group Abba. This was one of their most popular songs and it is about a girl who goes out on a Friday night and wants to dance. If you want to do this song with your SS there is a photocopiable activity on *p. 225*.

> **5.13**   CD2 Track 37
> You can dance, you can jive, having the time of your life
> See that girl, watch that scene, dig in the Dancing Queen
>
> Friday night and the lights are low
> Looking out for the place to go
> Where they play the right music, getting in the swing
> You come to look for a King.
> Anybody could be that guy
> Night is young and the music's high
>
> With a bit of rock music, everything is fine
> You're in the mood for a dance
> And when you get the chance
>
> You are the Dancing Queen, young and sweet, only seventeen
> Dancing Queen, feel the beat from the tambourine
> You can dance, you can jive, having the time of your life
> See that girl, watch that scene, dig in the Dancing Queen
>
> You're a teaser, you turn them on
> Leave them burning and then you're gone
> Looking out for another, anyone will do
> You're in the mood for a dance
> And when you get the chance, etc.

Extra photocopiable activities

Grammar
past simple irregular verbs *p. 158.*
Communicative
Boys' night out *p. 203* (instructions *p.180*).
Song
Dancing Queen p. 225 (instructions *p.220*).

HOMEWORK

Study Link **Workbook** *pp. 44–45.*

G past simple regular and irregular
V more irregular verbs
P past simple verbs

5 D Murder in a country house

Lesson plan

The aim of this lesson is to revise all forms of the past simple, regular and irregular. SS do not go to the **Grammar Bank**, but revise the past simple through reading, listening, and speaking, and learn several new irregular verbs. The lesson will work best if you can generate and maintain suspense so that SS want to find out who the murderer was. The story is presented in the form of a Graded Reader and is also on tape/CD (as many Graded Readers are). This provides a good opportunity to encourage SS to start reading Graded Readers if they haven't already done so.

Optional lead-in (books closed)

- Write the following types of texts on the board:
  novels   textbooks   song lyrics   the Internet
  newspapers   magazines
- Then ask SS *Which do you read in your language?* and get as much feedback as possible from different SS.
- Now ask SS *Which do you read in English?* Some SS may try to read e.g. song lyrics and information from the Internet in English.
- Then tell SS about Graded Readers and show them a few if possible, and tell them how important it is to read in English to improve their grammar and vocabulary.

1 READING

a • Focus on the photo of the house and ask SS a few questions, e.g. *What is it? How old do you think it is? Where do you think it is?* and elicit ideas/suggestions.
- Then focus on the text. Ask SS what kind of information is usually on the back of a book (an introduction to or summary of the story), and give SS a couple of minutes to read it.
- Go through the text with SS, explaining the meaning and pronunciation of *murder* /ˈmɜːdə/ and *country house*. Ask a few comprehension questions, e.g. *When does the story take place?* (in 1938), *Who is the main character and murder victim?* (Jeremy Travers), *Why was June 22nd an important day for him?* (it was his birthday), *What did he do that night?* (he had dinner with his wife, his daughter, and two guests).

b • Focus on the photos, and explain that they are the people who were in the house when the murder happened.
- Focus on the speech bubbles and get SS to practise in pairs saying who everybody is in relation to Jeremy, e.g. *Who's Claudia?* (she's Jeremy's secretary). This will help SS to remember who's who as they read/listen to the story and also revises using the possessive *'s*.
- Ask SS *Who do you think the murderer is?* and elicit ideas, suggestions.

c 5.14
- Now focus on the text and tell SS that they are going to read the story and listen to it at the same time.
- Play the tape/CD for SS to read and listen. Then set a time limit, e.g. four minutes and get SS in pairs to re-read the text together and mark sentences 1–7 T (true) or F (false).

5.14　　　　　　　　　　　　　　　CD2 Track 38

'Jeremy. Jeremy! Jeremy! Oh no!'

Inspector Granger arrived at about 9.00. He was a tall man with a big black moustache. Amanda, Barbara, Claudia, and Gordon were in the living room. The inspector came in.
'Mr Travers died between midnight last night and seven o'clock this morning,' he said. 'Somebody in this room killed him.' He looked at them one by one but nobody spoke.
'Mrs Travers. I want to talk to you first. Come into the library with me, please.'
Amanda Travers followed the inspector into the library and they sat down.
'What did your husband do after dinner last night?'
'When we finished dinner Jeremy said he was tired and he went to bed.'
'Did *you* go to bed then?'
'No, I didn't. I went for a walk in the garden.'
'What time did you go to bed?'
'About quarter to twelve.'
'Was your husband asleep?'
'I don't know, inspector. We… we slept in separate rooms.'
'Did you hear anything when you were in your room?'
'Yes, I heard Jeremy's bedroom door. It opened. I thought it was Jeremy. Then it closed again. I read in bed for half an hour and then I went to sleep.'
'What time did you get up this morning?'
'I got up at about 7.15. I had breakfast and at 8.00 I took my husband a cup of tea. I found him in bed. He was… dead.'
'Tell me, Mrs Travers, did you love your husband?'
'Jeremy is… was a difficult man.'
'But did you love him, Mrs Travers?'
'No, inspector. I hated him.'

- Check answers, getting SS to say why the F sentences are false.

> **1 F** He died between midnight and seven in the morning.
> **2 F** In the library.
> **3 T**
> **4 F** They slept in separate rooms.
> **5 T**
> **6** She got up at 7.15.
> **7 T**

- Deal with any vocabulary problems, e.g. *moustache, library* (contrast it with *bookshop*), *asleep*, but leave the new irregular verbs as SS are about to focus on them.

d • Focus on the instructions and on the highlighted verbs in the story. In pairs SS guess their infinitives (tell them they are all verbs that have come up before, and that the context will also help them).

e • Now tell SS to go to **Irregular Verbs** on *p. 154*. First get them to check their answers to **d**. Check answers with the whole class and model and drill the pronunciation. Pay particular attention to *read* /red/ which is spelt but not pronounced like the infinitive, and *said* /sed/ which has an unusual pronunciation.

2	say	7	think
3	speak	8	read
4	sit	9	take
5	sleep	10	find
6	hear		

• Explain that they will be coming back to the list at the end of the lesson.
• Tell SS to go back to the main lesson on *p. 59*.

2 PRONUNCIATION   past simple verbs

a 5.15

• Focus on the chart, and elicit the picture words and sounds, e.g. *cat* /æ/, *horse* /ɔː/, etc.
• Now ask SS how the first past simple verb is pronounced (*bought* /bɔːt/) and ask SS which column they think it goes in. Elicit that it is pronounced like *horse*. The *g* and *h* are silent.
• Get SS to continue in pairs. Then play the tape/CD for them to check.

⚠ Tell SS that it's not two verbs in each column. Some columns only have one verb, others two or three.

5.15		CD2 Track 39
cat	had, sat	
horse	bought, saw, thought, wore	
bull	could, took	
bird	heard	
egg	read, said, slept	
train	came	
phone	drove, spoke	
owl	found	

/æ/	/ɔː/	/ʊ/	/ɜː/	/e/	/eɪ/	/əʊ/	/aʊ/
had	bought	could	heard	read	came	drove	found
sat	saw	took		said		spoke	
	thought			slept			
	wore						

• Play the tape/CD again, pausing after each column for SS to repeat the verbs (or model them yourself) and give as much practice as is necessary.

b 5.16

• Remind SS how regular past simple verbs end (*-ed*) and get them to underline nine regular verbs in the story. Check answers, getting SS to say how they think they are pronounced.
• Play the tape/CD, pausing after each verb for SS to repeat it. Give SS more practice if necessary.

5.16		CD2 Track 40
arrived died killed looked followed		
finished opened closed hated		

Extra challenge

Get SS to *predict* how the *-ed* is pronounced for each verb, /d/, /t/ or /ɪd/. Then play the tape/CD for them to check.

(*arrived, died, killed, followed, opened, closed* are all /d/, *looked, finished* are /t/, and *hated* is /ɪd/.)

3 LISTENING

a 5.17

• Focus on the questions and Amanda's answers in the chart. Explain that SS are now going to hear the inspector interview the other three suspects, Barbara, Gordon, and Claudia. They have to complete the chart.
• Ask *Who's Barbara?* (Jeremy's daughter). Then play the tape twice for SS to complete the chart. Don't check answers yet, but get SS to compare answers with a partner between each listening.

5.17		CD2 Track 41

(tapescript in Student's Book on *p.117*.)
N = narrator, I = inspector, B = Barbara
N   Then the inspector questioned Barbara Travers.
I   What did you do after dinner yesterday evening?
B   After dinner? I played cards with Gordon, and then I went to bed.
I   What time was that?
B   It was about half past eleven. I remember I looked at my watch.
I   Did you hear anything in your father's room?
B   No. I didn't hear anything.
I   Did you have any problems with your father?
B   No, no problems at all. My father was a wonderful man and a perfect father.
I   Thank you, Miss Travers.

b 5.18

• Ask *Who's Gordon?* (Jeremy's business partner). Then play the tape twice for SS to complete the chart. Again, don't check answers yet, but let SS compare answers with a partner between each listening.

5.18		CD2 Track 42

(tapescript in Student's Book on *p.117*.)
G = Gordon
N   Next the inspector questioned Gordon Smith.
I   What did you do after dinner, Gordon?
G   I played cards with Barbara. Then she went to bed.
I   Did you go to bed then?
G   No. I stayed in the sitting room and I had a glass of whisky. Then I went to bed.
I   What time was that?
G   I don't remember exactly. I didn't look at the time.
I   Did you hear anything during the night?
G   No, I didn't. I was very tired. I slept very well.
I   You and Mr Travers were business partners, weren't you?
G   Yes, that's right.
I   And it's a very good business I understand.

G Yes, inspector, it is.
I And now it is *your* business.
G Listen, inspector, I did not kill Jeremy. He was my partner and he was my friend.

c (5.19)

- Ask *Who's Claudia?* (Jeremy's secretary). Then play the tape/CD twice for SS to complete the chart. Don't check answers yet, but get SS to compare answers with a partner between each listening.

5.19 CD2 Track 43

(tapescript in Student's Book on *p.117.*)

C = Claudia

N Finally the inspector questioned Claudia Simeone.
I What did you do yesterday evening, after dinner?
C I went to my room and I had a bath and I went to bed.
I What time was that?
C About 11.00.
I Did you hear anything?
C Yes. I heard somebody go into Jeremy's room. It was about 12.00.
I Who was it?
C It was Amanda, his wife.
I Are you sure? Did you see her?
C Well no, I didn't see her. But I'm sure it was Amanda.
I You were Mr Travers' secretary, Claudia.
C Yes, I was.
I Were you just his secretary?
C What do you mean?
I Were you in love with Mr Travers?
C No, I wasn't.
I The truth please, Claudia.
C Very well, inspector. Yes, I was in love with him and he said he was in love with me. He said he wanted to leave his wife – Amanda – and marry me. I was stupid. I believed him. He used me, inspector! I was very angry with him.
I Did you kill him?
C No, inspector, I loved Jeremy.

---

d ● Now check answers. You could copy these onto the board or OHT.

Barbara
She played cards with Gordon.
11.30.
No.
No motive, she loved him.

Gordon
He played cards with Barbara. He had a whisky.
He doesn't remember.
No.
Now he has the business.

Claudia
She went to her room and had a bath.
11.00.
She heard somebody go into Jeremy's room. She thinks it was Amanda.
She loved him but he used her. He said he wanted to marry her but he didn't.

Extra support

Play the three interviews again and get SS to listen and read the tapescript on *p. 117.*

Extra challenge

Get SS to roleplay an interview. Put them in pairs and get them each to choose a suspect they want to be. Give them a few minutes to read the tapescript on *p. 117.* Then get them to interview each other in pairs, using the chart as a prompt, with one student playing the part of the detective.

e ● Now tell SS to look at their charts and in pairs decide who they think the murderer is (they don't have to agree).

- Write the names of the four suspects on the board, and get a show of hands for each suspect.

f (5.20)

- Play the tape/CD for SS to see if they were right. Pause the tape after Amanda says 'Dinner everybody', and ask comprehension questions, e.g. *What happened before dinner? What did Gordon tell Jeremy?*, etc. to make sure SS are following the story.
- Now play the last part. Repeat it from the beginning if SS want to hear it again. Get SS to explain why Gordon killed him (because he wanted to marry Barbara *and* have all the money and Jeremy said that he couldn't).

5.20 CD2 Track 44

(tapescript in Student's Book on *p.118.*)

J = Jeremy

N Before dinner, Gordon had a drink with Jeremy in the library.
G Cheers, Jeremy. Happy birthday.
J Ah, thanks, Gordon.
G Listen, Jeremy, I want to talk to you about Barbara.
J Barbara? What's the problem?
G It's not exactly a problem. I am in love with her, and I want to marry her.
J Marry Barbara? Marry my daughter! Are you crazy? Never! You don't love Barbara. You only want her money!
G That's not true, Jeremy. I love her.
J Listen to me. If you marry Barbara, when I die all my money goes to Claudia.
G To Claudia? To your secretary?
J Yes.
G Is that your last word, Jeremy?
J Yes, it is.
A Dinner everybody!
N At midnight Gordon finished his whisky and went upstairs.
J Who is it? Gordon?

---

4 SPEAKING

- This activity will take at least 15–20 minutes. If you don't have time this lesson, go straight to the vocabulary and do it next lesson.
- Divide SS into groups of four, and then into pairs. One pair are both As (police officers) and the other Bs (friends/suspects). If you have odd numbers, have extra As (i.e. three police officers and two suspects).
- Tell SS to go to **Communication** *Police interview* A *p. 109*, B *p. 112.*
- Go through the instructions with them carefully. Then give at least five minutes for As to prepare their questions and for Bs to prepare their alibis.

- When they are ready, re-divide the groups of four, so that each A is with a different B. If possible, tell the As to take their suspects to different ends of the classroom to be interviewed. (It doesn't matter if they are near other police officers/suspects, they should just not be near their own 'partner'.)
- Allow at least five minutes for the interviews, making sure the police officers take notes.
- When the interviews are over, get the police officers (As) to compare the two friends' (Bs) alibis. If they are identical, the Bs are innocent. If there are any differences, they are guilty.
- Tell SS to go back to the main lesson on *p. 59.*

5 VOCABULARY irregular verbs

- Tell SS to go back to **Irregular verbs** on *pp. 154–155.*
- Tell SS that this is their reference list of irregular verbs. Explain that there are three columns, because irregular verbs also have irregular past participles, but that for the moment they should just concentrate on the first two columns.
- Show SS how to test themselves by covering the past simple column, looking at the present, and saying the sentences again but with the verb in the past.
- Go through the verbs one by one, eliciting/teaching the meaning of any new ones, and getting SS to highlight or tick the ones they already know. Tell them to choose three new verbs to learn, and tell them they should try to learn at least three more new ones every week.
- Finally go through the text about Graded Readers with them.

Extra idea

If you have a school library, get SS to take a book out and start reading. Put up a chart in your classroom so that SS can write down the name of the book they're reading, and you can keep track of how many they read.

If your school doesn't have a library, you could create a class library by getting each student to buy one Graded Reader (level 1) – they are relatively inexpensive. They then swap books with each other.

Extra photocopiable activities

Grammar
past simple regular and irregular *p. 159.*
Communicative
Past tense question time *p. 204* (instructions *p.180*).

HOMEWORK

Study Link **Workbook** *pp. 46–47.*

Vocabulary *T-shirt, mug*, etc.
Function Buying a present
Language *How much is that T-shirt?*, etc.

Lesson plan

In this lesson SS get practice in using and understanding basic shopping language in the context of shopping for souvenirs, as Allie buys a birthday present for Mark. Later Allie goes to the hotel to pick Mark up for dinner. She gives him the present but she drops it and it breaks. They set off together to the restaurant.

Study Link These lessons are also on the *New English File Elementary* Video, which can be used **instead of** the Class Cassette/CD (see introduction *p.9*).
The first section of the Video is also on the MultiROM, with additional activities.

VOCABULARY shopping

a • Focus on the pictures and give SS in pairs a few moments to match them to the words.
   • Check answers. Drill pronunciation.

> 1 postcards
> 2 a (camera) film
> 3 a mug
> 4 T-shirts
> 5 batteries

b • Tell SS to cover the words and test each other in pairs.

BUYING A PRESENT

a **5.21**
   • Focus on the picture and ask SS *Where's Allie?* (In a shop). Ask about the previous Practical English lesson, e.g. *What did Mark ask Allie to do?* (to have dinner with him). *Why?* (because it was his birthday). Elicit that Allie wants to buy Mark a small present.
   • Now either tell SS to close their books or cover the conversation and listen to find out what she buys.
   • Play the tape/CD once or twice. Check answers.

> She buys a large mug.

b • Now focus on the conversation and the gaps. Give SS a minute to read through the dialogue and guess the missing words. Then play the tape/CD again once or twice as necessary.
   • Get SS to compare their answers. Check answers.

> **5.21**   CD2 Track 45
>
> S = shop assistant, A = Allie
> S Can I help you?
> A How much is that T-shirt?
> S It's **15.60**.
> A Sorry, how much did you say?
> S **15.60**.
> A And how much are those mugs?

> S The big mugs are **10.25** and the small ones are **8.75**.
> A Can I have a big mug, please?
> S Sure. **Here** you are. **Anything** else?
> A Do you have birthday cards?
> S Sorry, *we've only got **postcards**.
> A Oh well, just the mug then.
> S That's **10.25**.
> A Here you are.
> S *Have you got the **25**?
> A Yes, here.
> S Thanks.
> A Thank you.
> S Bye.
> A Bye.

• Focus on the information box and the two starred examples in the dialogue. Go through the information.

Grammar notes
   have got
• *Have got* is often used in British English instead of *have* for possession, e.g. *I've got a car; Have you got any children?*, etc. It is a complex structure for low level SS as it involves a new auxiliary verb (*have*) and new contractions (*I've, he's*, etc.).
• We recommend at this level teaching *have got* for recognition only. However, if you want to teach it in more detail, the full table is in the **Grammar Bank** appendix *p. 138*.

c **5.22**
   • Now focus on the **YOU SAY** phrases. Tell SS they're going to listen to the dialogue again and they should repeat the **YOU SAY** phrases when they hear the beep.
   • Play the tape/CD, (pausing if necessary) and get SS to repeat the phrases. Encourage them to copy the rhythm and intonation.

> **5.22**   CD2 Track 46
>
> S Can I help you?
> A How much is that T-shirt?
> *repeat*
> S It's 15.60.
> A Sorry, how much did you say?
> *repeat*
> S 15.60.
> A And how much are those mugs?
> *repeat*
> S The big mugs are 10.25 and the small ones are 8.75.
> A Can I have a big mug, please?
> *repeat*
> S Sure. Here you are. Anything else?
> A Do you have birthday cards?
> *repeat*
> S Sorry, we've only got postcards.
> A Oh well, just the mug then.
> *repeat*
> S That's 10.25.
> A Here you are.
> *repeat*
> S Have you got the 25?
> A Yes, here.
> *repeat*
> S Thanks.
> A Thank you.
> S Bye.
> A Bye.

d ● Put SS in pairs, **A** and **B**. **A** is the shop assistant. Get SS to read the dialogue first. Then tell **B** to close his/her book and try to respond from memory. Then **A** and **B** swap roles.

SOCIAL ENGLISH

a 〔 5.23 〕

● Now focus on the next picture. Ask SS *Where are they?* (in Mark's hotel).

● Focus on sentences 1–4 and go through them.

● Play the tape/CD at least twice, and then give SS time to compare answers before checking. Ask why the F ones are false.

> **1** T
> **2** F He says 'Don't worry'
> **3** F She has her car.
> **4** F She has reserved a table for 8.00

> 〔 5.23 〕   CD2 Track 47
> (tapescript in Student's Book on *p.118.*)
> **M** Hi, Allie. **Wow! You look great.** Nice dress!
> **A** Oh, thank you. Er, this is for you – for your birthday. I bought you a little present. Oh! Oh no. I hope it's not broken.
> **M** It's a mug! It *was* a mug. Thanks, Allie!
> **A** **I don't believe it!** I'm sorry, Mark.
> **M** **No problem.** It was really nice of you.
> **A** I'll get you another one tomorrow.
> **M** Don't worry. Listen, did you call a taxi to go to the restaurant?
> **A** No, I have my car outside. **Come on, it's time to go.** I booked the table for 8.00 and I'm not sure exactly where the restaurant is.
> **M** Hey, Allie, **relax**. This isn't work. This is a night out.
> **A** Sorry. I'm a bit stressed today. OK. Let's go.

b ● Ask the question to the class. Elicit SS' ideas (because she broke the mug, because it's late, because she doesn't know where to park, because she's nervous about the dinner, etc.).

c ● Focus on the **USEFUL PHRASES**. For each phrase, ask SS *Who says it, Mark or Allie?* Then play the tape/CD for SS to check their answers.

● Play the tape/CD again for SS to check. Pause after each phrase and get SS to repeat it. In a monolingual class, tell them to decide together what the equivalent phrase is in their language.

> Wow! You look great. – Mark
> I don't believe it! – Allie
> No problem. – Mark
> Come on, it's time to go. – Allie
> Relax. – Mark

● Highlight that *Wow!* is a very useful expression to show either surprise or appreciation.

Extra challenge

Get SS in pairs to roleplay the second conversation using the tapescript on *p. 118*.

HOMEWORK

Study Link Workbook *p. 48*.

WRITING A HOLIDAY REPORT

Lesson plan

In this fifth writing lesson SS consolidate the past simple through a written report, and practise transferring information from a questionnaire into a written text.

a ● First focus on the questionnaire. Go through the questions, and highlight that the answers are not complete sentences but notes. Elicit/teach any expressions SS don't understand, e.g. *walked around*, *special atmosphere*, *cross the road*, etc.

● Now focus on the instructions. Give SS in pairs two minutes to match the questions and paragraphs. Check answers.

> paragraph 1: 1, 2, 3, 4
> paragraph 2: 5, 6
> paragraph 3: 7, 8
> paragraph: 4: 9, 10

● Ask SS to read the report and compare it with the questionnaire answers. Get SS to highlight or underline the words that have been added to make the answers into a text, e.g. in paragraph 1 *I went… with… We flew to Rome with…*

b ● Give SS five minutes or so to make notes about their last holiday, using the questionnaire's answers as a model.

Extra idea

Give SS extra oral practice by getting them to interview each other with the questions.

Write a holiday report

● Go through the instructions with SS. Stress the importance of checking writing after they've done it, and remind them that if they write on a computer, they should run a spell check in English when they've finished.

● Either give SS at least fifteen minutes to write the report in class, or set it for homework. Encourage SS to attach or scan in a photo if they do it at home.

● If SS do the writing in class, get them to swap and read each others' reports and correct any mistakes they find, before you collect them all in.

For instructions on how to use these pages, see *p.28*.

What do you remember?

GRAMMAR

a 1 b 2 b 3 a 4 a 5 a 6 b 7 b 8 b 9 a 10 a
b 1 studied
  2 went
  3 drove
  4 could
  5 waited
  6 said
  7 thought
  8 wrote
  9 stayed
  10 heard

VOCABULARY

a 1 actor 2 artist 3 painter 4 musician 5 scientist
b 1 have 2 get 3 go 4 get 5 have
c 1 for 2 out 3 by 4 to 5 in
d 1 three weeks ago
  2 yesterday morning
  3 last month
  4 last night
  5 last April

PRONUNCIATION

a 1 waited 2 landed 3 told 4 found 5 heard
b poli<u>ti</u>cian mu<u>si</u>cian <u>re</u>staurant a<u>go</u> <u>some</u>body

What can you do?

CAN YOU UNDERSTAND THIS TEXT?

a 2 smoked 3 cried 4 went
b 1 No. Because they went to McDonald's.
  2 Outside.
  3 No (but his father did).
  4 Because it was a barbecue and it rained.

CAN YOU HEAR THE DIFFERENCE?

a 1 b 2 b 3 a 4 a 5 b

5.24   CD2 Track 48
1 My mother was a writer.
2 We booked tickets on the Internet.
3 Where do you study English?
4 We meet every week.
5 They had a lot of money.

---

b 1 a 2 b 3 a 4 b 5 b

5.25   CD2 Track 49
1 A Where were you born?
  B I was born in Lyons, in France, but my parents are from Argentina.
2 A I like your shoes. Where did you get them?
  A At that new shop in the centre.
  A Wow! That's an expensive place!
  A Yes, but these were cheap.
3 A Did you like the film?
  A Well, I thought Tom Hanks was quite good but the film was terrible.
4 A What did you do on Saturday night?
  A We stayed at home. We were tired because we went out on Friday night.
5 A What time did you get up?
  A Well, I woke up at seven, but I didn't get up until half past.

Extra photocopiable activities

Quicktest 5 *p.235*.

6
A

G *there is / there are, some* and *any*
V houses and furniture: *living room, sofa,* etc.
P /ð/ and /eə/, sentence stress

A house with a history

Lesson plan

This lesson links back to the murder story in **5D**. Many years later, an American couple who are looking for a house to rent are shown round Jeremy Travers' house by an estate agent. It is only after they have decided to rent it that they discover that the house has a dark secret and that someone was murdered there. SS practise *there is / there are* and learn house and furniture vocabulary.

Optional lead-in (books closed)

- Copy the following sketch onto the board.

- Elicit/teach the names of the three rooms (bathroom, kitchen, and bedroom) and write them on the board. Model and drill pronunciation.
- Elicit from the class two items of furniture for each room, e.g. *bath, toilet, cooker, fridge, bed, cupboard.*
- Now tell SS to go to **Vocabulary Bank *Flats and houses*** on *p. 151* and continue from **1c** below.

1 VOCABULARY houses and furniture

a • Books open. Focus on the three anagrams. Tell SS that they are three rooms in a flat or house. SS in pairs re-order the letters.
- Check answers. Model and drill pronunciation.

| kitchen | bedroom | bathroom |

b • Elicit from the class two items of furniture for each room, e.g. *bath, toilet, cooker, fridge, bed, cupboard.*
- Write all the new words on the board and drill pronunciation, especially *cupboard* /ˈkʌbəd/.

c • Tell SS to go to **Vocabulary Bank *Flats and houses*** on *p. 151.*
- Give SS two minutes to do **1** in pairs. They should be able to do this quite quickly, as many of the rooms will be familiar to them
- Check answers. Model and drill pronunciation.

1 the bedroom	6 the living room
2 the study	7 the hall
3 the bathroom	8 the kitchen
4 the toilet	9 the garden
5 the dining room	10 the garage

- Now give SS five minutes to do **2a** in pairs. Check answers. Model and drill pronunciation.

1 shelves	9 a clock	16 a desk
2 a light	10 a fridge	17 central heating
3 a bed	11 a cooker	18 an armchair
4 carpet	12 a cupboard	19 a fireplace
5 a wall	13 floor	20 a picture
6 a shower	14 stairs	21 a sofa
7 a mirror	15 a lamp	22 a plant
8 a bath		

- Now get SS to cover the words and use the pictures to test themselves or each other with the words from **1** and **2**.
- Tell SS to close their books. In pairs they should try to tell each other what they have in at least two rooms in their own house/flat.

> **Study Link** SS can find more practice of these words on the MultiROM and on the *New English File Elementary* website.

- Tell SS to go back to the main lesson on *p. 64.*

2 LISTENING

a • Focus on the advertisement and photo and ask if SS would like to live in it and why (not)?
⚠ At this stage only tell SS that the house is the same house as **5D** if someone in the class realizes.
- Get ideas/feedback from a few SS. Check they understand *to rent* and *low price*. Ask SS why they think it is cheap. (Perhaps because nobody wants to live there because of the murder.)

b 🔊 **6.1**
- Focus on the picture and instructions. Ask *Who is the young man?* and elicit that he is an estate agent, a man who sells and rents houses and flats.
- Now either tell SS to close their books and listen, or to cover the conversation. Play the tape/CD once, and check answers.
⚠ Stress that SS should listen to find out which rooms they actually go into, not which ones they or the estate agent mention.

| the hall | the living room | the kitchen |

6.1   CD2 Track 50
E = estate agent, L = Larry, Lo = Louise
E   Well, this is the hall. There are six rooms on this floor. There's a kitchen, a dining room, a living room, a study, a library …
L   Wow! There's a library, Louise!
LO What's that room?
E   That's a bathroom, madam.
L   How many bathrooms are there?
E   There's one downstairs and three upstairs.
LO Are there any showers?

E   No, there aren't, madam. This is an old house… This is the living room.
LO Are those paintings original?
E   Yes, I think so, madam.
L   Is there a television?
E   No, there isn't, sir. But there's a piano… And the kitchen.
LO There isn't a fridge.
E   Yes, there is. It's over there.
LO You call that a fridge! Are there any glasses? I need a glass of water.
E   Yes, madam. There are some glasses in that cupboard. Now let's go upstairs.

c   • Focus on the gapped conversation. Play the tape/CD again for SS to complete it.

    • Get SS to compare with a partner and check answers.

1 dining room	6 television
2 study	7 piano
3 bathroom	8 fridge
4 upstairs	9 glasses
5 showers	10 cupboard

Extra support

Give SS time to read through the dialogue and think about what kind of words are missing (i.e. furniture or rooms) before you play the tape/CD.

d   6.2

    • Focus on the instructions. Then play the tape/CD twice. Get SS to compare with a partner before you check answers.

One of the bedrooms is very cold.
They decide to rent the house.

    • Ask a few more comprehension questions, e.g. *How old is the house?* (100 years old). *What kind of heating is there?* (central heating). *Why do they go back to the estate agent's office?* (to sign the contract). *Who lived in the house before?* (the Travers family). Elicit that this is the same house as in **5D**.

6.2   CD2 Track 51

(tapescript in Student's Book on *p.118*.)
E   OK. Let's have a look upstairs now. Follow me.
LO It's very old.
E   Yes, madam, the house is a hundred years old. The Travers family lived here for nearly eighty years. There are five bedrooms. This was Mr Travers' bedroom.
L   It's cold in here.
LO Yes, very cold.
E   Don't worry, madam. There is central heating in the house. And this room here is the second bedroom.
L   OK, well what do you think, Louise?
LO I like it.
L   Me too. Yup. We want it.
E   Excellent! Let's go back to my office and we can sign the contract.

---

3 GRAMMAR   *there is / there are*

a   • Focus on the chart and give SS a minute to complete it.

singular	plural
There's a piano.	There **are** some glasses in the cupboard.
There **isn't** a fridge.	There aren't any showers.
Is there a TV?	**Are there** any glasses?

b   • Give SS a moment to look at the question and discuss it in pairs. Elicit that *some* = we don't know how many exactly.

c   • Tell SS to go to **Grammar Bank 6A** on *p. 132*. Go through the rules with the class. Model and drill the example sentences.

Grammar notes

there is / there are

• *There is* is used with singular nouns, *there are* with plural nouns.

• Questions are formed by inversion (*There is – Is there…?*) and negatives by adding *not* or *n't* (*There is – There isn't*).

• There is no written contraction of *are* in *there are* (NOT ~~There're~~) but in speaking *are* is unstressed /ə/.

• When giving a list of things we use *there is* (NOT ~~there are~~) when the first word is singular, e.g. *In my living room there's a sofa and two armchairs*.

some and *any*

• *Some* and *any* are indefinite articles used here with plural countable nouns. *Some* and *any* with uncountable nouns is presented in **7A**.

• Focus on exercises **6A** on *p. 133*. SS do the exercises individually or in pairs.

• Check answers, getting SS to read out the full sentences.

a 1	There are	4	There's
2	There's	5	There are
3	There are	6	There's

b 1 There's a table in the kitchen.
  2 Is there a fireplace in the living room?
  3 There aren't any plants in the living room.
  4 Are there any cupboards in the kitchen?
  5 There isn't a shower in the bathroom.
  6 There are some shelves in the study.

• Tell SS to go back to the main lesson on *p. 65*.

4 PRONUNCIATION   /ð/ and /eə/, sentence stress

a   6.3

    • Focus on the dialogue and play the tape/CD. Elicit that all the examples of *th* are pronounced /ð/ like *mother*, and that the other highlighted letters all have the /eə/ sound, like *chair*.

    • Play the tape/CD again, pausing after each sentence for SS to repeat, copying the rhythm.

Extra support

Get SS to underline the stressed words (see tapescript) and remind them to pronounce them more strongly when they practise the dialogue.

    • Get SS to read the dialogue in pairs.

6.3	CD2 Track 52

A Where's the bathroom?
B It's upstairs.
A Is there a lift?
B No, there are stairs.
A Where are the stairs?
B They're over there.

b • Put SS in groups of three and give them roles (Larry, Louise, and the estate agent). SS read the dialogue in **2c**, focusing on getting the right rhythm. If you have time get them to change roles.

⚠ If you have odd numbers have one or two pairs. One student is the estate agent, the other should read the roles of Larry *and* Louise.

5 SPEAKING

a • Focus on the questions, and give SS two minutes to complete them with *Is there* or *Are there*. Check they have done this correctly by getting them to interview you about your flat/house.

In your house/flat
1 How many bedrooms **are there**?
2 How many bathrooms **are there**?
3 **Is there** a study?
4 **Is there** a garden?
5 **Is there** a garage?
6 **Is there** central heating?

In your bedroom
7 **Is there** a TV?
8 **Are there** any pictures on the wall?
9 **Are there** any plants?
10 **Is there** a mirror?
11 **Are there** any cupboards?
12 **Is there** a computer?

• Now get SS to interview each other. Get feedback.

Extra challenge

Write key words for the interview on the board, i.e. *bedrooms, bathrooms*, etc. and get SS to interview each other with books closed.

b • Focus on the instructions. To demonstrate quickly sketch a basic plan of your living room on the board and 'show' it to the class. (You don't need to draw everything in, just the main pieces of furniture.)
• SS do the same in pairs. Monitor and help SS with any other vocabulary they need.

6 LISTENING

a 6.4
• Focus on the picture and ask *Where are Louise and Larry?* (In a pub, near the house they've just rented.) Go through the instructions and questions.
• Play the tape/CD twice. Get SS to compare with a partner before checking answers.

1 Champagne; they want to celebrate their new house.
2 That a man (Mr Travers) was murdered there in 1938.
3 They leave the pub – Louise wants to find a hotel. She doesn't want to sleep in the house.

6.4	CD2 Track 53

(tapescript in Student's Book on *p.118*.)
L = Larry, Lo = Louise, B = barman
L Good evening.
B Good evening, sir, madam. What would you like to drink?
L Do you have champagne?
B Yes, sir.
L A bottle of champagne, please.
B Here you are!
LO Cheers, Larry.
L Cheers. To our new house.
B You're Americans, aren't you?
LO Yes, that's right. We're from Washington.
L My wife and I just rented the big house in the village. Tonight is our first night there.
B The Travers family's old house?
L Yes.
B Oh.
LO Is there a problem?
B Didn't they tell you?
L Tell us what?
B About the murder.
LO Murder??
B Yes, Mr Travers was murdered in that house in 1938… in his bed.
LO Oh, how horrible!
B That's why they always rent that house.
L Why?
B Because nobody wants to buy it.
LO Come on, Larry. Let's go and find a hotel.
L A hotel?
LO Yes – I don't want to sleep in a house where somebody was murdered. Come on.
L Louise… your champagne… Louise…

• Ask a few more comprehension questions, e.g. *Where are Louise and Larry from?* (Washington). *Why do they always rent the house?* (because nobody wants to buy it). *Does Louise finish her champagne?* (no). Finally ask SS if they would like to rent a house where somebody was murdered.

Extra support

Get SS to listen to the tape/CD for a final time with the tapescript on *p. 118* so they can see exactly what was said and see how much they understood. Translate/explain any new words or phrases.

Extra photocopiable activities

Grammar
there is/there are p. 160.
Communicative
Flat to rent *p. 205* (instructions *p.180*).

HOMEWORK

Study Link **Workbook** *pp. 49–50*.

G *there was / there were*
V prepositions of place: *in, on, under,* etc.
P silent letters

A night in a haunted hotel

Lesson plan

This lesson is based on a *Sunday Times* travel article about haunted hotels in the UK. A journalist was sent to stay at one and report on what happened during the night. This provides a context for SS to practise *there was/there were* and prepositions of place. Make sure SS realize that this is a true story, and that it is a real hotel where they could go and spend the night!

Optional lead-in (books closed)

- Play the 'long sentence game' with your SS to revise *there is* and furniture.
- You begin the game. Say : *In my living room there's a sofa.* Then choose a student to continue. He/She must repeat your sentence, and add one more piece of furniture, e.g. *In my living room there's a sofa and two armchairs.*
- Now point to another student who must continue, repeating the sentence and adding to it, e.g. *In my living room there's a sofa, two armchairs, and a table.*
- After ten SS have added their words, see if the whole class can repeat the list from memory.

1 VOCABULARY prepositions of place

a • Books open. Focus on the nine prepositions of place and the pictures.
- Ask *What can you see in every picture?* (a ghost). In pairs SS match the words and pictures. Some of these prepositions may be new to your SS, so go round monitoring and helping.

Extra support

Demonstrate the meaning of the prepositions using classroom objects before doing **a**.

- Check answers by asking SS *Where's the ghost in picture 1?* Model and drill the pronunciation.

1 behind
2 in
3 under
4 over
5 in front of
6 next to
7 between
8 opposite
9 on

- Highlight the difference between *in* (= inside) and *on*, and between *in front of* and *opposite* (= face to face) demonstrating with objects/people in the classroom.

Extra idea

Give more practice with the prepositions by asking questions about things/people in the classroom.

b • Focus on the example. SS cover the prepositions and

test each other in pairs pointing to pictures and asking *Where's the ghost?*

c • Tell SS to go to **Vocabulary Bank** *Flats and houses* on *p. 151.* Tell them to choose a room and to draw a ghost somewhere in it, e.g. in the cupboard, under the bed, etc. **They mustn't let their partner see their book.**
- If SS don't want to draw in their book tell them to choose a place where the ghost is and write it on a piece of paper.
- Get SS to sit face to face if possible. Now tell them that they have to 'find' their partner's ghost, but they can only ask ten questions, always beginning *Is it …? +* a preposition of place, e.g. *Is it in the living room? Is it behind the sofa?*
- ⚠ Make sure SS realize that first they need to identify what room the ghost is in.
- Demonstrate by 'hiding' the ghost yourself, and eliciting questions from SS until they 'find' it.
- Tell SS to go back to the main lesson on *p. 66.*

2 READING

a • Focus on the lesson title. Elicit / teach the meaning of a *haunted hotel* (a hotel where a ghost lives). Then focus on the title of the article and the two photos. Tell SS that this is a real hotel in England. SS now read the introduction (until *I don't believe in ghosts*) and in pairs answer the questions. Set a time limit, e.g. five minutes.
- Check answers. Make sure SS understood *priest* (a religious man), *appear* (suddenly come), *nervous* (a little bit worried/frightened before you do something).

1 In Cumbria, in the north of England.
2 A (*Sunday Times*) journalist.
3 People say there is a ghost there.
4 Stephen spent a night in Room 11.
5 Phone or speak to anybody.
6 Nervous.
7 No.

b • Ask the whole class and elicit responses.
c • Focus on the text, and explain that it's the journalist's account of his night in Room 11. Build suspense by asking SS if they think he sees the ghost or not.

6.5

- Focus on the three pictures. SS listen and read the text once and then label the pictures. Set another time limit for the first read (e.g. two minutes), and get SS to compare before checking answers. Model and drill pronunciation.

1 cemetery /ˈsemətri/
2 remote control
3 horror film

6.5 CD2 Track 54

I arrived at Gosforth Hall late in the evening. It was a very dark night but I could see there was a church with a cemetery next to the hotel. I checked in, and the receptionist gave me the key and showed me to my room.
I left my things in the room and came downstairs. There weren't many guests. There were only three including me. I sat in the sitting room and I talked to the manager, Sara Daniels, about her hotel. I had a drink and then at 12.00 I went upstairs to my room.
Room 11 was on the top floor. I opened the door and turned on the light. It was a very big room, quite old, and yes, it was a bit spooky. There was an old television on a table – but there wasn't a remote control. I turned on the TV. There was a film on. I was happy to see that it wasn't a horror film. I decided to watch the film and have the light on all night. But I was tired after my long journey and after half an hour I went to sleep.

d • Now focus on sentences 1–7 and the example. In pairs SS try to correct the information, and then read the text again to check.

Extra support

Let SS re-read the text *before* correcting the information.

• Check answers, and also make sure SS understand any vocabulary, e.g. *top floor, spooky, decided, have the light on, went to sleep,* etc.

> 2 two other guests
> 3 to the manager
> 4 on the top floor
> 5 It was a big room.
> 6 There was a film on, but not a horror film.
> 7 He went to sleep with the TV and the light on.

e • Ask the class again and see if they still think the same about whether Stephen saw a ghost or not. Tell SS that they will now find out what happened to Stephen.

3 LISTENING

a **6.6**
• Now tell SS they're going to hear Stephen being interviewed. Play the tape/CD once and elicit answers to the question.

Extra support

Pause the tape/CD first after … *turn it off.* Check comprehension by asking SS *What was strange about the room?* Pause again after *…something in the room…* and repeat the question. Elicit that he couldn't see anything but he could *feel* something. Then play until the end.

> He didn't see the ghost, but he felt something in the room.

b • Focus on the report form and go through it with SS. Highlight that sometimes they just have to circle *Yes* or *No*, in other places they have to write a word or number, and in 8 they have to tick a box.
• Play the tape/CD again, and repeat it if necessary. Get SS to compare with a partner and then check answers.

> 1 Yes   6 No
> 2 2.00 a.m. 7 Yes
> 3 Yes   8 very
> 4 TV   9 Yes
> 5 light   10 I want to see the ghost.

Extra support

Get SS to listen to the tape/CD for a final time with the tapescript on *p. 118* so they can see exactly what Stephen said and see how much they understood.
Translate/explain any new words or phrases.

6.6 CD2 Track 55

(tapescript in Student's Book on *p.118*.)
S = Stephen Bleach, I = interviewer
S In the middle of the night I suddenly woke up! It was two o'clock. The television was off! But how? There was no remote control, and I certainly didn't get up and turn it off. The light was still on, but suddenly the light went off too. Now I was really frightened! I couldn't see anything strange, but I could feel that there was somebody or something in the room. I got out of bed and turned on the TV again. Little by little I started to relax, and I went to sleep again. When I woke up it was morning. I had breakfast and I left the hotel about ten o'clock.
I So the question is, did you see the ghost?
S No, I didn't *see* the ghost, but I definitely *felt* something or somebody in the room when I woke up in the night.
I Were you frightened?
S Yes, I was! Very frightened!
I Would you like to spend another night in the hotel?
S Definitely, yes.
I Why?
S Well, I'm sure there was something strange in that room. I can't explain the television and the light. I want to go back because I want to *see* the ghost.

• Ask SS if they would now like to go to the hotel and stay in Room 11.

Extra idea

Get SS to read the tapescript on *p. 118*, and then roleplay the interview. The person playing Stephen should do it with books closed.

4 GRAMMAR *there was/there were*

a • Focus on the four sentences. Get SS to complete them in pairs. Check answers.

> 1 weren't
> 2 were
> 3 was
> 4 wasn't

b • Tell SS to go to **Grammar Bank 6B** on *p. 132*. Go through the rules with the class. Model and drill the example sentences.

Grammar notes

• *There is/there are* can be used in any tense simply by changing the tense of *be*, thus the past is *there was/there were.*

- Although it works in exactly the same way as *there is / there are*, SS have a tendency to forget the plural form *there were*.

- Focus on exercises **6B** on *p. 133*. SS do the exercises individually or in pairs. Remind them to use *some* and *any* in plural sentences where no number is mentioned.
- Check answers, getting SS to read the full sentences.

> **a 1** There were some double rooms.
> **2** There was a swimming pool.
> **3** There was a restaurant.
> **4** There wasn't a car park.
> **5** There weren't any shops.
> **b 1** There were   **7** was there
>   **2** There was   **8** There was
>   **3** there were   **9** Were there
>   **4** Was there   **10** there weren't
>   **5** there wasn't   **11** There was
>   **6** there was

- Tell SS to go back to the main lesson on *p. 67*.

5 SPEAKING

- Tell SS to go to **Communication Room 11** on *p.111*. Give them one minute to look at the picture.

a • Put students in pairs, A and B. Tell A to go to *p.109* and B to *p.112*. Give each student a couple of minutes to write their questions.

Extra support

Put SS in pairs, A and A and B and B, to prepare their questions together.

b • Get SS to sit face to face. A asks his/her questions to B who has to answer without looking back at the picture.
c • B now asks A his/her questions.
- When they have finished get SS to go back to *p.111* to check their answers and see who has the best memory.

Extra challenge

Get SS to make questions from the prompts orally, without writing them first.

- Tell SS to go back to the main lesson on *p. 67*.

6 PRONUNCIATION   silent letters

a • Go through the introductory text and model and drill the pronunciation of *cupboard* so SS can hear that the *p* isn't pronounced. Show them that the phonetics also make this clear. Highlight also that the second syllable in *cupboard* is shortened and is pronounced /bəd/ and not /bɔːd/.

Pronunciation notes

- Encourage and help SS to cross out silent letters when they learn new words, like this: *listen*.
- Emphasize that if SS can recognize the phonetic transcriptions next to words in the dictionary this will help them to identify silent letters.

- In pairs SS say the words aloud, decide which they think is the silent letter in each word, and cross it out.

b   **6.7**
- Play the tape/CD for them to check. Check answers (the silent letters are in red).

6.7	CD2 Track 56
guest	building
ghost	listen
half	friend
could	write
know	hour

- Highlight that in words that begin with *kn-* (e.g. *knee*) or *wr-* (e.g. *wrong*) the *k* and the *w* are always silent.

Extra idea

If your SS have dictionaries, you could get them to check their answers with the phonetics in their dictionary. This will help build their confidence in dictionary use.

Extra photocopiable activities

Grammar
there was / there were p. 161.
Communicative
Where is it? p. 206 (instructions p.181).

HOMEWORK

Study Link **Workbook** *pp. 51–52*.

6
C

G present continuous
V verb phrases: *make a noise*, etc.
P verb + *-ing*

Neighbours from hell

Lesson plan

This lesson is based on a newspaper survey about noisy neighbours. SS learn new verb phrases and practise the present continuous. The form (*be* + *-ing* form of the verb) is not a problem, but using it correctly can be difficult, especially for SS who do not have an equivalent in their L1 (e.g. French and Polish learners). The present simple and continuous are contrasted in the next lesson (**6D**). The use of the present continuous to express future arrangements is taught in *New English File Pre-intermediate*.

Optional lead-in (books closed)

- Do something which makes a noise, e.g. put a cassette on very loudly, bang the desk, etc., and elicit the word *noise*. Then elicit the verb we use with noise, *make a noise*, and the adjective *noisy*.
- Now elicit/teach the word *neighbours* (people who live in the flat/house next to you). Model and drill pronunciation /ˈneɪbəz/. Then give SS in pairs a few moments to think of three things noisy neighbours do.
- Get feedback and write SS' ideas on the board. When you start **1a**, get SS to see if any of the things they suggested are there.

1 VOCABULARY & SPEAKING

a ● Books open. Focus on the text and photo, and use it to teach the word *neighbours*. Model and drill pronunciation. Elicit that the man doesn't like his neighbours because they are *noisy*.
- Focus on the text and the verbs above it. Tell SS to read the text and, in pairs, to complete the problems. Get them to try to work out the meaning of the new verbs from the context.
- Check answers.

> They **talk** loudly.
> Their babies **cry**.
> They **have** noisy parties.
> Their dogs **bark**.
> They **watch** TV late at night.
> They **move** furniture.
> They **play** a musical instrument.
> They **argue** with their partner.

- Tell SS to cover the sentences and see how many they can remember.

b ● Focus on the survey and go through the questions.
- Get SS to interview you. Give as much (simple) information as you can to model the way you want the SS to answer the questions.
- SS interview each other in pairs or groups of three. Monitor and help with any new vocabulary they need.
- Get some feedback about their neighbours.

2 GRAMMAR present continuous

a ● Focus on the sentences and get SS to match them to the different flats on *p. 69*.
- Get SS to compare and then check answers. Model and drill pronunciation.

> 1 She's playing the violin.
> 2 They're arguing.
> 3 The dog's barking.
> 4 He's watching football.
> 5 The baby's crying.
> 6 They're moving furniture.
> 7 They're having a party.
> 8 He's listening to music.

6.8

b ● Get SS to cover the sentences and look at the picture. Play the tape/CD of eight sound effects (which tell you what the people in the flats are doing).
- Pause the tape/CD after each one and ask SS *What's happening?* (They're arguing) *Where?* (In flat 2) to elicit the eight sentences from **a**.

6.8	CD2 Track 57
1 He's watching football.	Flat 4
2 The baby's crying.	Flat 5
3 They're having a party.	Flat 7
4 She's playing the violin.	Flat 1
5 The dog's barking.	Flat 3
6 They're arguing.	Flat 2
7 They're moving furniture.	Flat 6
8 He's listening to music.	Flat 8

c ● Focus on the chart and on the three ⊞ sentences. Elicit that *'s* is the contraction of *is*, and *'re* is the contraction of *are*. The other verb is always verb + *-ing*.
- Get SS to complete the ⊟ and ? forms.

6.9

d ● Play the tape/CD and get SS to repeat the sentences and check their answers.

6.9	CD2 Track 58
The baby's crying.	
She's playing the violin.	
They're having a party.	
The baby **isn't** crying.	
She **isn't playing** the violin.	
They **aren't having** a party.	
Is the baby **crying**?	
Is **she playing** the violin?	
Are they **having** a party?	

- Elicit/teach that we use this form of the verb (present continuous) for something that's happening now, at the moment of speaking. Give a few more examples, e.g. *We're having a class. I'm talking to you and you're listening.*

e ● Tell SS to go to **Grammar Bank 6C** on *p. 132*. Go through the rules with the class. Model and drill the example sentences.

Grammar notes

Present continuous

● SS don't usually find the form of this tense difficult (*be + -ing* form of the verb), but they often have problems using it correctly, especially if they do not have an equivalent form in their L1. Their main mistake is to use the present simple, not continuous, for things which are happening now, e.g. *The baby cries* instead of *The baby's crying*.

● The present continuous is contrasted with the present simple in the next lesson (**6D**). Its use to talk about future arrangements will be presented in *New English File Pre-Intermediate*.

Spelling rules

SS learned the rules for making the *-ing* form in lesson **4B**. They will probably need to revise them (see *p. 128*).

● Focus on the exercises for **6C** on *p. 133*. SS do the exercises individually or in pairs.

● Check answers, getting SS to read the full sentences.

> **a 1** He's having a shower.
> **2** What are they doing? They're dancing.
> **3** What's she doing? She's listening to music.
> **b 1** It's raining
> **2** she's talking
> **3** are you doing
> **4** aren't you doing
> **5** we're studying
> **6** she's waiting
> **7** They're having
> **8** What's she wearing

Extra idea

Get SS in pairs to read the dialogue **b** in pairs.

● Tell SS to go back to the main lesson on *p.68*.

f ● Focus on the instructions. SS use the flats in **a** to practise making questions and answers.

Extra support

Get SS to practise making Yes/No questions, e.g. with Flat 1, A *Is she playing the piano?* B *No, (she isn't). She's playing the violin.*

g **6.10**

● Now tell SS to close their books and listen to six noises. They have to decide what they think is happening and write a sentence.

● Play the tape/CD once the whole way through, for SS just to listen. Then play it again, stopping after each sound effect, and give SS in pairs time to write a sentence. Emphasize that SS should write full sentences, not just the *-ing* form, e.g. *It's raining.*

● Check answers, accepting all appropriate sentences.

> **6.10**   CD2 Track 59
> 1 It's raining.
> 2 They're playing tennis.
> 3 He's having a shower/singing.
> 4 They're having lunch/dinner/a meal.
> 5 They're doing exercise.
> 6 She's cooking.

3 PRONUNCIATION verb + *-ing*

a ● Focus on the sound pictures and elicit the words and sounds (*car*, /ɑː/, *train*, /eɪ/, *horse*, /ɔː/, *bike*, /aɪ/, *boot*, /uː/, *phone*, /əʊ/).

● Now focus on the *-ing* forms/verbs. SS put two verbs in each column.

b **6.11**

● Play the tape/CD once for SS to check answers. Then play it again, pausing after each group for SS to repeat.

> **6.11**   CD2 Track 60
> car   dancing, asking
> train   playing, raining
> horse   calling, talking
> bike   crying, driving
> boot   doing, moving
> phone   smoking, going

c **6.12**

● Tell SS that when they're listening to the present continuous, it's often difficult to hear the verb *be*, as it's usually contracted.

● Now tell them they're going to listen to a man in a train talking on his mobile phone. They must listen and write down six present continuous sentences or questions.

● Play the tape/CD once the whole way through just for SS to listen. Get SS to compare with a partner what present continuous sentences they think they heard.

● Play the tape/CD twice more, pausing after each sentence to give SS time to write the answers.

> **6.12**   CD2 Track 61
> (tapescript in Student's Book on *p.118*.)
> Hi Bill, it's Rob. What are you doing?… I'm going to London…Who are you talking to?…I'm having a coffee… Is the baby crying?… My train's arriving. Bye!

● Check answers, and write them on the board. Get SS to spell the *-ing* forms.

> 1 What are you doing?
> 2 I'm going to London.
> 3 Who are you talking to?
> 4 I'm having a coffee.
> 5 Is the baby crying?
> 6 My train's arriving.

4 SPEAKING

A Use someone in class or pictures to pre-teach the use of *She's wearing…* to describe what clothes somebody has on. In your SS' language they may use the present simple to convey this idea.

- Put SS in pairs and get them to sit face to face. Now tell them to go to **Communication** *They're having a party!* **A** *p. 110,* **B** *p. 113.*
- Go through the instructions with them. Highlight that when we describe a picture, we use the present continuous for actions which are happening in the picture.
- Tell the **As** to describe the left-hand side of the picture and the **Bs** the right-hand side. Demonstrate the activity by sitting with an **A** and beginning to describe the left-hand side. Tell all the **Bs** to listen to you and to say when they hear something that's different.
- SS continue in pairs. When they've finished, they compare their pictures to see if they have correctly identified the differences.
- Check by getting pairs to explain the differences, e.g.
  A *In my picture the man and the woman are talking.*
  B *In my picture they're kissing.*

In A the parents are coming through the door / into the room; in B they are not there.
In A the boy and the girl are playing the guitar; in B they are talking.
In A the boy in the yellow shirt is opening a bottle of champagne; in B he's talking on his mobile.
In A the man and woman are dancing the tango; in B they are dancing rock'n'roll.
In B the boy in the orange shirt is looking at his watch; in A he's opening / having a drink.
In B the girl is wearing a blue dress; in A she's wearing a red dress.
In B two people are eating on the sofa; in A they're sleeping.
In B the people in the house next door are talking on the phone / calling the police; in A they are watching the television.

Extra idea

For more personalization with the present continuous, write the names of five family members or friends on the board, e.g. my mother, David (my brother), and explain who they are if necessary. Elicit from SS the question *What's (your mother) doing at the moment?* and answer, e.g. *I think she's (probably) having lunch.* When SS have asked about the other people, they do the same in pairs.

Extra photocopiable activities

Grammar
present continuous *p. 162.*
Communicative
Don't say a word *p. 207* (instructions *p.181*).

HOMEWORK

Study Link Workbook *pp. 53–54.*

G present simple or present continuous?
V places in a city: *square*, *castle*, etc.
P city names

When a man is tired of London...

Lesson plan

This lesson contrasts the present simple and present continuous. The context is provided by tourists' impressions of four of London's top attractions. SS also learn the vocabulary to describe tourist attractions in a city and they read an extract from a guidebook about the London Eye. The lesson finishes with the Kinks' 1967 song about London, *Waterloo Sunset*.

Optional lead-in (books closed)

- Write LONDON on the board and teach/elicit the right pronunciation (/ˈlʌndən/).
- Tell SS in pairs to write down three things they associate with London (e.g. red buses, Trafalgar Square, the River Thames, Big Ben, Oxford Street, Camden Market, etc.)
- Feedback their suggestions on the board.
- Ask SS *Have any of you visited London? Which of these did you see?* and get feedback.

1 GRAMMAR present simple or present continuous?

a • Books open. Focus on the lesson title and tell SS it's the beginning of a famous saying. Ask them if they have any idea how it finishes, and then tell them it is *When a man is tired of London, he's tired of life*, and was written by the 18th century writer Dr Johnson.
- Now focus on the photos and see if SS can identify them. Write the names on the board.

> The London Eye
> Tower Bridge
> Madame Tussaud's
> Buckingham Palace

- Ask SS which two attractions they would like to see and get responses. Ask *Why?*

b • Focus on the picture of Ivan and Eva. Revise the present continuous by asking SS *What are they doing? What's Ivan wearing? What's Eva wearing?*
- Tell SS that Ivan and Eva are in London for the day, and they visit all four attractions. Eva has a guidebook so she can tell Ivan about the attractions.

6.13 •
- Get SS to cover the dialogues and focus on the pictures. Play the tape/CD and get SS to number the pictures in order. Check answers.

> 1 Tower Bridge
> 2 Buckingham Palace
> 3 Madame Tussaud's
> 4 The London Eye

c • Now tell SS to uncover and look at the dialogues. Go through them and elicit/teach any new vocabulary, e.g. *ship, flag, guidebook*, etc.
- Now tell SS that the verbs in brackets are either in the

present continuous or the present simple. They are going to listen again to hear which tense it is, and should then write the verb in.

⚠ Remind SS to include the verb *be* in the present continuous. They should use contractions, as these are conversations.
- Play the tape/CD once the whole way through, telling SS just to read and listen. Then play it again, pausing after each verb (or after each dialogue) to give SS time to write.

Extra challenge

Give SS a few minutes to guess which tense the verbs are in before they listen.

- Check answers.

6.13   CD2 Track 62

I = **Ivan**, E = **Eva**

1 I Look! It's **opening**! A ship's **going** through!
E We're lucky. The guidebook says that it only **opens** two or three times a month!
2 E The flag's **flying** – that means the Queen is at home. She **doesn't live** here all the time. She often **stays** at Windsor Castle or in one of her other homes.
3 E That's Napoleon. He's **looking** at a model of the battle of Waterloo.
I Come on – let's go and see the next room.
E Yes, we **don't have** much time. It **closes** in twenty minutes.
4 I We're **going up**! Wow! Look – there's the Houses of Parliament! And Buckingham Palace over there!
E What a pity it's **raining**. The guidebook **says** you can see Windsor Castle on a clear day.

- Ask SS to go through the conversations with their partner, looking at the verbs. Give them two minutes to think about what the difference is between the two tenses (the present continuous and the present simple). Elicit/teach that the present continuous is for what's happening now, and the present simple is for what always or usually happens.

Extra support

Get SS to read the dialogues aloud in pairs.

d • Tell SS to go to **Grammar Bank 6D** on *p. 132*. Go through the rules with the class. Model and drill the example sentences.

Grammar notes

- There is a clear difference in use between the present simple and present continuous:
  The present simple is used for habitual actions (things which are always true or which happen every day).
  The present continuous is used for things happening now, at this moment.
- The use of these two tenses can cause problems either because SS don't have the present continuous in their

L1, or because English is 'stricter' about using it when talking about now.

If you know your SS' L1, contrast it with English to anticipate or correct errors.

- Some verbs are not normally used in the present continuous, e.g. *want*, *like*, *need*, *have* (= possession), and *know*.

- SS do **6D a** on *p.133* in pairs. Check answers, getting SS to correct the wrong sentences.

> **a 1** ✓
> **2** ✓
> **3** ✗ He's having a great time.
> **4** ✓
> **5** ✗ I normally go...
> **6** ✓
> **7** ✗ What do you do?

- Now focus on **b**. SS do it individually or in pairs. Check answers.

> **b 1** What are you doing I'm waiting
> **2** What does your mother do? She works...
> **3** They're having... They have
> **4** I'm going... Do you want...

Study Link SS can find an end-of-File grammar quiz on the MultiROM, and more grammar activities on the *New English File Elementary* website.

- Tell SS to go back to the main lesson on *p. 71.*

2 READING

a • Focus on the guidebook extract and photo of the London Eye.

- First go through the questions. Use the photo to explain *capsule*, and elicit/teach that *How long* = How much time. You could explain the use of *How* + adjective to make questions, e.g. *How high...? How far...? How fast...?*, etc. SS have already studied *How old.*

- Set a time limit, e.g. five minutes for SS to read the text to find the answers. Get them to compare with a partner and then check answers.

> **1** 135metres
> **2** 40km
> **3** 32
> **4** 25
> **5** 30 minutes
> **6** 15 metres a minute
> **7** 9 a.m.–10 p.m.; 10 a.m.–6 p.m.
> **8** Yes
> **9** in County Hall, next to the Eye
> **10** Waterloo

b • Now focus on the highlighted words. In pairs SS guess them from the context, and then match them to their meanings. Check answers, and explain/translate any other vocabulary SS want to know.

> **1** in advance
> **2** are available
> **3** Daily
> **4** to queue
> **5** room
> **6** Passengers

c • Ask the class and elicit why or why not.

3 VOCABULARY places in a city

a • Get ideas from the class and encourage them to tell you about the building(s), asking them *How high is it? What can you see?*, etc.

b • Tell SS to go to **Vocabulary Bank** *Town and city* on *p. 152.*

- Give SS five to ten minutes to do **a** in pairs. They have already seen a lot of the words.

- Check answers. Model and drill pronunciation.

> **1** a police station   **15** a road
> **2** a bus station   **16** a railway station
> **3** a river   **17** a supermarket
> **4** a shopping centre   **18** a theatre
> **5** a department store   **19** a street
> **6** a bridge   **20** a school
> **7** a hospital   **21** a travel agent's
> **8** a bank   **22** a chemist's/pharmacy
> **9** an art gallery   **23** a market
> **10** a church   **24** a town hall
> **11** a museum   **25** a park
> **12** a cinema   **26** a mosque
> **13** a sports centre   **27** a post office
> **14** a castle   **28** a square

- For **b** SS cover the words and use the pictures to test themselves or each other.

Study Link SS can find more practice of these words on the MultiROM and on the *New English File Elementary* website.

- Tell SS to go back to the main lesson on *p. 71.*

4 SPEAKING

- This speaking activity focuses on recycling the vocabulary SS have just learned.

- Focus on the questionnaire. If you are from a different town/city from your SS, get them to interview you about it.

- Put SS in pairs. If they are from the same town/city, get them to answer questions 1–3 together in English. Then tell them that for 4, they can only put one name, and to decide together which name to put. If SS are from different places, get them to answer the questions individually and then compare with a partner.

5 PRONUNCIATION city names

a 6.14

- Focus on the introductory sentence, and elicit the correct pronunciation of *Leicester* /ˈlestə/ getting SS to look at the phonetics.

- Tell SS that they're going to hear eight famous towns in the UK or Ireland, which they must write down (just the towns, not the whole sentences).

- Play the tape/CD once the whole way through for SS to listen. Then play it again, pausing after each sentence to give SS time to write. Check answers getting SS to spell the names and writing them on the board.

> **6.14** CD2 Track 63
>
> (tapescript in Student's Book on *p.119.*)
> 1 I'm from **Edinburgh**. /ˈedɪnbrə/
> 2 He's from **London**. /ˈlʌndən/
> 3 They live in **Brighton**. /ˈbraɪtən/
> 4 We went to **Oxford** for the weekend. /ˈɒksfəd/
> 5 She was born in **Dublin**. /ˈdʌblɪn/
> 6 We're studying in **Cambridge**. /ˈkeɪmbrɪdʒ/
> 7 I want to go to **Manchester**. /ˈmæntʃestə/
> 8 Do you like **Birmingham**? /ˈbɜːmɪŋəm/

b • Now repeat the tape/CD and get SS to repeat the names (or the whole sentence). Play it again, stopping after each sentence to ask SS if the town has the /ə/ sound (they all do except Dublin and Cambridge).

c • Get SS to practise saying the names.

d • Tell SS to go the **Sound Bank** on *p. 157*. Highlight that the /ə/ sound can be made by any combination of vowels and always occurs before or after a stressed syllable.

Extra idea

If your SS are more interested in the USA than the UK, teach them the pronunciation of famous towns/cities there, e.g. San Francisco, New York, Washington, etc.

6 SONG *Waterloo Sunset*

> **6.15**

• Here SS listen to one of the Kinks' most famous songs, about Waterloo Bridge, in central London. Waterloo Bridge and the station were named after the Battle of Waterloo. If you want to do this song with your SS there is a photocopiable activity on *p. 226.*

> **6.15** CD2 Track 64
>
> Dirty old river, must you keep rolling, flowing into the night
> People so busy, make me feel dizzy,
> Taxi light shines so bright
> But I don't need no friends
> As long as I gaze on Waterloo sunset I am in paradise
>
> Every day I look at the world from my window,
> But chilly, chilly is the evening time
> Waterloo sunset's fine
>
> Terry meets Julie, Waterloo station, every Friday night
> But I am so lazy, don't want to wander,
> I stay at home at night
> But I don't feel afraid
> As long as I gaze on Waterloo sunset I am in paradise
>
> Every day I look at the world from my window,
> But chilly, chilly is the evening time
> Waterloo sunset's fine
>
> Millions of people, swarming like flies round Waterloo underground,
> But Terry and Julie cross over the river
> Where they feel safe and sound
> And they don't need no friends
>
> As long as they gaze on Waterloo sunset, they are in paradise
> Waterloo sunset's fine

Extra photocopiable activities

Grammar
present simple or present continuous? *p. 163.*
Communicative
Find the differences *p. 208* (instructions *p.181*).
Song
Waterloo Sunset p. 226 (instructions *p.221*).

HOMEWORK

Study Link **Workbook** *pp. 55–56.*

Vocabulary directions: *turn left*, etc.
Function Asking for directions
Language *Could you tell me the way to …*

Lesson plan

The Mark and Allie story continues – they get lost, and Allie gets stressed trying to find the street where the restaurant is. Mark, rather irritatingly for Allie, always seems to be right.

In this lesson SS get practice with directions. The focus is more on asking for and understanding directions than on giving them, as this is difficult at their level.

Study Link These lessons are also on the *New English File Elementary* Video, which can be used **instead of** the Class Cassette/CD (see introduction *p.9*).

The first section of the Video is also on the MultiROM, with additional activities.

VOCABULARY directions

a • Focus on the pictures and give SS in pairs a few moments to match them to the words or phrases.
  • Check answers. Drill pronunciation. Highlight that when *opposite* is used to describe the position of a building it usually means facing on the other side of the road. Give an example by asking SS what there is opposite your school.

1 a roundabout	5 go straight on
2 on the corner	6 turn right
3 opposite	7 turn left
4 at the traffic lights	8 go past (the station)

b • Tell SS to cover the words and test each other in pairs.

ASKING FOR DIRECTIONS

a 6.16
  • Tell SS to cover the dialogue and look only at the map. Play the tape/CD at least twice and then ask them which street is King Street.
  • Get SS to compare answers in pairs. Check answers.

b • Now focus on the conversation and the gaps. Give SS a minute to read through the dialogue and guess the missing words. Then play the tape/CD again once.
  • Get SS to compare answers in pairs. Play the tape/CD again if necessary. Check answers.

> 6.16   CD3 Track 2
>
> **A = Allie, P = passer-by**
> A Excuse me. Where's King Street, please?
> P1 Sorry, I **don't** know.
> A Excuse me. Is King Street near here?
> P2 King Street? It's **near** here but I don't know exactly **where**. Sorry.
> A Thank you. Excuse me. Can you tell me the way to King Street?
> P3 Yes. Go **straight** on. Go past the church, and then turn **left** at the traffic lights. And then I think it's the **second** on the right.
> A Sorry, could you say that again, please?
> P3 Yes, go straight on. Go past the church, and then turn left at the traffic lights. And then I think it's the second on the right.
> A Thank you.

  • Go through the dialogue line by line. Highlight that *Can you tell me the way to …?* is the typical question to ask the route somewhere, and that *Could you say that again?* is more polite than *Repeat please!*

c 6.17
  • Now focus on the **YOU SAY** phrases. Tell SS they're going to hear the dialogue again. They repeat the **YOU SAY** phrases when they hear the beep.
  • Play the tape/CD, pausing if necessary for SS to repeat the phrases. Encourage them to copy the rhythm and intonation.

> 6.17   CD3 Track 3
>
> A Excuse me. Where's King Street, please?
> *repeat*
> P1 Sorry, I don't know.
> A Excuse me. Is King Street near here?
> *repeat*
> P2 King Street? It's near here but I don't know exactly where. Sorry.
> A Thank you.
> *repeat*
>   Excuse me. Can you tell me the way to King Street?
> *repeat*
> P3 Yes. Go straight on. Go past the church, and then turn left at the traffic lights. And then I think it's the second on the right.
> A Sorry, could you say that again, please?
> *repeat*
> P3 Yes, go straight on. Go past the church, and then turn left at the traffic lights. And then I think it's the second on the right.
> A Thank you.
> *repeat*

  • Put SS in pairs to practise the dialogue. **A** is Allie, **B** is all the passers by. Get SS to read the dialogue first. Then tell **A** to close his/her book and try to say the part from memory. Then **A** and **B** swap roles.

d • In pairs SS roleplay asking for and giving simple directions. Go through the instructions with them and give them time to find the places on the map and think about how to give directions to them.
  • Demonstrate first by asking a good student the way to the art gallery. SS then continue in pairs.

Extra idea

Give SS clear directions to a nearby restaurant or shop and see if they can work out where it is.

SOCIAL ENGLISH

a 6.18

- Focus on the picture. Ask SS *What's happening?*
- Write on the board: Who is right about where the street is, Mark or Allie? Play the tape/CD once and elicit that Mark is right.
- Focus on sentences 1–5 and go through them. Explain/translate *anywhere* (a possible place).
- Play the tape/CD at least twice, and then give SS time to compare answers before checking.

> 1 first 2 tourist 3 park 4 space 5 can't

6.18   CD3 Track 4

(tapescript in Student's Book on *p.119*.)

A OK. It's this street. No, it isn't. I'm sure she said the first on the right.
M No, she said the *second* on the right. Relax, Allie.
A Look, let's ask that man there.
M I don't think he knows. He's a **tourist**.
A Just ask him, please.
M OK, OK. Excuse me! We're lost. Do you know where King Street is?
P Sorry, I don't live here – I'm a tourist.
M You see. I was right.
A OK, let's try the second on the right.
M Here it is. King Street. I *knew* she said the second on the right.
A There's the restaurant, Donatella's. Can you see anywhere to **park**?
M That white car's going over there! Do you think you can park in that **space**?
A Are you saying I **can't** park?
M Allie, I'm only joking.
A OK, OK, I'm sorry.

---

b • Ask SS if they think Mark and Allie will enjoy their dinner. Elicit a few ideas.

c • Focus on the **USEFUL PHRASES**. For each phrase ask SS *Who says it, Mark or Allie?*
- Then play the tape/CD again for SS to check. Pause after each phrase and get SS to repeat it. In a monolingual class, tell them to decide together what the equivalent phrase is in their language.

> Let's ask that man there. – Allie
> Excuse me! We're lost. – Mark
> You see. I was right. – Mark
> Here it is. – Mark
> I'm only joking. – Mark

Extra support

If time, you could get SS to listen to the tape/CD for a final time with the tapescript on *p.119* so they can see exactly what Mark and Allie said and see how much they understood. Translate/explain any new words or phrases.

Extra challenge

Get SS in pairs to roleplay the second conversation using the tapescript on *p.119*.

HOMEWORK

Study Link **Workbook** *p. 57*.

WRITING A POSTCARD

Lesson plan

In this sixth writing lesson SS consolidate the present continuous and revise the present and past simple. The writing focus is on using the correct verb tense.

a • Ask SS if they send postcards when they're on holiday, who to, etc. Then focus on the two postcards and ask if SS know where they are from (they are both from Prague).
- If no one knows the answer, don't tell them and see if after reading the postcard and looking at the stamp they can guess where it is.

b • Give SS three minutes to read Melanie's postcard quickly. Tell SS it is one of the cards above. Tell them to ignore the gaps. Get them to discuss together which card it is.
- Check answers, and if they couldn't identify the city before, elicit more ideas and then tell them it's Prague, the capital of the Czech Republic.

> Postcard 1

c • Now tell SS to focus on the gaps and in pairs to put the verbs in the right tense. Ask them each time why it's that tense.
- Check answers.

> We're having
> arrived
> we're staying
> went
> visited
> we're sitting
> is
> are
> go
> have

- Check comprehension by asking a few questions, e.g. *Are they having a good time?* (Yes), *Where are they staying?* (in a small hotel), etc.

Write a postcard

Go through the instructions with SS. Stress the importance of checking writing after they've done it.

- Either give SS at least fifteen minutes to write the postcard in class, or set it for homework. Encourage SS to use a real postcard if they can get one.
- If SS do the writing in class, get them to swap and read each others' postcards and correct any mistakes they find, before you collect them all in.

For instructions on how to use these pages, see *p.28*.

What do you remember?

GRAMMAR

1 b 2 a 3 b 4 a 5 b 6 b 7 a 8 b 9 b 10 a

VOCABULARY

a 1 make 2 play 3 have 4 book 5 take
b 1 shelf (not a room)
   2 cooker (not in a living room)
   3 there (not a preposition)
   4 town hall (a building)
   5 square (not a building)
c 1 with 2 on 3 on 4 of 5 to

PRONUNCIATION

a 1 near 2 know 3 floor 4 church 5 theatre
b <u>o</u>pposite
  be<u>tween</u>
  be<u>hind</u>
  <u>cu</u>pboard
  mu<u>se</u>um

What can you do?

CAN YOU UNDERSTAND THIS TEXT?

a 1 B 2 F 3 E 4 A 5 D 6 G 7 C
b 1 T 2 F 3 F

CAN YOU HEAR THE DIFFERENCE?

a 1 b 2 a 3 b 4 b 5 a

6.19 CD3 Track 5

E = estate agent, C = customer
E Good afternoon, *Happy Homes*. How can I help you?
C Good afternoon. I'm calling about your advert in the local paper.
E Er, which one?
C The four-bedroomed house.
E Oh yes. I've got it.
C Where is it exactly?
E It's about thirteen miles from Cambridge.
C Sorry? Did you say thirty?
E Er, no. Thirteen.
C Oh, it's quite near. How many bathrooms are there?
E There's one upstairs and one downstairs.
C Is there a garden?
E A very small one.
C How old is the house?
E It's about ninety years old. Would you like to see it?
C Yes, please. When?
E Is Thursday afternoon OK?
C Yes. What time?
E At quarter to six?

C Where can we meet?
E Here in the office. Do you know where it is?
C Yes. OK then. Quarter to six on Thursday.
E Can you give me your name and your mobile number?

---

b 1 b 2 a 3 b 4 b 5 b

6.20 CD3 Track 6

1 A Was the hotel full?
  B No, it wasn't, it was empty. There were only five other guests, and us two.
2 A What's that noise?
  B It's the neighbours again. What do you think they're doing?
  A I think they're watching TV.
  B No. Listen, they're arguing!
3 A Can I speak to Jim, please?
  B Sorry, he's not here.
  A Do you know where he is?
  B Yes, he's at a restaurant. He's having dinner with friends.
4 A What are you reading, Maria?
  B An Agatha Christie book.
  A Oh, it's in English! Do you usually read in English?
  B No. My teacher told me to read this for homework.
5 A Is the gallery open every day?
  B Yes, but on Sundays it closes early, at 4.00 in the afternoon.

CAN YOU SAY THIS IN ENGLISH?

1 How many TVs are there in your house?
2 What was there on TV last night?
3 Is there a computer in your bedroom?
4 What time do the banks open in your country?
5 What are you wearing today?

Extra photocopiable activities

Quicktest 6 *p.236.*

7
A

G *a/an, some/any*
V food and drink, countable/uncountable nouns
P the letters *ea*

What does your food say about you?

Lesson plan

This lesson takes a light-hearted look at the food we eat and what it says about our personality type. The grammatical and lexical focus is on countable and uncountable nouns and how *a*, *some*, and *any* are used with them. SS also revise *there is/there are*. The pronunciation focus looks at the combination of vowels, *ea*, which can be pronounced in several different ways and which occurs in many food words.

Optional lead-in (books closed)

- Write BREAKFAST on the board. Put SS in pairs and give them two minutes to write as many words as they can for things people eat and drink for breakfast.
- Feedback their words onto the board. Model and drill pronunciation.

> (Possible answers)
> bread/toast/butter/jam
> cereal
> croissant
> cold meat
> cheese
> eggs
> fruit/fruit juice
> tea/coffee

- Get SS to say in pairs what they had for breakfast this morning.

1 VOCABULARY food

a • Focus on the picture. Ask SS what they think Laura writes in her Food Diary (what she eats and drinks every day) and why (to try to control her diet or her weight).
- Focus on the instructions and the food on the table. Give SS a minute to write the missing letters. Tell them that there is only one letter missing from each word.
- Get SS to check their answers by answering the question *What did Laura have to eat and drink yesterday?*, e.g. A *She had an apple.* B *She had a banana.*
- Now check answers getting SS to tell you the first letter for each word. Model and drill pronunciation. Remind SS that *some* = not an exact amount.

2 a banana	7 some sugar
3 some butter	8 a tomato
4 an egg	9 a biscuit
5 some meat	10 some coffee
6 some rice	

Extra idea

- Get SS to close their books and in pairs try to remember the ten things Laura had to eat and drink.
- Elicit from the whole class, making sure SS use *a/an* or *some*.

b • Focus on the two column headings and explain the difference, i.e. that countable words are used in the singular or plural and that they are things you can count (e.g. *a banana*, *two apples*). We think of them as individual units. Uncountable words are not normally used in the plural, and are not thought of as individual units (e.g. *rice*, *sugar*, etc.).
- SS in pairs put the words from **a** into the columns. Make sure they include *a/an* and *some*. Check answers.

countable nouns (singular or plural)	uncountable nouns (singular)
an apple	some butter
a banana	some meat
an egg	some rice
a tomato	some sugar
a biscuit	some coffee

c • Tell SS to go to **Vocabulary Bank** *Food* on *p. 153.*
- Focus on the groups of words and the tables, and the photos of food for breakfast, lunch, dinner and desserts and snacks.
- Give SS five minutes to do **a** in pairs. There are more words than usual but SS may already know many of them.
- Check answers. Model and drill pronunciation.

1 milk	13 ketchup	28 bananas
2 coffee	14 (*olive*) oil	29 apples
3 tea	15 a lettuce	30 a pineapple
4 jam	16 a salad	31 grapes
5 bread	17 potatoes	32 oranges
6 sugar	18 carrots	33 ice cream
7 cereal	19 rice	34 fruit salad
8 butter	20 fish	35 crisps
9 cheese	21 tomatoes	36 sandwiches
10 toast	22 an onion	37 biscuits
11 (*orange*) juice	23 meat	38 cake
12 eggs	24 mushrooms	39 chocolate
	25 pasta	40 sweets
	26 peas	
	27 chips	

- For **b** get SS to cover the words and use the pictures to test themselves or each other.

> **Study Link** SS can find more practice of these words on the MultiROM and on the *New English File Elementary* website.

- Tell SS to go back to the main lesson on *p. 76.*

2 GRAMMAR *a/an, some/any*

a • Focus on the questions and get SS to ask you first. Then they ask and answer in pairs.
- Get some feedback. Elicit that seeing what food people buy often tells you how healthy they are, if they cook much or not, how busy/stressed they are, etc.

b • Focus on the three baskets and elicit what is in each basket. Check answers.

> **Basket 1**
> carrots, lettuce, orange juice, mineral water, milk, grapes, pasta, oranges, tomatoes
> **Basket 2**
> champagne, smoked salmon, box of chocolates, a pineapple, ice cream, strawberries, steak, butter
> **Basket 3**
> chips, beer, peas, pizzas, chocolate, biscuits

• Now focus on the cartoon characters. Model and drill their names, and make sure SS understand *luxury* /ˈlʌkʃəri/. Give them a minute to decide which basket is whose. Check answers.

> 1 Healthy Hannah
> 2 Luxury Lucy
> 3 Fast Food Frank

c • Now focus on the sentences. Show SS that *There's some ice cream* is only true for basket 2. Get SS to continue in pairs. Check answers.

> **a** 2   **b** 3   **c** 2   **d** 3   **e** 1   **f** 1 and 3

d • Focus on the words in bold in sentences a–f and give SS a minute or two to complete the rules. Check answers.

> Use **a/an** with singular countable nouns.
> Use **some** (+) and **any** (− and ?) with plural nouns and uncountable nouns.

e • Tell SS to go to **Grammar Bank 7A** on *p. 134*. Go through the rules with the class. Model and drill the example sentences.

Grammar notes

Countable/uncountable nouns

• The concept of countable and uncountable nouns shouldn't cause too many problems (unless they do not exist in the SS' own language), but what may cause confusion is that some words are countable in English but uncountable in other languages or vice versa, e.g. *spaghetti* – uncountable in English, countable in Italian.

• You may need to give more examples of when a noun can be countable or uncountable. This occurs when we can think of e.g. *a chicken* (a whole chicken) and *chicken* (e.g. chicken pieces).
Others examples: *a beer* (= a can or glass of beer), *beer* (= the liquid in general); *a coffee* (= a cup of), *coffee* (= a quantity of coffee beans or powder in a jar).

a/an, some/any

• SS have already learnt the rules for *a/an*, *some*, and *any* plus singular and plural countable nouns in **6A**. Here they learn that *some* can also be used with singular uncountable nouns meaning not an exact amount, e.g. *some butter, some milk*.

• SS may find it strange using *some* and *any* with 'singular' words, e.g. *butter*, since they previously used them with plural nouns and may have translated them in their heads as plural words.

• Make sure you point out the exception of using *some* for offers and requests. SS usually assimilate this rule

instinctively through learning set phrases like *Would you like some coffee?*

• Focus on the exercises for **7A** on *p. 135*. SS do the exercises individually or in pairs.
• Check answers, getting SS to read the full sentences.

a 2	an orange	7	some coffee
3	a biscuit	8	some cheese
4	some peas	9	some chips
5	an ice cream	10	a pineapple
6	some cake		
b 1	some	6	any
2	some	7	an
3	an	8	any
4	any	9	a
5	some	10	some

• Tell SS to go back to the main lesson on *p. 77*.

f • Focus on the instructions. Then say a sentence yourself, e.g. *There isn't any chocolate*, and get SS to say which basket (1). SS continue in pairs taking turns to make sentences. A says a sentence, B has to say which basket it is. Set a time limit, e.g. five minutes.

Extra support

Get SS to write their (e.g. 6) sentences first and then read them to each other.

3 PRONUNCIATION the letters *ea*

Pronunciation notes

• The combination of vowels *e + a* has several possible pronunciations, several of which may seem quite irregular to SS, e.g. *great* /greɪt/. In this exercise we focus on common examples of this spelling which all occur in food words.

a • Focus on the words in the box and elicit that they all have the vowels *ea*, but that the pronunciation is not the same.

• Now focus on the sound pictures and elicit the three words and sounds (*tree* /iː/, *egg* /e/, *train* /eɪ/). Get SS in pairs to put the words in the three columns. Encourage them to say the words aloud to help them.

b 7.1
• Play the tape/CD once to check answers. Then play it again pausing after each word (or group of words) for SS to repeat. Elicit that the most common pronunciation is /iː/, but they will need to learn unusual ones, e.g. *steak*, by heart.

7.1		CD3 Track 7
tree	eat, ice cream, meat, peas, tea	
egg	bread, breakfast, health	
train	steak	

Extra challenge

Write up on the board some more words that SS know with *ea* for them to put in the columns, e.g. *sea, break, head, read* (/e/ and /iː/) *dead, great, leader, mean, please, speak*.

4 SPEAKING

a • Tell SS to go to **Vocabulary Bank** *Food* p. 153 and make a food diary for yesterday, i.e. to write down what they had to eat and drink. Monitor and help them with any new words they need, but try not to overdo new vocabulary. Encourage SS to use more general words, e.g. *meat, fish, vegetables*, rather than specific words (*lamb, hake, carrots*, etc.). Tell them to write *a / an* or *some* and *any* with each word, and to group them under meals.

b • Demonstrate first yourself. Tell SS what you had for breakfast, lunch, and dinner, and ask them if they think you are more like Healthy Hannah, Luxury Lucy, or Fast Food Frank.

• SS now do the same in pairs. Monitor and help with pronunciation and correct any mistakes with *a / an* or *some* and *any*.

• Get feedback from some pairs to find out what their diets are like.

5 LISTENING

a • Focus on the picture and ask SS what cooking programmes there are on TV in their country.

• Now focus on the question. Elicit ideas and write them on the board.

b 🔊 **7.2**

• Focus on the exercise. Tell SS they're going to hear the tape/CD twice, and that they should try to get some ingredients the first time, and then the rest the second time.

c • Play the tape/CD. Get SS to compare with a partner and then play it again.

• Check answers.

2 an onion	6 some tomato ketchup
3 some butter	7 some red wine
4 a carrot	8 some meat
5 some mushrooms	9 some cheese

Extra support

Pause the tape/CD after each ingredient to give SS time to write it down.

🔊 **7.2**   CD3 Track 8

(tapescript in Student's Book on *p.119*.)
B = Bob, A = audience, Be = Belinda, C = Colin
B Good evening. My name's Bob, and welcome to another edition of... *Can men cook?*
A Yes, they can!
B Well, Belinda, who's our first guest tonight?
BE This is Colin Davidson and he's from Bristol!
B Hello, Colin! What can you cook?
C Hello, Bob. My speciality is spaghetti bolognese.
B And what do you need to make it, Colin?
C Well, for four people you need some spaghetti. About half a kilo, Bob. And then for the bolognese sauce you need an onion, some butter, a carrot, some mushrooms, some tomato ketchup...
B Tomato ketchup, Colin?
C Yes, that's right, and you also need some red wine.
B Do you need any meat, Colin?
C Yes, Bob. You need some meat – about 300 grams. And some cheese.

B What kind of cheese?
C Any kind. It doesn't matter.
B OK. So those are all the ingredients. The question now is – Can men cook?
A Yes, they can!
B Colin, you have exactly 30 minutes to make us... spaghetti bolognese!
C Well, Bob, first you cut up the onion and you fry it. Then you take the...
B OK, Colin. That's your thirty minutes. And now it's time to taste the spaghetti bolognese. And it looks... mm, delicious. Belinda, can you try it for us? Well, Belinda, what do you think of it? Can men cook?
BE Mmm. Yes, Colin, it's er very interesting. I'm sure your wife loves your cooking.
C I'm not married, Belinda. Would you like to have dinner with me?
B Well, that's all we have time for. Until next week. It's goodbye from me Bob Keen, Belinda Leyton, and Colin Davidson from Bristol.

c • Play the tape / CD again for SS to check their answers. Ask if Belinda likes Colin's spaghetti bolognese (not really).

Extra support

Get SS to listen to the tape/CD for a final time with the tapescript on *p. 119* so they can see exactly what was said and see how much they understood. Translate/explain any new words or phrases.

d • If SS are all the same nationality, they can either all write the ingredients for the same dish (as they may well not agree), or choose different dishes. In pairs they list the ingredients. Get feedback and see whether SS agree, writing the name(s) of the dish and the ingredients on the board. Try to establish a 'definitive' list.

• If your SS are from different countries, put SS from the same country in pairs if possible. If not, they can work individually. Get them to write the ingredients for a dish from their country and then compare with other SS. Find out if they would they like to eat each other's dishes or not.

Extra photocopiable activities

Grammar
countable/uncountable nouns p. 164.
Communicative
Food families *p. 209* (instructions *p.181*).

HOMEWORK

Study Link Workbook *pp. 58–59*.

G *how much / how many?*, quantifiers: *a lot, not much,* etc.
V drinks: *water, wine,* etc.
P /w/, /v/, and /b/

How much water do we really need?

Lesson plan

This lesson continues the theme of diet and is based on the subject of how much water we need to drink every day. The text *Water – facts and myths* is based on several recent articles and studies and presents a controversial view which should provoke differing opinions in the class. The grammar builds on what SS learnt in the previous lesson, introducing different ways of talking and asking about quantity. SS have seen *much, many,* and *a lot of* previously in the book, so should be aware of their meaning, but have not focused on grammatical rules.

Optional lead-in (books closed)

- Write on the board SOFT DRINKS and ALCOHOLIC DRINKS. Elicit ideas from SS and write them up. Model and drill pronunciation.
- Ask SS if the words are countable or uncountable, and elicit that drinks words are generally uncountable (unless you mean *a glass of, a bottle of, a cup of,* etc.).
- Ask SS *What's your favourite drink?*

1 PRONUNCIATION /w/, /v/, and /b/

a (7.3)

- Focus on the three sound pictures and play the tape/CD for SS to repeat the words and sounds. Make sure SS can hear the difference between them, and show them the position of the lips/teeth to distinguish between /b/ and /v/.

7.3		CD3 Track 9
witch	/w/	water
vase	/v/	vodka
bag	/b/	beer

Pronunciation notes

- These three sounds can cause some nationalities difficulties because of LI interference. The rules are quite clear. See **Sound Bank** *p. 159.*

b (7.4)

- Now focus on the cartoon and dialogue. Play the tape/CD once and get SS to listen and read the dialogue. Then get SS to practise it in pairs.
- Monitor, helping and correcting. Finally, get one pair to 'perform' the dialogue for the rest of the class.

7.4	CD3 Track 10
V	Would you like a beer, Bill?
B	No, thanks, Vicky. A whisky and water.
V	Do you want some biscuits or a sandwich?
B	A sandwich.
V	Brown bread or white bread?
B	Brown bread. It's very good for you.

2 SPEAKING

a • Focus on the introduction to the questionnaire. Read it out loud, and ask SS if they think it's true that we need to drink lots of water. Then focus on the illustrations and use them to pre-teach *tap (water)* and revise *mineral water.*

b • Go through the questions and possible answers. Then get the class to interview you first. Answer the questions, giving a bit of extra information where you can as a model for the SS.

- SS interview each other in pairs. Get some quick feedback from the class for each question and find out how many SS think they need to drink more water.

3 GRAMMAR *how much / how many?*, quantifiers

a • Focus on the questions and elicit the answers from the class.

1 How many	2 How much

b • Now focus on the sentences and pictures, and get SS to match them. Check answers.

1 A	2 D	3 C	4 B

- Highlight that *much* and *many* are used with the negative verb. Ask SS what they think would change in sentence 2 if instead of *water,* it said *glasses of water,* and elicit that *much* would change to *many.*

c • Tell SS to go to **Grammar Bank 7B** on *p. 134.* Go through the rules with the class. Model and drill the example sentences. Highlight the pronunciation of *none* /nʌn/.

Grammar notes

a lot of

- In ⊕ sentences native speakers normally use *a lot of* for big quantities. It is also possible to use *a lot of* in negatives and questions, although it is more common to use *much / many.*
- We use *a lot* (NOT ~~a lot of~~) in short answers or when we don't give the noun, e.g. *I eat a lot of chocolate* but *I eat a lot.*
- In colloquial English people often use *lots of* as an alternative to *a lot of.* At this level it is best just to teach SS one form (*a lot of*).

much / many

- *Much* and *many* are used mainly in negative sentences and questions. *Many* is also sometimes used in ⊕ sentences in formal English, e.g. *Many people live in houses in the UK.* However *much* is not normally used in ⊕ sentences, e.g.
  NOT ~~British people drink much tea.~~
- Tell SS to think of *much* as singular and *many* as plural to help them to remember which one to use.

- Focus on the exercises for **7B** on *p. 135*. SS do the exercises individually or in pairs.
- Check answers, getting SS to read the full sentences.

> **a** 1 How many
> 2 How much
> 3 How much
> 4 How many
> 5 How many
> 6 How much
> 7 How many
> 8 How much
> **b** 1 a lot of
> 2 much
> 3 many
> 4 None
> 5 quite a lot of
> 6 Not much

- Tell SS to go back to the main lesson on *p. 79*.

d • Focus on the questions and the short answers (*a lot, quite a lot*, etc.) and get SS to complete the questions.
- Check answers by getting SS to ask you the questions. Use a short answer, and then add a bit more information where possible. You may want to teach a few words for containers, e.g. (*half*) *a bottle, a can, a carton.*

> 1 How many
> 2 How much
> 3 How many
> 4 How many
> 5 How much
> 6 How much
> 7 How much
> 8 How much

e • SS ask and answer in pairs.

Extra challenge

Have As asking the questions with books open and Bs answering with books closed, to encourage them to remember the short answers.

4 READING

a • Tell SS not to look at the article yet and go through the questions to make sure they understand them. Highlight the meaning of *too much* (= more than what is good for you). SS, in pairs, try to answer some of the questions.

⚠ Encourage SS to try to communicate their answers in English but not to worry too much about being accurate, as they may want to say more than they can express correctly.

Extra support

Ask the questions to the whole class, rather than having SS work in pairs, and help them to express their answers.

b • Now focus on the article, and instructions. Let SS take their time to read and match the questions, as this is probably the most challenging reading they've done so far.

Extra support

Get SS to go through the text together and do the task in pairs.

- Get SS to compare with a partner before checking answers. Get SS to write the questions in the spaces, as it will then make the article easier to re-read.

> B 5   C 2   D 4   E 6   F 3

c • SS read the text again and match the highlighted words to the phrases. Tell them also to underline any other words they're not sure of.

- Check answers and model and drill the pronunciation.

> 1 temperature /'temprɪtʃə/
> 2 sweat /swet/
> 3 experiments
> 4 recently
> 5 myths /mɪθs/
> 6 at least
> 7 contain
> 8 In fact

- Go through any other words or phrases that SS don't understand, either translating into SS' L1 if you prefer, or getting SS to check in their dictionaries.

d • Get SS to cover the text and look back at the questions. In pairs they should try to answer them from memory, i.e. say anything they can remember from the answers.

e • Do this as an open class question, and stress that this article is based on some doctors' theories. Some SS (and 'experts') may not agree with the answers to questions B and E.

Extra photocopiable activities

Grammar
how much/how many p. 165.
Communicative
Food questionnaire *p. 210* (instructions *p.182*).

HOMEWORK

Study Link Workbook *pp. 60–61.*

G *be going to* (plans)
V holidays *camping, the sights,* etc.
P sentence stress

7C Changing holidays

Lesson plan

This lesson is inspired by an episode of the BBC TV programme called *Holiday Swaps*, where two couples or families plan a holiday, which is then 'swapped' at the last minute with another couple's holiday. This provides a context for practising *going to* for future plans. The lesson is predominantly listening-based as SS follow the different stages of the programme.

Going to is the main future form taught in this level. *Going to* for predictions is practised in the next lesson. *Will* is introduced (in Practical English 8) but is not taught as a grammar point until *New English File Pre-intermediate*.

Optional lead-in (books closed)

- Copy the following onto the board:

  A HOLIDAY

How to get there	Where to stay	What to do
by car	in a friend's house	relax

- Get SS to copy this, and then in pairs SS write two more things in each column.
- Get feedback and write SS' answers under each heading.

  ⚠ Make sure you elicit/pre-teach *campsite* during this activity as SS will need this later.

(Possible answers)		
How to get there	**Where to stay**	**What to do**
by plane	in a hotel	go to the beach
		go shopping
by bus	at a campsite	do sport
		go for walks
by train	in a Youth Hostel	go to museums

1 READING

a ● Books open. Focus on the TV magazine extract and the photo. Give SS two minutes to read it. Then ask comprehension questions to check they understand how the programme works, e.g. *What's a couple?* (two people). *What do the couples plan?* (they plan a holiday). *What happens next?* (the programme chooses two couples and they exchange holidays). *Who are the two couples on tonight's programme?* (Lisa and Jon, Jerry and Sue).

2 GRAMMAR *be going to* (plans)

a 🔊 **7.5**

- Tell SS that the programme has chosen two couples, and now they're going to phone them. Get SS to cover the dialogue.
- Play the tape/CD once. Tell the whole class to listen to find out as much as they can about Lisa and Jon's holiday plans.
- Check their understanding by asking some comprehension questions, e.g. *Where are they going to go?* (New York). *How are they going to go?* (fly/by

plane). *Where are they going to stay?* (in a hotel – the Hotel Athena). *What are they going to do?* (go shopping, go clubbing, see a show, see the Statue of Liberty, Central Park, etc.).

b ● Now focus on the dialogue. Give SS time to read it through, and ask them what kind of words they think are missing (verbs). Then play the tape/CD once or twice for SS to fill in the missing words.

Extra support

Pause after each gap to give SS time to write.

- Check answers (see tapescript below). Elicit the meaning of *see the sights* (= visit the famous tourist places) and deal with any other new words or expressions.

🔊 7.5   CD3 Track 11

L = Lisa, P = Peter
L   Hello?
P   Hi! Lisa? This is Peter Douglas from *Changing Holidays*.
L   Oh! Hello!
P   Lisa, what are your holiday plans for next week?
L   Er… <u>I'm going to **fly**</u> to New York with my boyfriend, Jon.
P   Great. And where <u>are you going to **stay**</u>?
L   <u>We're going to **stay**</u> in the Hotel Athena in Manhattan.
P   What <u>are you going to **do**</u> in New York, Lisa?
L   <u>We're going to **go shopping**</u> – the shops in New York are fantastic – and in the evening we're going to **go** clubbing and **see** a show on Broadway.
P   <u>Are you going to **see**</u> the sights too?
L   Oh yes, we want to see the Empire State Building, the Statue of Liberty, Central Park…
P   Well, Lisa, say goodbye to New York. Because <u>we're going to **change**</u> your holiday!
L   Jon!! Jon!! We're going to be on TV.

Extra idea

Get SS to read the dialogue aloud in pairs.

c ● Tell SS to underline the examples of *going to* and to answer the questions in pairs. Stress that they should underline the whole expression (i.e. *I'm going to go*). Check answers (see tapescript above).

> 1 infinitive (e.g. *go, stay*)
> 2 the future

d ● Tell SS to go to **Grammar Bank 7C** on *p. 134*. Go through the rules with the class. Model and drill the example sentences, getting SS to copy the rhythm (I'm <u>going</u> to <u>have</u> a <u>ho</u>liday, Are you <u>going</u> to <u>have</u> a <u>ho</u>liday?, etc.).

Grammar notes

- *going to* + infinitive is the most common way to express future plans. It is often used with time expressions like *tonight*, *next week*. SS don't usually find the concept of *going to* a problem but the form needs plenty of practice. A typical error is the omission of the auxiliary *be*, i.e. *I going to have dinner*.
- In song lyrics *going to* is sometimes spelt *gonna* because of the way it is pronounced (see pronunciation below). Discourage SS from using this in written English.
- Some SS may know *will* and may ask if this is the future too. Explain that both *going to* and *will* are used to talk about the future. In *New English File going to* is presented first, as it is the right form for talking about plans and predictions (practised in **7D**). SS see *will* in **Practical English 8**, for expressing promises and it is dealt with in detail in *New English File Pre-Intermediate*.

- Focus on the exercises for **7C** on *p. 135*. Get SS to do the exercises individually or in pairs.
- Check answers, getting SS to read the full sentences.

> **a 2** She's going to speak Italian.
> **3** She's going to stay in a hotel.
> **4** She's going to take (some / a lot of) photos.
> **5** She's going to eat spaghetti.
> **6** She's going to see the Colosseum.
> **b 1** is going to cook
> **2** I'm going to study
> **3** Are (you) going to buy
> **4** aren't going to fly
> **5** is your (brother) going to do
> **6** isn't going to have

- Tell SS to go back to the main lesson on *p. 80*.

e 7.6

- Now focus on the chart, and tell SS they're going to hear the TV presenter, Peter Douglas, phone the second couple, Jerry and Sue.
- First elicit the questions 1–5 (*Where are you going to go? Who are you going to go with? How are you going to get there? What are you going to do? Where are you going to stay?*) and write them on the board.
- ⚠ Leave the questions on the board for the pronunciation exercise which comes next.
- Tell SS they don't need to write sentences in the chart, just the name of the place, the person, etc. Play the tape/CD. Get SS to compare with a partner and then play the tape/CD again. Check answers.

> **1** To Norway
> **2** Sue, his girlfriend
> **3** By train
> **4** clean a river, plant trees
> **5** at a campsite

> **7.6**   CD3 Track 12
> (tapescript in Student's Book on *p.119*.)
> **J = Jerry, P = Peter**
> J   Hello?
> P   Hello! Is that Jerry Harte?
> J   Speaking.

> P   This is Peter Douglas from the programme *Changing Holidays*.
> J   Oh, hello!
> P   Is your holiday planned for next week, Jerry?
> J   Yes, it is.
> P   **Where are you going to go?**
> J   We're going to go to Norway.
> P   **Who are you going to go with?**
> J   With Sue, my girlfriend.
> P   **How are you going to get there?**
> J   By train.
> P   **What are you going to do there?**
> J   We're going to clean a river and plant some trees. It's a working holiday!
> P   Oh, very interesting. **Where are you going to stay?**
> J   We're going to stay at a campsite.
> P   Well, Jerry, you're not going to go camping, because you're not going to go to Norway. We're going to *change* your *holiday*!
> J   Oh, so where are we going to go?

3 PRONUNCIATION   sentence stress

Pronunciation notes

When native speakers speak quickly, they tend to pronounce *going to* as *gonna* /ˈɡɒnə/. Elementary SS are unlikely to speak that quickly, so it is better to teach them to get the stress and rhythm right, i.e. to say, e.g. I'm <u>going</u> to be <u>late</u>, rather than trying to get them to contract *going to* to *gonna*.

a 7.7

- Focus on the questions (which you should still have on the board) and play the tape/CD. Ask SS which words are stressed (see tapescript below) and underline them on the board.

> **7.7**   CD3 Track 13
> <u>Where</u> are you <u>going</u> to <u>go</u>?
> <u>Who</u> are you <u>going</u> to <u>go</u> with?
> <u>How</u> are you <u>going</u> to <u>get</u> there?
> <u>What</u> are you <u>going</u> to <u>do</u> there?
> <u>Where</u> are you <u>going</u> to <u>stay</u>?

- Play the tape/CD again, pausing after each question for SS to repeat.

b • Now pretend that you are Jerry, and get SS to ask you the questions. Answer with full answers, e.g. *We're going to go to Norway*, etc.
- SS roleplay the interview in pairs. Get them to swap roles.

Extra challenge

Rub questions 1–5 off the board so that SS have to produce them from memory.

4 LISTENING & READING

a 7.8

- Tell SS that this is the moment in the programme when the two couples are at the airport (see photo on p.80). Explain that Peter, the presenter is going to give both couples an envelope with their new destinations. Ask SS whether they think they are going to like their new holidays.

- To help SS remember who's who, write up on the board:

  Lisa and Jon   Jerry and Sue
  (Planned to go to   (Planned to go to
  New York)   Norway)

- Play the tape/CD twice, pausing each time after *I hate camping*. Elicit that Lisa and Jon are not very happy with their new holiday. Ask *why* (because they don't want to work and Lisa hates camping).
- Then say *What about Sue and Jerry?* Play the rest of the tape/CD once or twice and elicit that Sue and Jerry are not very happy either because Jerry doesn't like shopping and they don't have the right clothes.

7.8   CD3 Track 14

(tapescript in Student's Book on *p.119*.)
P = Peter, J = Jon, L = Lisa, S = Sue, Je = Jerry

P   Well, here we are at the airport with Lisa and Jon and Jerry and Sue. And this is the moment of truth. I've got two envelopes here, and now I'm going to give the two couples their *new* holiday plans! Are you ready to play 'Changing Holidays'?
ALL Yes.
P   OK, so now you can open the envelopes. Jon and Lisa first.
J   A working holiday in Norway.
L   Oh no!
P   Oh yes! You're going to help clean a river and plant some trees.
J   Oh great. Working all day!
L   Where are we going to stay?
P   You're going to stay at a campsite!
L   A campsite? Oh no, I hate camping!
P   And now Sue and Jerry.
S   Oh! A week in New York.
Je   New York?
P   That's right. You're going to spend a week in the Big Apple, shopping, going out, and seeing the sights! Do you like shopping, Jerry?
Je   Not much.
S   What are we going to wear? We don't have the right clothes for New York.

Extra support

Get SS to listen again to the whole conversation with the tapescript on *p. 119*.

b
- Ask SS *Do you think the two couples are going to have a good time?* and elicit ideas. Then tell them they're going to find out.
- Focus on the holiday diaries and the photos. Set a time limit for SS to read and get them to compare ideas with a partner.
- Check answers, and get SS to give reasons.

> **Lisa and Jon** are not very happy (the weather is terrible, it's cold and raining a lot, the people are different, they can't cook, etc.)
> **Jerry and Sue** are (quite) happy (they like the food and the 'sights', they went to a famous nightclub, etc.)

c **7.9**
- Tell SS that the holidays are over and the two couples are back in the UK, and they go back to the programme. Focus on the instructions and get SS to

predict how the couples are going to answer the questions.
- Play the tape/CD once. SS compare in pairs. Play the tape/CD again if necessary. Check answers.

> Lisa and Jon didn't have a good time. Next year they're going to go to New York.
> Jerry and Sue had a good time.
> Next year they're going to go to another city, maybe Amsterdam or Barcelona.

d
- Focus on the exercise and play the tape/CD again. Check answers. Say, e.g. *Did Lisa and Jon like the work?* and elicit *No, they didn't*, etc.

Lisa and Jon		Jerry and Sue	
the work	✗	the hotel	✗
camping	✗	the sights	✓
the people	✓	the people	✓
the weather	✗	the food	✓
going to bed early	✗	the nightlife	✓

7.9   CD3 Track 15

(tapescript in Student's Book on *p.119*.)

P   OK, so it's hello again to our two couples from last week, Lisa and Jon, and Sue and Jerry. Welcome back. So what we all want to know is, did you have a good time? Jon and Lisa, what about you?
J   No, we didn't have a good time. It wasn't a holiday. I mean, we worked every day.
L   And it was hard work. That's not my idea of a holiday.
J   And we hated camping!
L   The people were very nice but…
J   It rained every day. We went to bed at 10.00 every night – not exactly exciting!
L   The thing is, what we really like is shopping, nightlife, big cities – and if that's what you want, Norway's not the place to go.
P   OK, OK. What about Sue and Jerry. Did you have a good time?
S   Well, we don't usually like big cities. But New York is special!
JE Yeah. The hotel wasn't very good – it was very big and impersonal. But we liked all the tourist sights – the Guggenheim was fantastic.
S   And the people were great, and we loved the food.
JE Yeah, we even liked the nightclub! We usually go to bed early, we're not really 'night' people, but the New York nightlife is great.
P   So where are you going to go next summer? Lisa and Jon?
L   Next summer we're really going to go to New York!
P   And Jerry and Sue?
S   We really liked New York. Next year we're going to go to another city, maybe Amsterdam or Barcelona!

Extra support

Get SS to listen to the tape/CD for a final time with the tapescript on *p. 119* so they can see exactly what was said and see how much they understood. Translate/explain any new words or phrases.

- Ask the whole class which holiday they would prefer and see which SS are more adventurous!

5 SPEAKING

a • Focus on the instructions and the example language in the speech bubbles. Tell SS that they are going to plan each part in pairs, beginning with **A** asking **B** *Where are we going to go?*, etc.

• Put SS in pairs, and give them about five minutes to make their plans for each of the four questions. Monitor and help, encouraging them to use *Why don't we…?* for making suggestions.

Extra idea

If your SS have been doing the *Practical English* lessons they will also know *What about…?* and *Let's….* Remind them of these expressions and write them on the board.

b • Now give each pair a piece of paper and tell them to write down their plans. Then collect them in.

c • Now give out a different plan to each pair and let them read them.

• Get one pair to come out to the front of the class. Act as TV presenter and interview them, using the prompts from **a**, e.g. *Where are you going to go?* Ask them if they are happy with their new holiday and why (not).

• Put each pair with another, and get them to interview each other about their new holidays. Ask each pair to tell the class what they're going to do, and if they're happy with their new holiday.

6 SONG *La Isla Bonita*

7.10

• Here SS listen to a song by Madonna about a summer holiday. If you want to do this song with your SS, there is a photocopiable activity on *p. 227*.

7.10   CD3 Track 16

Last night I dreamt of San Pedro
Just like I'd never gone, I knew the song
A young boy with eyes like the desert
It all seems like yesterday, not far away

Tropical the island breeze
All of nature wild and free
This is where I long to be
La isla bonita
And when the samba played
The sun would set so high
Ring through my ears and sting my eyes
Your Spanish lullaby

I fell in love with San Pedro
Warm wind carried on the sea, he called to me
'Te dijo te amo'

I prayed that the days would last
They went so fast

Tropical the island breeze, etc

I want to be where the sun warms the sky
When it's time for siesta you can watch them go by
Beautiful faces, no cares in this world
Where a girl loves a boy, and a boy loves a girl
Last night I dreamt of San Pedro
It all seems like yesterday, not far away

Tropical the island breeze, etc.

Extra photocopiable activities

Grammar
going to (plans) *p. 166.*
Communicative
What are you going to do? *p. 211* (instructions *p.182*).
Song
La Isla Bonita p. 227 (instructions *p.221*).

HOMEWORK

Study Link **Workbook** *pp. 62–63.*

G *be going to* (predictions)
V verb phrases: *be famous, get married*, etc.
P /ʊ/, /uː/, and /ʌ/

It's written in the cards

Lesson plan

This lesson continues with *going to*, but this time focuses on how the structure is used to express predictions (what we think or are sure is going to happen). The focus is on reading and speaking. SS read an original short story with a 'twist' about fortune telling, and then use the fortune teller's cards to tell each other's fortunes. The story is on tape/CD, so that SS can read and listen.

Optional lead-in (books closed)

- Revise *going to* for plans. Write the following prompts on the board:
  AFTER CLASS   TOMORROW NIGHT
  NEXT WEEKEND   NEXT SUMMER
- Get SS to ask you *What are you going to do…?* and the prompts.
- SS ask each other in pairs.

1 READING & LISTENING

a • Books open. Focus on the cards and ask SS what they think they are for. Elicit/tell them they are for fortune telling, i.e. predicting the future.

- In pairs, SS match the cards and verb phrases. Check answers, and model and drill pronunciation.

A be <u>lucky</u>	F meet <u>some</u>body new
B get <u>married</u>	G have a sur<u>prise</u>
C <u>tra</u>vel	H move house
D get a lot of <u>money</u>	I get a new job
E fall in love	J be <u>fa</u>mous

- Get SS to test each other's memory by covering the phrases and pointing at the cards.

b **7.11**

- Focus on the title of the story and help SS to explain/translate it. Then get them to cover all the text except paragraph 1. Tell SS that they are going to read and listen at the same time. Play the tape/CD for SS to listen to the first paragraph.

> **7.11**   CD3 Track 17
>
> **It's written in the cards**
> 'Come in,' said a voice. Jane Ross opened the door and went into a small room. There was a man sitting behind a table.
> 'Good afternoon,' said Jane. 'I want to see Madame Yolanda, the fortune teller.'
> 'Madame Yolanda isn't here today,' said the man. 'But don't worry. I'm going to tell you about your future. What questions do you want to ask?' Jane looked at the fortune teller. She couldn't see him very well because the room was very dark.

- Focus on questions 1–3. Get SS to answer them in pairs and then check answers. Elicit/teach the meaning of any words you think SS may not have understood, e.g. *a voice*.

> 1 Madame Yolanda, the fortune teller.
> 2 A man. Because Madame Yolanda isn't there.
> 3 Because the room is dark.

⚠ Although the story is in the past, it is more natural to ask and answer questions about it in the present.

7.12

- SS now uncover paragraph 2 and read and listen.

> **7.12**   CD3 Track 18
>
> 'Well,' she said, 'I have a problem with my boyfriend. We argue all the time. I don't think he loves me. I want to know if we're going to stay together.'
> 'Please choose five cards, but don't look at them.'
> Jane took five cards. The fortune teller put them on the table face down. He turned over the first card.
> 'Ah, this is a good card. This means you're going to be very lucky.'
> 'But am I going to stay with my boyfriend?' Jane asked.
> 'Maybe,' said the fortune teller. 'We need to look at the other cards first.'

- Focus on questions 4–6. Get SS to answer them in pairs and then check answers. Elicit/teach the meaning of any words you think SS may not have understood, e.g. *face down, turn over*.

> 4 She and her boyfriend always argue. She thinks he doesn't love her.
> 5 Five.
> 6 A She's going to be lucky.

7.13

- SS uncover paragraph 3 and read and listen.

> **7.13**   CD3 Track 19
>
> He turned over the second card.
> 'Mmm, a house. A new house. You're going to move, very soon, to another country.'
> 'But my boyfriend works here. He can't move to another country.'
> 'Let's look at the next card,' said the fortune teller. He turned over the third card.
> 'A heart. You're going to fall in love.'
> 'Who with?' asked Jane.
> 'Let me concentrate. I can see a tall man. He's very attractive.'
> 'Oh, that's Jim,' said Jane.
> 'Who's Jim? Your boyfriend?'
> 'No. Jim's a man I met at a party last month. He's an actor, and he says he's in love with me. It was his idea for me to come to Madame Yolanda.'
> 'Well, the card says that you're going to fall in love with him.'
> 'Are you sure?' asked Jane. 'But what about my boyfriend?'
> 'Let's look at the fourth card,' said the fortune teller.

- Focus on questions 7–10. Get SS to answer them in pairs and then check answers. Then elicit ideas for question 11.

> 7 H She's going to move house, to another country.
> 8 Because her boyfriend can't move to another country.
> 9 E She's going to fall in love.
> 10 An actor. She met him at a party.
> 11 A matter of opinion.

7.14

- SS uncover paragraph 4 and read and listen.

> **7.14**   CD3 Track 20
>
> The fortune teller turned over a card with two rings. 'Now I can see everything clearly. You are going to leave your boyfriend and go away with the other man, to another country. You are going to get married.'
> 'Married? But am I going to be happy with him?'
> 'You're going to be very happy.'
> Jane looked at her watch. 'Oh no, look at the time. I'm going to be late.'
> She stood up, left a £50 note on the table, and ran out of the room.

- Focus on questions 12–14. Get SS to answer them in pairs and then check answers. Elicit/teach the meaning of any words you think SS may not have understood, e.g. *ring*, *note*.

> 12 B She and Jim are going to get married.
> 13 Because she's going to be late.
> 14 £50

7.15

- SS uncover the last paragraph and read and listen.

> **7.15**   CD3 Track 21
>
> The fortune teller stood up. He turned on the light. At that moment an old woman came in. 'So, what happened?' she asked.
> 'She believed everything,' said Jim. 'I told you, I'm a very good actor!'
> He gave the woman £100.
> 'That's Jane's £50 and another £50 from me. Thanks very much, Madame Yolanda.'
> Madame Yolanda took the money. The fifth card was still on the table, face down. She turned it over. It was the ship. She looked at it for four or five seconds and then she said:
> 'Young man! Don't travel with that girl – you're going to…'
> But the room was empty.

- Let SS read the last paragraph again. Focus on questions 15–17. Get SS to answer them in pairs and then check answers.

> 15 Jim (the actor Jane had met).
> 16 Because she has helped him.
> 17 C (the travel card) – Accept any reasonable predictions – we assume they are going to have an accident of some sort.

Extra ideas

If SS have enjoyed the story and want to get more pronunciation practice, they could read it aloud in pairs.

Alternatively, you could give them extra listening practice by getting them to close their books and listen to the whole story on tape/CD.

You could also ask SS if anyone has ever been to a fortune teller, and to tell the class about it. They don't really have the language to do this accurately, but they could try to communicate what happened.

2 GRAMMAR   *be going to* (predictions)

a • Focus on the two sentences and make sure SS understand *a prediction* (= something you think is going to happen). SS answer the question in pairs. Check answers.

> **1** is a prediction   **2** is a plan

b • Tell SS to go to **Grammar Bank 7D** on *p. 134*. Model and drill the example sentences.

Grammar notes

> - SS learnt the use of *going to* to express future plans in the previous lesson. Here it is used to make predictions (what we think or are sure will happen). *Will* can also be used to make predictions. This is presented in *New English File Pre-intermediate*.

- Focus on the exercises for **7D** on *p. 135*. SS do the exercises individually or in pairs.
- Check answers, getting SS to read out the full sentences.

> **a 1** It's going to rain.
>   **2** She's going to have a baby.
>   **3** He's going to have an accident.
>   **4** They're going to play tennis.
> **b 1** 're going to win
>   **2** isn't going to pass
>   **3** 's going to be
>   **4** 're going to have
>   **5** 're going to break
>   **6** 's going to wake up

Study Link   SS can find an end-of-File grammar quiz on the MultiROM, and more grammar activities on the *New English File Elementary* website.

- Tell SS to go back to the main lesson on *p. 83*.

3 PRONUNCIATION   /ʊ/, /uː/, and /ʌ/

a • Focus on the three sound pictures and elicit the words and sounds (*bull*, /ʊ/, *boot* /uː/, *up* /ʌ/). Make sure they can hear the difference between the short /ʊ/ and long /uː/.

- Now focus on the first word in the list, *good*, and elicit that it's like *bull*. Then get SS to continue in pairs. Encourage them to say the words out loud to help them decide what the sound is.

b   **7.16**

- Play the tape/CD for SS to listen and check. Check answers (see tapescript). Then play it again, pausing after each word or group of words for SS to repeat.

7.16	CD3 Track 22
bull	good, look, put, couldn't, woman
boot	move, argue, you, new, soon
up	love, lucky, money, young, but

c • Tell SS to go the **Sound Bank** on *p. 157*. Go through the typical and less common spellings for each sound.
  • Tell SS to go back to the main lesson on *p. 83*.

4 SPEAKING

  • Go through the instructions with SS and focus on the example in the speech bubble. Highlight the use of *maybe* to express a possibility. Then put them in pairs, and get them to sit face to face.
  • SS individually number the cards 1–10. Stress that it should be in random order. Number the cards yourself too.
  • Demonstrate the activity. Get a student to tell you a number and 'tell his/her fortune', depending on the card he/she has chosen.
  • Tell SS to choose five numbers between 1 and 10, and write them on a piece of paper and give them to their partner. They then tell each other's fortunes.
  A If you have odd numbers, have a group of three, where A tells B's fortune, B tells C's, and C tells A's.
  • Get feedback, by asking a few SS what's going to happen to them.

Extra photocopiable activities

Grammar
be going to (predictions) *p. 167*.
Communicative
Pronunciation bingo *p. 212* (instructions *p.182*).

HOMEWORK

Study Link **Workbook** *pp. 64–65*.

Vocabulary a menu: *main course, dessert*, etc.
Function ordering a meal
Language *I'd like the onion soup.*

Lesson plans

In this lesson SS learn the language of menus and practise ordering a meal in a restaurant. In the story, Mark and Allie order their meal, but after they've had their main course, Mark tries to tell Allie something, but keeps getting interrupted by the waiter. Finally, he manages to ask her if she would like to come to a conference in the USA. Allie says she needs time to think.

Study Link These lessons are also on the *New English File Elementary* Video, which can be used **instead of** the Class Cassette / CD (see introduction *p.9*).
The first section of the Video is also on the MultiROM, with additional activities.

VOCABULARY a menu

a • Focus on the menu and give SS in pairs a few moments to fill the gaps. Check answers and model and drill the pronunciation of the words.

> Starters   Main courses   Desserts

b • Focus on the highlighted words and give SS in pairs a few minutes to try to work out what they think they mean.
  • Check answers, either by giving examples, translating into SS' L1 if you prefer, or getting SS to check in their dictionaries.

c • Get SS to cover the menu. Ask *What starters were there?* In pairs, see how many of the dishes they can remember. Repeat for the other courses then feedback asking the class to say what was on the menu.

ORDERING A MEAL

a 7.17
  • Focus on the picture and ask SS *Where are Allie and Mark?* (at the restaurant). *What are they doing?* (looking at the menu/ordering).
  • Now either tell SS to close their books or get SS to cover the conversation. Tell SS to listen to find out what Allie and Mark order.
  • Play the tape/CD once or twice. Check answers. Ask *What's Mark having for a starter?*, etc.

> Mark: onion soup and steak; red wine.
> Allie: goat's cheese salad and lasagne; mineral water.

b • Now focus on the conversation and the gaps. Give SS a minute to read through the dialogue and predict the missing words. Then play the tape/CD again once or twice as necessary.
  • Get SS to compare answers in pairs. Check answers.

7.17   CD3 Track 23

W = waiter, A = Allie, M = Mark
W Good **evening**. Do you have a reservation?
A Yes, a table for two. My name's Allie Gray.
W **Smoking** or non-smoking?
A Non-smoking, please.
W Come this **way**, please.

W Are you **ready** to order?
M Yes, I'd like the onion soup and then the steak, please.
A The goat's cheese salad and the lasagne for me, please.
W What would you like to **drink**?
M Would you like some wine?
A No, thanks. Just mineral water for me.
M OK. A glass of red wine and a bottle of mineral water, please.
W Thank you, sir.
M Thank you.

---

c 7.18
  • Now focus on the **YOU SAY** phrases. Highlight the two ways of ordering, e.g. *I'd like* (I would like) *the onion soup* or *The onion soup for me, please*.
  • Tell SS they're going to hear the dialogue again. They repeat the **YOU SAY** phrases when they hear the beep. Encourage them to copy the rhythm and intonation.
  • Play the tape/CD, pausing if necessary for SS to repeat the phrases.

7.18   CD3 Track 24

W Good evening. Do you have a reservation?
A Yes, a table for two. My name's Allie Gray.
repeat
W Smoking or non-smoking?
A Non-smoking, please.
repeat
W Come this way, please.
W Are you ready to order?
M Yes, I'd like the onion soup and then the steak, please.
repeat
A The goat's cheese salad and the lasagne for me, please.
repeat
W What would you like to drink?
M Would you like some wine?
repeat
A No, thanks. Just mineral water for me.
repeat
M OK. A glass of red wine and a bottle of mineral water, please.
repeat
W Thank you, sir.
M Thank you.
repeat

---

d • Put SS in groups of three, and choose a good student to be the 'waiter' for each group. Any extra SS can be customers.

Extra support

Get SS to read the dialogue through once or twice before roleplaying.

- If your classroom permits, get the 'customers' to stand up and come up to their 'waiter', who will show them to a table. Then tell the 'customers' to decide what they want from the menu.
- After a few minutes tell the waiters to go to the tables, and begin the conversation with *Are you ready to order?*

Extra challenge

Get the waiter to come back for SS to order desserts and coffee as well.

3 SOCIAL ENGLISH

a **7.19**

- Focus on the four questions. Play the tape/CD. Pause each time Mark tries to ask Allie his question (see * in the tapescript) and ask SS *What's he going to say?* to build up the suspense, and for SS to get the humour of the constant interruptions.
- Give SS time to compare answers before playing the tape/CD again. Check answers.

> 1 Allie fruit salad, Mark two espressos
> 2 To come to a conference in California
> 3 She's not sure – she needs time to think
> 4 Could we have the bill, please?

> **7.19**   CD3 Track 25
>
> (tapescript in Student's Book on *p.120*.)
> M How was the pasta?
> A It was delicious.
> M Listen, Allie. There's something I want to ask you.
> A Yes? What? *
> W Would you like a dessert?
> A Yes, please. What is there?
> W Tiramisu, ice cream, or fruit salad.
> A Fruit salad, please.
> W And you, sir?
> M Nothing for me, thanks. Allie?
> A Yes. Go on, Mark.
> M Well, tomorrow's my last day. And I think we… I mean, I really liked meeting you and… *
> W Here you are. Fruit salad. Would you like any coffee?
> A Yes, an espresso, please.
> M The same for me, please.
> A Sorry, Mark.
> M Do you want to come to California next month? There's a big conference. I'm going to be there. Why don't you come? What do you think?
> W Two espressos. Anything else? A little brandy? A grappa?
> M No, thank you. What do you say, Allie?
> A I'm not sure, Mark. I need some time to think about it, OK?
> M All right. But please tell me before I go.
> A OK.
> M Could we have the check, please?
> W Sorry? The check?
> A The bill, Mark. We're in Britain, remember?
> M Sorry. Could we have the bill, please?
> W Yes, sir.

b
- Ask the questions to the class. Elicit SS's ideas.

c
- Focus on the **USEFUL PHRASES**. For each phrase ask SS *Who says it, Mark or Allie?* Then play the tape/CD for SS to check their answers.

- Play the tape/CD again for SS to check. Pause after each phrase and get SS to repeat it (see the tapescript above). In a monolingual class, tell them to decide together what the equivalent phrase is in their language.

> It was delicious. – Allie
> What is there? – Allie
> Nothing for me, thanks. – Mark
> The same for me, please – Mark
> I'm not sure. – Allie
> Could we have the bill, please? – Mark

Extra support

If time, you could get SS to listen to the tape/CD for a final time with the tapescript on *p. 120* so they can see exactly what Mark and Allie said and see how much they understood. Translate/explain any new words or phrases.

Extra challenge

Get SS in pairs to roleplay the second conversation using the tapescript on *p. 120*.

HOMEWORK

Study Link **Workbook** *p. 66*.

Lesson plan

Here SS recycle food vocabulary, quantifiers, and imperatives in the context of a very simple recipe for a sandwich.

a • Focus on the photos and get SS to match them to the ingredients in the recipe. Check answers.

> A some brown bread
> B some black pepper
> C some cream cheese
> D some smoked salmon
> E a lemon

b • Quickly mime *cut* and *put* and elicit which is which. Then get SS to complete the gaps in the recipe.

> **A** Highlight the different pronunciation /kʌt/ and /pʊt/.

• Check answers. Go through the recipe. Make sure SS understand *pieces* and *on top*.

> 1 cut
> 2 put
> 3 Put
> 4 Cut
> 5 Put
> 6 put

• Ask SS if they'd like to eat this sandwich and why (not).

Extra challenge

Get SS to cover the recipe and see if they can remember the seven steps.

Write instructions

Go through the task with SS. Stress the importance of checking writing after they've done it.

• Give SS at least fifteen minutes to write the recipe in class. They could do it in pairs, and use a dictionary for any ingredients they don't know the words for. Alternatively, set it for homework.

• If SS do the writing in class, get them to swap and read each others' recipes and correct any mistakes they find, before you collect them all in.

Extra ideas

Put the recipes up round the classroom and get SS to vote for the best one.

You could also encourage SS to write their recipes on computer, or present them neatly, so you can make a class sandwich recipe book.

For instructions on how to use these pages, see *p.28.*

What do you remember?

GRAMMAR

1 a   2 b   3 b   4 a   5 b   6 a   7 b   8 a   9 b   10 a

VOCABULARY

a 1 stay
2 see
3 get
4 meet
5 move

b 1 dessert (not a meal)
2 strawberries (not vegetables)
3 sugar (not a drink)
4 tomatoes (not connected with potatoes)
5 coffee (not a dessert)

c 1 in
2 of
3 for
4 with
5 on

PRONUNCIATION

a 1 steak
2 tea
3 true
4 go
5 move

b des<u>s</u>ert
<u>m</u>enu
<u>v</u>egetables
ba<u>n</u>ana
<u>b</u>iscuit

What can you do?

CAN YOU UNDERSTAND THIS TEXT?

a 1 c 2 b 3 a 4 b

CAN YOU HEAR THE DIFFERENCE?

a 1 b 2 b 3 b 4 a 5 b

7.20   CD3 Track 26

1 **A** Is there any milk?
  B Yes, there's some in the fridge.
  A No, there isn't. I just looked.
  B Well, then go and get some. The supermarket's still open.
2 **A** How much coffee do you drink?
  B Quite a lot. Three or four cups a day.
  A That's not much! I drink six or seven.
3 **A** Where are you going to go on holiday?
  B Well, I wanted to go to Australia, but it's very expensive, so I'm going to go to Italy.
4 **A** What are we going to do tomorrow night?
  B I don't know. Are there any good films on at the cinema?
  A Not really. Why don't we try that new French restaurant?
  B That's a good idea.
5 **A** Do you think they're going to get married?
  B I don't know. Probably not. They're always arguing.
  A That's quite normal.

---

b 1 She buys oranges, strawberries and carrots.
   2 4.95

7.21   CD3 Track 27

G = greengrocer, C = customer
G Get your fresh fruit and vegetables here! Oh. Yes, love?
C Can I have three oranges, please?
G Help yourself. Anything else, love?
C Yes, do you have any grapes?
G Sorry, we haven't got any today. How about some strawberries? They're very cheap.
C How much are they?
G Five fifty a kilo.
C OK, half a kilo then. And half a kilo of carrots.
G Anything else, love? There are some nice tomatoes.
C No, thanks. How much is that?
G OK, let's see, that's two seventy-five for the strawberries, plus one for the carrots, and one twenty for the oranges. That's five ninety-five.
C Five ninety-five? Four ninety-five, you mean.
G Sorry love, you're right. Four ninety-five.
C Here you are.
G Here's your change. Thanks, love.

Extra photocopiable activities

Quicktest 7 *p.237.*

8 **G** comparative adjectives: *bigger, more dangerous,* etc.
V personality adjectives: *shy, generous,* etc.
P /ə/, sentence stress

A # The True False show

Lesson plan

In this lesson comparative adjectives are presented and practised in the context of a TV quiz show. One of the questions in the quiz refers to car colours, and at the end of the lesson SS listen to a psychologist talking about what your car colour says about your personality.

Optional lead-in (books closed)

- Revise adjectives by writing the following on the board:

tall   safe   good   cold   young
happy   expensive   clean   slow   poor

- Tell SS, in pairs, to write the opposites. Check answers.

> short   dangerous   bad   hot   old
> sad   cheap   dirty   fast   rich

1 SPEAKING & LISTENING

- Focus on the people and ask SS *What kind of programme do you think it is?* (a quiz show). Ask SS which programmes are popular in their country and which ones they like/don't like.

a • Now focus on the pictures and elicit from the class everything they can see. Write any new words, e.g. *mosquito, shark,* on the board, and model and drill pronunciation.

> a cat, a fish, a shark, brown and white eggs, Mars, a mosquito, the Earth, a tiger, a yellow and a white car

b • Focus on the sentences, and the first two comparatives, *more dangerous* and *healthier.* Elicit/teach that the sentences are comparing mosquitoes and sharks and brown and white eggs using the adjectives *dangerous* and *healthy.* Highlight that the *-er* ending in *healthier* means *more.* Get SS to read the sentences in pairs and decide whether they are true or false. **Don't check answers yet.**

c 8.1
- Play the tape/CD. Pause after the introduction (see * in the tapescript) and elicit how the quiz show works. (You have 10 seconds to say if each question is True or False. If you get the first question right, you win 10,000 euros. If you get the second question right, you win 20,000, etc. There are eight questions altogether. If you get a question wrong, you go home with nothing.)
- Now play the rest of the tape/CD, so SS can hear the show. Ask the question *What does Darren win?* and play it once the whole way through. (Darren doesn't win anything!)
- Then play it again, pausing after each answer. Check answers, and elicit any more information that SS heard.

> **1** T   **2** F   **3** T   **4** F   **5** T   **6** F   **7** F   **8** F

- Find out if any pair got all the answers right.

8.1 CD3 Track 28

(tapescript in Student's Book on *p.120*.)
P = presenter, D = Darren
P   Good evening. Welcome to *The True False Show.* Tonight's show comes from Dublin. My name's Annie O'Brian and I ask the questions. Remember, after each question you have ten seconds to say 'true' or 'false'. If you get the first answer right, you win 10,000 euros. If you get the second answer right, you win 20,000 euros, and you win 30,000 euros for the third correct answer. For eight correct answers you win 80,000 euros. But if you get an answer wrong, you go home with ... nothing.*
  Our first contestant is Darren from London. Right, Darren, for 10,000 euros. Mosquitoes are more dangerous than sharks. True or false?
D   Er, true.
P   Correct. Mosquitoes are more dangerous than sharks. More people die every year from mosquito bites than from shark attacks. Now, for 20,000 euros, brown eggs are healthier than white eggs. True or false?
D   Er... false.
P   Correct. It's false. Brown eggs *look* nicer than white ones, but they are exactly the same. For 30,000 euros, the Earth is hotter than Mars.
D   I think it's true, Annie.
P   Correct. The Earth is much hotter than Mars. Next, for 40,000 euros, coffee is more popular than tea in the UK. True or false?
D   Er, false.
P   Correct. British people drink 185 million cups of tea every day. Next, for 50,000 euros, tigers are better swimmers than cats. True or false?
D   Er... false. No – true.
P   Is that your answer?
D   Yes, true.
P   Correct. Tigers are very good swimmers. For 60,000 euros, an adult is shorter in the morning than in the evening.
D   Er... false.
P   Correct. Adults are one centimetre taller in the morning than in the evening. OK Darren, for 70,000 euros. White cars are safer than yellow cars. True or false?
D   Er, I'm sure that's false, Annie.
P   Correct. Yellow cars are safer – they are easier to see during the day, so they don't have as many accidents. And finally, the last question. Be very careful, Darren. If you get it right, you win 80,000 euros, but if you get it wrong, you lose everything. Are you ready?
D   Yes, ready.
P   OK, so for 80,000 euros. The word 'yes' is more common than the word 'no'. True or false?
D   Er... er...
P   Quickly Darren, time's running out.
D   True.
P   No, Darren. It's false. 'No' is more common than 'yes'. You had 70,000 euros, but now you go home with *nothing.*

Extra support

Get SS to listen to the tape/CD for a final time with the tapescript on *p. 120* so they can see exactly what was said and see how much they understood. Translate/explain any new words or phrases.

2 GRAMMAR comparative adjectives

a ● Focus on the instructions. Give SS two minutes to answer the questions in pairs. Check answers.

> 1 *-er*
> 2 because an extra *t* is also added
> 3 the y changes to *i* before the *-er*
> 4 *more*
> 5 *than*

b ● Tell SS to go to **Grammar Bank 8A** on *p. 136*. Go through the rules with the class. Model and drill the example sentences.

Grammar notes

- There are clear rules governing the formation of comparative adjectives.

⚠ To simplify the rules even further tell SS that for short adjectives (one syllable) add *-er*. For all the rest (two syllables or more) add *more* (except adjectives ending in *–y*).

- The spelling rules for *big, hot*, etc. are the same as for verbs ending in *-ing* (see *p.128*), e.g. *big, bigger*.
- Depending on your SS' L1, they may try to use *that* instead of *than* after comparative adjectives.

- Focus on the exercises for **8A** on *p. 137*. SS do the exercises individually or in pairs.
- Check answers. Get SS to spell the *-er* adjectives in **a** and write them on the board. In **b**, get them to read the full sentences.

> **a 1** shorter
> 2 more difficult
> 3 more beautiful
> 4 noisier
> 5 thinner
> 6 nearer
> 7 easier
> 8 richer
> **b 1** Canada is bigger than Brazil.
> 2 Tessa is prettier than Deborah.
> 3 Driving is more dangerous than flying.
> 4 My English is worse than your English.
> 5 This chair is more comfortable than that chair.
> 6 Her husband is younger than her.
> 7 Buses are cheaper than trains.
> 8 French wine is better than English wine.

- Tell SS to go back to the main lesson on *p. 89*.

3 PRONUNCIATION /ə/, sentence stress

a 〈8.2〉

- Focus on the comparative adjectives. Play the tape/CD once, pausing after each adjective for SS to underline the stressed syllable (it's always the first). Check answers, and elicit that the final *er* is always

pronounced /ə/, like *computer*, and is never stressed, e.g. ~~safer~~ NOT ~~safer~~.

- Play the tape/CD again, pausing for SS to repeat the adjectives.

〈8.2〉		CD3 Track 29
healthier	shorter	
hotter	safer	
better		

b 〈8.3〉

- Now get SS to look back at the quiz sentences in **1b**. Play the tape/CD for them to repeat, encouraging them to copy the rhythm. Highlight that *is/are* and *than* are **not** stressed.

〈8.3〉	CD3 Track 30
1 Mosquitoes are more dangerous than sharks.	
2 Brown eggs are healthier than white eggs.	
3 The Earth is hotter than Mars.	
4 Coffee is more popular than tea in the UK.	
5 Tigers are better swimmers than cats.	
6 An adult is shorter in the morning than in the evening.	
7 White cars are safer than yellow cars.	
8 The word 'yes' is more common than the word 'no'.	

c ● Put SS in pairs A and B and tell them to go to **Communication** *True False Show* A *p. 110*, B *p. 113*.

- Go through all the instructions with them. Then give SS five minutes to complete their sentences with comparative adjectives.
- Write the amounts of money that they win up on the board, e.g. 1–10,000 (euros, dollars, or a currency that your SS are familiar with), 2–20,000, 3–40,000, etc. (up to 80,000) and check SS can say the numbers correctly. Explain that if you get e.g. question 4 wrong, you lose all your money and start again, i.e. for question 5 you get 10,000, question 6 20,000, etc.
- Now get SS to sit face to face. A reads his/her sentences to B. Monitor and help SS to get the rhythm right when they read their quiz sentences.

Student A	Student B
1 faster	1 better
2 more expensive	2 safer
3 nearer	3 older
4 bigger	4 more intelligent
5 more common	5 smaller
6 worse	6 shorter
7 more dangerous	7 more popular
8 richer	8 longer

Extra support

You could do the above activity in groups of four instead of pairs. Divide class into groups of four and have two As and two Bs. They prepare their quiz sentences together, and take turns to read them to the other pair.

Extra challenge

Encourage A to 'play the role' of the presenter. Give SS a few minutes to look at the tapescript and make a note of any useful language (e.g. *Good evening, I ask the questions*).

- When both SS have played the game get feedback to see who won the most money.
- Tell SS to go back to the main lesson on *p. 89*.

4 VOCABULARY personality adjectives

- Focus on the adjectives in the box, and get SS in pairs to match the words to their meanings. Check answers and model and drill pronunciation.

> 2 careful
> 3 serious
> 4 quiet
> 5 generous
> 6 stylish
> 7 aggressive

- Get SS to cover the first half of the sentences (i.e. the adjectives) with a piece of paper and to remember the adjectives by reading the rest of the sentence (e.g. *a/an … person is open and kind*).
- Get SS to work in pairs and write down the comparative form of the seven adjectives. Check answers.

5 LISTENING

a
- Ask SS if they can remember from the quiz which cars are safer, white cars or yellow cars? (Yellow cars: both are good colours at night, but yellow cars are easier to see during the day.)
- Focus on the question. Tell them about your car, if you have one, and why you chose the colour.
- In a small class, ask all SS. In a big class get them to ask a partner and feedback a few answers.

b 8.4
- Focus on the chart. Tell SS they're going to hear the programme twice. The first time they should just write the colours in the chart in the order the speaker mentions them.
- Play the tape/CD once and let SS compare in pairs. **Don't check answers yet.**

Extra idea

You could keep back the last four lines of the conversation until the end of the activity so that SS can appreciate the doctor's reply to the last question more fully.

c
- Now tell SS to listen again and complete the missing adjectives (they are all ones they have just learnt in the previous **VOCABULARY** exercise). Play the tape/CD again.
- Get SS to compare with a partner, and then play the tape/CD again if necessary. Check answers. *Silver* may be a new word for many SS.

> 1 yellow – friendly
> 2 white – careful
> 3 red – aggressive
> 4 blue – quiet
> 5 green – generous
> 6 black – serious
> 7 silver – stylish

- Ask SS what colour Dr Baker's car is and what it says about him. (The interviewer suggests white, as he's a doctor, but in fact it's red which means he's aggressive.)

8.4 CD3 Track 31

(tapescript in Student's Book on *p.120*.)

P = presenter, A = Alan Baker

P Hello again. Today we talk to Dr Alan Baker, a psychologist, about car colour and personality. Good evening, Dr Baker.

A Good evening!

P So, what does the colour of our cars say about our personality?

A Well, let's start with yellow. People who drive yellow cars are usually very friendly. This colour is more popular with women than with men.

P And white?

A A white car shows that you are careful. It's the favourite colour car for doctors – they buy more white cars than any other colour.

P What about other colours?

A Well, let's take red. People who choose red cars are usually more aggressive drivers than normal. With blue cars, it's the opposite. If you have a blue car it means you are probably quiet.

P What about green?

A People with green cars are usually generous.

P And what about black?

A Well, people who like black cars are usually serious people. Business people often choose black cars.

P We've got time for one more colour. What about silver?

A Yes, well if you have a silver car it means you are stylish.

P Er, what colour is your car, Dr Baker? White?

A No, it's red, actually.

P Thank you very much, Dr Baker. And now we turn our attention…

Extra support

Get SS to listen to the tape/CD for a final time with the tapescript on *p. 120* so they can see exactly what was said and see how much they understood. Translate/explain any new words or phrases.

d
- Get SS to do this in pairs, and then get some feedback from the class.

Extra photocopiable activities

Grammar
comparative adjectives *p. 168*.
Communicative
Guess the comparative *p. 213* (instructions *p.183*).

HOMEWORK

Study Link Workbook *pp. 67–68*.

8 B

G superlative adjectives: *the biggest, the best,* etc.
V the weather, more common adjectives
P consonant groups

The highest city in the world

Lesson plan

In this lesson SS make the logical progression from comparatives to superlatives. The magazine article on which the lesson is based describes three 'extreme' places to live in, the highest city, the hottest country, and the coldest place. In the second half of the lesson SS do a superlative quiz (about world capitals) and talk about their own country.

Optional lead-in (books closed)

- Write on the board **Russia** and **China**. Ask SS if they are big or small countries, and elicit that they are big. Then ask which is bigger, and elicit that Russia is bigger. (For reference, Russia is about 17 million km², China about 9.6 million km²).
- Now rub **China** off the board. Ask SS if they know any country which is bigger than Russia (there isn't one). Elicit/teach *Russia is the biggest country in the world.* Write the sentence on the board.

1 READING

a • Books open. Focus on the photos and elicit ideas but don't tell SS the answers yet.

b • Now focus on the article and the three superlative phrases.
- Set a time limit, e.g. three minutes, for SS to read it, complete the headings, and match the places to the photos. Check answers.

> **The hottest** country in the world
> **The highest** capital city in the world
> **The coldest** place in the world

c • Focus on the instructions, and set another time limit, e.g. two minutes. Get SS to compare with a partner and check their answers.

> 2 La Paz
> 3 Mali
> 4 Siberia (Yakutia)
> 5 Siberia (Yakutia)
> 6 La Paz

Extra challenge

Get SS to answer the questions from memory and then read the article again to check.

d • Now tell SS to focus on the highlighted words and in pairs try to guess what they mean. Check answers, either drawing, miming, translating into SS' L1 if you prefer, using the glossary below, or getting SS to check in their dictionaries. Model and drill pronunciation.

cotton	a material, typical for, e.g. T-shirts
roof	the top part of a house
sea level	how high the sea is
breathe /briːð/	take in air
altitude	how high something is above sea level

hit	strike with your hand or a tool, e.g. hit a ball
freezer	place where you keep frozen food
nose	the part of your face that you use to breathe
snows	soft frozen water falls to the ground

e • Tell SS to choose five new words (or phrases) to learn from the text and write them in their vocabulary notebooks. Get them to compare the words they've chosen with a partner. Get some feedback of the words they've chosen.

2 GRAMMAR superlative adjectives

a • Focus on the chart and elicit the meaning of *the coldest* (= colder than all others). SS then complete the chart with more superlatives.
- Check answers. Model and drill pronunciation.

> the highest
> the hottest
> the most dangerous
> the best
> the worst

- Elicit/explain how superlatives are formed, e.g. for one-syllable adjectives add *-est* to the **end** of the adjective, for adjectives with two or more syllables, use *the most* **before** the adjective. Highlight that we use *the* before superlatives.
- Get SS to underline a sentence where each superlative occurs in the text.

b • Tell SS to go to **Grammar Bank 8B** on *p. 136*. Go through the rules with the class. Model and drill the example sentences.

Grammar notes

Superlatives
- Make sure SS are clear about the difference between comparatives (to compare two things or people, etc.) and superlatives (to say which is e.g. the smallest in a group of three or more). In your SS' L1 they may just use the comparative form + *the*. (Typical error: *the better place in the world …*)
- Formation of superlatives is very easy once SS know comparatives. *-er* changes to *-est* in short adjectives and *more* changes to *the most* before long adjectives.

Spelling rules
These are exactly the same as for comparatives, e.g. hotter/the hottest; prettier/the prettiest.

⚠ Use *in* the world, *in* the class, etc. after superlatives, NOT *of.*

- Focus on the exercises for **8B** on *p. 137*. SS do the exercises individually or in pairs.
- Check answers. Get SS to spell the *-est* adjectives in **a** where there's a spelling change and write them on the

board. In **b**, get them to read the full sentences, helping them with the rhythm.

a 1 the smallest
2 the highest
3 the most expensive
4 the oldest
5 the most difficult
6 the driest
7 the most beautiful/the prettiest
8 the poorest
b 1 the tallest
2 the oldest
3 the best
4 the hottest
5 the most famous
6 the worst
7 the most difficult
8 the prettiest

• Tell SS to go back to the main lesson on *p.91*.

3 PRONUNCIATION consonant groups

a 8.5
  • Focus on the chart and get SS to listen and repeat.

8.5		CD3 Track 32
cold	colder	the coldest
high	higher	the highest
hot	hotter	the hottest
dangerous	more dangerous	the most dangerous
good	better	the best
bad	worse	the worst

  • Get SS to cover the comparatives and superlatives in the chart and try to remember them.

b 8.6
  • Focus on the instructions and the superlatives. Play the tape/CD once for SS to listen. Then play it again pausing after each superlative for SS to repeat.

8.6	CD3 Track 33
the most expensive	
the most crowded	
the driest	
the coldest	
the most beautiful	
the smallest	
the fastest	
the strongest	

c • Focus on the World Capitals Quiz and the adjectives in brackets. Elicit/teach *crowded* (= full of people).

Extra idea

As the quiz is on capital cities, give SS a quick oral quiz first and revise countries by asking SS where each city is.

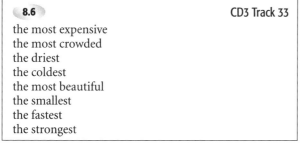

Tokyo – Japan
Madrid – Spain
Rome – Italy
Buenos Aires – Argentina
Mexico City – Mexico
Nairobi – Kenya
Lagos – Nigeria

Cairo – Egypt
London – England
Washington – the USA
Copenhagen – Denmark
Canberra – Australia
Oslo – Norway
Beijing – China
Bangkok – Thailand
New Delhi – India

• SS complete the questions with the correct superlative. Check answers.

1 the noisiest
2 the biggest
3 the driest
4 the most expensive
5 the safest
6 the most crowded

• Now get SS to take turns asking each other the questions. They should circle their partner's answer, and then say if they agree.
• Check answers to the quiz.

1 Tokyo
2 Tokyo
3 Cairo
4 Tokyo
5 Oslo
6 New Delhi

4 VOCABULARY the weather

a • Teach the question *What's the weather like?* Focus on the pictures and the sentences and give SS time to match them together. Check answers and model and drill pronunciation.

1 D **2** A **3** E **4** C **5** B

b • Do this as a whole class activity.

5 SPEAKING

  • Focus on the questions. If you are not from the same country as your SS, get them to interview you first, and see how much you know about your country.
  ⚠ Don't be afraid to say *I don't know but I think it's…* This will provide a good model for SS.
  • Get SS in pairs to ask and answer the questions. If they are from different countries they can interview each other. If they are from the same country, they should ask and answer the questions together to see if they both know/agree on the answers. They should note their answers after the questions.

Extra challenge

Tell SS not to write the superlatives but to produce them orally.

  • Get feedback. In a class where SS are from the same country, see if they agree, especially on the answers about tourism.

6 SONG *The Best*

8.7

- Here SS listen to one of Tina Turner's most famous songs, *The Best*. If you want to use this song with your SS there is a photocopiable activity on *p. 228*.

8.7   CD3 Track 34

I call you when I need you
And my heart's on fire
You come to me, come to me
Wild and wired
You come to me, give me everything I need

You bring a lifetime of promises
And a world of dreams
You speak the language of love
Like you know what it means
And it can't be wrong
Take my heart and make it strong

You're simply the best
Better than all the rest
Better than anyone
Anyone I ever met
I'm stuck on your heart
I hang on every word you say
Tear us apart
Baby I would rather be dead

In your heart
I see the start
Of every night and every day
And in your eyes I get lost
I get washed away
Just as long as I'm here in your arms
I could be in no better place

You're simply the best, etc.

Each time you leave me I start losing control
You're walking away with my heart and my soul
I can feel you even when I'm alone
Oh baby, don't go

Oh, you're the best, etc

Extra photocopiable activities

Grammar
superlative adjectives *p. 169.*

Communicative
What do you know about the UK? *p. 214* (instructions *p.183*).

Song
The Best p. 228 (instructions *p.221*).

HOMEWORK

Study Link **Workbook** *pp. 69–70.*

8 C

G *would like to* + infinitive / *like* + gerund
V adventures: *parachute jump*, etc.
P sentence stress

Would you like to drive a Ferrari?

Lesson plan

In the UK today many people, instead of traditional presents, give people 'adventure experiences' as gifts, e.g. spending a day learning to fly a plane or going up in a balloon. This lesson uses this context for SS to practise *would like to* (*do*) and contrast it with *like* (*doing*). First they read about different possible presents, discuss which ones they would like to do, and finish by listening to one person's experience of doing a parachute jump.

Optional lead-in (books closed)

- Revise verb phrases. Quickly write the following on the board:

1 ____ a car		5 ____ a meal
2 ____ a new language		6 ____ salsa
3 ____ a plane		7 ____ a song
4 ____ a motorbike/a horse		8 ____ money/time

- Give SS in pairs two minutes to write the verbs. Check answers.

1 drive	**5** cook / have
2 learn/study	**6** dance
3 fly	**7** sing
4 ride	**8** spend

1 READING & SPEAKING

a • Books open. Focus on the questions, and get SS to answer in pairs. Get feedback, and tell SS about your family.

b • Focus on the advert and get SS to read it, or read it with them. Tell SS that these are now very popular presents in the UK, especially for 'the person who has everything'. Ask SS what they think of the idea.

- Now focus on the pictures and tell SS they are different 'experience' presents. Set a time limit, e.g. five minutes for SS in pairs to read the information and match the presents to the information.

- Check answers.

1 F	**2** C	**3** E	**4** B	**5** D	**6** A

c • Get SS to do this in pairs. The first two are facts, the rest are a matter of opinion. Get feedback, to see if SS agree about the *Which do you think… ?* questions.

> The cheapest is E.   The most expensive is A.

- Go through the text making sure SS understand the new words and phrases, e.g. *record (v)*, *recording studio, go back in time, recipes, lasts.*

d • Get SS to ask you the questions first. Then they answer them in pairs.
- Get feedback from a few SS.

Extra idea

Get SS to rank the experiences in order, 1–6 (1 = their favourite).

2 GRAMMAR *would like to/like*

a • Focus on the dialogue and get SS to answer the questions in pairs, or ask the whole class. Check answers.

> **1** *to* + infinitive
> **2** b
> **3** I like dancing = I like dancing in general; I'd like to dance = I want to dance now or in the future

b • Tell SS to go to **Grammar Bank 8C** on *p. 136.* Go through the rules with the class. Model and drill the example sentences.
⚠ Remind SS that the *l* in *would* is silent /wʊd/.

Grammar notes

- This is the first time 'the infinitive with *to*' is referred to. Explain that the infinitive can be with or without *to*, e.g. without *to* after *can*, but with *to* after *would like*. Other verbs they know which are followed by the infinitive with *to* are *want, need,* and *learn.*

- Focus on the exercises for **8C** on *p. 137.* SS do the exercises individually or in pairs.
- Check answers. Get SS to use contractions *'d* and *wouldn't* when they read their answers.

> **a 1** I'd like to be a millionaire.
>   **2** Would you like to be famous?
>   **3** I wouldn't like to go up in a balloon.
>   **4** He'd like to learn to cook.
>   **5** She wouldn't like to be on TV.
>   **6** Would they like to have children?
>   **7** I wouldn't like to live in a foreign country.
>   **8** We'd like to buy a bigger flat.
> **b 1** to have   **5** to get
>   **2** to go flying   **6** to open cooking
>   **3** to be   **7** living
>   **4** seeing to go   **8** to learn

- Tell SS to go back to the main lesson on *p. 93.*

3 PRONUNCIATION sentence stress

a 🔊 **8.8**

- Focus on the dialogue, and play the tape/CD once just for SS to listen. Then play it again and pause after each line for SS to repeat.

> 🔊 **8.8**   CD3 Track 35
> A <u>Would</u> you <u>like</u> to <u>learn</u> to <u>fly</u> a <u>plane</u>?
> B <u>No</u>, I <u>wouldn't</u>.
> A <u>Why</u> <u>not</u>?
> B Because I <u>don't</u> <u>like</u> <u>flying</u>, and I <u>think</u> it's <u>dangerous</u>.

8
C

b 8.9

- Focus on the second dialogue. Play the tape/CD and pause at the end of each line for SS to underline the stressed words.
- Get SS to compare with a partner, and then check answers (see tapescript).

8.9	CD3 Track 36

A <u>Would</u> you <u>like</u> to <u>drive</u> a <u>Ferrari</u>?
B <u>Yes</u>, I'd <u>love</u> to.
A <u>Why</u>?
B Because I <u>like</u> <u>driving</u>, but my <u>car's</u> very <u>slow</u>.

c • SS practise reading the dialogue in pairs.
d • Focus on the pictures in **1b**. SS take turns to interview their partner using the pictures.

4 LISTENING

a • Focus on the photo, instructions, and the two questions. Elicit that the present was a parachute jump, and ask SS if they think Russell enjoyed it.

b 8.10

- Focus on the phrases and pictures. Tell SS that the phrases are from the interview they are going to hear.
- Play the tape/CD once, and get SS to match them. Check answers, and teach *land* (= touch the ground), *float* (= move gently on top of the water or through the air), *jump* (= push your body into the air).

8.10	CD3 Track 37

1 We learned how to land.
2 I sat on the floor and waited.
3 Then the instructor said 'Jump!' and I jumped.
4 Suddenly the parachute opened, and I floated down.
5 One of the people in my group broke his leg.

1 D   2 C   3 A   4 E   5 B

c 8.11

- Now tell SS they're going to hear the whole interview. Tell SS just to relax and listen to see if it was a good experience or not. Play the tape/CD once.
- Ask SS *Did he enjoy it?* (Yes, especially after the jump). *Would he like to do it again?* (No, because he thinks it's dangerous – one of his group broke his leg, and he heard that another person died two months after he jumped).

8.11	CD3 Track 38

(tapescript in Student's Book on *p.121*.)
I = interviewer, R = Russell
I Russell, can you describe your day?
R Well, first we had some classes and **we learned how to land.**
I What happened then?
R Well, when we finished the classes we went up in the plane.
I How high did you go up?
R About 800 metres.
I Then what happened?
R Well, **I sat on the floor and waited.**
I How did you feel?
R Very frightened! That was the worst part, waiting to jump.

I And then?
R **Then the instructor said 'Jump!' and I jumped.**
I How was it?
R It was incredible. First I fell very fast. I couldn't think. I forgot all the instructions. **Suddenly the parachute opened, and I floated down.**
I Did you land OK?
R Yes, I did – perfectly.
I How did you feel afterwards?
R Great – I felt fantastic. I was really happy. I thought 'I did it!'
I Would you like to do it again?
R Well no, I wouldn't.
I Why not?
R Because it can be dangerous. **One of the people in my group broke his leg.** And two months after that I heard that someone died.
I How?
R His parachute didn't open and he fell…

d • Now focus on the sentences. In pairs, SS number them 1–9 based on what they heard the first time and on what they think is a logical order.

- Play the tape/CD once for SS to check their order. Get them to compare answers with their partner. Play the tape/CD again if necessary. Check answers.

2 He went up in the plane.
3 He waited to jump.
4 He felt frightened.
5 He jumped.
6 He fell very fast.
7 His parachute opened.
8 He landed.
9 He felt fantastic.

Extra support

Get SS to listen to the tape/CD for a final time with the tapescript on *p. 121* so they can see exactly what was said and see how much they understood. Translate/explain any new words or phrases.

- Ask the whole class if they would like to do a parachute jump. See if the majority would like to or not. Elicit a few reasons.

A You may want to do the photocopiable activity on *p. 215* at this point, where SS design their own 'experience' present.

Extra photocopiable activities

Grammar
would like to / like p. 170.
Communicative
Make your own 'experience' present *p. 215* (instructions *p.183*).

HOMEWORK

Study Link Workbook *pp. 71–72.*

G adverbs
V common adverbs: *slowly, fast,* etc.
P word stress in adjectives and adverbs

They dress well but drive badly

Lesson plan

This lesson is based on real interviews with people who live abroad, where they rate different aspects of their 'new' country, and talk about what surprised them when they first arrived. This provides the context for SS to practise forming and using adverbs.

Optional lead-in (books closed)

- Tell SS to imagine that they have to go and live for a year in a foreign city. Then tell them, in pairs, to say which two cities they would like to go to, and why.
- Get feedback about the cities SS chose, and their reasons.

1 READING & SPEAKING

a • Books open. Focus on the cities and elicit where they are.

> Rio de Janeiro – Brazil, Milan – Italy, Barcelona – Spain, Tokyo – Japan, Los Angeles – USA, Sydney – Australia.

b • Go through the instructions. Tell SS which cities you would find easy or difficult to live in and why.
- Give SS in pairs a few minutes to mark the cities **E** or **D** and compare with a partner. Get feedback from a few SS.

c • Focus on the text. Set a time limit, e.g. five minutes, for SS to read and complete the texts with a city. Get them to compare with a partner and then check answers.

> Nuria lives in Los Angeles.
> Mónica lives in Tokyo.
> Kevin lives in Milan.

d • Tell SS to read the text again slowly and try to remember at least three things about each city. Move around helping SS with any vocabulary they don't understand.
- Write on the board on one side the three cities, and on the other side the headings from the text, i.e. **driving**, **social life**, **people**, **safety**, **clothes**, **food**.
- Tell SS to cover the text and in pairs say what they can remember about the three cities.
- Get feedback, and ask SS if they found anything about the cities surprising.

2 GRAMMAR adverbs

a • Focus on the four sentences, and elicit that you normally make adverbs by adding *-ly* to the adjective.

b • Focus on the underlined phrase in the text *drive quite slowly.* SS underline eight more verb + adverb phrases. Check answers and elicit that *hard, fast,* and *well* are also adverbs but they don't end in *-ly*.

> work very hard; walk safely; drive carefully; speak very quietly; change completely; sang very loudly and badly; dresses well; drive very fast

c • Tell SS to go to **Grammar Bank 8D** on *p. 136.* Go through the rules with the class. Model and drill the example sentences.

Grammar notes

- The most common word order with these kinds of adverbs is after a verb or verb phrase, e.g. *He drives very quickly, I speak English very well* (typical error: *I speak very well English*).
- SS may try to use *hardly* instead of *hard,* e.g. *I work hardly.* Explain that *hard* is irregular and doesn't add *-ly. Hardly* is another word which means *almost not,* e.g. *I hardly slept last night, I hardly ever go to the theatre.* SS learnt *hardly ever* in lesson **3C**.

- Focus on the exercises for **8D** on *p. 137.* SS do the exercises individually or in pairs.
- Check answers. Get SS to read the whole sentence. Help with rhythm, and tell them that adverbs are always stressed.

> **a** 1 slowly   5 carefully
>   2 perfect   6 safely
>   3 quickly   7 well
>   4 good   8 terrible
> **b** 1 badly   5 hard
>   2 slowly   6 carefully
>   3 quietly   7 healthily
>   4 easily   8 beautifully

Study Link SS can find an end-of-File grammar quiz on the MultiROM, and more grammar activities on the *New English File Elementary* website.

- Tell SS to go back to the main lesson on *p. 95.*

d **8.12**

- Tell SS they're going to hear six sound effects and for each sound they must write a sentence using the present continuous and an adverb to describe what's happening.
- Play the tape/CD and pause after number 1, so SS can see how the example sentence (*They're speaking quietly*) describes the sounds. Ask *Why?* and elicit that it's because the baby is asleep.
- Now play the other five sounds, pausing after each one for SS to write sentences in pairs. Check answers.

> **2** She's driving aggressively.
> **3** He's dancing badly.
> **4** He's eating noisily.
> **5** She's singing beautifully/well.
> **6** He's talking/speaking loudly.

> **8.12**   CD3 Track 39
> 1 *speaking quietly*   4 *eating noisily*
> 2 *driving aggressively*   5 *singing beautifully*
> 3 *dancing badly*   6 *talking loudly*

3 PRONUNCIATION   adjectives and adverbs

a ● Focus on the adjectives, and tell SS in pairs to underline the stressed syllable.

Extra support

Play the tape/CD first to remind them where the stress is.

b **8.13**

● Play the tape/CD once for SS to check answers. Then play it again pausing after each adjective for SS to repeat.

8.13	CD3 Track 40
aggressive	beautiful
stylish	quiet
dangerous	careful
polite	complete

c **8.14**

● Now focus on the adverbs. Tell SS to listen to see if the stress changes, and elicit that it stays the same, although the extra syllable has been added.

8.14	CD3 Track 41
aggressively	beautifully
stylishly	quietly
dangerously	carefully
politely	completely

d ● In pairs SS practise saying the adverbs. Alternatively play the tape/CD again, pausing for them to repeat.

4 SPEAKING

a ● Focus on the pictures and gapped sentences. Tell SS that in different countries or cities people do things in different ways. In pairs, SS complete the sentences. Have one group of three if you have an odd number.

b ● Put two pairs together, to make groups of four (or five), and get them to compare their sentences.

⚠ SS may want to use comparative adverbs here, e.g. *People dress more stylishly in ___ .* You could explain they just have to put *more* before the adverb, except the irregular ones which are the same as the comparative adjectives, e.g. *harder, faster, better,* and *worse.*

c ● Then focus on SS' own country (or city) and the verbs. Demonstrate first if you are from a different country/city, by telling SS, e.g. *In Britain people drive very carefully.*

● Put SS in groups to make sentences. Get feedback to see if SS agree.

Extra photocopiable activities

Grammar
adverbs *p. 171.*
Communicative
Mime the phrase *p. 216* (instructions *p.184*).

HOMEWORK

Study Link Workbook *pp. 73–74.*

---

8 PRACTICAL ENGLISH GOING HOME

Vocabulary verb phrases: *pay the bill*
Function Checking out
Language *Can I have my bill, please?*

Lesson plan

In this final Practical English lesson SS revise some verb phrases and practise checking out of a hotel. Allie is supposed to be taking Mark to the airport but is delayed. Mark is nervously waiting to hear if she is going to come to the States or not. She finally turns up at the airport to give him her answer...

Study Link These lessons are also on the *New English File Elementary* Video, which can be used **instead of** the Class Cassette/CD (see introduction p.9). The first section of the Video is also on the MultiROM, with additional activities.

VOCABULARY   verb phrases

a ● Focus on the phrases and give SS in pairs a few moments to complete them with the right verb. Check answers and model and drill pronunciation.

1 check out	**2** ask	**3** pay	**4** sign /saɪn/	**5** need
6 call				

b ● Put SS in pairs. Get one student to close his/her book. A reads the phrase (e.g. *of a hotel*) and B has to remember the verb (e.g. *check out*). SS swap roles.

CHECKING OUT

a **8.15**

● Focus on the picture and ask SS *Where's Mark?* (At the hotel). *What's he doing?* (He's checking out).

● Now write the two questions on the board and tell SS to close their books, or get SS to cover the conversation.

● Play the tape/CD once or twice. Check answers.

> He asks for the bill. He doesn't need a taxi or help with his luggage.

b ● Now focus on the conversation and the gaps. Give SS a minute to read through the dialogue and try to predict the missing words. Then play the tape/CD once for SS to complete the dialogue.

● Get SS to compare answers in pairs. Then play the tape/CD again. Check answers (see tapescript).

8.15	CD3 Track 42

R = receptionist, M = Mark
R Good morning, sir.
M Good morning. Can I have my bill, please? I'm checking out.
R Which room **is** it?
M Room 425.
R **Did** you have anything from the minibar last night?
M Yes, a mineral water.
R Here you are. How **would** you like to pay?
M American Express.
R Thank you. OK. **Can** you sign here, please? Thank you. **Would** you like me to call a taxi for you?

M No, thanks.
R **Do** you need any help with your luggage?
M No, I'm fine, thanks.
R Have a good trip, Mr Ryder.
M Thank you.
R Goodbye.
M Goodbye.

c 8.16

- Tell SS they're going to hear the dialogue again. They repeat the **YOU SAY** phrases when they hear the beep. Encourage them to copy the rhythm and intonation.
- Play the tape/CD, pausing for SS to repeat the phrases.

8.16 CD3 Track 43

R Good morning, sir.
M Good morning. Can I have my bill, please? I'm checking out.
repeat
R Which room is it?
M Room 425.
repeat
R Did you have anything from the minibar last night?
M Yes, a mineral water.
repeat
R Here you are. How would you like to pay?
M American Express.
repeat
R Thank you. OK. Can you sign here, please? Thank you. Would you like me to call a taxi for you?
M No, thanks.
repeat
R Do you need any help with your luggage?
M No, I'm fine, thanks.
repeat
R Have a good trip, Mr Ryder.
M Thank you.
R Goodbye.
M Goodbye.

---

d • Put SS in pairs. A is the receptionist. Get SS to read the dialogue first. Then tell B to close his/her book and answer from memory. Then A and B swap roles.

SOCIAL ENGLISH

a 8.17

- Now focus on the next picture. Write the following on the board:

Mark phones Allie.	**Mark asks for a taxi.**
Mark gets his plane.	**Allie and Mark meet.**
Allie phones Mark.	

- Play the tape/CD once. Get SS to tell you in which order things happen.

1 Allie phones Mark.	**4** Allie and Mark meet.
2 Mark asks for a taxi.	**5** Mark gets his plane.
3 Mark phones Allie.	

- Focus on the five sentences. Play the tape/CD twice and SS choose the correct option. Check answers.

1 terrible	**2** train	**3** airport	**4** forty	**5** can

8.17 CD3 Track 44

(tapescript in Student's Book on *p.121*.)
M Hello?
A Hi, Mark, it's Allie. I'm really sorry but the traffic this morning is terrible. I'm going to be very late.
M OK.
A I think the best thing is for you to take a taxi to the station and then get the train to the airport.
M No problem, **I'll call a taxi. Well, thanks for everything…**
A No listen, **I'll meet you at the airport** – we can say goodbye there.
M All right. **Where can we meet?**
A At the information desk.
M OK, see you there.
A Bye.
M Excuse me, change of plan. **Could you call me a taxi, please?** To the station.
Hello. Sorry I can't take your call. Please leave a message after the tone.
M Hi, Allie, this is Mark. Where are you? I'm at the information desk. My flight leaves in forty minutes.
A Mark! Mark! **Sorry I'm late!**
M Don't worry – I'm just happy you got here.
A Come on. You're going to miss your flight.
M Wait a minute. Are you going to come to the conference in California? Am I going to see you again?
A The plane's going to leave without you.
M Allie?
A I asked my boss this morning, and he said yes. I can go!
M Great! Oh, I don't have your home phone number.
A Don't worry. I'll e-mail it to you tomorrow.
This is the final call for all passengers on flight BA287 to San Francisco. Please proceed immediately to Gate 12.
M Goodbye, Allie. And thanks for everything.
A Goodbye, Mark. **Have a safe trip!**
M See you in California. Bye.

---

b • Focus on the question and elicit some ideas from the class. Tell SS to use *going to* in their answers.

c • Focus on the **USEFUL PHRASES**. Ask SS *Who says it, Mark or Allie?* Then play the tape/CD for SS to check their answers.

- Play the tape/CD again for SS to check. Pause after each phrase and get SS to repeat it. (See the tapescript above). In a monolingual class, ask them what the equivalent phrase is in their language.

I'll call a taxi. – Mark
Well, thanks for everything. – Mark
I'll meet you at the airport. – Allie
Where can we meet? – Mark
Could you call me a taxi, please? – Mark
Sorry I'm late. –Allie
Have a safe trip! – Allie

- Focus on the note about *will*. Explain that it's used here to make an instant decision or promise about the future, e.g. *I'll call a taxi*. The uses of *will* are dealt with in *New English File Pre-intermediate* but are included here for reference in the **Grammar Bank** appendix on *p. 139*.

HOMEWORK

Study Link Workbook *p. 75*.

Lesson plan

In this last writing lesson, SS learn to write a formal e-mail to book a hotel room. They compare and contrast the conventions of a formal e-mail with an informal one. There is no focus on a formal letter as it is more likely today that SS will need to write an e-mail. However, if you think your SS also need to learn how to write a formal letter, the conventions are highlighted below under **Extra idea**.

a • Focus on the three hotels. Give SS a few minutes to read them. Ask SS which hotel they'd like to go to and why. Explain/translate any words SS want to know, e.g. *roof terrace, views, lagoon*, etc.

b • Now focus on the e-mail. Tell SS to read it quickly, ignoring the gaps, and to answer the question. Check answers.

> The Residence, Tunisia

c • Focus on the words/expressions and get SS to complete the e-mail. Get them to compare with a partner and check answers.

> 2 reservation
> 3 room
> 4 nights
> 5 view
> 6 information
> 7 Please
> 8 Yours

d • Focus on the chart and get SS to complete it. Check answers.

> Dear confirm Yours surname

Extra idea

If your SS also need to write formal letters, not just e-mails, tell them that they can use exactly the same language to begin and end as in an e-mail, but should put:
– their address in the top right hand corner
– the name and address of the person/company they're writing to on the left hand side, slightly lower down
– the date under the name and address
– *Yours faithfully* (if the letter is addressed *Dear Sir/Madam*) or *Yours sincerely* (if it is addressed to a name, e.g. *Dear Mrs Richards*).

You could also teach as a set phrase *I look forward to hearing from you.*

Write an e-mail

• Go through the instructions with SS. Stress the importance of checking writing after they've done it.
• Either give SS at least fifteen minutes to write the e-mail in class, or set it for homework.
• If SS do the writing in class, get them to swap and read each others' e-mails and correct any mistakes they find, before you collect them all in.

GRAMMAR

| 1 b | 2 a | 3 b | 4 a | 5 a | 6 b | 7 a | 8 a | 9 b | 10 b |

VOCABULARY

a 1 slowly 2 dangerous 3 badly 4 quiet
  5 the worst
b 1 tall (physical, not personality)
  2 dangerous (not to do with climate)
  3 leader (not a comparative)
  4 friendly (not an adverb)
  5 safe (not a negative adjective for a town/city)
c 1 in 2 of 3 for 4 up 5 than

PRONUNCIATION

a 1 car 2 slowly 3 boring 4 serious 5 big
b aggressive, ambitious, adventure, politely, dangerously

CAN YOU UNDERSTAND THIS TEXT?

b 1 a 2 b 3 a 4 c

CAN YOU HEAR THE DIFFERENCE?

b 1 a 2 a 3 b 4 a 5 b

8.18 CD3 Track 45

I = interviewer, N = Nicolas
I Tell me about Edinburgh.
N Er, well, at first I had a problem with the language. People here speak with a Scottish accent, and they also use some different words.
I Different words? For example?
N For example, they don't say 'little' they say 'wee' – 'a wee boy', 'a wee drink', things like that.
I Was the weather a problem?
N Not really. Well, people told me that it rained a lot in Scotland. But in fact it doesn't rain very much. I read the other day that it rains more in Paris than Edinburgh. But it *is* very windy, and I didn't expect that. And people talk about the weather all the time!
I What about the food?
N Well, I love Scotland but I don't think the diet is very healthy. My Scottish friends eat a lot of chocolate bars, biscuits – things like that. They don't eat much fruit or vegetables.
I What about the whisky? Do you like it?
N Well, my friends say the whisky is fantastic – and there are many different kinds. In some pubs they have special whisky menus. But unfortunately I don't like whisky. I only drink wine!
I Would you like to stay in Scotland when you finish university?
N I don't know yet. It depends if I can find a good job here.

Extra photocopiable activities

Quicktest 8 *p.238.*

G present perfect for past experiences
V *been to*
P sentence stress

Before we met

Lesson plan

The idea for this lesson comes from a novel called *Before we met* by Julian Barnes, about a couple where the man is pathologically jealous of his girlfriend's ex-boyfriend. However, the 'extract from a novel' is invented and is not based on the original novel. The present perfect (for past experiences) is presented, but confined to one past participle (*been to…*) to talk about cities and countries which SS have visited. This allows SS to get to grips with *have* as an auxiliary verb, and with making questions and negatives. In **9B** they learn other regular and irregular past participles, and contrast the present perfect with the past simple.

Optional lead-in (books closed)

- Revise the adjectives of personality SS learned in **8A**. Write on the board:

What's the word for a person who…

is open and kind ?	f_____
thinks a lot and doesn't make jokes?	s_____
likes arguing and can be violent?	a_____
doesn't talk much?	q_____
likes giving people things?	g_____
dresses well?	s_____
thinks their partner is interested in another person	j_____

- Give SS a minute to try and think of the adjectives (tell them the last one may be new).
- Check answers.

> friendly
> serious
> aggressive
> quiet
> generous
> stylish
> jealous

- Model and drill the pronunciation of *jealous* /ˈdʒeləs/ and elicit that the *ea* is pronounced /e/, like *bread*, *breakfast*, etc.

1 SPEAKING & READING

a
- Books open. Focus on the questionnaire. If you didn't do the lead in, elicit/teach the meaning of *jealous*.
- Get SS to ask you the questions. They then interview each other in pairs or small groups.
- Get feedback from the class. Find out what the majority opinion is for question **4**.

b 9.1
- Now focus on the 'extract from the novel' and questions 1–3. Play the tape/CD once for SS to read and listen.

A If SS ask at this point what *I've been* is say that *I've* = *I have* and *been* is the past participle of *be*. The meaning here is *visited*.

Extra challenge

As an alternative, you could do **b** as a listening, i.e. get SS to cover the text and listen and answer the questions. Play the tape/CD twice and check answers. Then get them to read the story and guess the meaning of the highlighted words.

- Get SS to compare with a partner and then check answers.

> 1 Barcelona Rome Florence
> 2 His ex-girlfriend.
>   She's in Canada.
> 3 Because Rob went there with Jessica.

> **9.1**   CD3 Track 46
>
> It was a Thursday evening in June when we sat down in Charlotte's living room with the holiday brochures. 'I got these from the travel agent's today,' said Charlotte. 'This is going to be fun! <u>Have you been to Italy?</u>'
> 'Yes, I have,' I replied. '<u>I've been to Rome and Florence.</u>'
> 'On holiday?'
> 'Yes… with Jessica.'
> 'Oh.' There was a long silence.
> 'But I haven't been to Venice. What about Venice?'
> 'No. Forget Italy. <u>Have you been to Spain?</u>'
> 'Yes. <u>I've been to Barcelona.</u>'
> 'With Jessica?'
> 'Yes, but…'
> She picked up a brochure for Lisbon. 'Don't tell me. <u>You've been there too.</u> With Jessica.'
> 'No. <u>I've never been to Portugal.</u> Look, what's the problem? Jessica's not my girlfriend now. She's thousands of miles away. She lives in Canada. Why are you so jealous of her?'
> 'Me? Jealous? I'm not jealous.'
> There was another long silence.

c
- SS read the text again and focus on the meaning of the highlighted words. Check answers by explaining or translating the words, letting SS check with a dictionary or using the glossary below.

holiday brochures	magazines with photos and information about holidays
fun	enjoyable, entertaining
replied	answered
silence	when there is no noise/nobody is talking
picked up	took from the floor or from a table

- Ask SS *Do you think Charlotte is jealous?* Note: the story continues in **LISTENING**.

2 GRAMMAR present perfect

a • Focus on the instructions and get SS to answer in pairs. Check answers.

> **1** yes   **2** no   **3** *have*   **4** *be*

b • SS underline examples of *have been to*. Check answers (see tapescript above), and elicit that *have been to = have visited*.

c • Focus on the chart. Give SS a few minutes to complete it. Check answers.

	+	−	?
I, you, we, they	I **have** been to Rome.	I **haven't** been to Venice.	**Have** you been to Lisbon?
he, she, it	She **has** been to Rome.	She **hasn't** been to Venice.	**Has** he been to Lisbon?

d • Tell SS to go to **Grammar Bank 9A** on *p. 138*. Go through the rules with the class. Model and drill the example sentences.

Grammar notes

• The present perfect is probably the tense which causes most problems for foreign learners, mainly because of L1 interference. For this reason in *New English File Elementary* we introduce it through one simple and common use, i.e. to talk about past experiences (things that we have done in our lives up till now, but *without* saying exactly when). SS will study further uses of the present perfect in *New English File Pre-intermediate*.

• Although the use of the present perfect is usually considered the main difficulty for SS, the form is also problematic, as it is the first time SS see *have* used as an auxiliary verb with all its contractions (*I've… he's…*, etc.).

• The meaning of *been to* can cause problems. SS naturally expect either *been in* or *gone to*. It is probably best to explain that *been to* in the present perfect = visited (and come back), *gone to* = travelled to and not returned.

• Focus on the exercises for **9A** on *p. 139*. SS do the exercises individually or in pairs.

• Check answers. In **a** write the contracted forms on the board, and in **b** tell SS to use contractions in + and − after *I, he*, etc.

> **a 1** She **hasn't** been to the USA.
> **2** They **haven't** been to China.
> **3** He**'s** been to an opera.
> **4** You **haven't** been to my house.
> **5** I **haven't** been there.
> **6** We**'ve** been to Madrid.
> **b 1** I haven't been to Rome.
> **2** Have you been to Barcelona?
> **3** Mark hasn't been to South America.
> **4** My parents have been to Africa.
> **5** Has Ann been to Argentina?
> **6** We haven't been to Budapest.

• Tell SS to go back to the main lesson on *p. 101*.

3 PRONUNCIATION sentence stress

a 9.2
• Focus on the dialogue. Play the tape/CD once for SS to listen. Then play it again, pausing after each line for SS to repeat. Highlight that the underlined words are the ones which SS should stress more strongly.

> | **9.2** | CD3 Track 47 |
> |---|---|
> A   Have you been to Italy?
> B   Yes, I have. I've been to Venice.
> A   Have you been to New York?
> B   No, I haven't. I haven't been to the USA.

• Get SS to practise the dialogue in pairs.

b • Demonstrate the activity. Write on the board six place names (countries or cities), three of which you've been to and three of which you haven't.

• Tell SS to decide in pairs which three they think you *have* been to, and write them on a piece of paper.

• SS ask you *Have you been to …?* for all six places to check their guesses. Get feedback to see which pair(s) guessed right.

• Put SS in pairs and get them to write their own lists of six cities. In a monolingual class, if your SS haven't travelled abroad restrict the activity to cities in their country. Monitor and help SS write their lists.

• SS swap lists, and try to guess which three places their partner has been to. They then ask *Have you been to…?* questions to check. Monitor, helping SS get the right rhythm in their questions. Get feedback to see who had the most correct guesses in each pair.

4 LISTENING

a 9.3
• If you are doing this activity on a different day to when you did the first part of the Rob and Charlotte story you could read the text again to refresh SS' memories.

• Tell SS they're now going to see what happens to Rob and Charlotte. Focus on the question, and play the tape/CD once and elicit the answer.

> Jessica phones.

b • Now focus on sentences 1–6. Play the tape/CD once for SS to complete them with a name. Get them to compare answers with their partner. Play the tape/CD again and check answers.

> **1** Rob
> **2** Charlotte
> **3** Rob
> **4** Jessica
> **5** Rob, Jessica
> **6** Charlotte, Rob

> | **9.3** | CD3 Track 48 |
> |---|---|
> (tapescript in Student's Book on *p.121*)
> **R = Rob, C = Charlotte**
> R   Why don't we go to Paris? I haven't been there.
> C   Are you sure?
> R   Look, I promise. I've never been to Paris.

C OK. Let's look at the brochure. I love Paris. It's one of my favourite cities.

R You choose a hotel then.

C What about this one? It's very near the Eiffel Tower. It looks nice. Very romantic. Let's go there.

R Is that your phone?

C No, it's yours.

R Oh yeah. You're right. Hello?… Who?… Oh hi. What a surprise… Fine, fine. How are you?… Sorry?… It's seven o'clock here. In the evening. What time is it in Canada?… Sorry?… No, I'm not. I'm with… I'm with a friend… Can I call you back later?… I said, can I call you back later this evening?… Sorry? I can't hear you… OK I'll call you back later… Yes, OK. Bye… Sorry, Charlotte, what did you say about the hotel?

C Forget it, Rob. I don't want to go away with you this weekend. In fact I don't want to do anything with you. See you sometime.

R Charlotte, don't go. Listen, I can explain. It isn't what you think…

Extra support

Get SS to listen to the tape/CD for a final time with the tapescript on *p. 121* so they can see exactly what was said and see how much they understood. Translate/explain any new words or phrases.

5 SPEAKING

- Focus on the questionnaire and go through the questions. Then focus on the instructions and make sure SS understand them.
- Set a time limit, e.g. five minutes. Tell SS to stand up and start. Mix in with them yourself.
- Stop the activity after five minutes (or when you think SS have had enough, or when someone has found people for all the questions). Get SS to sit down again.
- Get feedback. Ask *Who has been to a very hot country?* and elicit the student's name. Then ask him or her *Where? When?*
- Do the same for the other questions, getting a bit more information each time.

A Be careful to elicit short answers here, not full sentences, as SS may try (incorrectly) to use the present perfect.

Extra challenge

Tell SS they must try to find a *different* person for each question.

Extra photocopiable activities

Grammar
present perfect *p. 172.*
Communicative
Where have you been? p. 217 (instructions *p.184*).

HOMEWORK

Study Link Workbook *pp. 76–77.*

G present perfect or past simple?
V past participles: *seen, broken,* etc.
P irregular past participles

9B I've read the book, I've seen the film

Lesson plan

In this final lesson SS learn more about the present perfect (for past experiences). They get practice in forming regular and irregular past participles and in asking questions with *ever*. The main context of the lesson is a survey asking about 'Cinema experiences'. Finally, the lesson contrasts the present perfect and the past simple in a natural context: *Have you read the book? Have you seen the film? Which did you prefer?*

Optional lead-in (books closed)

- Write on the board in two columns:
  PAST PARTICIPLE INFINITIVE
- Now write *been* under past participle and elicit that the infinitive is *be*, and write it under infinitive.
- Then write these past participles in the column:
  spoken, seen, cried, bought, left, slept, kissed
- Give SS in pairs one minute to decide what they think the infinitive is. Check answers, and model and drill the pronunciation. Ask which two are regular past participles (*cried, kissed*).

speak, see, cry, buy, leave, sleep, kiss

1 SPEAKING

a • Books open. Focus on the questionnaire and the beginning of the question *Have you ever...?* Elicit/teach that *ever* = (at any time) in your life.
- Focus on the example *Have you ever spoken to a film actor or actress?* If you didn't do the lead-in, ask SS what the infinitive of *spoken* is (*speak*). Explain that *spoken* is the 'past participle' of the verb *speak*.
- If you didn't do the lead-in, focus on the past participles in the box (*slept, bought,* etc.) and elicit the infinitive and the meaning of each verb.
- In pairs, give SS two minutes to complete the questionnaire with the past participles. Check answers.

2 seen **3** cried **4** bought **5** left **6** slept **7** kissed

b • Get SS to ask you the first question. If you answer *Yes*, get them to ask the two follow-up questions. If you answer *No*, get them to ask question 2, etc. until you answer *Yes*.

⚠ These questions are in the past simple *not* the present perfect. If SS ask about this, reassure them that you will explain this in detail later in the lesson.

- SS interview each other in pairs. Get them to sit face to face. A should give B a complete interview and then swap roles. Monitor and help, but don't correct them too much in their answers to the follow-up questions. The focus should be on communication not accuracy.
- Get feedback from a few SS. Ask *Who has spoken to a film actor?* and then get the details.

2 VOCABULARY past participles

a • Focus on questions 1–3 and the questionnaire in **1**. Give SS, in pairs, two minutes to answer the questions. Check answers.

1 cried kissed   **2** bought left slept   **3** spoken seen

b • Tell SS to go to **Irregular verbs** on *p. 154*. Focus on the third column, and go through them with SS, getting them to tick the past participles that are different from the past simple. Model and drill the pronunciation of these only.
- Tell SS they only need to learn the ones that are different (assuming they have assimilated the past simple verbs whose past participles are the same.) Give them five minutes to focus on them and then get them to close their books and see how many they can remember.
- Tell SS to go back to the main lesson on *p. 102*.

3 PRONUNCIATION irregular participles

a • Focus on the five sound pictures and elicit the word and sound (fish, /ɪ/, train /eɪ/, up /ʌ/, phone /əʊ/, horse /ɔː/)
- In pairs SS put three past participles into each column.

Extra support

Model the pronunciation of the participles first and then get SS to put them in columns.

b 9.4
- Play the tape/CD once for SS to check their answers. Then play it again pausing after each group for SS to repeat. Give extra practice as necessary. Make sure SS don't pronounce the *gh* in *bought* and *caught*.

9.4		CD3 Track 49
fish	driven, given, written	
train	made, paid, taken	
up	begun, done, drunk	
phone	broken, known, spoken	
horse	bought, caught, worn	

4 GRAMMAR present perfect or past simple?

a • Focus on the dialogue and give SS time to answer the questions in pairs. Check answers.

1 present perfect
2 past simple
3 A
4 B and C

b • Tell SS to go to **Grammar Bank 9B** on *p. 138*. Go through the rules with the class. Model and drill the example sentences.

Grammar notes

Regular and irregular past participles

- Regular verbs should not cause any problems for SS since they are the same as the past simple. SS simply have to remember the pronunciation rules for *-ed* endings.
- Many irregular past participles also have the same form as the past simple. However, ones which are different (e.g. *speak spoke spoken*) may cause problems as SS may confuse the two forms (e.g. *I have spoke…*) For this reason it is worth focusing especially on these verbs.

Present perfect or past simple?

- It is almost impossible to teach the present perfect for experiences without dealing with the contrast with the past simple, since when people talk about an experience, *I've been to Morocco*, they are frequently asked *When…?* or another question which focuses on a specific moment in time (i.e. when you were in Morocco), when the past simple must be used, e.g. *Did you like it?*

- Focus on the exercises for **9B** on *p. 139*. SS do the exercises individually or in pairs.

Extra challenge

Get SS to try to do **a** without checking with the irregular verb list.

- Check answers.

a 1 met
2 read
3 fallen
4 cried
5 travelled
6 met
7 seen
8 written
b 1 Have you ever spoken…
2 Yes, I have.
3 Who was it?
4 Where did you see him?
5 I saw…
6 What did you say…
7 I asked him for…
8 Has your brother been to South Korea?
9 Yes he has.
10 He's been to Seoul.
11 When did he go there?
12 He went there…
13 Did he like it?
14 Yes, he loved it.

Study Link SS can find an end-of-File grammar quiz on the MultiROM, and more grammar activities on the *New English File Elementary* website.

Extra idea

Get SS to read the two dialogues in **b** to practise their pronunciation.

- Tell SS to go back to the main lesson on *p.103*.

5 LISTENING & SPEAKING

a • Focus on the books. Model and drill the two questions. Get SS to ask you the questions for each one, and answer them.

⚠ SS may need help with the titles, which may have been translated differently in their country.

- Either get SS to ask each other in pairs, or ask round the class. If anyone has both read the book and seen the film ask *Which did you like best? Why?*

b • Focus on the website information and give SS a minute to read it. Then ask the whole class the questions and elicit answers. (It's about whether good books make good films, and listeners are going to phone and say what they think.)

c **9.5**

- Focus on the question. Then play the tape/CD once and elicit that the person who is the most positive about films made from books is Linda.

9.5 CD3 Track 50

(tapescript in Student's Book on *p.121*.)

P = presenter, C = Carl, L = Linda, S = Sam

P Our next caller is Carl from Essex. Hello, Carl.
C Hi.
P What do you think, Carl? Do good books make good films?
C Well, I've read a lot of books and then seen the films, and I usually think that the books are better. For example, I loved the *Lord of the Rings* books but I didn't like the films very much.
P Thank you, Carl. Our next caller is Linda from Manchester. Hello, Linda.
L Hi. Well, what I think is that today people don't read very much. But they do go to the cinema. And sometimes *after* they've seen a film of a book then they go and buy the book, so that's a good thing because they read more.
P But do you think good books make good films?
L Yes. I've read a lot of good books and then I've seen the films and I've loved them all, *The Exorcist*, *Harry Potter*, *Gone with the Wind*. They're all great books and great films.
P Thank you, Linda. And our last caller is Sam from Cardiff. Hello, Sam. What do you think about our question today?
S I think it depends. I think good books *don't* usually make good films. But I've seen some films which I think are *better* than the books. That's usually because the book *wasn't* very good.
P So bad books can make good films?
S That's right.
P Give me an example.
S Well, the James Bond films. The books aren't very good but some of the films are great, like *Goldfinger*, or *From Russia with Love*.
P Thank you, Sam. Bye.

---

d • Focus on the true/false sentences and give SS a moment to read them. Then play the tape/CD again and get SS to compare their answers with a partner. Play the tape/CD again and then check answers. Ask why the F sentences are false.

1 T
2 F He didn't like them very much.
3 F They don't read much.
4 T
5 T
6 F He preferred the films.

e ● Write up on the board the name of a recent film based on a book (preferably one you've seen). Then get SS in pairs to think of one each. Get each pair to tell you the film they have thought of and write them on the board.

⚠ In a monolingual class don't worry about translating film titles into English unless your SS want you to.

f ● Focus on the flow chart. Tell SS in pairs to decide what the full questions are. Tell them that all the questions are either present perfect or past simple. They should write the full questions on a separate piece of paper, **not on the flow chart**.

● Check answers, eliciting which tense each question is.

Have you seen the film? (present perfect)
Yes, I have.
No, I haven't.
Did you like it? (past simple)
Have you read the book? (present perfect)
Yes, I have.
No, I haven't.
Did you like it? (past simple)
Which did you prefer, the film or the book? (past simple)

g ● Get SS to ask you about the first film in the list on the board. Get them to use the name, i.e. *Have you seen* (name)? and then follow the flow chart.

● Now SS interview each other in pairs. Encourage them to ask the questions using just the prompts in the flow chart.

Extra support

Let SS refer to the full questions on their piece of paper for this activity.

● Monitor and help. Finally get feedback to find out who has both seen the film and read the book for any of the titles and which they preferred.

Extra photocopiable activities

Grammar
present perfect or past simple? *p. 173.*
Communicative
Have you ever …? *p. 218* (instructions *p.184*).

HOMEWORK

Study Link Workbook *pp. 78–79.*

The last two sections in File 9, **Revise and Check Grammar** and **Revise and Check Vocabulary and Pronunciation** are intended to help SS revise for a final end-of-course test.

GRAMMAR

The grammar is divided up by Files, and gives the **Grammar Bank** page reference. SS should read through the rules again, and then test themselves with the exercises. They can either do this File by File or all at once. We suggest doing them in pairs or small groups in a final class, where SS can talk together about which is the right answer and why, but they can also be done individually or at home.

File 1
1 b 2 c 3 b 4 a 5 c
File 2
1 c 2 b 3 a 4 c 5 b
File 3
1 b 2 b 3 a 4 c 5 a
File 4
1 a 2 b 3 a 4 c 5 b
File 5
1 c 2 a 3 b 4 c 5 b
File 6
1 b 2 b 3 c 4 b 5 a
File 7
1 c 2 b 3 a 4 c 5 a
File 8
1 c 2 b 3 c 4 b 5 a
File 9
1 b 2 c 3 a 4 b 5 c

VOCABULARY

This section provides exercises to test SS on all the **Vocabulary Banks** of *New English File Elementary*. If possible, give SS time to revise the **Vocabulary Banks** before doing the exercises. If this is not feasible, the exercises should highlight which ones SS need to look back over. We suggest doing them in pairs or small groups, where SS can talk together about which is the right answer and why, but they can also be done individually or at home.

a 1 Polish (not a country)
  2 cooker (not a job)
  3 grandmother (the others are all male words)
  4 fast (not a feeling)
  5 yesterday (not an adverb of frequency)
  6 buy (not past)
  7 living room (not furniture)
  8 square (not a building)
  9 strawberries (not a vegetable)
  10 good (not an adverb)
b 1 fifty   6 three times
  2 Tuesday   7 hour
  3 third   8 winter
  4 thirtieth   9 April
  5 evening   10 next week

c	1	June	6	the post office
	2	my aunt	7	Spanish
	3	the bathroom	8	a waiter
	4	dirty	9	hate
	5	thought	10	generous
d	1	get	6	take
	2	have	7	turn
	3	go	8	give
	4	do	9	play
	5	make	10	wait
e	1	keys	6	bath
	2	glasses	7	bridge
	3	rich	8	church
	4	high	9	(some) cheese
	5	cupboard	10	(some) meat
f	1	from	6	in
	2	about	7	of
	3	at	8	for
	4	to	9	to
	5	up	10	to

PRONUNCIATION

This section provides exercises to test sounds and word stress.

a	1	bread	9	see
	2	famous	10	give
	3	work	11	have
	4	four	12	daughter
	5	three	13	don't
	6	get	14	cinema
	7	love	15	food
	8	hour		
b	1	American	11	sunglasses
	2	afternoon	12	magazine
	3	thirteen	13	chocolate
	4	breakfast	14	umbrella
	5	July	15	receptionist
	6	musician	16	grandmother
	7	between	17	dangerous
	8	bathroom	18	museum
	9	tomorrow	19	supermarket
	10	pronunciation	20	newspaper

Extra photocopiable activities

Grammar
revision of prepositions *p. 174.*
Communicative
Revise and Check *p. 219* (instructions *p.184*).
End-of-course test *p. 239* (tapescript opposite).

TA   CD3 Track 51

Part A

1 A Can you tell me your phone number?
   B Yes, it's 7734056.
   A Sorry?
   B 7734056.
2 A Do you like shopping?
   B Not really. Shopping for CDs and DVDs is OK, but I hate shopping for clothes and things like that.
3 A Where were you last night between 9 o'clock and 10.30?
   B I was at home all evening. I watched TV for an hour. Then I had a bath and I went to bed early, at about 10.00.
4 A Hi Simon. Where are you?
   B I'm in the office. I'm working.
   A But it's Saturday. You don't usually work on Saturdays.
   B I know, but this week I'm really busy.
5 A Where are you going to go for your summer holidays next year?
   B Portugal.
   A Portugal, really? Have you been there before?
   B No, I haven't. This is my first time.

TB   CD3 Track 52

Part B

A = Alex, S = Sylvie, T = travel agent

A Good morning. We'd like to go to Dublin on Friday, for the weekend.
T How would you like to travel? You can go by train, bus, or by plane.
S Which is the cheapest?
T Bus. By plane is the most expensive.
S How much is a return train ticket?
T It's 150 euros.
S 150 euros. For that price, we could get a flight on the Internet.
A But we haven't got time. Anyway, I like travelling by train. And it's much more comfortable than going by bus. We'd like to leave on Friday morning. What time is the first train?
T There's one at 6.45 and one at 7.45.
S Let's get the first one. Then we'll get there earlier. How long does it take?
T It takes about nine hours. You arrive in Dublin at 15.50.
S Great.
T When do you want to come back?
A On Monday evening.
S I think it'd be better to come back after lunch. Then we'll get back earlier.
T There's a train that leaves at 15.10 and gets to London at midnight.
A Fine.

CONTENTS

Photocopiable material

- There is a **Grammar activity** for each main (A, B, C, and D) lesson of the Student's Book.
- There is a **Communicative activity** for each main (A, B, C, and D) lesson of the Student's Book.
- There are seven **Song activities**. These can be used as part of the main lesson in the Student's Book or in a later lesson. The recording of the song can be found in the main lesson on the Class Cassette / CD.
- There is a **Quicktest** for Files 1–8. These are short tests of the main Grammar, Vocabulary, and Pronunciation to be used at the end of each File.
- There is an **End-of-course test** which tests Grammar, Vocabulary, and Pronunciation from the course as well as Reading, Listening, and Writing.

Using extra activities in mixed ability classes

Some teachers have classes with a very wide range of levels, and where some SS finish SB activities much more quickly than others. You could give these fast-finishers a photocopiable activity (either Communicative or Grammar) while you help the slower students. Alternatively some teachers might want to give faster SS extra oral practice with a communicative activity while slower students consolidate their knowledge with an extra grammar activity.

Tips for using Grammar activities

The Grammar activities are designed to give SS extra practice in the main grammar point from each lesson. How you use these activities depends on the needs of your SS and time you have available. They can be used in the lesson if you think all of your class would benefit from the extra practice or you could set them as homework for some or all of your SS.

- All of the activities start with a writing stage. If you use the activities in class, get SS to work individually or in pairs. Allow SS to compare before checking the answers.
- Many of the activities have a final section that gets SS to cover the sentences and to test their memory. If you are using the activities in class, SS can work in pairs and test their partner. If you set them for homework, encourage SS to use this stage to test themselves.
- If SS are having trouble with any of the activities, make sure they refer to the relevant Grammar Bank in the Student's Book.
- Make sure that SS keep their copies of the activities and that they review any difficult areas regularly. Encourage them to go back to activities and cover and test themselves. This will help with their revision.

1A pronouns + verb *be*

a 2 You're 3 She's 4 It's 5 We're 6 They're 7 I'm
8 You're 9 He's

b 2 You are 3 She is 4 It is 5 We are 6 They are
7 I am 8 You are 9 He is

1B verb *be* [−] and [?]

a 2 Are 3 am 4 Are 5 're 6 's 7 's 8 are 9 'm
10 'm 11 Are 12 'm 13 'm 14 's 15 's 16 Is 17 's
18 are 19 're 20 're

1C possessive adjectives

a 2 My 3 his 4 Her 5 Their 6 our 7 your 8 her
9 my 10 His

1D *a / an, the, this, that, these, those*

a 3 What's that? It's a 4 What's this? It's an
5 What's that? It's an 6 What are these? They're
7 What are those? They're 8 What's this? It's a
9 What's this? It's a 10 What's that? It's an

c 2 the 3 a 4 the; the 5 the 6 an 7 an; a 8 the

2A present simple [+] and [−]

a 2 drinks 3 don't have 4 live 5 doesn't watch 6 wear
7 works

c 2 goes 3 don't read 4 watches 5 drink 6 don't stop
7 does 8 doesn't like 9 don't do 10 studies
11 don't live 12 finishes

2B present simple [?]

a 2 Is 3 are 4 do 5 Do 6 Do 7 is 8 does 9 Are
10 do 11 Are 12 Do 13 Is 14 does 15 is

2C *a / an* + jobs

a 2 do they They're actors. 3 does he He's a doctor.
4 do they They're builders. 5 does she She's a secretary.
6 do they They're waiters. 7 does he He's a hairdresser.
8 do they They're police officers. 9 does he He's a
politician. 10 do they They're musicians.

2D possessive *s*

3 It's Fiona's bag. 4 It's Matt's CD. 5 It's Fiona's coat.
6 It's Nicola's dictionary. 7 It's Matt's piano.
8 It's Luke's shirt. 9 They're Nicola's pens.
10 It's Fiona's car. 11 They're Luke's football boots.
12 It's Nicola's book.

3A adjectives

a 2 He's an old waiter. 3 It's a cheap hotel.
4 It's an expensive car. 5 It's an easy exercise.
6 They're dirty glasses. 7 It's a small mobile (phone).
8 It's a big city. 9 He's a tall man. 10 It's a long snake.

3B telling the time; present simple

a 2 It's five to four. 3 It's twenty-five past twelve.
4 It's quarter to two. 5 It's twenty to nine.
6 It's twenty past eleven. 7 It's twenty-five to five.
8 It's ten to ten.

c 3 at quarter to nine 4 at nine o'clock 5 at quarter past
one 6 at six o'clock 7 at quarter to eight
8 at half past eight 9 at half past eleven

3C adverbs of frequency

Possible answers

a 2 She never goes to the gym. 3 She hardly ever does
exercise. 4 She hardly ever has breakfast.
5 She sometimes goes to the pub. 6 She sometimes gets
up late. 7 She often smokes. 8 She often drinks wine.
9 She usually goes to bed at 12.00. 10 She usually has
lunch at one o'clock. 11 She always goes to work by train.
12 She always gets home at 9.00.

3D prepositions of time

a 2 on 3 at 4 at 5 in 6 at 7 in 8 at 9 in 10 at
11 on 12 on 13 in 14 in 15 in 16 on 17 in
18 in 19 on 20 on

4A *can / can't*

a 3 Can open 4 can't draw 5 can't smoke 6 can't hear
7 can't swim 8 Can help 9 can't speak 10 can't play
11 Can open 12 can't find

4B *like* + (verb +/-*ing*)

a 2 loves cooking 3 doesn't like doing 4 likes watching
5 loves reading 6 doesn't like dancing 7 likes playing
8 hate getting up 9 loves playing 10 hates taking

4C object pronouns

a 2 us 3 them 4 him 5 her 6 him 7 you 8 it
9 them 10 us 11 it 12 her 13 me 14 them 15 us

4D possessive pronouns

a 2 ours 3 his 4 yours 5 ours 6 theirs 7 hers
8 mine

5A *was / were*

a 2 weren't 3 was 4 was 5 was 6 wasn't 7 wasn't
8 weren't 9 weren't 10 weren't 11 wasn't 12 wasn't
13 was 14 weren't 15 was

5B past simple regular verbs

a 3 He waited for the plane. 4 He didn't smoke.
5 He landed in Milan. 6 He travelled by bus to the hotel.
7 He arrived at the hotel. 8 He stayed at the hotel for two
nights. 9 He didn't visit the city. 10 He trained for three
hours. 11 He didn't play the match. 12 Milan scored
five goals.

5C past simple irregular verbs

a 2 had 3 was 4 was 5 saw 6 went 7 couldn't.
8 went 9 met 10 drove 11 had 12 got 13 went
14 drove 15 were 16 went 17 saw 18 didn't see
19 left 20 didn't see

b 2 did Lali have? 3 did she meet Nestor?
4 did they drive / go? 5 did they do 6 did they get home?
7 did Lali go 8 Did Nestor see 9 did she do?
10 Did she see him

5D past simple regular and irregular

2 didn't come   3 did you see   4 woke up   5 had
6 drove   7 went   8 was   9 made   10 did you come
11 came   12 sat   13 read   14 had   15 went   16 had
17 slept   18 Did you speak   19 came   20 did she say
21 didn't speak   22 said   23 took   24 didn't say
25 heard   26 didn't see

6A *there is / there are*

a 2 Is there an armchair in the living room? Yes, there is.
3 Is there a window in the study? No, there isn't.
4 Are there any plants in the kitchen? Yes, there are.
5 Is there a mirror in the hall? Yes, there is.
6 Are there any pictures in the house? No, there aren't.
b 2 There isn't a clock in the hall.
3 There's a shower in the bathroom.
4 There isn't a television in the bedroom.
5 There are some cupboards in the kitchen.
6 There aren't any flowers in the living room.

6B *there was / there were*

a 2 there weren't   3 Was there   4 there were   5 there
wasn't   6 were there   7 there were   8 Were there
9 there wasn't   10 Was there   11 There was   12 there
weren't   13 Was there   14 There were   15 There wasn't

6C present continuous

2 's happening?   3 're winning   4 aren't playing
5 aren't watching   6 'm driving   7 's doing   8 Is working?
9 're travelling   10 are doing   11 'm not working
12 'm looking for   13 are doing?   14 're counting
15 aren't counting   16 're playing   17 's doing?
18 's looking

6D present simple or present continuous?

2 do do   3 are going   4 Do go   5 'm listening
6 do listen   7 are having   8 Do have   9 Do wear
10 are wearing   11 's working   12 do work

7A countable / uncountable nouns

a 2 Is there any butter? Yes, there is.   3 Are there any
mushrooms? Yes, there are.   4 Is there any beer? No, there
isn't.   5 Is there any cheese? Yes, there is.   6 Is there a
lettuce? No, there isn't.   7 Are there any carrots? Yes, there
are.
b 2 There aren't any onions.   3 There is some milk.
4 There is some orange juice.   5 There aren't any bananas.
6 There are some grapes.   7 There isn't any meat.

7B *how much / how many?*

a 2 How many She eats a lot of vegetables.   3 How much
She doesn't drink much diet cola.   4 How much He eats a
lot of pasta.   5 How many He eats a lot of tomatoes.
6 How much He doesn't drink any beer.   7 How many
He doesn't eat any vegetables.   8 How many He eats a lot
of hamburgers.   9 How much He doesn't drink any
mineral water.   10 How much She drinks a lot of milk.
11 How many She doesn't eat many biscuits.   12 How
much She doesn't drink any coffee.

7C *be going to* (plans)

2 's going to bring   3 're going to buy   4 are going to do
5 aren't going to give   6 isn't going to teach   7 's going to
go back   8 Are going to watch   9 're going to watch
10 'm not going to go out   11 'm going to go   12 are
going to do   13 'm going to stay   14 Are going to take
15 're going to stay

7D *be going to* (predictions)

Possible answers
a 2 He's going to kiss her.   3 She's going to buy some shoes.
4 He's going to go to his Italian class.   5 He's going to have
/ eat a sandwich.   6 She's going to buy a dog.   7 He's
going to do the housework.   8 She's / They're going to
have a baby.

8A comparative adjectives

a 2 New York is more dangerous than London.   3 A Rolex
Daytona is more expensive than a Cartier Roadster.
4 Germany is smaller than France.   5 Water is healthier
than beer.   6 Seville is hotter than Toronto.
7 A Fiat Uno is slower than a Lamborghini Countach.
8 Compact discs are newer than cassettes.   9 Rio de
Janeiro is wetter than Moscow.   10 The Leaning Tower of
Pisa is older than the Taj Mahal.

8B superlative adjectives

a 2 What is the tallest animal in the world?
3 What is the fastest bird in the world?
4 What is the heaviest snake in the world?
5 What is the biggest land animal in the world?
6 What is the noisiest land animal in the world?
7 What is the noisiest sea animal in the world?
8 What is the slowest land animal in the world?
9 What is the most dangerous insect in the world?
b 2 the giraffe   3 the ostrich   4 the Burmese python
5 the African elephant   6 the Howler monkey   7 the blue
whale   8 the three-toed sloth   9 the Anopheles mosquito

8C *would like to / like*

a 2 Would you like to have   3 would like to have
4 would like to travel   5 Would you like to play
6 wouldn't like to be   7 would like to buy
c 1 Do   2 Would   3 Does   4 Would   5 Would

8D adverbs

a badly, carefully, dangerously, fast, well, hard, loud, quietly,
slowly
b 2 He's talking loudly.   3 He's driving slowly.   4 He's
opening quietly.   5 He's singing badly.   6 He's playing
well.   7 He's working hard.   8 He's riding dangerously.
9 He's writing carefully.

9A present perfect

a 2 She's been to Moscow.   3 Have they been to Sydney?
4 He's been to Rome.   5 Have you been to San Francisco?
6 They've been to London.   7 Has she been to Paris?
8 We haven't been to Rio.   9 They haven't been to Athens.
10 I've been to Dublin.

9B present perfect or past simple?

a 2 stayed   3 Have been   4 went   5 Have read   6 studied
7 did have   8 wasn't   9 Have spoken   10 've met
11 Did cry   12 was   13 Have seen   14 Did do
15 didn't have

9 revision of prepositions

a 2 at   3 for   4 at   5 in   6 to   7 to   8 on   9 at   10 to
11 by   12 for   13 in   14 for   15 to   16 for   17 on
18 in   19 in   20 for

New English File Teacher's Book Elementary
Photocopiable © Oxford University Press 2004

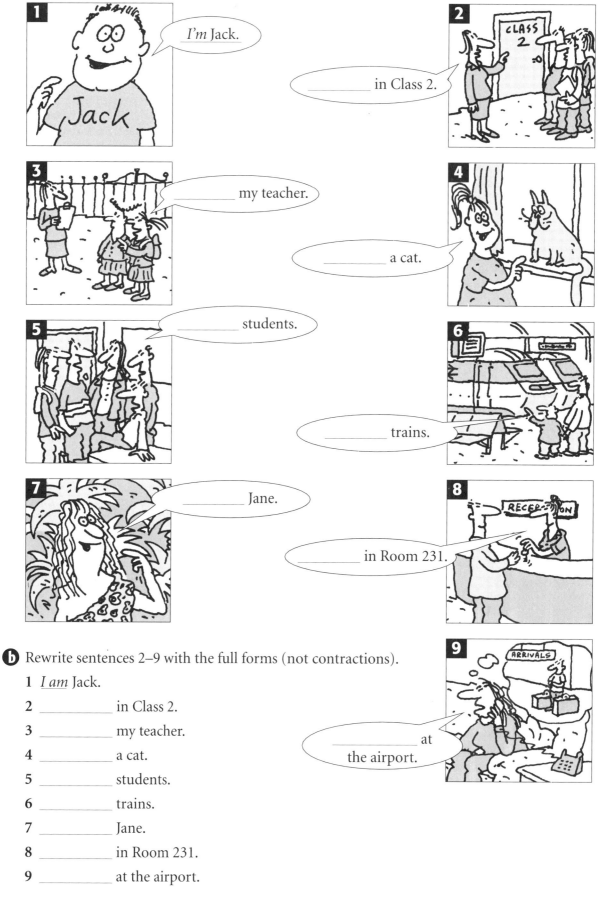

a Complete the sentences with a pronoun (*I*, *you*, etc.) and *'m*, *'re*, or *'s*.

1 *I'm* Jack.

_____ in Class 2.

_____ my teacher.

_____ a cat.

_____ students.

_____ trains.

_____ Jane.

_____ in Room 231.

b Rewrite sentences 2–9 with the full forms (not contractions).

1 *I am* Jack.

2 _____ in Class 2.

3 _____ my teacher.

4 _____ a cat.

5 _____ students.

6 _____ trains.

7 _____ Jane.

8 _____ in Room 231.

9 _____ at the airport.

_____ at the airport.

c **Test your memory.** Cover the sentences in **a**. Look at the pictures and say the sentences. Use contractions.

New English File Teacher's Book Elementary
Photocopiable © Oxford University Press 2004

ⓐ Complete the conversation with *is*, *are*, or *am*. Use contractions where possible.

PETRA Hello.

JUAN Hi.

PETRA [1] *Is* this Class 2?

JUAN Yes. [2]_____ you here for the English class?

PETRA Yes I [3]_____. [4]_____ you in this class too?

JUAN Yes. We [5]_____ in the same class. My name [6]_____ Juan.

PETRA Hello. My name [7]_____ Petra.

JUAN Where [8]_____ you from, Petra?

PETRA I [9]_____ from the Czech Republic. And you?

JUAN I [10]_____ from Madrid in Spain.

PETRA [11]_____ you Spanish?

JUAN No, I [12]_____ not. I [13]_____ Mexican, but I live in Spain.

PETRA Who [14]_____ our teacher?

JUAN Her name [15]_____ Diane.

PETRA [16]_____ she English?

JUAN No, she isn't. She [17]_____ Canadian.

PETRA Where [18]_____ the other students?

JUAN They [19]_____ in the classroom! We [20]_____ late!

ⓑ Practise the conversation with a partner.

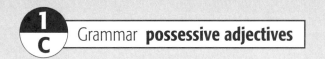
New English File Teacher's Book Elementary
Photocopiable © Oxford University Press 2004

a Look at the pictures. Complete the sentences with *my*, *your*, etc.

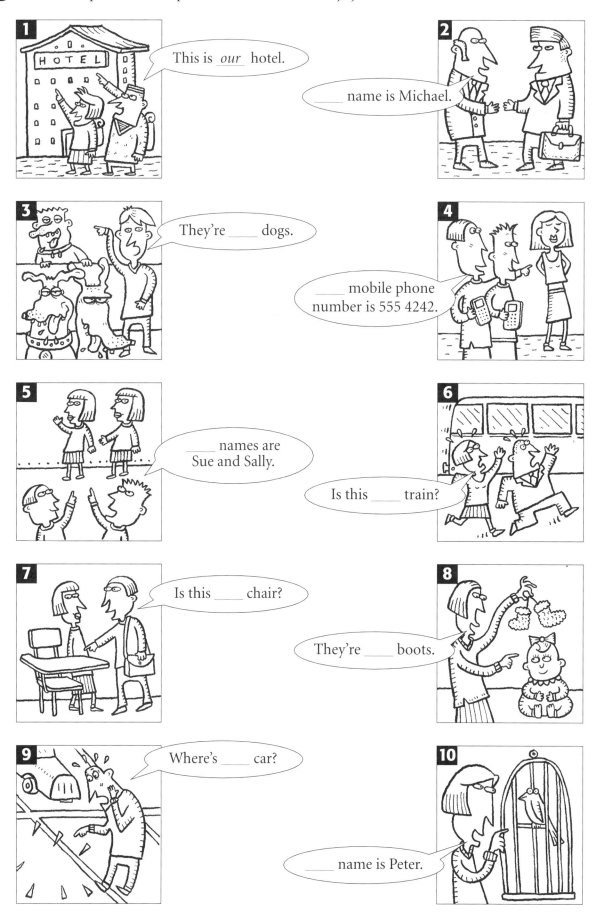

1 This is _our_ hotel.

2 ____ name is Michael.

3 They're ____ dogs.

4 ____ mobile phone number is 555 4242.

5 ____ names are Sue and Sally.

6 Is this ____ train?

7 Is this ____ chair?

8 They're ____ boots.

9 Where's ____ car?

10 ____ name is Peter.

b **Test your memory.** Cover the sentences. Look at the pictures and say the sentences.

New English File Teacher's Book Elementary
Photocopiable © Oxford University Press 2004

ⓐ Look at the pictures. Write the questions with *this, that, these,* and *those* and the answers.

What's that?
  It's a hotel.

What are these?
  They're glasses.

_____?
_____ TV.

_____?
_____ identity card.

_____?
_____ umbrella.

_____?
_____ coins.

_____?
_____ dictionaries.

_____?
_____ mobile phone.

_____?
_____ lighter.

_____?
_____ egg sandwich.

ⓑ **Test your memory.** Look at the pictures and say the sentences.

A *What's this/that?*
  What are these/those?

B *It's a …*
  They're …

ⓒ Complete the sentences with *a, an,* or *the*.

1 Open *the* window.

2 I don't know ____ answer.

3 She's from ____ city in Poland. I don't remember its name.

4 Read ____ text and answer ____ questions.

5 Where's ____ hotel?

6 It's ____ identity card.

7 **A** Is that ____ address book?
  B No, it's ____ diary.

8 Please close ____ door.

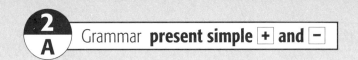

2A Grammar present simple + and −

New English File Teacher's Book Elementary
Photocopiable © Oxford University Press 2004

a Write a + or − sentence for each picture.

1 I *don't smoke.*

2 He _____ a lot of coffee.

3 They _____ children.

4 We _____ in that house.

5 He _____ TV.

b **Test your memory.** Cover the sentences. Look at the pictures and say the sentences.

c Complete the sentences using the correct form of the verb in brackets.

1 Jane and I _go_ to the cinema every Wednesday. (go)

2 Mario _____ to English classes on Tuesday and Thursday. (go)

3 I _____ in the evening. I watch TV. (not/read)

4 My mother _____ cooking programmes on TV. (watch)

5 British people _____ a lot of tea. (drink)

6 In Spain cars _____ at zebra crossings. (not/stop)

7 She _____ her homework in the evening. (do)

8 Amanda _____ dogs. (not/like)

9 A lot of men _____ housework. (not/do)

10 Gary _____ German. (study)

11 My parents _____ in a flat, they live in a house. (not/live)

12 It's a good film but it _____ at 12.00. (finish)

6 I _____ glasses.

7 She _____ in an office.

a Complete the conversation with *do*, *does*, *is*, or *are*.

ROB   Hi. I'm Rob.

MARTINA   I'm Martina. Nice to meet you.

ROB   ¹ *Do* you want a glass of wine?

MARTINA   Yes, please. Thank you.

ROB   Martina. ²_____ that a Spanish name?

MARTINA   I don't know, but I'm not Spanish.

ROB   Where ³_____ you from?

MARTINA   From Prague, but I live in the USA.

ROB   Where ⁴_____ you live in the USA?

MARTINA   In Boston.

ROB   ⁵_____ you like it there?

MARTINA   Yes, I love it. But I miss my family.

ROB   ⁶_____ your parents live in the Czech Republic?

MARTINA   Yes, and my brother too.

ROB   How old ⁷_____ he?

MARTINA   He's 24.

ROB   What ⁸_____ he do?

MARTINA   He's a student. He studies law at Prague University.

ROB   ⁹_____ you a student?

MARTINA   No, I teach Russian literature.

ROB   Where ¹⁰_____ you work?

MARTINA   At Harvard.

ROB   Harvard! ¹¹_____ you married?

MARTINA   Yes, I am.

ROB   Oh. ¹²_____ you have any children?

MARTINA   No, I don't.

ROB   ¹³_____ your husband American?

MARTINA   No, he's Russian.

ROB   And what ¹⁴_____ your husband do?

MARTINA   He's a policeman. Ah. here he is. Boris, this is … sorry, what ¹⁵_____ your name?

b Practise reading the conversation.

New English File Teacher's Book Elementary
Photocopiable © Oxford University Press 2004

a Look at the pictures. Write the question and the answer.

1 What _does she_ do?
She's a lawyer.

What _____ do?
_____ .

3 What _____ do?
_____ .

What _____ do?
_____ .

5 What _____ do?
_____ .

What _____ do?
_____ .

7 What _____ do?
_____ .

What _____ do?
_____ .

9 What _____ do?
_____ .

What _____ do?
_____ .

b **Test your memory.** Cover the sentences. Look at the pictures and say the sentences.

A *What does he do?*
B *He's a doctor.*

New English File Teacher's Book Elementary
Photocopiable © Oxford University Press 2004

Nicola
an English teacher

Luke
a footballer

Fiona
a doctor

Matt
a music student

a Look at objects 1–12. Whose are they?
Write ten more sentences.

1 *It's Luke's football.*
2 *They're Matt's books.*

3 _____ .
4 _____ .
5 _____ .
6 _____ .
7 _____ .
8 _____ .
9 _____ .
10 _____ .
11 _____ .
12 _____ .

b Cover the sentences. Test a partner.

A *Whose is this?*
B *It's Luke's football. Whose are these?*
A *They're Matt's books.*

New English File Teacher's Book Elementary
Photocopiable © Oxford University Press 2004

ⓐ Write sentences for pictures 1–10. Use an adjective from the box.

~~beautiful~~	big	cheap	dirty	easy
expensive	long	old	small	tall

1 *She's a beautiful actress* .

2 _____ .

3 _____ .

4 _____ .

5 _____ .

6 _____ .

7 _____ .

8 _____ .

9 _____ .

10 _____ .

ⓑ Test your memory. Cover the sentences and adjectives. Remember the sentences.

New English File Teacher's Book Elementary
Photocopiable © Oxford University Press 2004

a What's the time?

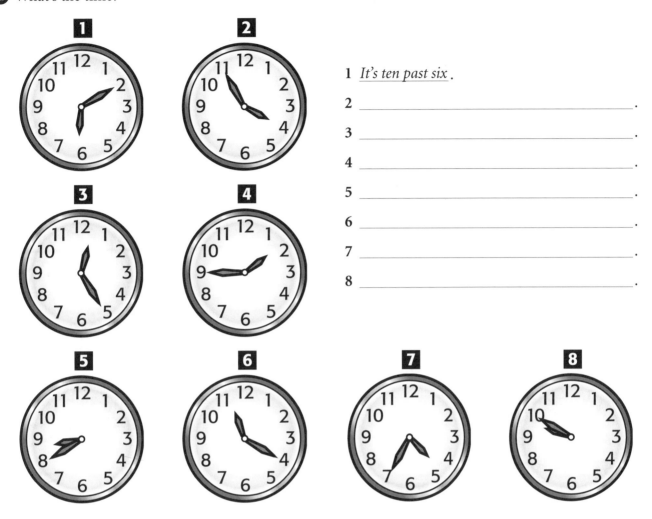

1 *It's ten past six* .

2 _____ .

3 _____ .

4 _____ .

5 _____ .

6 _____ .

7 _____ .

8 _____ .

b **Test your memory.** Cover the sentences and remember the times.

c Look at the clocks and complete the text.

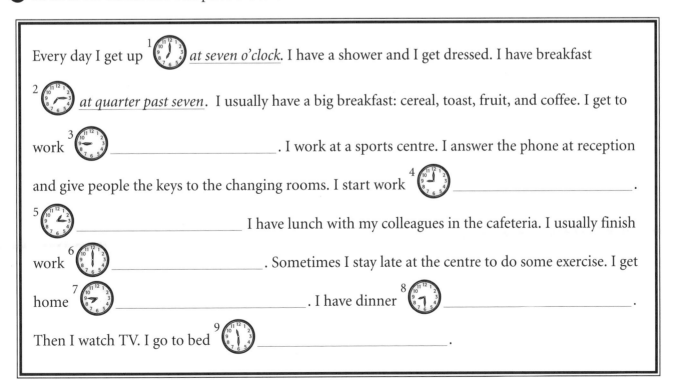

Every day I get up ¹ *at seven o'clock*. I have a shower and I get dressed. I have breakfast

² *at quarter past seven*. I usually have a big breakfast: cereal, toast, fruit, and coffee. I get to

work ³ _____ . I work at a sports centre. I answer the phone at reception

and give people the keys to the changing rooms. I start work ⁴ _____ .

⁵ _____ I have lunch with my colleagues in the cafeteria. I usually finish

work ⁶ _____ . Sometimes I stay late at the centre to do some exercise. I get

home ⁷ _____ . I have dinner ⁸ _____ .

Then I watch TV. I go to bed ⁹ _____ .

New English File Teacher's Book Elementary
Photocopiable © Oxford University Press 2004

a Look at the pictures and write sentences with the adverbs of frequency.

never

1 *She never goes to the cinema*.

2 _____ .

hardly ever

3 _____ .

4 _____ .

sometimes

5 _____ .

6 _____ .

often

7 _____ .

8 _____ .

usually

9 _____ .

10 _____ .

always

11 _____ .

12 _____ .

b **Test your memory.** Cover the sentences. Look at the pictures and say the sentences.

New English File Teacher's Book Elementary
Photocopiable © Oxford University Press 2004

a Complete the sentences with the correct preposition.
Write in the **in, on, at** column.

in, on, at

1 I wake up ____ 7.00.   *at*

2 I sometimes work ____ Saturdays.   ____

3 I never work ____ the weekend.   ____

4 I see my family ____ Christmas.   ____

5 I go on holiday ____ August.   ____

6 I go to bed ____ 11.00 p.m.   ____

7 I watch TV ____ the evening.   ____

8 I do my English homework ____ night.   ____

9 I read the newspaper ____ the morning.   ____

10 I have lunch ____ 1.30 p.m.   ____

11 I always go out ____ Friday nights.   ____

12 I go to a restaurant ____ New Year's Eve.   ____

13 I start a new school year ____ September.   ____

14 I go skiing ____ the winter.   ____

15 I have my holiday ____ the summer.   ____

16 I get up late ____ Saturday mornings.   ____

17 I usually have a cup of coffee ____ the afternoon.   ____

18 My birthday is ____ July.   ____

19 The party is ____ the 21st October.   ____

20 We have a meeting ____ the first Thursday of the month. ____

b **Test your memory.** Cover the **in, on, at** column and say the sentences.

a Look at the pictures. Complete the sentences with *can/can't* and a verb.

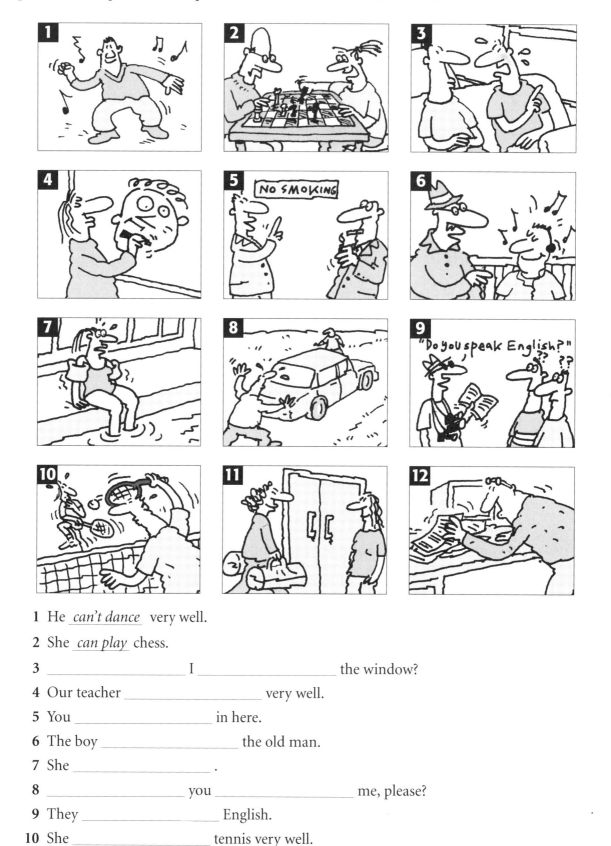

1 He _can't dance_ very well.

2 She _can play_ chess.

3 _____ I _____ the window?

4 Our teacher _____ very well.

5 You _____ in here.

6 The boy _____ the old man.

7 She _____ .

8 _____ you _____ me, please?

9 They _____ English.

10 She _____ tennis very well.

11 _____ you _____ the door for me, please?

12 He _____ his glasses.

b **Test your memory.** Cover the sentences. Look at the pictures and say the sentences.

New English File Teacher's Book Elementary
Photocopiable © Oxford University Press 2004

a Look at the pictures and write the sentences.

1 He *hates shopping*.

2 She _____ .

3 She _____
the housework.

4 He _____ TV.

5 She _____ novels.

6 He _____ .

7 She _____
computer games.

8 They _____ early.

9 He _____ the guitar.

10 She _____
the dog for a walk.

b **Test your memory.** Cover the sentences. Look at the pictures and say the sentences.

153

a Complete the sentences with *me, you, him, her, it, us,* or *them.*
Write in the **PRONOUN** column.

PRONOUN

1 It's an awful song. I hate ____ .   *it*

2 We have a meeting with the manager. She wants to speak to ____ .   ____

3 I like these clothes but I can't buy ____ . They are very expensive.   ____

4 I have a new baby son. I love ____ very much.   ____

5 My aunt lives in Prague. I like visiting ____ .   ____

6 My husband gets home late, but I always have dinner with ____ .   ____

7 Can you go to the office? The secretary wants to see ____ .   ____

8 It isn't a great film, but I like ____ because it has good special effects.   ____

9 **A** Do you like the Rolling Stones?

   B No, I don't like ____ . They are too old.   ____

10 We don't know the city very well. Can you help ____ ?   ____

11 This exercise is very difficult. I can't do ____ .   ____

12 My daughter is at university. We hardly ever see ____ .   ____

13 Hello again! Do you remember ____ ? My name's Jane.   ____

14 Where are my keys? I can't find ____ .   ____

15 We often write to Anne, but she never writes to ____ .   ____

b **Test your memory.** Cover the **PRONOUN** column. Say the sentences again
with the pronoun.

New English File Teacher's Book Elementary
Photocopiable © Oxford University Press 2004

a Look at the pictures and complete the sentences with *mine*, *yours*, *his*, *hers*, *ours*, or *theirs*.

1. I think that's *mine*.

2. It's not _____.

3. Is this _____?

4. I think this is _____.

5. Hey! That's _____.

6. Hello Jo, Hi Tim.
   They know our names but we don't know _____.

7. That's _____.

8. It's not _____.

b **Test your memory.** Cover the sentences. Look at the pictures and say the sentences.

New English File Teacher's Book Elementary
Photocopiable © Oxford University Press 2004

a Complete with *was/wasn't* or *were/weren't* to make true sentences.

1 Julius Caesar _wasn't_ the first Roman emperor.

2 The Olympic Games _____ in Barcelona in 1996.

3 Mozart _____ the composer of the *Marriage of Figaro*.

4 Albert Einstein _____ born in Germany.

5 Valentina Tereshkova _____ the first woman in space.

6 Vincent Van Gogh _____ from Belgium.

7 The 2002 football World Cup _____ in China.

8 The Incas _____ from Mexico.

9 The Beatles _____ from Manchester.

10 Socrates and Plato _____ Roman philosophers.

11 Che Guevara _____ born in Cuba.

12 Bill Clinton _____ President of the United States in 2002.

13 Marie Antoinette _____ Louis XVI's wife.

14 The Vikings _____ from Germany.

15 Garibaldi _____ born in Italy.

DR. GUEVARA

b Make questions and test your partner's memory.

A *Was Julius Caesar the first Roman Emperor?*

B *No, he wasn't.*

New English File Teacher's Book Elementary
Photocopiable © Oxford University Press 2004

1 arrive at Manchester airport   **2** check in   **3** wait for the plane   **4** not smoke

5 land in Milan   **6** travel by bus to the hotel   **7** arrive at the hotel   **8** stay at the hotel for two nights

9 not visit the city   **10** train for three hours   **11** not play the match   **12** Milan score five goals

ⓐ Look at the pictures. Write sentences in the past simple.

1 *Steve arrived at Manchester airport* .

2 *He checked in* .

3 _____ .

4 _____ .

5 _____ .

6 _____ .

7 _____ .

8 _____ .

9 _____ .

10 _____ .

11 _____ .

12 _____ .

ⓑ **Test your memory.** Cover the sentences and look at the pictures. Remember the story.

ⓐ Complete the story with the past simple of the verbs in brackets.

Lali's story

L ALI [1] _went_ into the Café Paris and [2]_____ (have) a coffee. The waiter's name [3]_____ (be) Nestor. He [4]_____ (be) tall and handsome. Lali fell in love with him the first time she [5]_____ (see) him.

The next day Lali [6]_____ (go) into the same café. 'Do you want to go out for lunch?' she asked Nestor. He [7]_____ (not / can). He finished work at six. 'But I can meet you after work,' he said.

Lali [8]_____ (go) back to the café and [9]_____ (meet) Nestor at 6.00. They [10]_____ (drive) to the beach in Nestor's car. At the beach they [11]_____ (have) a drink and danced at a disco. They [12]_____ (get) home after midnight.

Every day, Lali [13]_____ (go) to the café at 6.00 in the evening and they [14]_____ (drive) to the beach. They [15]_____ (be) very happy.

On Nestor's birthday, Lali wanted to surprise him. She [16]_____ (go) to the café in the morning. She [17]_____ (see) Nestor, but Nestor [18]_____ (not / see) Lali. He was with another girl. Lali [19]_____ (leave). She [20]_____ (not / see) Nestor again.

ⓑ Complete these questions about the text.

1 Where _____ _did Nestor and Lali meet_ _____? They met at the Café Paris.

2 What _____? She had a coffee.

3 What time _____? She met Nestor at 6.00.

4 Where _____? They drove to the beach.

5 What _____ at the beach? They had a drink, had dinner, and danced at a disco.

6 What time _____? They got home after midnight.

7 Where _____ on Nestor's birthday? She went to the café.

8 _____ her? No, he didn't.

9 What _____? She left.

10 _____ again? No, she didn't.

ⓒ **Test your memory.** Cover the answers. Can you remember them?

● Complete the conversation with the past tense of the verb in brackets.
Be careful with +, −, and ?.

A NEW LIFE

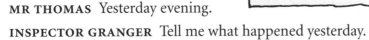

INSPECTOR GRANGER OK Mr Thomas. Relax and tell me the problem.

MR THOMAS It's my wife. She ¹*went* (go) out yesterday to buy some milk. And she ²_____ (not / come) back.

INSPECTOR GRANGER When ³_____ (/ you see) your wife for the last time?

MR THOMAS Yesterday evening.

INSPECTOR GRANGER Tell me what happened yesterday.

MR THOMAS Well, we ⁴_____ (wake up) at about 8.00 as usual. We ⁵_____ (have) breakfast and then I ⁶_____ (drive) to work. I think she ⁷_____ (go) shopping. It ⁸_____ (be) a Wednesday. She always goes shopping on Wednesdays. Then she ⁹_____ (make) the dinner.

INSPECTOR GRANGER When ¹⁰_____ home? (/ you come)

MR THOMAS I ¹¹_____ (come) home at six o'clock. I ¹²_____ (sit) down in my chair and ¹³_____ (read) the newspaper. Then we ¹⁴_____ (have) dinner. After dinner, my wife ¹⁵_____ (go) to the kitchen. I ¹⁶_____ (have) a glass of whisky and ¹⁷_____ (sleep) in my chair.

INSPECTOR GRANGER ¹⁸_____ (/ you speak) to your wife when you ¹⁹_____ (come) home? Or ²⁰_____ (/ she say) anything to you?

MR THOMAS I ²¹_____ (not / speak) to her, but after about an hour she ²²_____ (say), 'This isn't a life. I'm going out.' She ²³_____ (take) her bag and her coat. She ²⁴_____ (not / say) goodbye. I ²⁵_____ (hear) the door close. But I ²⁶_____ (not / see) her again.

INSPECTOR GRANGER I see sir. I think I can guess the answer to this mystery.

159

New English File Teacher's Book Elementary
Photocopiable © Oxford University Press 2004

a Write the questions and short answers.

1 sofa / living room? *Is there a sofa in the living room*?   *Yes, there is*.

2 armchair / living room? _____ ? _____.

3 window / study? _____ ? _____.

4 plants / kitchen? _____ ? _____.

5 mirror / hall? _____ ? _____.

6 pictures / house? _____ ? _____.

b Write ⊞ or ⊟ sentences.

1 sofa / living room *There's a sofa in the living room* .

2 clock / hall _____ .

3 shower / bathroom _____ .

4 television / bedroom _____ .

5 cupboards / kitchen _____ .

6 flowers / living room _____ .

New English File Teacher's Book Elementary
Photocopiable © Oxford University Press 2004

a Complete the sentences with *there was / there wasn't,*
there were / there weren't, or *was there / were there.*

1   a rock concert in the park last night.   *There was*

2 I looked in the fridge, but   any eggs.   _____

3   a supermarket in the town when you were a child?   _____

4 When we arrived,   only three people in the restaurant.   _____

5 It was an expensive hotel, but   a swimming pool or a gym, so I couldn't do any exercise.   _____

6 How many students   in class yesterday?   _____

7 When I got home,   two men in a car outside our house.   _____

8   many tourists in Rome when you went in January?   _____

9 It was a nice house, but we didn't buy it because   a garden.   _____

10   a party last night in the flat upstairs? I heard a lot of noise in the middle of the night.   _____

11   a good film on TV last night. Did you watch it?   _____

12 I went to that new shop, but   any clothes that I liked and I didn't buy anything.   _____

13   a cooker in the kitchen?   _____

14   80,000 people at the football match last night.   _____

15 We didn't go to the British Museum.   time.   _____

b **Test your memory.** Cover the right-hand column and say the sentences.

New English File Teacher's Book Elementary
Photocopiable © Oxford University Press 2004

● Complete the sentences with the verb in brackets in the present continuous.

A ¹*Are* you *watching* the match (watch)?

B Of course we are.

A What ²_____ (happen)?

B We ³_____ (win) 1–0, but we ⁴_____
(not/play) very well. Why ⁵_____ you _____
(not/watch) the match?

A I ⁶_____ (drive) home from work but the traffic is
terrible.

A How's your sister?

B She's fine.

A What ⁷_____ she _____ (do) now? ⁸_____ she
_____ (work)?

A No, she's in Thailand at the moment with two friends. They
⁹_____ (travel) round the world.

A What ¹⁰_____ you _____ (do) now?

B I ¹¹_____ (not/work) at the moment but
I ¹²_____ (look for) a job.

A What can you see?

B There are three men downstairs.

A What ¹³_____ they _____ (do)?

B They ¹⁴_____ (count) money I think. No, sorry.
They ¹⁵_____ (not/count) money. They
¹⁶_____ (play) cards.

A Can you see Jim?

B Yes, he's upstairs.

A What ¹⁷_____ he _____ (do)?

B He ¹⁸_____ (look) at us!

New English File Teacher's Book Elementary
Photocopiable © Oxford University Press 2004

● Put the verbs in the present simple or present continuous.

1 A _Are_ you _doing_ anything at the moment? (**do**)
   B No, I'm free today.

2 A What _____ you _____? (**do**)
   B I'm a student.

3 A Where _____ you _____? (**go**)
   B To the cinema.

4 A _____ you _____ to the gym every day? (**go**)
   B No, just Mondays, Wednesdays, and Fridays.

5 A What is the answer to number 5?
   B Shh! I _____ to the teacher. (**listen**)

6 A When _____ you _____ to music? (**listen**)
   B In the evening, when I get home from work.

7 A What is that loud music?
   B My neighbours _____ a party. (**have**)

8 A _____ you _____ any brothers and sisters? (**have**)
   B Just one sister.

9 A _____ you _____ a uniform for work? (**wear**)
   B Yes. I hate it!

10 A Why _____ you _____ your best clothes? (**wear**)
    B I'm going out to dinner with Mark.

11 A Where's Simon?
    B He _____ in the garden at the moment. (**work**)

12 A Where _____ you _____? (**work**)
    B In a bank.

    12

10–12 Excellent. You understand the difference between the
   present continuous and the present simple.

8–11 Quite good, but check the rules in the Grammar Bank
   (Student's Book *p.132*) and look at the exercise again.

1–7 This is difficult for you. Read the rules in the
   Grammar Bank (Student's Book *p.132*).
   Then ask your teacher for another photocopy and do
   the exercise again at home.

a Write the questions and short answers.

1 eggs   *Are there any eggs?*   *No, there aren't.*

2 butter   _____ ?   _____ .

3 mushrooms   _____ ?   _____ .

4 beer   _____ ?   _____ .

5 cheese   _____ ?   _____ .

6 lettuce   _____ ?   _____ .

7 carrots   _____ ?   _____ .

b Write ⊞ or ⊟ sentences with *a/an*, *some*, or *any*.

1 bread   *There isn't any bread.*

2 onions   _____ .

3 milk   _____ .

4 orange juice   _____ .

5 bananas   _____ .

6 grapes   _____ .

7 meat   _____ .

c **Test your memory.** Cover the sentences. Look at the picture and say what there is and isn't in the fridge.

New English File Teacher's Book Elementary
Photocopiable © Oxford University Press 2004

ⓐ Cross out the wrong word. Then answer the question with a complete sentence with *a lot of, not … much, not … many, not … any.*

Valerie the vegetarian

1 How much/~~many~~ meat does she eat?
   She doesn't eat any meat .

2 How *much/ many* vegetables does she eat?

   _____ .

3 How *much/ many* diet cola does she drink?

   _____ .

Fabio the Italian Food Fan

4 How *much/ many* pasta does he eat?

   _____ .

5 How *much/ many* tomatoes does he eat?

   _____ .

6 How *much/ many* beer does he drink?

   _____ .

Fast Food Phil

7 How *much/ many* vegetables does he eat?

   _____ .

8 How *much/ many* hamburgers does he eat?

   _____ .

9 How *much/ many* mineral water does he drink?

   _____ .

Baby Belinda

10 How *much/ many* milk does she drink?

   _____ .

11 How *much/ many* biscuits does she eat?

   _____ .

12 How *much/ many* coffee does she drink?

   _____ .

ⓑ **Test your memory.** Cover the sentences and look at the pictures. Remember what they eat and drink.

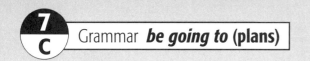

New English File Teacher's Book Elementary
Photocopiable © Oxford University Press 2004

● Complete the sentences with *be + going to* . Use the verb in brackets.

A ¹ _Is_ Anna _going to be_ at your party? (**be**)

B Yes, and she ²_____ her new boyfriend. (**bring**)

A Where are your parents?

B They're out shopping. They ³_____ a new TV. (**buy**)

A What ⁴_____ they _____ with the old one? (**do**)

B I don't know, but they ⁵_____ it to me. (**not / give**)

A Mike ⁶_____ us next year. (**not teach**)

B Why not?

A Because he ⁷_____ to the USA. (**go back**)

A ⁸_____ you _____ the football match tonight ? (**watch**)

B No, we ⁹_____ the film on the other channel. (**watch**)

A I ¹⁰_____ tonight. (**not / go out**)

B Why not?

A I'm too tired. I ¹¹_____ to bed at 10.00. (**go**)

A What ¹²_____ you _____ next weekend? (**do**)

B I ¹³_____ with my sister in Brighton. (**stay**)

A ¹⁴_____ you _____ the children? (**take**)

B No, they ¹⁵_____ with their grandmother. (**stay**)

15

12–15 Excellent. You can use *going to* very well.

8–11 Quite good, but check the rules in the Grammar Bank (Student's Book *p.134*) and look at the exercise again.

1–7 This is difficult for you. Read the rules in the Grammar Bank (Student's Book *p.134*). Then ask your teacher for another photocopy and do the exercise again at home.

a What are they going to do? Write your predictions for each picture.

1 *He's going to watch TV*.

2 _____ .

3 _____ .

4 _____ .

5 _____ .

6 _____ .

7 _____ .

8 _____ .

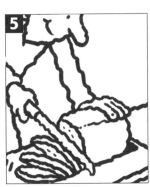

Note to teacher: Cut here and give out exercise a.
Then give out exercise b for students to compare their answers.

b Look at the pictures. Were your predictions correct?

New English File Teacher's Book Elementary
Photocopiable © Oxford University Press 2004

● Use the information to make comparative sentences.

1
Diameter
– Mars 6,786 km
– Earth 12,756 km

big

1 *Earth is bigger than Mars*.

2 _____ .

2
Murders in 2001
– New York 643
– London 200

dangerous

3
Price
– A Rolex Daytona €5204
– A Cartier Roadster €3828

expensive

3 _____ .

4 _____ .

4
Area
– Germany 356,840 km^2
– France 543,965 km^2

small

5
Calories per glass
– beer 130
– water 0

healthy

5 _____ .

6 _____ .

6
Average temperature
– Seville 18°C
– Toronto 7°C

hot

7
Maximum speed
– A Fiat Uno 165 km/h
– A Lamborghini Countach 330 km/h

slow

7 _____ .

8 _____ .

8
Invented
– compact discs 1981
– cassettes 1963

new

9
Annual rainfall
– Moscow 575mm
– Rio de Janeiro 1086mm

wet

9 _____ .

10 _____ .

10
Built
– The Leaning Tower of Pisa 1350
– The Taj Mahal 1653

old

● **Test your memory.** Cover the sentences and look at the pictures. Compare the things.

New English File Teacher's Book Elementary
Photocopiable © Oxford University Press 2004

a Write the questions.

1 fast / land animal / world.
   What is the fastest land animal in the world ?

2 tall / animal / world
   _____ ?

3 fast / bird / world
   _____ ?

4 heavy / snake / world
   _____ ?

5 big / land animal / world
   _____ ?

6 noisy / land animal / world
   _____ ?

7 noisy / sea animal / world
   _____ ?

8 slow / land animal / world
   _____ ?

9 dangerous / insect / world
   _____ ?

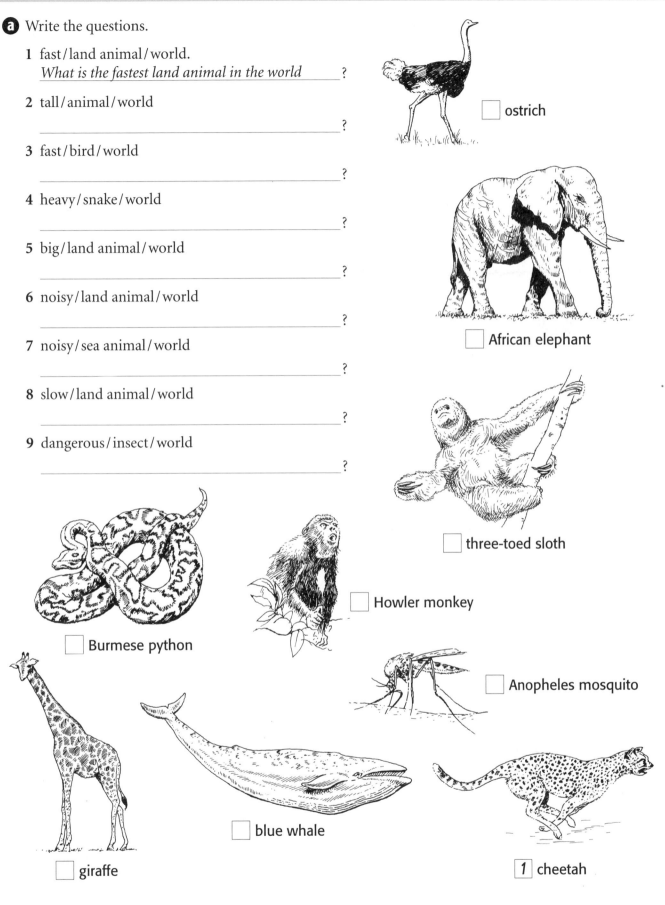

☐ ostrich

☐ African elephant

☐ three-toed sloth

☐ Howler monkey

☐ Anopheles mosquito

☐ Burmese python

☐ giraffe

☐ blue whale

1 cheetah

b Match the questions with the answers.

c **Test your memory.** Cover the sentences. Look at the pictures and say the sentences.

The cheetah is …

8 C Grammar *would like to / like*

New English File Teacher's Book Elementary
Photocopiable © Oxford University Press 2004

a Look at the pictures. Write a ⊕ or ⊖ sentence or ?. Use *would like* and a verb.

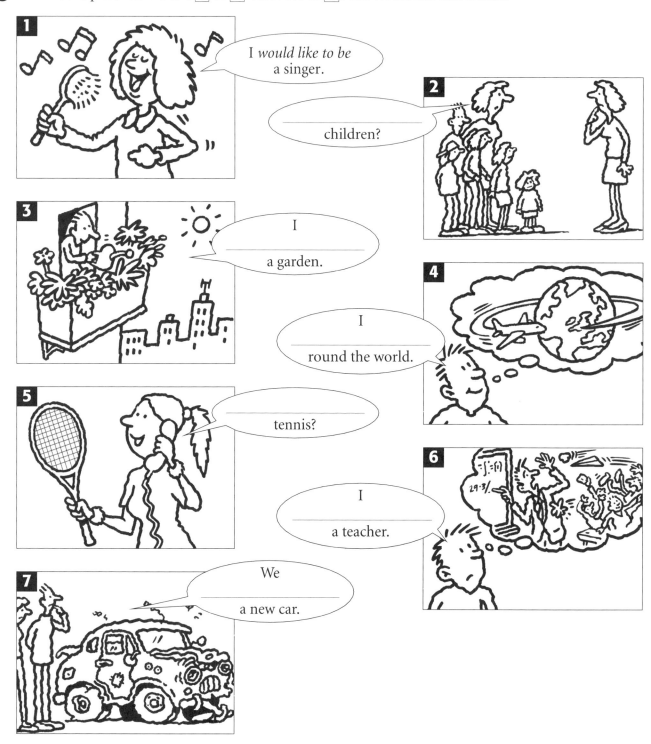

1 I *would like to be* a singer.

2 _____ children?

3 I _____ a garden.

4 I _____ round the world.

5 _____ tennis?

6 I _____ a teacher.

7 We _____ a new car.

b **Test your memory.** Cover the sentences. Look at the pictures and say the sentences.

c Complete the dialogues with *would* or *do / does*.

1 A _____ you like classical music?
  B No, I prefer pop.

2 A _____ you like to have dinner with me tonight?
  B I'm sorry. I'm busy tonight.

3 A _____ your sister like cooking?
  B Yes, she loves it.

4 A _____ you like another drink?
  B Yes, please.

5 A _____ your parents like to come to dinner?
  B I don't know. Why don't you ask them?

New English File Teacher's Book Elementary
Photocopiable © Oxford University Press 2004

a Make adverbs from the adjectives.

bad_____   careful_____   dangerous_____   fast_____

good_____   hard_____   loud_____   quiet_____   slow_____

b Write sentences for pictures 1–8. Use a verb and an adverb from **a**.

She's running fast.

_____.

_____.

_____ the door _____.

_____.

_____.

_____.

_____.

_____.

c **Test your memory.** Cover the sentences. Look at the pictures and say the sentences.

171

a Look at the city names.
Write a +, –, ? sentence in the present perfect.

He – **New York**

1 *He hasn't been to New York*.

She + **Moscow**

2 _____ .

They ? **Sydney**

3 _____ ?

He + **Rome**

4 _____ .

You ? **San Francisco**

5 _____ ?

They + **London**

6 _____ ?

She ? **Paris**

7 _____ ?

We – **Rio**

8 _____ .

They – **Athens**

9 _____ .

I + **Dublin**

10 _____ .

b Cover the sentences. Look at the cities and say the sentences.

New English File Teacher's Book Elementary
Photocopiable © Oxford University Press 2004

● Write the verbs in the present perfect or past simple.

A [1] _Did_ you _go_ to the cinema last night. (**go**)
B No, I [2]_____ at home. (**stay**)

A [3]_____ you ever _____ to Mexico? (**go**)
B Yes, I have. I [4]_____ last year. (**go**)

A [5]_____ you _____ any Latin American novels? (**read**)
B Yes. I [6]_____ Spanish when I was at university. (**study**)

A What [7]_____ you _____ for dinner last night? (**have**)
B Nothing, I [8]_____ hungry. (**not be**)

A [9]_____ you ever _____ to a famous actor? (**speak**)
B No, I [10]_____ never _____ a famous person. (**meet**)

A [11]_____ you _____ at the end of *Titanic*? (**cry**)
B Yes. It [12]_____ very sad. (**be**)

A [13]_____ you _____ the new James Bond film? (**see**)
B No. Is it good?

A [14]_____ you _____ your homework last night? (**do**)
B No, I [15]_____ time. (**not / have**)

☐ **15**

13–15 Excellent. You understand the difference between the Present perfect and the Past simple.

8–12 Quite good, but check the rules in the Grammar Bank (Student's Book *p.138*) and look at the exercise again.

1–7 This is difficult for you. Read the rules in the Grammar Bank (Student's Book *p.138*). Then ask your teacher for another photocopy and do the exercise again at home.

a Complete the sentences with a preposition. Write in the **PREPOSITION** column.

at	by	for	from	in	on	to	up

PREPOSITION

1 My name's Carlos and I'm ____ Chile.   *from*

2 Look ____ the board please.   ____

3 My father works ____ IBM in France.   ____

4 Our son is ____ school today.   ____

5 My parents live ____ a small flat.   ____

6 I don't like listening ____ the radio.   ____

7 We go ____ the cinema twice a week.   ____

8 My sister never goes out ____ Friday nights.   ____

9 Her husband gets home very late ____ night.   ____

10 It's quarter ____ eight.   ____

11 This morning I came to work ____ bus.   ____

12 Would you like a salad ____ lunch?   ____

13 The fortune teller said I'm going to fall ____ love.   ____

14 Wait ____ me!   ____

15 The lamp is next ____ the bed.   ____

16 I'm looking ____ my car keys. I can't find them.   ____

17 We live ____ the first floor.   ____

18 Are there any biscuits ____ the cupboard?   ____

19 This is the most expensive street ____ the city.   ____

20 Water is very good ____ you.   ____

b Test your memory. Cover the **PREPOSITION** column. Say the sentences with the preposition.

174

Tips for using Communicative activities

- We have suggested the ideal number of copies for each activity. However, you can often manage with fewer, e.g. one copy per pair instead of one per student.

- Many of the activities will provide useful reference for SS, e.g. **Food questionnaire 7B**, and **Guess the comparative 8A**. Encourage SS to keep these activities in their files.

- When SS are working in pairs, if possible get them to sit face to face. This will encourage them to really talk to each other and also means they can't see each other's sheet.

- If your class doesn't divide into pairs or groups, take part yourself, get two SS to share one role, or get one student to monitor, help, and correct.

- If some SS finish early, they can swap roles and do the activity again, or you could get them to write some of the sentences from the activity.

- With some activities we have left space for you to add information to make them more relevant to your students.

Fancy dress party
A / A mingle activity

SS introduce themselves to everybody in the class and then try to remember who was who. Copy and cut up one sheet per 16 SS.

> **LANGUAGE**
> Hello / Hi.   I'm … / My name's …   Nice to meet you.

- Give each student one card. If you have more than 16 SS, either invent some more names and write them on strips of paper, or have some characters repeated.

- Write the phrases in **LANGUAGE** on the board and drill pronunciation.

- Tell SS they're at a fancy dress party. They are dressed up as the 'character' on the card. They must introduce themselves to everybody else at the party. They mustn't show anybody their card. Tell SS to stand up and begin the activity.

- When SS have finished, ask them to sit down again.

- Ask SS 'Can you remember who is who?' Elicit complete answers, using the language on the board (e.g. *He's Dracula. She's Lara Croft.*)

Extra idea Put on some lively, party music in the background while SS do this activity.

Where are they from?
B / A pairwork information gap activity

SS ask and answer where famous people are from. Copy one sheet per pair and cut into **A** and **B**.

> **LANGUAGE**
> *Is Kylie Minogue American?   No she isn't. She's Australian.*
> *Where's she from?   She's from Melbourne.*

- Write the example dialogue from **LANGUAGE** on the board. Model and drill the questions and answers.

- Put SS in pairs and give out the sheets. Sit **A** and **B** so they can't see each other's paper. Explain to SS that they have different information. Focus on the instructions and examples.

- **A** and **B** take turns to ask and answer the questions about the famous people. **A** starts. **They must not show their partner the piece of paper.**

- When SS have finished, ask them if they were surprised by the nationalities of any of the people in the photos.

Personal information
C / A mingle activity

Students ask and answer questions to complete business cards with personal information about each other. Copy and cut up one sheet per eight SS.

> **LANGUAGE**
> *What's your name, please?   And your surname?*
> *What's your e-mail address? Can you spell it?* (+ alphabet)
> *What's your phone number?* (+ numbers 0–10)

- If necessary, revise the alphabet and numbers before you start.

- Divide the class into groups of eight (or fewer, e.g. if you have 20 SS, have two groups of eight and one of four). Use one set of cards per group

- Give each student one strip with a card and two blanks. Focus on the first card and tell them that they are that person. Check that they know how to say the @ sign (*at*) and the . (*dot*). Tell them not to worry if they can't pronounce the names perfectly.

- Now focus on the blank cards and elicit the questions they need to ask to get that information (see **LANGUAGE**). Write the questions on the board.

- Tell SS they are at a conference. They must complete the blank business cards with information about two other people from their group. Demonstrate with one of the students first.

- SS mingle and complete their forms.

Mystery objects
D / A pairwork guessing game

SS talk about close-up photos of everyday objects. Copy one sheet per pair.

> **LANGUAGE**
> *What's this?*   *I think it's a (credit card).*
> *What are these?*   *I think they're (keys)*
> Common objects

- Copy the phrases in **LANGUAGE** onto the board. Model and drill pronunciation.
- In pairs SS take turns to ask and answer questions pointing at the photos.
- If a pair has answered all the questions they can, but still don't know what some of the objects are, they can ask other pairs of students.
- At the end of the activity, go through all the pictures and ask SS what they are.

1	a bag	11	a lipstick
2	stamps	12	cigarettes
3	coins	13	matches
4	sunglasses	14	a lighter
5	a file	15	tissues
6	a credit card	16	keys
7	a newspaper	17	a mobile (phone)
8	a pencil	18	an identity card
9	a purse	19	an umbrella
10	a book	20	a comb

2 A — They're brothers but they're different

A pairwork activity

SS use picture prompts to speak about two brothers. They have to find out how many things the brothers have in common. Copy one sheet per pair and cut into **A** and **B**.

> **LANGUAGE**
> Present simple: *he*
> ⊞ *He lives in a flat.* ⊟ *He doesn't watch TV.*

- Write the names Steve and Simon on the board. Explain that Steve and Simon are brothers, but they are different. SS have to find out how many things the brothers have in common.
- Give out the copies to SS in pairs, **A** and **B**. **SS must not show each other their worksheet.**
- Demonstrate the activity by eliciting one sentence about Steve and one sentence about Simon.
- In pairs, SS use the pictures to describe Steve and Simon to each other.
- Ask SS how many things the brothers have in common. (they wear glasses, they have a car)
- Elicit correct sentences on the board with the whole class. Focus on the spelling of, e.g. *plays, watches, doesn't.*

A Steve		
	He does yoga.	He doesn't watch TV.
	He lives in a flat.	He drives an old car.
	He drinks beer.	He wears glasses.
	He eats Chinese food.	He smokes.
B Simon	He plays tennis.	He watches TV.
	He lives in a big house.	He drives a new car.
	He drinks wine.	He wears glasses.
	He eats pasta.	He doesn't smoke.

Extra idea When you have finished checking the answers, clean the board. Tell SS to look at their pictures together again and remember the sentences.

2 B — Somebody like you

A mingle activity

SS answer questions about themselves, and then ask other SS the questions to find somebody similar to them. Copy and cut up one sheet per three SS.

> **LANGUAGE**
> Present simple *Wh-?* questions and answers:
> *What sports do you play? I play football.*

- Give one section to each student. Ask SS to fill in the information about themselves in the first part (YOU).
- Tell SS they are all at a party together. They must ask each other questions to find a person who is similar to them. Elicit and drill the questions from the second part of the worksheet (OTHER PEOPLE). You could get SS to interview you first.
- SS mingle and ask and answer questions. Make it clear that they must try to talk to as many different people as possible at the party. Set a time limit.
- When they have finished, ask individual SS who is similar to them in the class.

Extra idea Put on some lively, party music in the background while SS do this activity.

2 C — What do they do?

A group board game

SS move around a board making sentences about different jobs and collecting points. Make one copy of the board game for every four students. You also need a dice to play this game, one dice per group.

> **LANGUAGE**
> Present simple: *he/she* ⊞ *He works in a bank.*
> Jobs vocabulary

- Quickly revise the language in 'Guess my job' (Student's Book *p. 21*).
- Write on the board 'A nurse'. Ask SS 'What does a nurse do?' Elicit different sentences, e.g. 'She works in a hospital/ She wears a uniform/ She works with other people.'
- Put SS in small groups (3 or 4). Give each group a copy of the board game and a dice.
- Write on the board: 3 correct sentences = 3 points; 2 correct sentences = 2 points; 1 correct sentence = 1 point.
- Explain the rules of the game. SS throw a dice and move the corresponding number of squares on the board. When they land on a square, they must try to make a maximum of three sentences about the job. If they can make three sentences they get 3 points, if only two, 2 points, etc. One student keeps the scores for the group.
- If a student lands on a square which another student has previously landed on, they must make *different* sentences.
- SS play the game in groups. The game finishes when someone reaches the FINISH square. SS add up their points. The student with the most points wins.

⚠ If you don't have dice tell SS to write numbers 1–6 on separate pieces of paper and put them in an envelope. Each SS picks a number when it's his/her turn and then puts it back.

2
D Who's who?

A pairwork information gap activity

SS complete a family tree. Copy one sheet per pair, and cut into A and B.

> **LANGUAGE**
> *Who's Andrew's mother? Rita.*
> *How do you spell it? R-I-T-A*
> *What does she do? She's retired.*
> Family vocabulary: *mother, father, etc.*

- Give out the copies to SS in pairs, A and B. Sit A and B so they can't see each other's paper. **They must not look at each other's family tree.**

- Explain that they have to find out the names of all the people in Andrew's family and what they do. Focus on the instructions and examples.

- Demonstrate the activity. Take the part of A and ask the Bs. 'Who's Andrew's mother?' When the class answers, ask them to spell her name and write it on the board.

- Ask 'What does she do?' When the class answers, write *Retired* next to Rita's name. Then take the part of B and ask the As 'Who's Andrew's father? How do you spell it? What does he do?'

- SS take turns to ask and answer questions to complete their family trees in pairs. Tell them to ask all questions in relation to Andrew. Remind them to ask each other to spell the names.

- When they have completed their family trees, SS compare to check they have the right names and jobs.

3
A The same or different?

An information gap activity

SS describe different pictures to each other and decide if they are the same or different. Copy one sheet per pair and cut into A and B.

> **LANGUAGE**
> Adjectives and nouns: *an old house, wet jeans*

- Give out copies and sit A and B so they can't see each other's picture. Explain to SS that they have 15 pictures. Five are the same and ten are different.

- They have to write same (S) or different (D) on each one. They must find ten different pictures.

- Demonstrate the activity. Take the part of A and say 'My number 1 is an old house'. Elicit from the Bs, 'My number 1 is a new house'. Then tell both As and Bs to write D on square 1, because their pictures are different.

- In pairs, SS describe their pictures to each other and find which ten are different.

- When SS have finished check answers by asking which pictures are different, and get SS to compare their sheets.

> **A** 1 an old house D   2 a very tall waiter D
> 3 an expensive watch S   4 an empty glass D
> 5 a high mountain S   6 wet jeans S   7 an old woman D
> 8 short legs D   9 a poor man D   10 a dirty floor D
> 11 fair hair D   12 a small bag D   13 a fast car S
> 14 two thin men D   15 two beautiful women S

> **B** 1 new house D   2 short waiter D   3 expensive watch S
> 4 full glass D   5 high mountain S   6 wet jeans S
> 7 young woman D   8 long legs D   9 rich man D
> 10 clean floor D   11 dark hair D   12 big bag D
> 13 fast car S   14 two fat men D
> 15 two beautiful women S

3
B A day in the life of an English teacher

A picture story

SS tell an English Teacher's day in the present simple. Copy one sheet per student.

> **LANGUAGE**
> Present simple, routine verbs:
> *He gets up at 9.30. He has a shower.*
> Telling the time

- Give out one sheet per student. Use the pictures to elicit and drill the following suggested sentences about the English teacher:

  1 He wakes up at 9.30.
  2 He gets up.
  3 He has a coffee.
  4 He has a shower.
  5 At 10.30 he has breakfast and reads the newspaper.
  6 He gets dressed.
  7 He goes to work by train at 11.30.
  8 He gets to work at 12.00.
  9 He teaches/works from 12.00 to 2.00.
  10 He has lunch at 2.30.
  11 He teaches from 4.00 to 9.30.
  12 He has a drink with friends at 10.00.
  13 He goes home at 11.30.
  14 He corrects homework from 12.00 to 1.00.
  15 He goes to bed at 1.30.

- After every five sentences, see if the class can remember his day from the beginning.

- Put SS in pairs and get them to try to tell his day from the beginning. Ask SS if they think he is stressed.

  Extra idea Get SS to use the pictures to ask you about your day, e.g. What time do you wake up? What time do you get up? Do you have a coffee?

  Ask SS if you are similar or different to the teacher in the picture story.

3
C How often … ?

A pairwork question and answer activity

SS ask each other questions about regular activities. Copy one sheet per pair and cut into A and B.

> **LANGUAGE**
> *How often do you (go to the cinema)?*
> Adverbs of frequency: *never, always, hardly ever, etc.*
> Time expressions: *every day, once a week, etc.*

- SS work in pairs. Get one pair to demonstrate the activity. Student A asks 'How often do you go to the hairdresser's?' Student B chooses one of the answers from the language in the triangle. Then Student B asks 'How often do you go to the dentist's?' and student **A** chooses an answer from the language in the triangle.

EXTRA challenge Encourage SS to ask for / give more information, e.g. '*Why(not)?*', '*What kind of films do you like?*', '*What hairdresser do you go to?*', etc.

- SS take it in turns to ask and answer questions in pairs.
- Follow up by asking individual students to report on their partner.

3 Dates and times survey
D · A pairwork activity

SS complete a table with personal information about dates and times, then interview a partner. Copy one sheet per student.

> **LANGUAGE**
> *When is (your birthday)?*
> *What time do you (get up)?*
> *What is your favourite time (to watch TV)?*
> Prepositions of time: *at 8 o'clock, in February, on March 5th.*
> Days of the week, months, and times

- If necessary, quickly revise prepositions *on* (for days and dates), *in* (for months and seasons), *at* (for times).
- Focus on instruction **a**. Go through the instructions. SS answer each question for themselves in the column marked YOU. Do the first two examples with the class, using true information about yourself. Tell students they only need to write the day, date, or time. Allow them time to finish the first column.
- Now tell them to complete the last question themselves, and answer it.
- SS work in pairs. Focus on instruction **b**. SS interview each other and complete the column YOUR PARTNER with information about their partner. Demonstrate with a student. Ask them the first two questions, and elicit the answer with the preposition, e.g. 'When is your birthday?' 'On March 5th'. SS interview each other in pairs using the form. Encourage them to answer with the prepositions or in whole sentences. Monitor and correct prepositions.
- Get some feedback from individual students.

4 Find somebody who …
A · A class mingle

SS find somebody in the class for each category and ask follow-up questions. Copy and cut up one survey per student.

Before photocopying, to personalize the activity, complete number 8 with a relevant activity, e.g. *can / can't play* (+ a game), *can/can't make* (+ recipe /drink), *can / can't understand* (+ a language), etc. (Local examples are often the best, e.g. in Spain *Find somebody who can make a good paella*.). Give out the sheets.

> **LANGUAGE**
> can + activity verbs: *Can you (cook well)? Yes, I can. No, I can't.*
> Follow up questions: *What's your speciality?*

- Elicit the questions 1–8, i.e. *Can you (+ verb)?* Do the same for the follow up questions.

 Make sure SS don't try to use a negative question for question 7 (NOT ~~Can't you~~…?).

- Demonstrate the activity. Ask a student the first question: 'Can you play a musical instrument?' Elicit 'Yes, I can' or 'No, I can't'. If the student answers 'Yes, I can' write their name in the column on your sheet, then ask the follow up questions 'Which instrument (can you play)?' 'How well (can you play)?' If the student answers 'No, I can't' then say 'Thank you' and ask another student until somebody answers 'Yes, I can'.
- Tell SS to find and write the name of a different student for each category. SS mingle, asking each other the questions, and the follow-up questions if appropriate, and writing in names.
- Feedback to find out who can do what. You may need to teach *nobody*.

4 A partner for the perfect weekend?
B · A mingle activity

SS complete a table with information about their free time activities and then find a partner who has the same likes and dislikes. Copy and cut up one card per student.

> **LANGUAGE**
> *Do you like + verb + ing?   Yes, I do. No, I hate it.*

- Give each student a card. Explain that the form contains weekend activities.
- Go through the instructions. Tell SS they're going to find a partner to spend a perfect weekend with. First they must tick the boxes which are true for them.
- SS stand up and move around asking other SS questions based on their cards, e.g. 'Do you like cooking?' 'No, I hate it.' Tell them they have to talk to as many SS as possible to try to find somebody who has very similar tastes to them. Set a time limit, e.g. five minutes.
- Feedback. See if SS found one or several ideal partners.

4 What do you think of …?
C · A pairwork activity

SS ask each other what they think of local singers, restaurants, TV programmes etc. Copy one sheet per student.

> **LANGUAGE**
> *What do you think of (Milan)?   I love it./I hate it.*
> Object pronouns: *it, him, her, them*
> Adjectives: *fantastic, awful, great*

- Give SS the sheet and focus on instructions for **a**. Give SS time to write a name for each picture.
- Focus on instructions for **b**. Model and drill the language in the **USEFUL LANGUAGE** box. Emphasize the intonation of *great/fantastic* and *awful/terrible*.
- Demonstrate the activity. Write the name of a singer you like (or don't like) on the board and get SS to ask you, *What do you think of…?* Answer using phrases from **USEFUL LANGUAGE**, e.g. *I don't like him. He's awful!*

- SS in pairs take turns to ask *What do you think of…?* (singer/restaurant, etc.) and answer each other's questions.
- Get feedback.

⚠️ If you have a multi-lingual class, tell SS to use internationally famous people and a restaurant/shop in the town where they are studying.

Extra idea When they have finished the activity, you could ask SS to ask you what you think of some of the things they wrote down on their sheets.

4 Vowel sounds dominoes
D A group domino game

SS match different words according to their vowel sounds. Copy and cut up one sheet for every three or four SS.

> **LANGUAGE**
> Vowel sounds: /iː/, /ɔː/, /ɜː/, /ʌ/, /aɪ/, /eə/

- Write the following words on the board: s**o**n, f**a**ll, w**ear**, m**i**ne, m**e**, h**er**s. Drill pronunciation and elicit the English File sound word and sound (see *p. 156*) for each one, e.g.: son – up /ʌ/; fall – horse /ɔː/; wear – chair /eə/, mine – bike /aɪ/; me – tree /iː/; hers – bird /ɜː/
- Then write the word b**uy**. Ask SS which word has the same vowel sound. (*mine*). Do the same with th**ir**d (hers).
- Put SS in groups of three. Give each group a set of dominoes. Tell them to distribute them evenly (each student should have six dominoes).
- Explain the rules for dominoes. The first student puts down a domino. The next student must try to put down a domino with the same vowel sound.

| m**i**ne | l**u**nch | s**o**n | f**a**ll | sh**or**t | m**ee**t |

- SS must say the two matching words aloud as they put down the domino. The rest of the group decides if they are the same or not. If they aren't the same, the student keeps the card. If a student doesn't have a matching sound, he or she says 'Pass' and it is the next student's turn.
- Tell SS that the youngest person in each group starts the game. The winner is the person who puts down all their dominoes first. Circulate and monitor.
- When the game finishes, model and drill the pronunciation of any words students were having difficulties with.

Extra idea If one group finishes early, tell them to write down all the words on the dominoes in six different groups according to their vowel sounds.

5 Where was James?
A An information gap picture story

SS practise *was/ were + at/ in*. Copy one sheet per pair and cut into **A** and **B**.

> **LANGUAGE**
> *Where was James (in 1998)?*
> *He was at university.*

- SS in pairs. Give out copies to **A** and **B**. Sit **A** and **B** so they can't see each other's paper.
- Demonstrate the activity. Take the part of **B** and ask **A**s 'Where was James in 1998?' Elicit 'He was at university'. Then take the part of **A** and ask **B**s 'Where was Silvia in 1998?' SS ask and answer questions in turn to complete the information about James and Silvia.
- When finished, SS compare and join their pictures, and work out when and where James and Silvia were together. Check their answers.

> They were together a week ago, last Wednesday night, and yesterday afternoon.

Extra idea SS turn over their sheets. Write the time phrases on the board in a vertical column. In pairs, SS write down where they both were for each time, e.g. *James was at university. Silvia was at school.* Check answers, especially prepositions *in / at*.

5 Where's the match?
B A pairwork activity

SS put together a jumbled story, then retell the story. Copy and cut up one sheet for every pair of SS.

> **LANGUAGE**
> Past simple regular verbs: *checked, booked, played*

- Write on the board The Champions League. Ask SS which football team was the winner last year. Tell them that they are going to read a true story about some fans who wanted to see their team play in a Champions League match. Pre-teach *fan*.
- Write the first sentence of the story on the board: *A few years ago Manchester United played the Spanish team Deportivo de La Coruña in the Champions League.*
- SS work in pairs. Give each pair a set of cards. Tell them to find the first sentence and then try to put the rest of the story in order.
- Check answers. Get students to underline the regular verbs and drill the pronunciation of the past tense verbs.
- SS work in pairs again. One student holds the cards so that the other can't see them. The other student tries to remember the story line by line. The first student helps and corrects pronunciation. When the first student has finished, change roles.
- Feedback and see if any pairs can tell the whole story from memory.

Extra idea For extra suspense you could keep back the last sentence and give SS only eight cards. When they've got the story in order then get SS to guess what the last sentence is. Elicit any ideas and then give out the last card.

Extra challenge With a strong class, divide them into groups of three and give them three cards each. **They mustn't show their cards to the other SS**. SS read their sentences out loud, and the group try to decide which is the first sentence. They then decide on the second, etc. Each time they tell the story from the beginning before deciding on the next sentence. When they think they've got the story in the right order, they lay the cards down and read it to check.

1 A few years ago Manchester United played the Spanish team Deportivo de La Coruña in the Champions League.
2 Two Manchester United fans wanted to travel to Spain to see the match.
3 It wasn't possible to fly to La Coruña direct, so they needed to fly to Santiago de Compostela, and then get a taxi.
4 They booked tickets to Santiago on the Internet.
5 They checked in at Heathrow Airport at 9.00 p.m. because the flight was at 11.00 at night.
6 When the plane landed they were very surprised! It was morning!
7 They walked out of the airport and stopped a taxi.
8 They asked the taxi driver, 'Where's the match?' The taxi driver answered 'What match?'
9 They weren't in Spain. They were in Santiago, the capital of Chile!

5 Boys' night out
C A picture story

SS tell a story in the past simple. Copy one story sheet per student or pair.

> **LANGUAGE**
> Past simple irregular verbs
> *They met at 7.00. They went to a football match.*

- Give out one sheet per student. Use the pictures to elicit and drill the following suggested sentences about a boys' night out. Tell SS to use the past tense of the verbs on the pictures.

1 They met at 7.00.
2 They wore football shirts.
3 They went to a restaurant.
4 They had beer and pizza.
5 They talked about girls and football.
6 Then they went to the stadium.
7 They watched the football match.
8 After the match they had a drink.
9 Then they went to a disco.
10 They danced.
11 They went home by taxi.
12 They got home at 2.00.

- After every three sentences, see if the class can remember the story from the beginning.
- Put SS in pairs and get them to try to tell the story from the beginning.

EXTRA support If time you could elicit the story from the beginning and write it on the board for SS to copy, or write half sentences (e.g. *They talked ...*) to see if SS can remember the missing words.

EXTRA idea Get SS in pairs to ask each other questions about the story. A turns his/her sheet over. B asks questions for two minutes e.g. *What time did they meet? What did they wear?* Then they swap roles.

5 Past tense question time
D A pairwork activity

SS practise with question prompts. Copy and cut up one sheet per pair (or if you are short of time copy one sheet per student).

> **LANGUAGE**
> Past simple questions and answers: *What time did you get up? I got up at 7.00. Did you have breakfast? Yes, I did.*

- Tell the SS the object of the activity is to revise the past simple by asking and answering as many questions as they can.
- Demonstrate the activity. Take a card and ask different students the questions. Then copy a couple of question prompts from your card on the board and elicit the questions. Elicit and drill the rhythm of the two questions.
- SS work in pairs. Give each pair a set of cards. Set a time limit, e.g. ten minutes. SS take turns to take a card and ask their partner questions. (If you haven't cut up the sheets just get the students to choose a group of questions to ask)
- Monitor, help, and correct.

EXTRA challenge Encourage the student who is answering the questions to give more information where possible, and the student who is asking to try to ask extra questions where appropriate.

6 Flat to rent
A A pairwork guided roleplay

SS roleplay a phone call for information about a flat to rent. Copy one worksheet per pair. Cut into A and B.

> **LANGUAGE**
> *There is/are* [+] and [?] *Is there a garden? Yes, there is.*
> House vocabulary

- Put SS in pairs A and B, and give out the sheet. Explain that they are going to roleplay a phone conversation to rent a flat.
- Tell the SS who have sheet A that they have a flat that they want to rent out. They must read the instructions and information about the flat.
- Tell the SS who have sheet B that they need to rent a flat. They have a list of questions that they want to ask. They must read the instructions and prepare their questions. Encourage the Bs not to write the missing words but to remember them.
- Monitor making sure the As understand all their information and the Bs are clear what questions they have to ask.
- After a few minutes tell SS to start the conversation. Remind SS that the conversation is on the phone. Tell As to start with *Hello?*
- At the end of the conversation get feedback to see which Bs decided to rent the flat.

6 B Where is it?

A pairwork information gap activity

SS practise prepositions of place. Copy one sheet per pair and cut into A and B.

> **LANGUAGE**
> *next to, in, on, under   Where is/ are …? Is/ Are …?*
> Furniture and common objects

- Divide SS into pairs A and B. (If you have an odd number of SS, have two As in one group.)
- Give each A and B their pictures. Sit A and B so they can't see each other's paper. **Tell them not to show their pictures to their partners.**
- Go through the instructions and explain the task. Student As complete picture 1 by asking questions about the position of the six objects to the right of their picture. They then draw the objects in the right place.
- Then student Bs asks A about the position of the objects in picture 2.
- Monitor to make sure they don't look at each other's pictures. When SS finish, tell them to compare their pictures.

  EXTRA idea Fast finishers can test each other, asking about other objects in the pictures.

6 C Don't say a word

A group drawing game

SS practise the present continuous. Copy and cut up one set of cards per groups of four/five SS. Each group also needs paper and pencils for drawing.

> **LANGUAGE**
> *He's (eating spaghetti). They're (speaking Chinese).*

- SS work in small groups. Give each group a set of cards.
- Explain the rules of the game: When you say 'Start', S1 in each group takes a card and has to draw the sentence. **S1 mustn't speak, or write any words or letters.** Tell the other SS they must guess the sentence. They must guess exactly what's on the card. As soon as the team have guessed S1's sentence, S2 takes a card and draws, etc.
- Demonstrate by doing a blackboard drawing to elicit a present continuous sentence, e.g. *He's playing the guitar.*
- The first team to finish all the cards wins.

6 D Find the differences

A pairwork information gap activity

SS revise the present continuous. Copy one sheet per pair and cut into A and B.

> **LANGUAGE**
> *There's a woman. She's carrying a baby.*
> *There are two people. They are running.*
> *It's the same in my picture.*
> Prepositions of place

- Pre-teach *zebra crossing* and revise any words in the picture you think SS may have forgotten.

- Divide SS into pairs A and B and give out the sheets, face down. **Tell SS they mustn't look at each other's picture.** If possible get them to sit face to face.
- Explain the activity. SS describe their pictures to each other and find ten differences (there are 14 altogether). Demonstrate how to find differences by playing the parts of both A and B, e.g. A 'In my picture, there's a man and a woman. They're running.' B 'In my picture, they're not running.'
- In pairs SS work together and try to find and circle nine more differences.
- Feedback the differences orally with the class, writing up any difficult sentences for SS to copy.

  EXTRA idea Fast finishers can first start writing sentences to describe the differences. There are 14 differences.

A A cat is sitting on a car.
B The cat is standing on a car.
A A dog is looking at a cat.
B The dog is barking at a cat.
A A boy is wearing a cap.
B The boy isn't wearing a cap.
A The boy is wearing sunglasses.
B The boy isn't wearing sunglasses.
A A police officer is looking at her watch.
B The police officer is putting a ticket on a car.
A A man and woman are running.
B The man and woman aren't running.
A A man is looking at clothes in the window.
B The man is coming out of the shop.
A A woman with a baby is waiting to cross the road.
B The woman is crossing the road.
A A man is walking with two dogs.
B The man is walking with one dog.
A A couple are kissing.
B The couple are looking at a map.
A A man is riding a bike.
B The man is riding a motorbike.
A Two children are eating ice cream.
B The children are buying ice cream.
A The children are crossing the road.
B The children aren't crossing the road.
A A woman is carrying a baby.
B A man is carrying a baby.

7 A Food families

A group card game

SS practise countable and uncountable food words and *a/ an/ any*. Copy and cut up one set of cards per group of three or four students.

> **LANGUAGE**
> *Do you have a/ any …? Yes, I do./ No, I don't.*
> *Can I have it, please? Here you are.*
> Food vocabulary: *an apple, ice cream*

- Tell the SS that in this card game there are five sets of cards, and write across the board: FRUIT, DESSERT, VEGETABLES, DRINKS, BREAKFAST. Elicit the four words for each set, and write them under each heading, e.g. FRUIT: apple, banana, orange, and grapes. (To save time you could make an overhead projector transparency of the page and use this to elicit the words.)

- Check pronunciation of the words, and if they are countable or uncountable. Then rub them off the board leaving just the five headings.
- Put SS in groups of three or four. Give each group one full set of cards. One student shuffles and deals the cards face down.
- SS look at their cards. Explain that the four little pictures at the bottom of each card are to remind them of the others in the set.
- To collect a set of cards, SS ask each other for ones they don't have using 'Do you have a/any…?' They can ask any group member for any card, e.g.

S1 *Do you have a banana?*   S4 *Yes, I do.*
S1 *Can I have it, please?*   S4 *Here you are.*

- S1 keeps asking until someone answers 'No, I haven't.' Then it's the turn of the student who answered 'no'. Remind SS to use *any* with plural and uncountable nouns, e.g. 'Do you have any toast?'
- Demonstrate with one group first. Either set a time limit, and tell SS that the winner is the person with the most sets, or stop the game when one student has a complete set. Then the cards are re-dealt and a new game starts.

Food questionnaire

B / A pairwork questionnaire

SS revise *How much/How many* questions and food vocabulary. Copy one questionnaire per student.

> **LANGUAGE**
> *How much (fruit) do you eat a day? Quite a lot.*
> *How many (cups of coffee) do you drink a day? Not many.*

- Tell SS that they are going to complete a food questionnaire to see if their diet is healthy or unhealthy.
- Give each student a copy of the questionnaire. Tell them first to complete the spaces with *How much* or *How many*. **They mustn't answer the questions at this point.** Ask them to write two extra questions in the spaces provided at the end. Check answers and make sure SS's new questions are correct.
- SS work in pairs. B turns over his/her paper. A interviews B and notes the answers on the sheet. Then they change roles. Tell SS to ask the questions in random order so their partner really has to listen. Encourage SS to try and say a bit more than just the answer to the question where possible.
- When they finish, SS can compare their diets and decide if they are healthy or unhealthy. Get some feedback.

Extra idea Get SS to turn over the questionnaire and interview you. They ask you all the questions they can remember.

What are you going to do?

C / A group survey

SS ask questions about future plans. If you have more than eleven students, or if you want to personalize this activity more, before making copies of the sheet, fill in the last five cards with local or relevant information for your students, e.g. *How many people are going to see* (a popular film that is on at the cinema), *How many people are going to go to*

(a popular weekend destination), etc. Copy and cut up one sheet per group of 16 students.

> **LANGUAGE**
> *Are you going to (go home after class)? Yes, I am. No, I'm not.*

- Write on the board 'How many people are going to go to a restaurant this evening?' Show how you change the question to ask individual SS, e.g. 'Are you going to go to a restaurant this evening?' For every student that says 'Yes, I am', put a tick next to the original question. After you have asked the class count up the number of ticks and tell the class the result, e.g. *Four people are going to go to a restaurant this evening.*
- Tell SS they are going to do a similar survey. Give each student a slip of paper. Elicit/teach the meaning of *Find out.* Tell SS that they must ask everybody in the class their question and keep a record of the number of people who answer 'yes'. SS mingle and ask their questions to other SS.
- When SS finish, feedback to get the results of the survey.

EXTRA challenge Encourage SS to ask other questions to follow up as well, e.g. 'Are you going to go home after class?' 'No, I'm not.' 'What are you going to do?' 'I'm going to go to the cinema.'

Pronunciation bingo

D / A class game

SS practise pronunciation with Bingo cards. Copy and cut out one game card per pair.

> **LANGUAGE**
> Vowel sounds

- Revise the pronunciation of vowel sounds using the pictures in the Student's Book *p.156*.
- Put SS in pairs and give each pair a bingo card. Explain that you are going to call out a word. If this word has the same vowel sound as one of the pictures on their card they must write the word under it on the **first line on the card**. Demonstrate by holding up a card. Say a word and ask 'Where do I write the word?'.
- When one pair has a word under each of the six pictures they call out 'Bingo'.
- Call out the words from the list below in order. Say the word clearly at least twice. Continue until a pair has written in a word for each of their pictures and shouts 'Bingo!' Tick the last word you call out so that you know where to start again if you want to repeat the game. Check the answers by asking the winning students to read you back the words they wrote down. If they have made a mistake, the game continues.
- If you want to play again, collect the cards and redistribute them. Tell SS now to write their answers on the second line. You can play a third game, making sure that you use different words.

1 fast	/ɑː/	2 her	/ɜː/
3 light	/aɪ/	4 much	/ʌ/
5 fruit	/uː/	6 road	/əʊ/
7 grapes	/eɪ/	8 tea	/iː/
9 French	/e/	10 house	/aʊ/
11 job	/ɒ/	12 door	/ɔː/
13 bread	/e/	14 hot	/ɒ/

15 how	/aʊ/	16 sport	/ɔː/
17 food	/uː/	18 smoke	/əʊ/
19 cake	/eɪ/	20 cheese	/iː/
21 lunch	/ʌ/	22 wine	/aɪ/
23 work	/ɜː/	24 dark	/ɑː/
25 please	/iː/	26 page	/eɪ/
27 spell	/e/	28 juice	/uː/
29 card	/ɑː/	30 learn	/ɜː/
31 ice	/aɪ/	32 cup	/ʌ/
33 hall	/ɔː/	34 stop	/ɒ/
35 brown	/aʊ/	36 when	/e/
37 love	/ʌ/	38 rice	/aɪ/
39 girl	/ɜː/	40 dance	/ɑː/
41 school	/uː/	42 close	/əʊ/
43 say	/eɪ/	44 sweets	/iː/
45 twelve	/e/	46 now	/aʊ/
47 from	/ɒ/	48 talk	/ɔː/
49 blue	/uː/	50 cold	/əʊ/
51 day	/eɪ/	52 meat	/iː/
53 bed	/e/	54 town	/aʊ/
55 watch	/ɒ/	56 tall	/ɔː/
57 come	/ʌ/	58 nice	/aɪ/
59 word	/ɜː/	60 glass	/ɑː/
61 pen	/e/	62 hour	/aʊ/
63 song	/ɒ/	64 walk	/ɔː/
65 beach	/iː/	66 change	/eɪ/
67 go	/əʊ/	68 do	/uː/
69 park	/ɑː/	70 nurse	/ɜː/
71 why	/aɪ/	72 one	/ʌ/

8 A Guess the comparative

A pairwork activity

SS read sentences and guess what the missing comparative adjective is. Copy one sheet for each pair and cut into **A** and **B**.

> **LANGUAGE**
> Comparative adjectives: *friendlier, colder, more expensive*

- Demonstrate the activity. Write an example sentence on a piece of paper, e.g. *A Rolex watch is more expensive than a Swatch watch*. Tell SS they have to guess the sentence on your piece of paper.

- Then write on the board *A Rolex watch is _____ than a Swatch watch*. Elicit from SS several possible comparatives to fill the gap, e.g. *more beautiful, better, more expensive*, before telling them what you have on your piece of paper and show it to them.

- Give out copies to **A** and **B**. **Make sure SS can't see each other's paper.** Tell SS to work individually at first and complete the blanks on their paper. Remind them that all the missing words are comparative adjectives.

- Monitor to make sure SS are writing correct and logical comparative adjectives.

- Put SS in pairs. Explain the activity. Student **B** has to read out his/her first sentence. If it is the same as on **A**s card (i.e. *Russia is colder than Spain*) **A** says *That's right*. If it's not the same **A** says 'Try again', and **B** guesses using more comparatives until he/she gets the right one. Then **A** reads his/her second sentence, etc.

- Finally tell SS to put their pieces of paper face down and see if they can remember the 12 comparative sentences. Say the first half of the sentences to jog their memory, i.e. *Russia is …*

8 B What do you know about the UK?

A quiz about Britain

SS revise superlatives. Copy one sheet per student or pair/group.

> **LANGUAGE**
> Superlatives: *most popular, busiest*

- If necessary quickly revise the formation of superlatives with examples on the board, e.g. *The (tall) person in the class is… The (popular) sport in the country is…*

- SS work in groups of three/four. Give out copies. Set a time limit (e.g. five minutes) for SS to choose the correct answer. Monitor and help.

- Check answers.

> 1 a 2 c 3 c 4 a 5 a 6 a 7 a 8 a 9 a 10 c 11 b 12 a

8 C Make your own 'experience' present

An advertisement activity

SS create their own advertisement for an experience present and then try to 'sell' it to others. Make one copy of the sheet for every pair of SS.

> **LANGUAGE**
> *Do you like (driving)?*
> *Would you like to (drive a Formula 1 car)?*

- Remind SS of the adventure presents on *p. 92* of the Student's Book. Tell the SS that they are going to design their own adventure present.

- SS in pairs. Give each pair a sheet. Go through the advertisement and show SS how instructions 1–5 below tell them what kind of words they must write in.

- Demonstrate by giving your own examples.

- Set a time limit, e.g. five minutes for SS to make their own experience present following the instructions on the sheet. Monitor and help, correcting spelling where necessary.

- Finally get SS to draw a picture of their present in the space at the top. You can ask all SS to do this after they have completed the form.

- When SS have finished, tell them that they are going to try to 'sell' their present to other SS. Demonstrate with one pair of SS. Ask a question, e.g. 'Do you like driving? Would you like to drive a Formula 1 car?' Continue reading through the sheet and providing your own information, e.g. 'Now you CAN! For only €1,000 you can have this experience present.' Let the SS decide if they would like to buy it or not.

- SS mingle and read out the information about their adventure gifts to each other. Feedback at the end. Ask which adventure gifts were the most popular in the class.

8 Mime the phrase
D A miming game

SS practise adverbs by miming actions in different manners. Copy and cut up one set of cards for every five / six SS in the class.

Before photocopying the worksheet, you could personalise the activity by completing the blank cards with extra verb and adverb combinations that suit your class, e.g. *sing* (a well-known song) *badly*.

> **LANGUAGE**
> Adverbs: *badly, carefully, fast*

- If necessary revise adverb formation by writing the following adjectives on the board and asking SS to change them to adverbs: *careful, bad, fast, quiet, polite, good.*

- SS work in groups of five / six. Give each group a set of cards in an envelope. Explain the game. S1 takes a card and mimes the action. The others in the group try to guess exactly what is on the card. If the other SS can guess the phrase on the card then S1 keeps the card. If other SS can't guess the phrase then S1 puts it back in the envelope.

- Demonstrate by taking a card and miming the action for the class. Emphasize that SS only have to say the verb and the adverb e.g. *dance badly.*

- SS take turns miming actions until all the cards are used. The winner is the person with the most cards at the end.

   EXTRA idea For groups that finish early, ask the SS to put all the cards back in the envelope and try to write down all the verbs and adverbs from memory.

9 Where have you been?
A A pairwork information gap

SS practise asking and answering present perfect questions. Copy and cut up one worksheet for each pair of students.

> **LANGUAGE**
> Present perfect simple
> *Have you been to …?   Yes, I have.   No, I haven't.*

- Divide SS into pairs and give each student an **A** or **B** sheet. Sit **A** and **B** so they can't see each other's paper.

- Explain that the countries with ticks are the countries that they have visited.

- Demonstrate the activity. Write two or three countries on the board and put a tick next to one of them. Elicit the question, *Have you been to …?*. If you have a tick next to this country say 'Yes, I have.' If you don't have a tick, say, 'No, I haven't.'

- Explain the activity. SS work in pairs and ask questions to find three countries that neither of them has visited (the USA, Australia, and Morocco).

- When they finish they must decide which of the three countries they'd most like to go to.

- Get feedback. Ask a few pairs where they'd like to go together.

9 Have you ever …?
B A class mingle speaking activity

SS practise the present perfect and past simple with question prompts. Copy and cut up one sheet for the class / per group.

Before you make copies of the sheet, you could personalize the activity by writing two questions of your own that are relevant to your SS, e.g. 'Have you / eat at (a local restaurant)? Have you / be (to a country)?'.

> **LANGUAGE**
> Present perfect: *Have you ever met a famous politician? Yes, I have. No, I haven't.*
> Follow up questions: *Who? Which one? When?*

- Give every student in the class a question. Tell them not to show their question to anybody. If you have a class of more than 12 SS, divide the class into two or more groups.

- Explain that they're going to do a survey. SS must move around asking the question on their card to all the other SS in their class or group. If somebody answers 'Yes, I have', then they ask the second question.

- Remind SS that they must put the verb into the past participle form.

- Get feedback when SS have finished. Find out e.g. how many people have been on TV.

9 Revise and check
Prompts to revise speaking / question formation

SS practise key structures from Files 1–9. This could be used as a final 'pre-test' revision, e.g. before SS's oral exam. Copy and cut up one set of cards per pair.

> **LANGUAGE**
> Questions and answers: past, present, and future

- Tell SS the object of the activity is to ask and answer as many questions as they can to revise the English they know. Demonstrate by taking a card and asking one student the questions. Then take another card and quickly copy it onto the board. Get SS to use the prompts to ask you complete questions. Remind SS that each '/' = a missing word or words.

- SS work in pairs. Give each pair a set of cards. Set a time limit, e.g. ten minutes. SS take turns to take a card and ask their partner the questions. Encourage SS to follow up their partner's answers with further questions. Monitor, help, and correct.

New English File Teacher's Book Elementary
Photocopiable © Oxford University Press 2004

You're **Dracula.**

You're **Lara Croft.**

You're **Mickey Mouse.**

You're **Robin Hood.**

You're **Frankenstein.**

You're **Mary Poppins.**

You're **Tarzan.**

You're **Bart Simpson.**

You're **Batman.**

You're **Harry Potter.**

You're **Napoleon.**

You're **Barbie.**

You're **Cleopatra.**

You're **Snow White.**

You're **Julius Caesar.**

You're **Sherlock Holmes.**

New English File Teacher's Book Elementary
Photocopiable © Oxford University Press 2004

A Ask **B** the questions about the famous people. Answer **B**'s questions with the information you have.

A *Is Martin Scorsese Italian?*
B *No, he isn't, he's ...*
A *Where's he from?*
B *He's from ...*

Martin Scorsese
/ Italian?
Where / from? _____

Nicole Kidman
Australian
Sydney, Australia

Pierce Brosnan
/ English?
Where / from? _____

Ricky Martin
Puerto Rican
San Juan, Puerto Rico

Celine Dion
/ American ?
Where / from? _____

Christina Aguilera
American
New York, USA

Ewan McGregor
/ Irish?
Where / from? _____

Shakira
Colombian
Barranquilla, Colombia

B Ask **A** the questions about the famous people. Answer **A**'s questions with the information you have.

B *Is Nicole Kidman American?*
A *No, she isn't, she's ...*
B *Where's she from?*
A *She's from ...*

Martin Scorsese
American
New York, USA

Nicole Kidman
/ American?
Where / from? _____

Pierce Brosnan
Irish
Navan, Ireland

Ricky Martin
/ Mexican ?
Where / from? _____

Celine Dion
Canadian
Quebec, Canada

Christina Aguilera
/ Argentinian?
Where / from? _____

Ewan McGregor
Scottish
Crieff, Scotland

Shakira
/ Brazilian?
Where / from? _____

New English File Teacher's Book Elementary
Photocopiable © Oxford University Press 2004

Name **Jane** Surname **DUKE** E-mail **jane.duke@comet.com** Phone **020 7934 3374**	Name _____ Surname _____ E-mail _____ Phone _____	Name _____ Surname _____ E-mail _____ Phone _____
Name **Rachel** Surname **HARVEY** E-mail **r.harvey@basol.com** Phone **01189 221 6944**	Name _____ Surname _____ E-mail _____ Phone _____	Name _____ Surname _____ E-mail _____ Phone _____
Name **Donna** Surname **WILLIAMS** E-mail **donna.williams@mail.com** Phone **415 786 2251**	Name _____ Surname _____ E-mail _____ Phone _____	Name _____ Surname _____ E-mail _____ Phone _____
Name **Celine** Surname **CARSON** E-mail **carson.c@compu.com** Phone **212 327 9472**	Name _____ Surname _____ E-mail _____ Phone _____	Name _____ Surname _____ E-mail _____ Phone _____
Name **David** Surname **RICHARDS** E-mail **d.richards@speedon.com** Phone **09794 487 3524**	Name _____ Surname _____ E-mail _____ Phone _____	Name _____ Surname _____ E-mail _____ Phone _____
Name **Patrick** Surname **MANNERS** E-mail **p.manners@freemail.com** Phone **02243 767 9574**	Name _____ Surname _____ E-mail _____ Phone _____	Name _____ Surname _____ E-mail _____ Phone _____
Name **Dale** Surname **PITT** E-mail **dale.pitt@over.com** Phone **650 836 4825**	Name _____ Surname _____ E-mail _____ Phone _____	Name _____ Surname _____ E-mail _____ Phone _____
Name **Wayne** Surname **EASTWOOD** E-mail **w.eastwood@yonder.com** Phone **719 475 9718**	Name _____ Surname _____ E-mail _____ Phone _____	Name _____ Surname _____ E-mail _____ Phone _____

New English File Teacher's Book Elementary
Photocopiable © Oxford University Press 2004

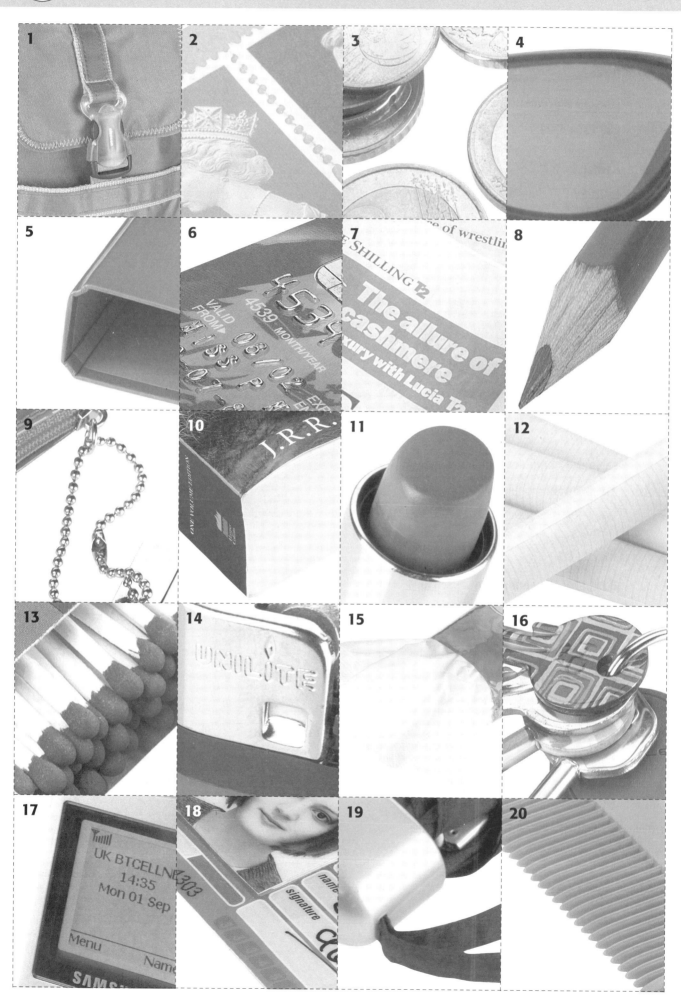

A ● Use the pictures to tell **B** about Steve.
Steve does yoga.

● What do they have in common?

B ● Use the pictures to tell **A** about Simon.
Simon plays tennis.

● What do they have in common?

New English File Teacher's Book Elementary
Photocopiable © Oxford University Press 2004

a Fill in the information for **YOU**.

b Imagine you're at a party. Talk to **OTHER PEOPLE** to find somebody like you.

YOU

smoke? Yes ☐ No ☐

have a pet? Yes _____ No ☐

play a sport? Yes _____ No ☐

I like _____ food (e.g. Italian)

I listen to _____ (music)

I watch _____ (TV programme)

I read _____ (magazine or paper)

OTHER PEOPLE

/ smoke ?

/ have a pet? What pet / have?

/ play sport ? What sport / play?

What food / like?

What music / listen to?

What TV programme / watch?

What paper or magazine / read?

---

a Fill in the information for **YOU**.

b Imagine you're at a party. Talk to **OTHER PEOPLE** to find somebody like you.

YOU

smoke? Yes ☐ No ☐

have a pet? Yes _____ No ☐

play a sport? Yes _____ No ☐

I like _____ food (e.g. Italian)

I listen to _____ (music)

I watch _____ (TV programme)

I read _____ (magazine or paper)

OTHER PEOPLE

/ smoke ?

/ have a pet? What pet / have?

/ play sport ? What sport / play?

What food / like?

What music / listen to?

What TV programme / watch?

What paper or magazine / read?

---

a Fill in the information for **YOU**.

b Imagine you're at a party. Talk to **OTHER PEOPLE** to find somebody like you.

YOU

smoke? Yes ☐ No ☐

have a pet? Yes _____ No ☐

play a sport? Yes _____ No ☐

I like _____ food (e.g. Italian)

I listen to _____ (music)

I watch _____ (TV programme)

I read _____ (magazine or paper)

OTHER PEOPLE

/ smoke ?

/ have a pet? What pet / have?

/ play sport ? What sport / play?

What food / like?

What music / listen to?

What TV programme / watch?

What paper or magazine / read?

New English File Teacher's Book Elementary
Photocopiable © Oxford University Press 2004

A Ask **B** questions about Andrew's family to complete the family tree.

Who's Andrew's mother?
What does she do?

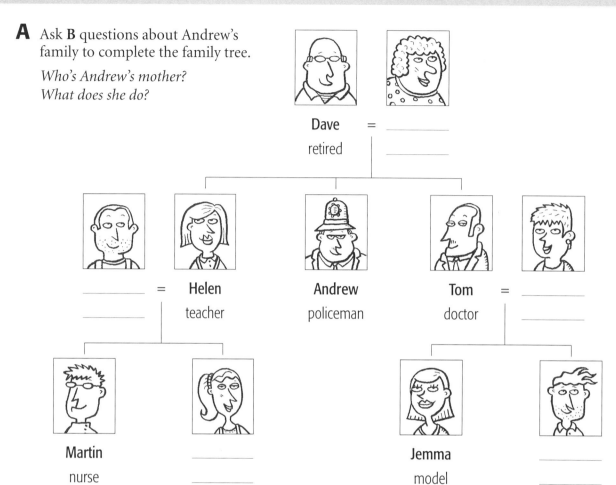

Dave = _____
retired _____

_____ = Helen   Andrew   Tom = _____
_____   teacher   policeman   doctor _____

Martin   _____   Jemma   _____
nurse   _____   model   _____

B Ask **A** questions about Andrew's family to complete the family tree.

Who's Andrew's father?
What does he do?

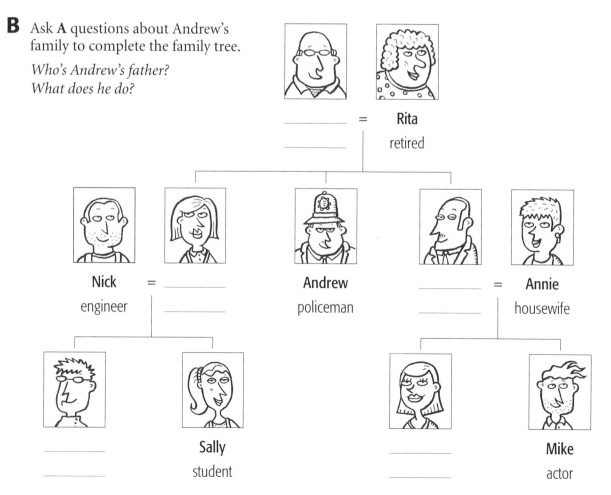

_____ = Rita
_____ retired

Nick = _____   Andrew   _____ = Annie
engineer _____   policeman   _____ housewife

_____   Sally   _____   Mike
_____   student   _____   actor

A Describe your pictures to **B**.

Number 1 It's an old house.

Are the pictures the same or different? Write **S** or **D** on the picture. Find ten differences.

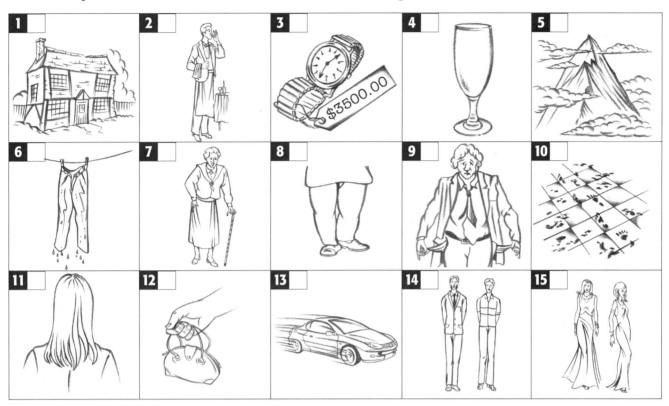

B Describe your pictures to **A**.

Number 1 It's a new house.

Are the pictures the same or different? Write **S** or **D** on the picture. Find ten differences.

New English File Teacher's Book Elementary
Photocopiable © Oxford University Press 2004

New English File Teacher's Book Elementary
Photocopiable © Oxford University Press 2004

A Ask and answer questions.

How often do you go to the hairdresser's …?

Once a week. What about you?

never

hardly ever

sometimes

(not) often

once a week / month / year

every day / week / month

go to the hairdresser's

eat chocolate

go to the theatre

be late for work / school

get a taxi

do housework

see your best friend

read the newspaper

B Ask and answer questions.

How often do you go to the dentist's …?

Hardly ever. What about you?

never

hardly ever

sometimes

(not) often

once a week / month / year

every day / week / month

go to the dentist's

eat in a restaurant

go to the cinema

listen to classical music

have a holiday

cook

do sport or exercise

drink tea

195

New English File Teacher's Book Elementary
Photocopiable © Oxford University Press 2004

a Answer the questions in the **YOU** column.

b Ask the questions to a partner and write their answers in the
YOUR PARTNER column.

A *When's your birthday?*

B *On March 5th.*

A *What time do you usually get up?*

	You	Your partner
When's your birthday?		
What time do you usually get up?		
When do you have a shower or bath?		
What time do you usually have lunch?		
What time do you finish work / school?		
What time do you usually have dinner?		
When do you usually go shopping?		
When do you usually have your summer holiday?		
When do you go to English class?		
When do you do your homework?		
When do you usually read?		
When do you usually listen to music?		
What's your favourite time to watch TV?		
When do you usually do sport or exercise?		
When do you usually see your friends?		
What's your favourite day of the week?		
When's the next public holiday in your country?		
What's your favourite public holiday?		
When is it?		
When do you usually _____?		

	Find someone who …	Student's name	More information
1	can play a musical instrument		*Which? How well?*
2	can cook well		*What's your speciality?*
3	can speak three languages		*Which? How well?*
4	can play a racket sport		*Which? How well?*
5	can ski or water ski		*How well? Where do you usually do it?*
6	can drive		*What car do you have?*
7	can't swim		*Why?*
8			

	Find someone who …	Student's name	More information
1	can play a musical instrument		*Which? How well?*
2	can cook well		*What's your speciality?*
3	can speak three languages		*Which? How well?*
4	can play a racket sport		*Which? How well?*
5	can ski or water ski		*How well? Where do you usually do it?*
6	can drive		*What car do you have?*
7	can't swim		*Why?*
8			

A Tick (✓) the boxes which are true for you.

WEEKEND

	I love	I like	I don't like	I hate
cooking	☐	☐	☐	☐
watching football on TV	☐	☐	☐	☐
doing sport or exercise	☐	☐	☐	☐
going to the cinema	☐	☐	☐	☐
shopping for clothes	☐	☐	☐	☐
dancing	☐	☐	☐	☐

B Tick (✓) the boxes which are true for you.

WEEKEND

	I love	I like	I don't like	I hate
cooking	☐	☐	☐	☐
watching football on TV	☐	☐	☐	☐
doing sport or exercise	☐	☐	☐	☐
going to the cinema	☐	☐	☐	☐
shopping for clothes	☐	☐	☐	☐
dancing	☐	☐	☐	☐

a Write the name of real places/things/people you love (or hate) for each picture, for example **1** a singer you love (or hate).

1 a singer

2 a restaurant

3 a TV programme

4 a shop

5 a famous actor

6 a music group

7 a sportsperson

8 a city

9 a book

10 a classic film

b Take turns. Ask your partner *What do you think of...?*

USEFUL LANGUAGE

I love	him.
I like	her.
I don't like	it.
I hate	them.

He's	great / fantastic.
She's	(very) good.
It's	OK / all right.
They're	awful / terrible.

s**o**n	f**a**ll	th**ere**	b**uy**
y**ou**ng	th**eir**s	w**or**k	n**igh**t
wh**y**	ch**air**	th**ir**d	sp**ea**k
m**i**ne	l**u**nch	h**air**	str**ee**t
m**e**	h**er**s	f**ir**st	wh**ere**
sh**or**t	m**ee**t	st**o**ry	w**or**d
d**oo**r	l**o**ve	s**ee**	ch**i**ld
y**our**s	l**ear**n	wr**i**te	h**u**ngry
w**ear**	l**ea**ve	m**u**ch	b**oar**d

A

ⓐ Ask **B** questions to complete the chart.
Answer **B**'s questions.

A *Where was Silvia in 1998?*
B *She was .... Where was James?*

B

ⓐ Ask **A** questions to complete the chart.
Answer **A**'s questions.

A *Where was James in 1998?*
B *He was .... Where was Silvia?*

Silvia		James	Silvia		James
	1998			1998	
		at university		at school	
	2001			2001	
	at work			at university	
	last year			last year	
	in Mexico			in France	
	six months ago			six months ago	
	in Berlin			in Paris	
	last month			last month	
	in Paris			in Paris	
	a week ago			a week ago	
	at the Louvre			at the Louvre	
last Wednesday night			last Wednesday night		
at a restaurant			at a restaurant		
yesterday afternoon			yesterday afternoon		
in church			in church		

ⓑ Compare your pictures. When were they together?

ⓑ Compare your pictures. When were they together?

201

New English File Teacher's Book Elementary
Photocopiable © Oxford University Press 2004

A few years ago Manchester United played the Spanish team Deportivo de La Coruña in the Champions League.

Two Manchester United fans wanted to travel to Spain to see the match.

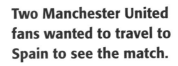

It wasn't possible to fly to La Coruña direct, so they needed to fly to Santiago de Compostela, and then get a taxi.

They booked tickets to Santiago on the Internet.

They checked in at Heathrow Airport at 9.00 p.m. because the flight was at 11.00 at night.

When the plane landed they were very surprised! It was morning!

They walked out of the airport and stopped a taxi.

They asked the taxi driver, 'Where's the match?' The taxi driver answered 'What match?'

They weren't in Spain. They were in Santiago, the capital of Chile!

New English File Teacher's Book Elementary
Photocopiable © Oxford University Press 2004

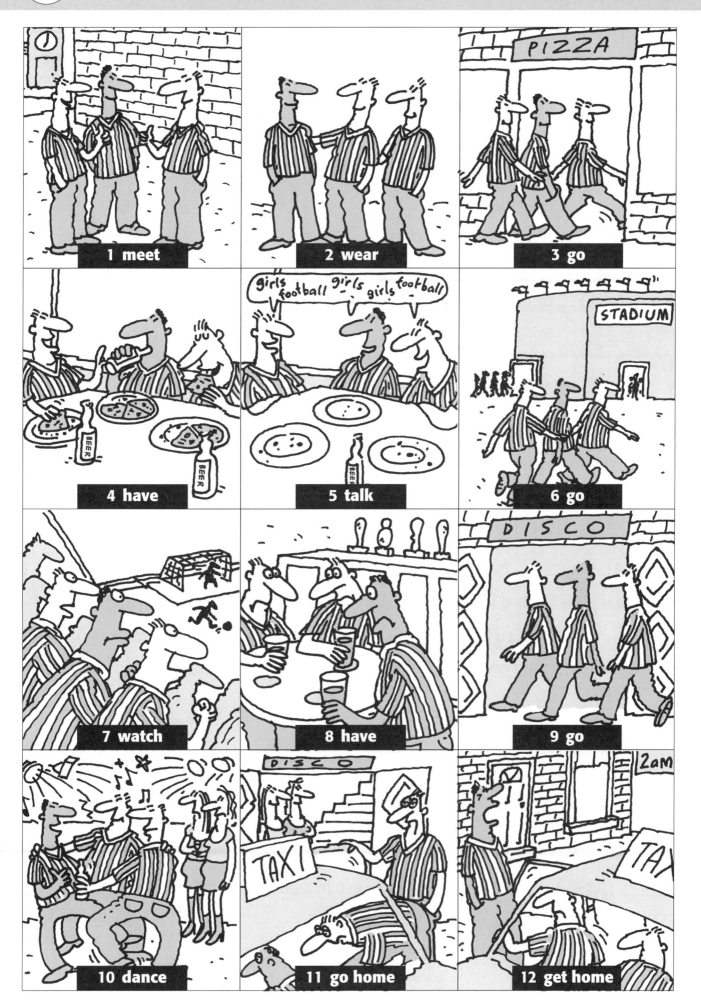

New English File Teacher's Book Elementary
Photocopiable © Oxford University Press 2004

This morning

What time / wake up?

What time / get up?

/ have breakfast?

What / have?

What time / leave the house?

How / get to work or school?

When you were 10 years old

Where / live?

What school / go to?

/ like school?

Which teachers / like?

What / do after school?

What TV programmes / you watch?

Yesterday

What / have for breakfast?

Where / have lunch?

Who / have lunch with?

Where / be / 6.30 p.m.?

What / do / evening?

/ go to bed late?

What time / go to bed?

Last Saturday

/ go shopping?

What / buy?

/ go out in the evening?

Where / go?

What / have to eat and drink?

/ have a good time?

What time / go to bed?

Your last holiday

Where / go?

Who / go with?

How / get there?

/ stay in a hotel?

What / do?

New English File Teacher's Book Elementary
Photocopiable © Oxford University Press 2004

A

a You want to rent your flat. Look at the advertisement that you put in the paper, and the information about the flat. Try to remember the information.

Large Flat to Rent
Phone
01189 885 6270
for more
information.

HOME PAGE

PROPERTIES TO LET

RENT YOUR PROPERTY

MORE ABOUT US

Best Buy & Co

City centre. Rent: £850 a month

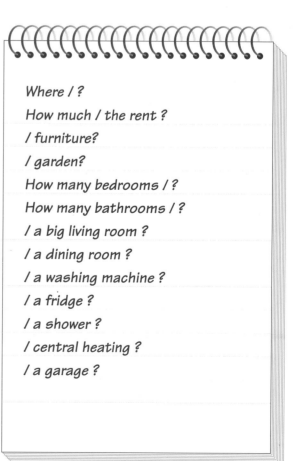

Quiet, ground floor flat with sunny garden. Beautifully furnished with central heating. Two large bedrooms + living room with doors to garden. Dining room and new kitchen with washing machine and fridge freezer. Modern bathroom with new shower. 5 minutes from city centre. Good shops and transport.

b Answer **B**'s questions.

B *Where is it?*
A *It's …*
B *How much is the rent?*
A *It's _____ a month.*

B

a You want to rent a flat. Look at your notebook. What questions do you need to ask?
Where is it?
How much is the rent?
Is there any furniture?

b Phone **A** and ask for information. Write **A**'s answers in your notebook.
Hello. Can you tell me about the flat?

Where / ?

How much / the rent ?

/ furniture?

/ garden?

How many bedrooms / ?

How many bathrooms / ?

/ a big living room ?

/ a dining room ?

/ a washing machine ?

/ a fridge ?

/ a shower ?

/ central heating ?

/ a garage ?

A

ⓐ Look at picture **1**. Ask **B** questions and draw your six objects in the correct place.

Where are the books?   Where's the mirror?

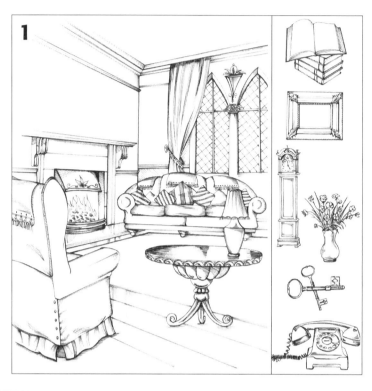

ⓑ Look at picture **2**. Listen to **B**. Answer the questions.

It's in the …   They're behind the …

B

ⓐ Look at picture **1**. Answer **A**'s questions.

It's in the …   They're behind the …

ⓑ Look at picture **2**. Ask **A** questions and draw your six objects in the correct place.

Where's the book?   Where's the mirror?

New English File Teacher's Book Elementary
Photocopiable © Oxford University Press 2004

He's watching football.

They're playing volleyball.

They're having a party.

They're arguing.

He's eating spaghetti.

He's making a pizza.

She's driving a fast car.

She's teaching English.

They're speaking Chinese.

They're running a marathon.

The baby's crying.

They're dancing a tango.

She's phoning her boyfriend.

She's doing yoga.

They're drinking champagne.

He's painting his house.

He's playing chess.

They're waiting for a bus.

The dog's barking.

She's taking photos.

New English File Teacher's Book Elementary
Photocopiable © Oxford University Press 2004

A Describe your picture to **B**. Find ten differences.

In my picture a man and a woman are sitting outside. They are having a coffee.

B Describe your picture to **A**. Find ten differences.

In my picture a man and a woman are sitting outside. They are having a coffee.

New English File Teacher's Book Elementary
Photocopiable © Oxford University Press 2004

New English File Teacher's Book Elementary
Photocopiable © Oxford University Press 2004

ⓐ Complete the questions with *How much* or *How many*. Add two more questions.

ⓑ Interview a partner. Put a [✓] tick in the right column.

ⓒ Look at your partner's answers. Do you think his/her diet is healthy or unhealthy?

Food Questionnaire

	A lot	Quite a lot	Not much or Not many	None
_____ sugar do you have in your coffee or tea?	☐	☐	☐	☐
_____ cups of coffee do you drink a day?	☐	☐	☐	☐
_____ salt do you put on your food?	☐	☐	☐	☐
_____ sweets do you eat a day?	☐	☐	☐	☐
_____ meat or fish do you eat a week?	☐	☐	☐	☐
_____ butter do you put on your bread?	☐	☐	☐	☐
_____ eggs do you eat a week?	☐	☐	☐	☐
_____ water do you drink a day?	☐	☐	☐	☐
_____ chocolate do you eat a week?	☐	☐	☐	☐
_____ fruit do you eat a day?	☐	☐	☐	☐
_____ alcohol do you drink a week?	☐	☐	☐	☐
How much _____?	☐	☐	☐	☐
How many _____?	☐	☐	☐	☐

New English File Teacher's Book Elementary
Photocopiable © Oxford University Press 2004

How many people are going to go home after class? **Find out.** ☐

How many people are going to watch television tonight? **Find out.** ☐

How many people are going to go to the gym this week? **Find out.** ☐

How many people are going to go shopping tomorrow? **Find out.** ☐

How many people are going to cook tonight? **Find out.** ☐

How many people are going to go to the cinema this weekend? **Find out.** ☐

How many people are going to go to another country next year? **Find out.** ☐

How many people are going to go out tonight? **Find out.** ☐

How many people are going to study English tonight? **Find out.** ☐

How many people are going to use the Internet this evening? **Find out.** ☐

How many people are going to have a drink after class? **Find out.** ☐

How many people are going to … ☐

How many people are going to … ☐

How many people are going to … ☐

How many people are going to … ☐

How many people are going to … ☐

New English File Teacher's Book Elementary
Photocopiable © Oxford University Press 2004

1 uː	2 ʌ	3 e	1 əʊ	2 ʌ	3 e
4 ɔː	5 ɒ	6 eɪ	4 ɜː	5 ɒ	6 eɪ
1 iː	2 aʊ	3 aɪ	1 ɒ	2 aʊ	3 aɪ
4 uː	5 əʊ	6 ɔː	4 eɪ	5 uː	6 e
1 ɔː	2 ɜː	3 ʌ	1 əʊ	2 iː	3 aɪ
4 iː	5 ɒ	6 aʊ	4 ɒ	5 ɒ	6 ɜː

A

1 Russia is **colder** than Spain.

2 The Americans are _____ than the British.

3 Swimming is **better** exercise than walking.

4 A sofa is _____ than a chair.

5 A Rolls Royce is **more expensive** than a Citroen.

6 Driving is _____ than flying.

7 Men are **more aggressive** drivers than women.

8 Basketball players are _____ than footballers.

9 Red wine is **healthier** than whisky.

10 Canada is _____ than Brazil.

11 The weather in Britain is **worse** than the weather in Portugal.

12 Italian men are _____ than British men.

B

1 Russia is _____ than Spain.

2 The Americans are **friendlier** than the British.

3 Swimming is _____ exercise than walking.

4 A sofa is **more comfortable** than a chair.

5 A Rolls Royce is _____ than a Citroen.

6 Driving is **more dangerous** than flying.

7 Men are _____ drivers than women.

8 Basketball players are **taller** than footballers.

9 Red wine is _____ than whisky.

10 Canada is **bigger** than Brazil.

11 The weather in Britain is _____ than the weather in Portugal.

12 Italian men are **more stylish** than British men.

New English File Teacher's Book Elementary
Photocopiable © Oxford University Press 2004

1 What's the busiest London airport?

   a Heathrow   **b** Gatwick   **c** Stansted

2 What's the most popular kind of food?

   a British   **b** Chinese   **c** Indian

3 Which is the biggest city (after London)?

   a Edinburgh   **b** Manchester   **c** Birmingham

4 Where's the highest mountain?

   a Scotland   **b** England   **c** Wales

5 Which part of Britain is the sunniest?

   a South West   **b** South East   **c** North East

6 Which is the most popular tourist town (after London)?

   a Oxford   **b** Cambridge   **c** Edinburgh

7 What is the most popular free time activity?

   a gardening   **b** watching TV   **c** reading

8 What is the most popular sport?

   a fishing   **b** football   **c** darts

9 Which is the oldest university?

   a Oxford   **b** Cambridge   **c** London

10 What is the most common religion?

   a Islam   **b** Roman Catholicism   **c** Protestantism

11 What's the most common foreign language that people learn?

   a Spanish   **b** French   **c** German

12 What's the biggest animal?

   a horse   **b** bull   **c** bear

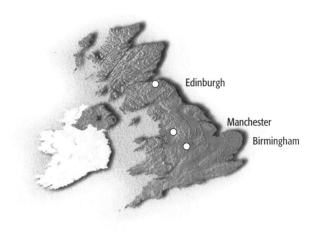

Edinburgh

Manchester

Birmingham

New English File Teacher's Book Elementary
Photocopiable © Oxford University Press 2004

a Make your own 'experience' present. Complete the gaps with your own ideas.

1 Write your name or the name of your company.

2 Write a verb in the *-ing* form, for example, *cooking, flying, driving.*

3 Write a verb phrase, for example, *spend a day with a famous person, ride an Olympic horse.*

4 Write a price.

5 Write a person for example, *your mother, your best friend.*

6 Draw a picture of your present in the box.

b Try to 'sell' your present to other students.
Do you like …?
Would you like to …?

Are you looking for an amazing present?

- ¹_____ has the perfect original present for you!

- Do you like ²_____?

- Would you like to ³_____?

- For only ⁴_____ you can give this unique experience to ⁵_____.

New English File Teacher's Book Elementary
Photocopiable © Oxford University Press 2004

drive carefully	play football aggressively
get dressed quickly	work hard
eat noisily	play chess well
speak English badly	wake up slowly
sing beautifully	dance badly
draw (on the board) well	close the door quietly
walk sexily	ask for a coffee politely
drink fast	say goodbye sadly

New English File Teacher's Book Elementary
Photocopiable © Oxford University Press 2004

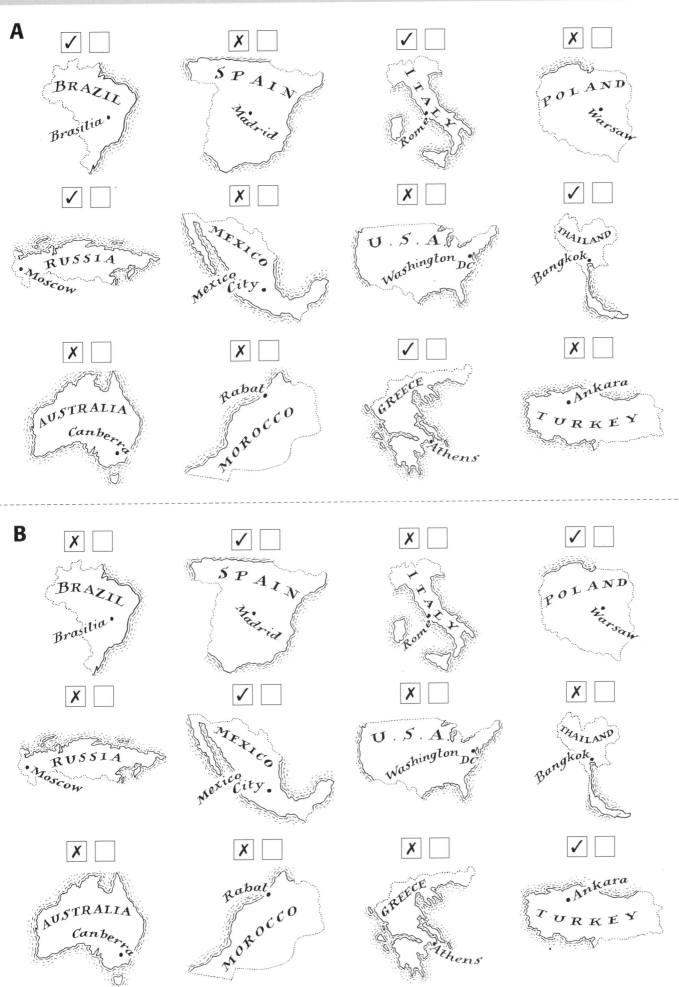

New English File Teacher's Book Elementary
Photocopiable © Oxford University Press 2004

Have you ever _____ (be) in a very expensive car?
What kind of car?

Have you ever _____ (go) to sleep in class?
What class?

Have you ever _____ (meet) a famous politician?
Who?

Have you ever _____ (read) a newspaper or magazine in English?
Which one?

Have you ever _____ (speak) to a tourist in English?
Why?

Have you ever _____ (cook) for a lot of people?
What did you make?

Have you ever _____ (be) near a dangerous animal?
Which?

Have you ever _____ (win) a cup or medal?
What for?

Have you ever _____ (be) on TV?
What programme?

Have you ever _____ (phone) a radio or TV programme?
Which?

Have you ever

Have you ever

Personal Information

What / surname?
How / spell it?
Where / from?
/ married?
What / phone number?
What / do?
Where / work (study)?
How many languages / speak?

Free time

What sports / play?
What kind of music / like?
What TV programmes / like?
How often / go to the cinema?
What / like doing at weekends?
/ like reading?
What books / like?

Your flat or house

/ live in a house or flat?
How many bedrooms / there?
/ there a TV in your bedroom?
/ there any plants in your living
    room?
/ have a bath in your house or flat?
What / your favourite room?
/ there any shops near you?

Your possessions

/ have a car? What car / have?
    What colour / ?
/ have a mobile phone?
/ have pets? What pets / have?

What can you do?

/ play a musical instrument?
/ sing or dance?
/ drive?
/ cook?
/ speak another foreign language?
/ ski or waterski?

Lifestyle

What time / usually get up?
What / usually have for breakfast?
/ smoke? How many cigarettes /
    smoke a day?
/ often drink alcohol?
/ drink coffee? How many cups /
    drink a day?
/ do exercise? How often? When?
How many hours / sleep?

Which do you prefer? Why?

/ tea or coffee?
/ the summer or the winter?
/ travelling by train or by car?
/ pop or classical music?
/ Saturday or Sunday?
/ Italian food or Chinese food?

Describe a friend

What / his (her) name?
Where / live?
What / do?
How old / ?
/ study English?
/ tall? / dark? / good-looking?

What do you think of ...? Why?

(an actor/actress)
(a TV programme)
(a singer or group)
(a town or city)
(a politician)
(a sports team)

Time

What / the time?
What day / it today?
When / your birthday?
What time / have lunch?
When / favourite time of day?
When / this course end?
When / usually go on holiday?

The past (be)

When / born?
Where / born?
/ busy yesterday?
Where / yesterday at
    8.00. a.m.
    12.15 p.m.
    9.30 p.m.
    12.45 a.m.?

The past simple

/ study English yesterday?
What / do last night?
What time / go to bed last night?
/ have breakfast this morning?
What / do last weekend?
Where / go for your last holiday?
Who / go with?

Now

Why / study English?
What book / reading at the
    moment?
/ it raining?
What / doing now?
What / wearing?

Future

What / do after class?
/ watch TV tonight?
What / have for dinner tonight?
What / do tomorrow?
/ go away this weekend?
Where / go for your next holiday?
/ study English next year?

1 D Eternal Flame
Listening for the correct phrase

1.34   CD1 Track 35

> **LANGUAGE**
> Verb *be*, *this* / *that*, common verbs and phrases

- Give each student a sheet. Go through the words and phrases at the ends of the lines and check the meaning and pronunciation of each one. Play the tape/CD once. SS should underline the word or phrase they hear. Play the song again for SS to check their answers. Check answers with the whole class, going through the song line by line.

1 Close	5 to be	9 my name
2 understand	6 you are	10 don't want
3 am I	7 am I	
4 Is this	8 Is this	

- Give SS a few minutes to read through the song with the glossary. If you think students would like to hear the song again, play it to them one more time. If your class likes singing, they can sing along.

2 B Something Stupid
Common verbs

2.8   CD1 Track 47

> **LANGUAGE**
> Present simple, common verbs

- Give each student a sheet. Go through the words in the two word pools and and check the meaning and pronunciation of each one. Play the tape/CD once for SS to try to put one word in each gap. Repeat if necessary. Check answers, going through the song line by line.

1 think	5 go	9 wait
2 find	6 love	10 get
3 know	7 practise	11 go
4 have	8 make	12 love

- Give SS a few minutes to read through the song with the glossary. If you think students would like to hear the song again, play it to them one more time. If your class likes singing, they can sing along. Ask SS what they think the 'something stupid' is.

> I love you.

3 A Oh Pretty Woman
Rhyming words

3.4   CD1 Track 62

> **LANGUAGE**
> /iː/, /aɪ/, /eɪ/

- Check that SS remember the sounds above either using the Sounds Chart on *p.156* or the *New English File* pronunciation wall chart if you have it. Elicit example words for each sound.

- Give each student a sheet and put SS in pairs. Explain they should put the words from the circle into the correct column, according to the vowel sound. Feedback answers onto the board or OHT.

/iː/	me, meet, see, street
/aɪ/	by, cry, right, tonight
/eɪ/	late, stay, wait, way

- Tell SS that they are now going to listen to the song and that they have to put the words from **a** into the correct place in the song. Explain that, as with the majority of pop songs in English, the words at the end of each line rhyme. Play the tape/CD once for SS to fill the gaps. Repeat if necessary. Check answers, going through the song line by line.

- Give SS a few minutes to read through the song with the glossary.

- If you think students would like to hear the song again, play it to them one more time. If your class likes singing, they can sing along

1 street	5 way	9 by
2 meet	6 stay	10 cry
3 me	7 right	11 late
4 see	8 tonight	12 wait

5 C Dancing Queen
Listening for specific words

5.13   CD2 Track 37

> **LANGUAGE**
> General vocabulary revision

- Give SS a worksheet and ask where the girl is. Get SS to look at the pictures and to tell you what they think is happening.

- Go through the words in **bold** from the song and check the meaning and pronunciation of each one.

- Tell SS that some of the words are right and some words are wrong. The first time they listen, they should just decide if they are right or wrong. Play the tape/CD once. Check answers.

- Now tell SS they are going to try to correct all the wrong words. Play the tape/CD again. Let SS compare their answers with a partner. Repeat if necessary. Check answers, going through the song line by line.

1 ✗ dance	10 ✗ high	19 ✔			
2 ✔	11 ✗ fine	20 ✗ See			
3 ✗ See	12 ✗ dance	21 ✗ on			
4 ✗ Friday	13 ✔	22 ✔			
5 ✔	14 ✔	23 ✔			
6 ✗ music	15 ✗ seventeen	24 ✗ dance			
7 ✔	16 ✔	25 ✔			
8 ✗ king	17 ✔				
9 ✔	18 ✗ dance				

- Give SS a few minutes to read through the song with the glossary.
- If you think students would like to hear the song again, play it to them one more time. If your class likes singing, they can sing along.

6 Waterloo Sunset

D

Adjectives

6.15   CD2 Track 64

> **LANGUAGE**
> Revision and extension of common adjectives

- Give each student a worksheet. SS work in pairs to complete **a**. Check answers.

1 safe	4 afraid	7 bright
2 dizzy	5 lazy	8 busy
3 fine	6 dirty	9 chilly

- Tell SS they are now going to listen to the song and that they have to fill the blanks in the song with an adjective from **a**. Make sure they realize that some adjectives are used more than once. Play the tape/CD once. Let SS compare their answers with a partner. Repeat if necessary. Check answers, going through the song line by line.

1 Dirty	5 chilly	9 afraid
2 busy	6 chilly	10 safe
3 dizzy	7 fine	
4 bright	8 lazy	

- Give SS a few minutes to read through the song with the glossary. Then get SS to work in pairs or small groups and answer the questions in **c**.

> Possible answers
> **a** London is beautiful at sunset. It is busy with people going home from work, cars etc.
> **b** A solitary person who prefers to stay at home and likes looking at the world from inside.
> **c** A pair of young lovers who only have eyes for each other

- If you think students would like to hear the song again, play it to them one more time. If your class likes singing, they can sing along.

7 La Isla Bonita

C

Holiday words

7.10   CD3 Track 16

> **LANGUAGE**
> Holiday vocabulary

- Give each student a worksheet. Get SS to look at the pictures in **a** and elicit some ideas of what they can see in each picture.
- Get SS to work in pairs and match the sentences with the pictures in **a**. Check answers. Get SS to cover the sentences and look at the pictures. Elicit the story.

1 e	3 a	5 d	7 h
2 g	4 c	6 f	8 b

- Now focus on the words in **b**. Check meaning and pronunciation.
- Play the tape/CD once. Let SS compare their answers with a partner. Repeat if necessary. Check answers, going through the song line by line.

1 boy	5 sea	9 sky
2 island	6 days	10 siesta
3 samba	7 fast	11 girl
4 sun	8 island	12 island

- Give SS a few minutes to read through the song with the glossary.
- If you think students would like to hear the song again, play it to them one more time. If your class likes singing, they can sing along.

8 The Best

B

Choosing the correct word

8.7   CD3 Track 34

> **LANGUAGE**
> General vocabulary revision

- Give each student a worksheet.
- Explain the activity. SS have to listen and choose from two similar-sounding words.
- Go through the words in brackets from the song and check the meaning and pronunciation of each one.
- Play the tape/CD once. Let SS compare their answers with a partner. Repeat if necessary. Check answers, going through the song line by line.

1 need	6 anyone	11 here
2 everything	7 say	12 start
3 bring	8 dead	13 can
4 means	9 heart	
5 wrong	10 night	

- Give SS a few minutes to read through the song with the glossary.
- If you think students would like to hear the song again, play it to them one more time. If your class likes singing, they can sing along.

D Song **Eternal Flame**

New English File Teacher's Book Elementary
Photocopiable © Oxford University Press 2004

a Listen and underline the correct words in the box.

b Listen again and check. Write the words in the song.

Eternal Flame

1_____ your eyes, give me your hand, darling
Do you feel my heart beating
Do you 2_____ ?
Do you feel the same, 3_____ only dreaming?
4_____ burning an eternal flame?

I believe it's meant 5_____, darling
I watch you when 6_____ sleeping,
You belong with me
Do you feel the same, 7_____ only dreaming?
8_____ burning an eternal flame?

Say 9_____, sun shines through the rain
A whole life so lonely
and then you come and ease the pain
I 10_____ to lose this feeling, oh…

Open / Close

remember / understand
am I / are you
Is this / Is that

to be / not to be
I am / you are

am I / are you
Is this / Is that

my name / your name

don't like / don't want

Eternal Flame was a number 1 in the UK and the US in 1989 for the American all-girl group The Bangles. It was a number 1 hit again for the British girl group Atomic Kitten in 2001.

Glossary

eyes 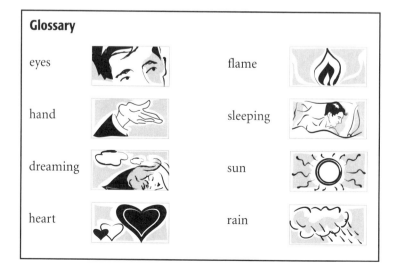 flame

hand sleeping

dreaming sun

heart rain

222

a Listen to the song and complete each verse with the correct verb.

Something stupid

find	go	have	know	love	think

I know I stand in line, until you **1**_____ you have the time
To spend an evening with me
And if we **2**_____ some place to dance, I **3**_____ that there's a chance
You won't be leaving with me
And afterwards we drop into a quiet little place
And **4**_____ a drink or two
And then I **5**_____ and spoil it all, by saying something stupid
Like: I **6**_____ you

I can see it in your eyes you still despise the same old lies
You heard the night before
And though it's just a line to you, for me it's true
It never seemed so right before

get	go	love	make	practise	wait

I **7**_____ every day to find some clever lines to say
To **8**_____ the meaning come through
But then I think I'll **9**_____ until the evening gets late
And I'm alone with you
The time is right, your perfume fills my head, the stars **10**_____ red
And oh the night's so blue
And then I **11**_____ and spoil it all, by saying something stupid
Like: I **12**_____ you

The time is right, etc.

b Listen again. What is the 'something stupid'?

Glossary

spend an evening = pass an evening

chance = possibility

won't = will not (future)

drop into = go into

spoil = ruin, make something bad

like = for example

despise = hate

lies = things that are not true

heard = past simple of hear

clever = intelligent

come through = be clear

Something Stupid was originally a hit for father and daughter duo Frank and Nancy Sinatra in 1967. Robbie Williams and Nicole Kidman made a new recording of the song in 2001.

New English File Teacher's Book Elementary
Photocopiable © Oxford University Press 2004

a Which words have the same sound? Write them in the correct column.

stay
me   street
wait   by   cry
late   tonight   meet
see   way
right

tree	bike	train

b Listen and complete the song with pairs of rhyming words.

Oh Pretty Woman

Pretty woman, walking down the ¹_____
Pretty woman, the kind I like to ²_____
Pretty woman
I don't believe you, you're not the truth
No one could look as good as you
Mercy

Pretty woman, won't you pardon ³_____
Pretty woman, I couldn't help but ⁴_____
Pretty woman
That you look lovely as can be
Are you lonely just like me?

Pretty woman, stop a while
Pretty woman, talk a while
Pretty woman, give your smile to me

Pretty woman, yeah yeah yeah
Pretty woman, look my ⁵_____
Pretty woman, say you'll ⁶_____ with me

'Cause I need you, I'll treat you ⁷_____
Come with me baby, be mine ⁸_____

Pretty woman, don't walk on ⁹_____
Pretty woman, don't make me ¹⁰_____
Pretty woman, don't walk away, hey ... okay
If that's the way it must be, okay
I guess I'll go on home, it's ¹¹_____
There'll be tomorrow night, but ¹²_____
What do I see?
Is she walking back to me?
Yeah, she's walking back to me
Oh, oh, Pretty woman

Glossary

lovely as can be = very beautiful
mercy = don't make me suffer
won't you pardon me = please forgive me
I couldn't help but see = It was impossible not to see
a while = a short time
I'll treat you right = I'll be good to you
walk on by = walk past without stopping
If that's the way it must be = If that is the situation
I guess I'll go on home = I think I'll go home

Oh Pretty Woman was originally a big hit for the Texan Roy Orbison in 1964 but was a hit again in 1990 when it provided the inspiration for the title of the film *Pretty Woman*, starring Julia Roberts and Richard Gere.

a Listen to the song. Are the words in **bold** right or wrong?
Tick ✔ or cross ✘ the lines.

b Listen again. Correct the wrong words.

Dancing Queen

You can **sing**, you can jive,	1 _____
Having the **time** of your life	2 _____
Watch that girl, watch that scene,	3 _____
Dig in the Dancing Queen	
Monday night and the lights are low	4 _____
Looking out for the **place** to go	5 _____
Where they play the right **songs**,	6 _____
Getting in the **swing**	7 _____
You come to look for a **boyfriend**	8 _____
Anybody could be **that** guy	9 _____
The night is young and the music's **low**	10 _____
With a bit of rock music, everything is **great**	11 _____
You're in the mood for a **beer**	12 _____
And when you get the **chance**	13 _____
You are the Dancing Queen, **young** and sweet,	14 _____
only **sixteen**	15 _____
Dancing Queen, feel the **beat**	16 _____
from the **tambourine**, oh yeah	17 _____
You can **sing**, you can jive,	18 _____
Having the **time** of your life	19 _____
Watch that girl, watch that scene	20 _____
Dig in the Dancing Queen	
You're a teaser, you turn them **off**	21 _____
Leave them burning and **then** you're gone	22 _____
Looking out for another, anyone will **do**	23 _____
You're in the mood for a **coffee**	24 _____
And when you get the **chance**, etc.	25 _____

Glossary
jive = a way of dancing
dig in = (informal) get ready
guy = (informal) man, boy
you're in the mood for = you want, you feel like
chance = opportunity
tambourine = musical instrument
teaser = a person who flirts, provokes
anyone will do = it doesn't matter who

Dancing Queen was a Number 1 all round the world in 1976 for the Swedish group Abba. The group broke up in 1982, but their records are still popular in discos and parties today.

New English File Teacher's Book Elementary
Photocopiable © Oxford University Press 2004

a Complete sentences 1–9 with adjectives from the list.

afraid	bright	busy	chilly	dirty	dizzy	fine	lazy	safe

1 The opposite of dangerous is _____
2 When you feel _____, everything is going round in circles.
3 How are you? I'm _____ thanks.
4 Some people never travel by plane because they are _____ of flying.
5 Somebody who doesn't like working is _____.
6 The opposite of clean is _____.
7 The lights in a TV studio are always very _____.
8 When you have a lot of things you need to do, you are very _____.
9 Another way of saying quite cold is _____.

b Now listen to the song. Complete the gaps with an adjective. Some adjectives are used more than once.

Waterloo Sunset is a song about the view of London over the River Thames in the evening, when millions of people are going home from work. It was a big hit for The Kinks in the mid 1960s.

Waterloo Sunset

1 _____ old river, must you keep rolling, flowing into the night
People so 2 _____, make me feel 3 _____,
Taxi light shines so 4 _____
But I don't need no friends
As long as I gaze on Waterloo sunset I am in paradise

Every day I look at the world from my window,
But 5 _____, 6 _____ is the evening time
Waterloo sunset's 7 _____

Terry meets Julie, Waterloo station, every Friday night
But I am so 8 _____, don't want to wander,
I stay at home at night
But I don't feel 9 _____
As long as I gaze on Waterloo sunset I am in paradise

Every day, etc.

Millions of people, swarming like flies round Waterloo underground,
But Terry and July cross over the river, where they feel 10 _____ and sound
And they don't need no friends
As long as they gaze on Waterloo sunset, they are in paradise
Waterloo sunset's fine

c Read the song with glossary. Use the pictures to help you, too. Then listen to the song again. What impression do you get of

1 London?   3 Terry and Julie?
2 the singer?

Glossary	
keep rolling = continue to move	gaze on = look at
so (+ adjective) = very	be in paradise = be very happy
I don't need no = I don't need any	wander = go for a walk
as long as = if I can	swarming like flies = moving like little insects

ⓐ Match the pictures with the sentences below.

e
te amo

f
JULY 11

1 He told her he loved her. ☐
2 She went home. ☐
3 A girl went to a tropical island
  on holiday. ☐
4 Every night a band played the samba. ☐
5 She met a boy. ☐
6 The days went very fast. ☐
7 She had a dream about her holiday. ☐
8 Every afternoon she watched the people
  go by. ☐

ⓑ Listen and complete the song with the right word.

| boy | days | fast | girl | island (x3) |
| samba | sea | siesta | sky | sun |

La Isla Bonita

Last night I dreamt of San Pedro
Just like I'd never gone, I knew the song
A young [1]_____ with eyes like the desert
It all seems like yesterday, not far away

Tropical the [2]_____ breeze
All of nature wild and free
This is where I long to be
La isla bonita
And when the [3]_____ played
The [4]_____ would set so high
Ring through my ears and sting my eyes
Your Spanish lullaby

I fell in love with San Pedro
Warm wind carried on the [5]_____, he called to me
'*Te dijo te amo*'
I prayed that the [6]_____ would last
They went so [7]_____

Tropical the [8]_____ breeze, etc.

I want to be where the sun warms the [8]_____
When it's time for [10]_____ you can watch them go by
Beautiful faces, no cares in this world
Where a [11]_____ loves a boy, and a boy loves a girl
Last night I dreamt of San Pedro
It all seems like yesterday, not far away

Tropical the [12]_____ breeze, etc.

Glossary
desert = a very dry place with sand
breeze = a light wind
wild = not controlled
long to = really want to
sting my eyes = make my eyes hurt
lullaby = song to make a child go to sleep
pray = ask God for something
warm (v) = make hot
face = front part of your head
cares = worries

La Isla Bonita was recorded by Madonna in 1986. Its Latin
flavour helped to make it a big hit around the world.

New English File Teacher's Book Elementary
Photocopiable © Oxford University Press 2004

● Listen and underline the correct word in every pair.

The Best

I call you when I ¹_____ you   need / see
And my heart's on fire
You come to me, come to me
Wild and wired
You come to me, give me ²_____ I need   everything / anything

You ³_____ a lifetime of promises   give / bring
And a world of dreams
You speak the language of love
Like you know what it ⁴_____   feels / means
And it can't be ⁵_____   wrong / long
Take my heart and make it strong

You're simply the best
Better than all the rest
Better than ⁶_____   everyone / anyone
Anyone I ever met
I'm stuck on your heart
I hang on every word you ⁷_____   said / say
Tear us apart
Baby I would rather be ⁸_____   there / dead

In your ⁹_____   head / heart
I see the start
Of every ¹⁰_____ and every day   light / night
And in your eyes I get lost
I get washed away
Just as long as I'm ¹¹_____ in your arms   here / there
I could be in no better place

You're simply the best, etc.

Each time you leave me I ¹²_____ losing control   start / stop
You're walking away with my heart and my soul
I ¹³_____ feel you even when I'm alone   can / can't
Oh baby, don't go

Oh, you're the best, etc.

Glossary

on fire = burning
wild = not controlled
wired = electrified
simply = completely, absolutely
all the rest = all the other people
anyone = any other person

stuck on = connected to
hang on = wait for
tear us apart = separate us
I would rather = I would prefer
soul = spiritual part of a person

The Best was recorded in 1989 by Tina
Turner. It was a big hit all over the world
and is one of her best known songs.

Instructions

There are eight photocopiable Quicktests, one for each File 1–8. These test the Grammar, Vocabulary, and Pronunciation from the A, B, C, and D lessons.

There is one mark for each answer so SS will get a total mark out of 50 for each test.

Each test should take between 20 and 30 minutes.

Answers

1 Quicktest

GRAMMAR

a 1 b   2 c   3 b   4 b   5 c   6 a
7 a   8 b   9 c   10 b

b 11 I   16 aren't / 're not
12 What   17 Is
13 are   18 His
14 is / 's   19 Our
15 Where   20 an

VOCABULARY

a 1 seven   2 thirty   3 Thursday
4 Polish   5 Ireland

b 6 player   7 number   8 phone
9 name   10 card

c 11 Good   16 number
12 meet   17 off
13 from   18 Open
14 spell   19 speak
15 old   20 Read

PRONUNCIATION

a 1 door   2 Thursday   3 Monday
4 what   5 their

b 6 Internet   7 Japa<u>nese</u>   8 fif<u>teen</u>
9 <u>fif</u>ty   10 ad<u>dress</u>

2 Quicktest

GRAMMAR

a 1 a   2 b   3 b   4 b   5 c   6 a
7 a   8 c   9 a   10 a

b 11 lives   16 do
12 don't   17 does
13 has   18 Do
14 doesn't   19 an
15 open   20 Who

VOCABULARY

a 1 watch   2 listen   3 play   4 eat
5 read

b 6 men   7 women   8 children
9 people

c 10 brother   11 husband
12 grandfather   13 nephew
14 uncle

d 15 in   16 retired / unemployed
17 journalist   18 footballer   19 at
20 cousin

PRONUNCIATION

a 1 cook   2 cinema   3 politician
4 nephew   5 has

b 6 re<u>cep</u>tionist   9 poli<u>ti</u>cian
7 <u>grand</u>mother   10 <u>u</u>niform
8 <u>hus</u>band

3 Quicktest

GRAMMAR

a 1 c   2 a   3 b   4 c   5 b   6 a
7 c   8 a   9 a   10 c

b 11 's / is   12 It's   13 at   14 What
15 Then   16 never   17 ever   18 in
19 on   20 at

VOCABULARY

a 1 easy   2 cheap   3 dirty   4 ugly
5 short

b 6 March   7 August   8 third
9 seventh   10 spring

c 11 very   16 go
12 hungry   17 watch
13 have   18 every
14 Do   19 times
15 up   20 date

PRONUNCIATION

a 1 this   2 throw   3 shopping
4 don't   5 worried

b 6 <u>beau</u>tiful   7 <u>dan</u>gerous
8 <u>au</u>tumn   9 Au<u>gust</u>   10 Sep<u>tem</u>ber

4 Quicktest

GRAMMAR

a 1 b   2 c   3 b   4 c   5 b   6 a
7 b   8 a   9 b   10 a

b 11 speak   16 us
12 can't   17 me
13 watching   18 it
14 going   19 Whose
15 him   20 yours/ours

VOCABULARY

a 1 dance   6 give
2 wait   7 use
3 take   8 go
4 ride   9 sing
5 play   10 draw / paint

b 11 take   16 with
12 for   17 the
13 on   18 song
14 on   19 orchestra
15 Why   20 lyrics

PRONUNCIATION

a 1 thanks   2 cinema   3 leave
4 clothes   5 mine

b 6 <u>shop</u>ping   7 <u>clas</u>sical   8 <u>trav</u>el
9 <u>in</u>strument   10 <u>bas</u>ketball

5 Quicktest

GRAMMAR

a 1 c   2 b   3 c   4 a   5 c   6 b
7 a   8 b   9 b   10 c

b 11 was   16 stopped
12 were   17 do
13 Did   18 went
14 watched   19 wore
15 studied   20 go

VOCABULARY

a 1 writer   2 musician   3 artist
4 leader   5 politician

b 6 left   7 said   8 slept   9 thought
10 could

c 11 get   12 have   13 go   14 get
15 have

d 16 We didn't go out last night.
17 I started learning English three years ago.
18 She didn't come to class yesterday afternoon.
19 We went out on Friday night.
20 My sister got married last year.

PRONUNCIATION

a 1 bought   2 came   3 said
4 drove   5 could

b 6 <u>pres</u>ident   7 com<u>pos</u>er
8 <u>jour</u>ney   9 a<u>go</u>   10 in<u>spec</u>tor

6 Quicktest

GRAMMAR

a 1 b 2 c 3 a 4 b 5 c 6 c
7 b 8 b 9 a 10 b

b 11 a 12 any 13 were 14 There
15 Is 16 watching 17 isn't
18 doing 19 goes 20 do

VOCABULARY

a 1 bathroom 4 dining room
2 kitchen 5 garage
3 living room

b 6 a sofa 9 shelves
7 a fridge 10 a cooker
8 a carpet

c 11 chemist's 14 station
12 bridge 15 art gallery
13 post office

d 16 next 17 front 18 with
19 make 20 bark

PRONUNCIATION

a 1 there 2 near 3 wrong
4 fridge 5 ghost

b 6 sofa 7 hospital
8 department store 9 mirror
10 behind

7 Quicktest

GRAMMAR

a 1 c 2 c 3 b 4 b 5 a 6 a
7 a 8 c 9 b 10 c

b 11 some 16 're / are
12 an 17 Are
13 lot 18 be
14 much 19 isn't
15 to 20 it's

VOCABULARY

a 1 have 2 drink 3 do 4 go
5 stay 6 see 7 say 8 fall/be
9 get 10 be

b 11 meat 14 oil
12 rice 15 lettuce
13 pasta

c 16 for 17 Next 18 Tomorrow
19 breakfast 20 vegetables

PRONUNCIATION

a 1 bread 2 meat 3 sugar
4 peas 5 rice

b 6 pineapple 9 biscuits
7 tomatoes 10 potatoes
8 chocolate

8 Quicktest

GRAMMAR

a 1 c 2 b 3 b 4 a 5 c 6 c
7 a 8 a 9 b 10 a

b 11 than 16 to
12 more 17 Do
13 most 18 Would
14 in 19 slowly
15 wouldn't 20 badly

VOCABULARY

a 1 poorer 2 bigger 3 more expensive
4 happier 5 worse

b 6 the hottest 9 the tallest/the longest
7 the easiest 10 the prettiest
8 the best

c 11 quickly 12 quietly 13 badly
14 dangerously

d 15 weather 16 snows 17 windy
18 hard 19 for 20 fly

PRONUNCIATION

a 1 stylish 2 healthy 3 carefully
4 fast 5 world

b 6 popular 9 fantastic
7 generous 10 imagine
8 beautifully

END-OF-COURSE TEST

Instructions

The End-of-course test is a test of all of the Grammar, Vocabulary, and Pronunciation from the A, B, C, and D lessons. It also includes Reading, Listening, and Writing.

Grammar
25 marks one mark for each answer
Vocabulary
25 marks one mark for each answer
Pronunciation
10 marks one mark for each answer
Reading
10 marks one mark for each answer
Listening
10 marks one mark for each answer
Writing
10 marks We suggest you allocate 6 marks for grammar, vocabulary, and spelling, and 4 marks for content, presentation, and layout.
Speaking
10 marks Either give a mark for their speaking during the course, or use Communicative activity Revise & Check on *p.219* as an oral test. Give SS a mark out of 10.

Answers

GRAMMAR

a 1 c 2 b 3 c 4 a 5 c 6 c
7 a 8 b 9 a 10 c 11 c 12 c
13 b 14 a 15 b

b 16 Her 21 see
17 does 22 are
18 me 23 any
19 were 24 much
20 didn't 25 well

VOCABULARY

a 1 French 6 August
2 fifty 7 third
3 daughter 8 bought
4 musician 9 vegetables
5 cheap

b 10 do 14 go
11 play 15 have
12 get 16 wear
13 eat/have 17 wait

c 18 key 22 fridge
19 identity card 23 garage
20 pilot 24 chemist's
21 dirty 25 post office

PRONUNCIATION

a 1 word 2 weather 3 their
4 worse 5 big

b 6 fifteen 7 behind 8 Chinese
9 expensive 10 October

READING

a 1 False 6 False
2 False 7 True
3 False 8 True
4 True 9 False
5 False 10 False

LISTENING

a 1 b 2 c 3 b 4 c 5 a

b 6 train 9 15.50 / 3.50 p.m.
7 150 euros 10 midnight
8 Friday

(For tapescripts, see *p.136*)

GRAMMAR

a Circle a, b, or c.

Example: My name ____ David.
   a am ⓑ is   c are

1   Maria is a student. ____ 's in Class 4.
   a He   b She   c It

2   **A** Are you English?
   B ____ .
   a Yes, I'm   b No, I not   c Yes, I am

3   They ____ from Milan, they're from Rome.
   a not are   b aren't   c isn't

4   Mr Jamieson is the director. That's ____ room.
   a her   b his   c he

5   Pavel and Marc are in class 7. ____ teacher is Sally.
   a They're   b Her   c Their

6   **A** What's ____ name?
   B I'm Jack.
   a your   b you   c his

7   **A** What are those?
   B They're ____ .
   a watches   b watch   c watchs

8   **A** What's ____ ?
   B It's my identity card.
   a these   b that   c those

9   Egypt and Morocco are African ____ .
   a countrys   b country   c countries

10   ____ cars are Japanese.
   a This   b These   c That

b Complete the sentences.

Example: I'm English. I'm _from_ London.

11   Hello. ____'m Mike.
12   ____'s your name?
13   How ____ you?
14   He ____ in Class 2.
15   ____ are you from?
16   We ____ German, we're French.
17   ____ your mother Scottish?
18   He's from Mexico. ____ name's Pablo.
19   We're new students. ____ names are Jan and Kasia.
20   **A** What's that?
   B It's ____ umbrella.

[20]

VOCABULARY

a Write the missing word.

Example: one, two, _three_

1   ten, nine, eight, ____
2   twenty, ____ , forty, fifty
3   Tuesday, Wednesday, ____
4   China – Chinese; Poland – ____
5   Scotland – Scottish; ____ – Irish

b Complete the objects with a word from the list.

~~book~~   card   name   number   phone   player

Example: address _book_

6   CD ____   9   first ____
7   phone ____   10   identity ____
8   mobile ____

c Complete with one word.

11   ____ morning. How are you?
12   **A** I'm Kay.   **B** Nice to ____ you.
13   **A** Where are you ____ ?   **B** Berlin.
14   **A** How do you ____ your name?
   B G-A-R-Y.
15   **A** How ____ are you?   **B** I'm 18.
16   **A** What's your phone ____ ?   **B** 375 4604.
17   Turn ____ your mobile phone.
18   ____ your books on page 76, please.
19   Please don't ____ Italian. This is an English class.
20   ____ the text on page 12.

[20]

PRONUNCIATION

a Write the words from the list in the chart.

d**oo**r   M**o**nday   th**ei**r   Th**ur**sday   wh**a**t

board	her	umbrella	not	where
1 ____	2 ____	3 ____	4 ____	5 ____

b Underline the stressed syllable.

Example: after_noon_

6   Internet   8   fifteen   10   address
7   Japanese   9   fifty

[10]

Total [50]

GRAMMAR

a Circle a, b, or c.

Example: My name ____ David.
  a am (b) is c are

1 Neil and Angela ____ to the cinema every weekend.
  a go b goes c gos

2 My brother ____ economics at university.
  a studys b studies c study

3 **A** Does Jane live with her mother?
  B ____ .
  a Yes, she likes b Yes, she does c Yes, she is

4 Where ____ ?
  a he works b does he work c does he works

5 ____ speak Spanish in class?
  a Do your teacher b Your teacher does
  c Does your teacher

6 **A** What ____ ?
  B They're doctors.
  a do they do b they do c do they work

7 **A** Who's that boy?
  B He's ____ .
  a Chloe's brother b the brother of Chloe
  c Chloes brother

8 Is that ____ ?
  a the your parents' car b your parent's car
  c your parents' car

9 He's ____ .
  a my sister's boyfriend b my boyfriend's sister
  c the boyfriend of my sister

10 This is ____ .
  a the end of the exercise b the exercise's end
  c the end's exercise

b Complete the sentences.

Example: I'm English. I'm *from* London.

11 I live in London but my sister _____ in New York.
12 We _____ drive to work, we go by bike.
13 My mother _____ three sisters.
14 He _____ work. He's retired.
15 The shops _____ at 9.30 a.m. and close at 6.00 p.m.
16 Where _____ you live?
17 What _____ your brother do?
18 _____ your parents have a car?
19 My boyfriend's _____ engineer.
20 **A** _____ 's that woman?
   B She's Sandra's aunt.

☐ **20**

VOCABULARY

a Write the missing verb.

Example: *speak* German

1 _____ TV
2 _____ to the radio
3 _____ the guitar
4 _____ fast food
5 _____ the newspaper

b Write the plurals.

Example: book *books*

6 man _____   8 child _____
7 woman _____   9 person _____

c Write the missing words.

Example: mother *father*

10 sister _____   13 niece _____
11 wife _____   14 aunt _____
12 grandmother _____

d Complete with one word.

15 Do you work _____ an office?
16 I don't have a job. I'm _____ .
17 She's a _____ . She works for *The Times* newspaper.
18 He's a _____ . He plays for Manchester United.
19 My niece is 13. She's _____ school.
20 My aunt's daughter is my _____ .

☐ **20**

PRONUNCIATION

a Write the words from the list in the chart.

cinema cook has nephew politician

actor	speak	sushi	footballer	music
1 ____	2 ____	3 ____	4 ____	5 ____

b Underline the stressed syllable.

Example: after*noon*

6 receptionist
7 grandmother
8 husband
9 politician
10 uniform

☐ **10**

Total ☐ **50**

New English File Teacher's Book Elementary
Photocopiable © Oxford University Press 2004

GRAMMAR

a Circle a, b, or c.

Example: My name ____ David.
       a am (b) is   c are

1 This is a ____ .
a very house nice   b house very nice
c very nice house

2 Do you like my ____ ?
a new boots   b news boots   c boots new

3 **A** What's the time?
B ____ .
a It's past half four   b It's half past four
c It's four past half

4 What time ____ ?
a get you home   b you get home
c do you get home

5 What time ____ Louisa get up in the morning?
a do   b does   c is

6 ____ to bed late.
a We usually go   b We usually are
c We go usually

7 The boss is angry with me. ____ .
a I always late   b I'm late always
c I'm always late

8 He ____ on Saturdays.
a never works   b doesn't never work
c works never

9 I never study ____ the evening.
a in   b on   c at

10 All my family go home ____ Christmas.
a on   b in   c at

b Complete the sentences.

Example: I'm English. I'm *from* London.

11 **A** What _____ the time?
12 **B** _____ eight o'clock
13 Our daughter always wakes up _____ half past five.
14 **A** _____ time do you get up in the morning?
    B 7.00 p.m.
15 I have a shower. _____ I have breakfast.
16 He's _____ late for class. He's always on time.
17 I'm very healthy. I'm hardly _____ ill.
18 I only drink coffee _____ the morning.
19 I work in a bar _____ Saturday evenings.
20 My wife is a doctor. She often works _____ night.

| 20 |

VOCABULARY

a Write the opposite adjectives.

Example: big   *small*

1 difficult _____
2 expensive _____
3 clean _____
4 beautiful _____
5 tall _____

b Write the missing word.

Example: one, two, *three*

6 January, February, _____
7 June, July, _____
8 first, second, _____
9 fifth, sixth, _____
10 autumn, winter, _____

c Complete with one word.

11 It's a good restaurant and it isn't _____ expensive.
12 **A** Do you want a sandwich?
    B No, thanks. I'm not _____ .
13 I never _____ breakfast in the morning.
14 _____ your homework before you go to bed.
15 He always wakes _____ two or three times at night.
16 When the class finishes I _____ home.
17 My parents never _____ TV.
18 I get up early _____ day.
19 They go on holiday three _____ a year.
20 **A** What's the _____ today?
    B the second of April.

| 20 |

PRONUNCIATION

a Write the words from the list in the chart.

don't	shopping	this	throw	worried

ð	θ	ɒ	əʊ	ʌ
the	Thursday	job	go	son
1 ____	2 ____	3 ____	4 ____	5 ____

b Underline the stressed syllable.

Example: after*noon*

6 beautiful
7 dangerous
8 autumn
9 August
10 September

| 10 |

Total | 50 |

233

New English File Teacher's Book Elementary
Photocopiable © Oxford University Press 2004

GRAMMAR

a Circle a, b, or c.

Example: My name ＿＿＿ David.
   a am　(b) is　c are

1　＿＿＿ help me? I'm lost.
　a You can　b Can you　c Can you to

2　She ＿＿＿ drive. She walks to work.
　a doesn't can　b can't to　c can't

3　**A** Do you like shopping?
　B ＿＿＿ .
　a Yes, I like　b Yes, I love it　c No, I do

4　Fiona hates ＿＿＿ up early.
　a geting　b get　c getting

5　She doesn't like ＿＿＿ alone.
　a live　b living　c liveing

6　I don't like ＿＿＿ . I think she's a terrible actress.
　a her　b him　c them

7　The children are very quiet. I can't hear ＿＿＿ .
　a they　b them　c their

8　Is that ＿＿＿ book?
　a your　b yours　c you

9　They have a cat. ＿＿＿ name is Felix.
　a It's　b Its　c Their

10　Martha and Dick live in London, but I don't know ＿＿＿ address.
　a their　b theirs　c hers

b Complete the sentences.

Example: I'm English. I'm *from* London.

11　I can ＿＿＿＿＿ three languages.
12　You ＿＿＿＿＿ park here. It's 'No Parking'.
13　My mother hates ＿＿＿＿＿ football on TV.
14　Emily loves ＿＿＿＿＿ to the cinema.
15　Carl loves Molly but she doesn't love ＿＿＿＿＿ .
16　We can't find our hotel. Can you help ＿＿＿＿＿ ?
17　I love you but you don't love ＿＿＿ .
18　**A** What do you think of this music?
　B I like ＿＿＿＿＿ .
19　**A** ＿＿＿＿＿ is that bag?
　B It's mine.
20　**A** Are these coats ＿＿＿＿＿ ?
　B No, they're not. Ours are black.

[20]

VOCABULARY

a Write the missing verb.

Example: *speak* German

1　＿＿＿＿＿ the tango
2　＿＿＿＿＿ for the bus
3　＿＿＿＿＿ photos
4　＿＿＿＿＿ a bike
5　＿＿＿＿＿ chess
6　＿＿＿＿＿ someone a present
7　＿＿＿＿＿ a computer
8　＿＿＿＿＿ out together
9　＿＿＿＿＿ karaoke
10　＿＿＿＿＿ a picture

b Complete with one word.

11　Don't forget to ＿＿＿＿＿ your umbrella when you go to London.
12　I can't find my glasses. Help me to look ＿＿＿＿＿ them.
13　It's very dark in here. Please turn ＿＿＿＿＿ the lights.
14　Can I try ＿＿＿＿＿ these jeans please?
15　**A** ＿＿＿＿＿ don't you like the book?
　B Because it's boring.
16　In *Pretty Woman* Richard Gere falls in love ＿＿＿＿＿ Julia Roberts.
17　Can you play ＿＿＿＿＿ piano?
18　My father's favourite ＿＿＿＿＿ is *Imagine* by John Lennon.
19　He's a violinist. He plays in an ＿＿＿＿＿ .
20　I like this group's music but I can't understand their ＿＿＿＿＿ .

[20]

PRONUNCIATION

a Write the words from the list in the chart.

| cinema | clothes | leave | mine | thanks |

thing	his	me	no	money
1 ＿＿	2 ＿＿	3 ＿＿	4 ＿＿	5 ＿＿

b Underline the stressed syllable.

Example: after*noon*

6　shopping
7　classical
8　travel
9　instrument
10　basketball

[10]

Total [50]

New English File Teacher's Book Elementary
Photocopiable © Oxford University Press 2004

GRAMMAR

a Circle a, b, or c.

Example: My name _____ David.

     a am (b) is c are

1 Chopin and Mozart _____ famous composers.
  a is b was c were

2 _____ your mother born in India?
  a Were b Was c Is

3 Joan of Arc _____ English. She was French.
  a doesn't b weren't c wasn't

4 He _____ work yesterday. He was ill.
  a didn't b doesn't c wasn't

5 They _____ tennis yesterday.
  a playd b plays c played

6 I _____ last night.
  a not cooked b didn't cook c didn't cooked

7 **A** What _____ on Friday night?
  B I went out with my friends.
  a did you do b did you c you did

8 Did you _____ a good time?
  a had b have c has

9 I _____ my boyfriend yesterday. He was in London.
  a didn't saw b didn't see c don't see

10 He _____ me some beautiful flowers for my birthday.
  a buy b buyed c bought

b Complete the sentences.

Example: I'm English. I'm _from_ London.

11 Washington _____ the first American president.

12 **A** Where _____ you born?
  B In Liverpool.

13 **A** _____ you book your tickets on the internet?
  B No, I didn't.

14 We _____ TV last night.

15 **A** Did you study French at school?
  B No, I _____ German.

16 The bus didn't stop in Lyon. It only _____ in Paris.

17 **A** What did you _____ on Saturday night?
  B I went to a party.

18 I _____ to a Japanese restaurant yesterday.

19 **A** What did you wear?
  B I _____ my new jacket.

20 I didn't _____ out last night. I was very tired.

                         20

VOCABULARY

a Write the person.

Example: act _actor_

1 write _____
2 music _____
3 art _____
4 lead _____
5 politics _____

b Write the past simple.

Example: go _went_

6 leave _____
7 say _____
8 sleep _____
9 think _____
10 can _____

c Write _have_, _go_, or _get_.

Example: _have_ a shower

11 _____ dressed
12 _____ a drink
13 _____ out on a Friday night
14 _____ an e-mail
15 _____ breakfast

d ~~Cross out~~ the wrong expression.

Example: I didn't go to work **yesterday** / ~~the yesterday~~.

16 We didn't go out **last night** / **the last night**.

17 I started learning English **ago three years** / **three years ago**.

18 She didn't come to class **yesterday afternoon** / **the last afternoon**.

19 We went out on **Friday night** / **the Friday night**.

20 My sister got married **the last year** / **last year**.

                         20

PRONUNCIATION

a Write the words from the list in the chart.

bought	came	could	drove	said

b**ough**t	m**a**de	w**e**nt	sp**o**ke	t**oo**k
w**o**re	m**a**de	w**e**nt	sp**o**ke	t**oo**k
1 _____	2 _____	3 _____	4 _____	5 _____

b Underline the stressed syllable.

Example: after_noon_

6 president
7 composer
8 journey
9 ago
10 inspector

                         10

Total   **50**

New English File Teacher's Book Elementary
Photocopiable © Oxford University Press 2004

GRAMMAR

a Circle a, b, or c.

Example: My name _____ David.

    a am   (b) is   c are

1 How many bedrooms _____ in your flat?
  a is there   b are there   c there are

2 There are _____ glasses in the cupboard.
  a any   b a   c some

3 _____ many guests in the hotel.
  a There weren't   b They weren't   c There wasn't

4 _____ a very noisy party in the street last night.
  a There is   b There was   c There were

5 _____ any good programmes on TV yesterday?
  a Was there   b Are there   c Were there

6 What _____ ?
  a you are doing   b you doing   c are you doing

7 She _____ lunch.
  a is make   b is making   c is makeing

8 **A** What does he do?
  B _____ .
  a He's reading   b He's a student   c Yes, he does

9 My sister _____ on Friday nights.
  a usually goes out   b is usually going out
  c goes usually out

10 **A** Where's Ann?
  B She's in the bathroom. _____ .
  a She has a shower   b She's having a shower
  c She having a shower

b Complete the sentences.

Example: I'm English. I'm _from_ London.

11 There's _____ big table in the living room.
12 There aren't _____ chairs.
13 How many people _____ there in class yesterday?
14 _____ wasn't a bar in the hotel.
15 _____ your brother working at the moment?
16 Don't make a noise! Your father's _____ TV.
17 She _____ drinking vodka! It's water.
18 **A** What's Mark _____ ?
  B He's playing tennis.
19 Simon usually _____ to bed early.
20 **A** What does he _____ ?
  B He's a pilot.

      20

VOCABULARY

a Write the rooms in the house.

Example: The room where you sleep   _the bedroom_

1 The room where you have a shower _____
2 The room where you cook _____
3 The room where you relax and watch TV _____
4 The room where you have dinner _____
5 The place where you leave your car _____

b Write the furniture.

Example: You sleep in this   a **b**_ed_

6 Two people can sit here   a **s**_____
7 You put food and drinks here   a **f**_____
8 You have this on the floor   a **c**_____
9 You put books etc on these   **sh**_____**s**
10 You cook on this   a **c**_____

c Write the places.

Example: A place where you can see old things _museum_

11 A place where you can buy medicine _____
12 A place where you go over a river _____
13 A place where you can buy stamps _____
14 A place where you get a train _____
15 A place where you can see famous paintings _____

d Complete with one word.

16 There's a small table _____ to the bed.
17 There's a plant in _____ of the window.
18 Don't argue _____ me!
19 Our neighbours always _____ a lot of noise
20 My dogs always _____ when they see the postman.

      20

PRONUNCIATION

a Write the words from the list in the chart.

fri**dge**   **gh**ost   **near**   **there**   **wr**ong

eə	eɪ	r	dʒ	g
st**air**s	**here**	**r**oad	**j**ob	**g**arden
1 _____	2 _____	3 _____	4 _____	5 _____

b Underline the stressed syllable.

Example: after_noon_

6 sofa
7 hospital
8 department store
9 mirror
10 behind

      10

Total   **50**

GRAMMAR

a Circle a, b, or c.

Example: My name _____ David.
       a am (b) is c are

1 Is there _____ milk in the fridge?
  a a b an c any

2 There are _____ chairs in the kitchen.
  a any b an c some

3 I don't want _____ coffee, thanks.
  a some b any c many

4 _____ cigarettes do you smoke a day?
  a How much b How many c How

5 _____ water do you drink?
  a How much b How many c How

6 **A** How many oranges do you eat a week?
  B _____ . I don't like oranges.
  a None b Any c A lot

7 I _____ a new car.
  a am going to buy b go to buy c am going buy

8 What _____ do next summer?
  a you are going to b do you go to
  c are you going to

9 We _____ have a holiday this summer.
  a don't go to b aren't going to c aren't go to

10 **A** What do you think is going to happen?
  B I think _____ leave her husband.
  a she goes b she's going c she's going to

b Complete the sentences.

Example: I'm English. I'm _from_ London.

11 We need _____ butter.
12 Do you want _____ apple?
13 They eat a _____ of fruit.
14 I don't drink _____ coffee – only two cups a day.
15 Is your brother going _____ go to university?
16 We _____ going to drive to Paris.
17 _____ you going to come and see us next summer?
18 I'm sure they're going to _____ very happy.
19 She _____ going to come. She's not well.
20 Take your umbrella. I think _____ going to rain.

| 20

VOCABULARY

a Write the verb.

Example: _go_ on holiday

1 _____ coffee and toast for breakfast
2 _____ a lot of water
3 _____ sport or exercise
4 _____ shopping
5 _____ in a hotel
6 _____ the sights
7 _____ goodbye
8 _____ in love
9 _____ married
10 _____ lucky

b Complete the food words.

Example: I usually have t_oast_ for breakfast.

11 Vegetarians don't eat m_____ .
12 They eat a lot of **r**_____ in Japan and China.
13 Macaroni and spaghetti are kinds of **p**_____ .
14 In the Mediterranean they use a lot of olive **o**_____ .
15 People often put **l**_____ in salads.

c Complete with one word.

16 Let's have ice cream _____ dessert.
17 It's January. _____ month is February.
18 Today is Monday. _____ is Tuesday.
19 I usually have coffee and toast for _____ .
20 Peas and carrots are my favourite _____ .

| 20

PRONUNCIATION

a Write the words from the list in the chart.

bread   meat   peas   rice   sugar

when	see	mushrooms	eggs	sweets
1 _____	2 _____	3 _____	4 _____	5 _____

b Underline the stressed syllable.

Example: after_noon_

6 pineapple
7 tomatoes
8 chocolate
9 biscuits
10 potatoes

| 10

Total | 50

GRAMMAR

a Circle a, b, or c.

Example: My name ____ David.

        a am (b) is c are

1 Today is ____ than yesterday.
   a cold   b more cold   c colder

2 My sister is ____ than me.
   a prettyer   b prettier   c more pretty

3 A Porsche is ____ than a Seat.
   a expensiver   b more expensive   c most expensive

4 What's ____ river in the world?
   a the longest   b the longer   c longest

5 This is ____ restaurant I know.
   a the better   b the goodest   c the best

6 People say rugby is ____ sport.
   a the dangerous   b the more dangerous
   c the most dangerous

7 She ____ learn Spanish.
   a 'd like to   b likes   c like to

8 ____ to go skiing?
   a Would you like   b Do you like   c You would like

9 My brother speaks French ____ .
   a very good   b very well   c very goodly

10 The Americans don't drive very ____ .
   a fast   b fastly   c faster

b Complete the sentences.

Example: I'm English. I'm *from* London.

11 Martin is taller _____ James.

12 Russian is difficult, but Chinese is _____ difficult.

13 She's the _____ intelligent girl in the class.

14 Everest is the highest mountain _____ the world.

15 She _____ like to go up in a balloon. She hates flying.

16 **A** Would you like to drive a Ferrari?
   B Yes I'd love _____ .

17 _____ you like cooking?

18 _____ you like to learn to cook well?

19 You speak very fast. Can you speak more _____, please?

20 I can't understand him. He speaks English very _____ .

        | 20 |

VOCABULARY

a Write the opposite comparative.

Example: hotter   *colder*

1 richer _____   4 sadder _____

2 smaller _____   5 better _____

3 cheaper _____

b Write the opposite superlative.

Example: the biggest   *the smallest*

6 the coldest _____

7 the most difficult _____

8 the worst _____

9 the shortest _____

10 the ugliest _____

c Write the opposite adverb.

Example: healthily   *unhealthily*

11 slowly _____   13 well _____

12 loudly _____   14 safely _____

d Complete with one word.

15 **A** What's the _____ like?
   B It's hot and sunny.

16 It _____ a lot in Siberia in the winter.

17 It was very _____ last night. Some trees fell down.

18 If you want to pass the exam, you need to work _____ .

19 This is a present _____ you.

20 He'd like to learn to _____ a plane.

        | 20 |

PRONUNCIATION

a Write the words from the list in the chart.

| carefully | fast | healthy | stylish | world |

high	wet	square	hard	learn
1 ____	2 ____	3 ____	4 ____	5 ____

b Underline the stressed syllable.

Example: after*noon*

6 popular

7 generous

8 beautifully

9 fantastic

10 imagine

        | 10 |

Total | 50 |

New English File Teacher's Book Elementary
Photocopiable © Oxford University Press 2004

GRAMMAR

a Circle a, b, or c.

1 Where _____ from?
   a she is   b are she   c is she

2 **A** What's _____ ?
   B It's a statue.
   a those   b that   c these

3 The film _____ at 10.30 p.m.
   a finish   b finishs   c finishes

4 They _____ any foreign languages.
   a don't speak   b doesn't speak   c not speak

5 Is she your _____ ?
   a brothers' girlfriend   b girlfriend's brother
   c brother's girlfriend

6 I like your _____ .
   a shoes new   b news shoes   c new shoes

7 My father _____ TV.
   a never watches   b watches never   c never watch

8 She _____ drive very well.
   a don't can   b can't   c can't to

9 I don't like _____ late at night.
   a studying   b studing   c study

10 **A** Is that Mark and Anna's house?
    B No, _____ is at the end of the road.
    a his   b their   c theirs

11 **A** Where's Dad?
    B He's in the kitchen. He _____ the dinner.
    a makes   b making   c is making

12 What _____ do next summer?
    a you are going   b are you going
    c are you going to

13 Angela is _____ person in the class.
    a the taller   b the tallest   c the most tall

14 _____ see a film tonight?
    a Would you like to   b Do you like
    c Would you to

15 Have you ever _____ Paris?
    a been   b been to   c be to

b Complete the sentences.

16 She's French. _____ name's Sandrine.

17 What time _____ your brother usually get up?

18 That's my book. Give it to _____ .

19 Where _____ you born?

20 I _____ go out last night because I had a lot
    of homework.

21 **A** I went to the cinema on Saturday night.
    B What film did you _____ ?

22 How many rooms _____ there in this hotel?

23 Is there _____ water in the fridge?

24 How _____ water do you drink a day?

25 She's a good driver. She drives very _____ .

| 25 |

VOCABULARY

a Write the missing word.

1 Britain – British;   France – _____

2 20 – twenty;   50 – _____

3 father – son;   mother – _____

4 act – actor;   music – _____

5 big – small;   expensive – _____

6 January, February;   July, _____

7 1st – first;   3rd – _____

8 go – went;   buy – _____

9 apples – fruit;   carrots – _____

b Write the missing verb.

10 _____ your homework

11 _____ the piano

12 _____ dressed

13 _____ cereal for breakfast

14 _____ to bed late

15 _____ a good time

16 _____ glasses

17 _____ for the bus

c Complete with one word.

18 You're in room 208. Here's your _____ .

19 When you travel to another country you need to
    show your passport or _____ .

20 He's a _____ . He flies planes.

21 These windows aren't clean. They are very
    _____ .

22 People usually put milk and fresh food in the
    _____ .

23 **A** Did you put the car in the _____ ?
    B No, I left it in the street.

24 You can buy aspirins or antibiotics in
    a _____ .

25 You can buy stamps and send letters in
    the _____ .

| 25 |

PRONUNCIATION

a Underline the word with a different sound.

1 /ɔː/   saw   floor   thought   word

2 /iː/   meet   weather   easy   cheap

3 /ɜː/   their   work   nurse   dirty

4 /ʃː/   sugar   Polish   worse   she

5 /dʒː/   Japan   big   bridge   dangerous

b Underline the stressed syllable.

6 fifteen
7 behind
8 Chinese
9 expensive
10 October

| 10 |

READING

Read this newspaper article and circle the correct answer.

The long way home

A British couple went to France for the day – and they got home seven days later.

Everything began well for Mr and Mrs Long on their day trip to France. They went by train from London to Dover and got the ferry to Boulogne in France.

They went for a short walk around the town but they got completely lost. 'We walked and walked,' said Mrs Long, 'but we couldn't find our way back to the ferry port'. They walked all night and finally a motorist picked them up and drove them to a small village. Here they caught a train to Paris. Their plan was to travel from Paris to London. But they caught the wrong train and the next morning they arrived in Luxembourg! They went to the police station for help, and two hours later the police put them on the train back to Paris. But the train divided into two and unfortunately they were in the wrong half, and they arrived in Basle in Switzerland! A lorry driver took them back to Paris and they went to the railway station again where they nearly got a train to Bonn in Germany. Finally, they got on the right train, and they arrived back in Boulogne a week after their 'short walk around the town'. Mr Long said, 'This was our first trip abroad and probably our last!'

Example: Mr and Mrs Long are from France. (True)/ False

1 They wanted to spend a week in France. True / False
2 They flew from London to Dover. True / False
3 They caught the ferry from London to Boulogne. True / False
4 They went from Boulogne to a small village by car. True / False
5 They wanted to travel from Paris to London by car. True / False
6 They went to the police station in Paris. True / False
7 One half of the train went from Luxembourg to Paris. True / False
8 They went from Luxembourg to Switzerland by train. True / False
9 They went from Switzerland to Paris by train. True / False
10 Mr Long wants to go on holiday in France next year. True / False

[ ] 10

LISTENING

a Listen and circle the correct answer.

1 Her phone number is _____.
   a 7734856
   b 7734056
   c 734056

2 a He hates shopping for CDs.
   b He likes shopping.
   c He doesn't like shopping for clothes.

3 a He was in bed from 9.00 a.m. to 10.30 p.m.
   b He didn't go out last night.
   c He went out at about 10.00 p.m.

4 a Simon usually works on Saturdays.
   b Simon isn't busy this week.
   c Simon is working today.

5 a She has never been to Portugal.
   b She went to Portugal last summer.
   c She has been to Portugal three times.

b Listen and write the correct answer in the space.

Destination: _Dublin_
Travel by 6 _____
Price of ticket: 7 _____
Leave London on 8 _____ morning at 6.45 a.m.
Arrive in Dublin at 9 _____
Leave Dublin on Monday at 3.10 p.m.
Arrive in London at 10 _____

[ ] 10

WRITING

Hello!
My name's Jaime and I'm from Buenos Aires. I'm studying medicine at university. I live with my family – my parents and my two sisters. They're younger than me, and they're at school. In my free time I like watching football on TV, chatting on the Internet, and going out with my friends. Last weekend we went to see a football match. My team, River Plate, won 4-0. It was fantastic.
Please write soon.

Answer Jaime's e-mail. Give similar information about you.

[ ] 10

SPEAKING

[ ] 10

Total [ ] 100

149170